FILM AND VIDEO INTERMEDIALITY

FILM AND VIDEO INTERMEDIALITY

THE QUESTION OF MEDIUM SPECIFICITY IN CONTEMPORARY MOVING IMAGES

Janna Houwen

Bloomsbury Academic India
An imprint of Bloomsbury Publishing Inc

B L O O M S B U R Y
NEW DELHI • LONDON • OXFORD • NEW YORK • SYDNEY

BLOOMSBURY INDIA
Bloomsbury Publishing India Pvt. Ltd
Second Floor, LSC Building No. 4, DDA Complex, Pocket C–6&7,
Vasant Kunj, New Delhi 110070

BLOOMSBURY, BLOOMSBURY ACADEMIC INDIA and the Diana logo are
trademarks of Bloomsbury Publishing Plc

First published in India 2024
First published 2017

This edition published with permission from Bloomsbury Publishing Plc,
50 Bedford Square, London, WC1B3DP, UK

British Library Cataloguing-in-Publication Data
A catalogue record for this book is available from the British Library.

Library of Congress Cataloging-in-Publication Data
A catalog record for this book is available from the Library of Congress

ISBN: 978-93-61316-92-0

Cover design: Eleanor Rose
Cover image: Julien Ten Thousand Waves
Typeset by RefineCatch Limited, Bungay, Suffolk
Printed and bound in India by Replika Press Pvt. Ltd.
To find out more about our authors and books
visit www.bloomsbury.com and sign up for our newsletters

To Erik, Midas and Anna

CONTENTS

INTRODUCTION

Ten Thousand Waves, two media, and *A Voyage on the North Sea*

The viewfinder of a surveillance video camera frantically scans the dark waving surface of the ocean. The images of dizzying, frantic camera movements over undulating stretches of grey, pixelated water are accompanied by alarming reports to the coastguard. First, a panicky woman's voice is telling how a group of Chinese cockle-fishers is stuck in Morecambe Bay. "Can you please, just please get something out there now," she begs. As the water has already risen above the waist of the young men (most of whom are unable to swim) the woman continues to plead: "They need a plane or something. They have got to get out!" A few minutes later, police officers report that they are arriving on scene. From their rescue helicopter, they search for the twenty-five Chinese immigrants who were caught by the rapidly rising tides in the so-called quicksand bay near Lancaster on the night of February 5, 2004.

In Isaac Julien's installation *Ten Thousand Waves* (2010), the impressive archival video footage of the rescue operation is projected onto nine large screens. Together, seven of these screens form an oval, with two screens placed in the middle. As a consequence, the viewer of the installation is surrounded by nine stretches of moving, foaming water which can never be seen all at once. While the police officers report from their helicopter how they can only recover one person, and while the camera keeps scanning the rolling waves, the spectator is spurred to move, to turn from screen to screen, in order to join the search for signs of life in the dark blur of grainy water. Later on in *Ten Thousand Waves*, handheld images of Morecambe Bay by daylight show deserted sandbanks and vast expanses of water. The cockle-fishers are nowhere to be found. A short sample from a video documentary on the Morecambe Bay tragedy proves that the rescue operation was not completely successful. The scene focuses on a family member of one of the twenty-three drowned immigrants, who is going through the personal effects of a deceased loved one.

In between these instances of poignant, grainy video footage, the images of *Ten Thousand Waves* turn into something else. First, the pixelated grey ocean is replaced by smooth, sharp waves. Instead of blurred moving images, the installation's nine screens are now filled with bright images in which we can see each ripple on the ocean's surface. When the camera dips under the water's surface, it shows in medium close-up how three drowned Chinese fishermen sink slowly into the depth of the sea, their lifeless bodies swaying in the rocking ocean. Suddenly, a woman with long, waving black hair and piercing dark eyes appears on the installation's screens. Dressed in a sumptuous white gown, she seems to float in midair. What is more, like the helicopter's surveillance camera, the woman is looking downwards from her airborne viewpoint, which suggests that she too is scanning the ocean's surface.

When both the flying woman and the drowning men reappear within a densely grown Chinese landscape instead of the North Sea as their backdrop later on in the installation, the mysterious woman can be identified as the goddess Mazu; the most revered female deity in China. The age-old "Tale of Yishan Island" tells how Mazu—savior and protector of ocean travelers, rescuer of the drowning—once saved a group of twenty fishermen from a sudden squall at sea. First, she leads them to an unknown, thickly wooded island. When the storm has subsided, the goddess shows them the way to their home port, where the fishermen all arrive safe and sound. This story is especially meaningful in relation to the Morecambe Bay tragedy because it originates from the Chinese province of Fujian, where Mazu has been worshipped since around CE 1000. Twenty of the twenty-three drowned cockle-fishers were impoverished farmers and workers from Fujian province—the home of most Chinese workers who emigrate to Europe.

The medium by which *Ten Thousand Waves* retells this age-old myth, however, is not as old as the "Tale of Yishan Island" itself. The installation narrates the story of Mazu through *filmic* means. First of all, the smooth and sharp images which depict Mazu's rescue of the cockle-fishers look like film images because of their contrast with the preceding low-quality video footage. As the difference between the media of film and video has long been marked particularly by the discrepancy between video's low resolution and low contrast ratio on the one hand, and film's high-quality images on the other hand, it seems obvious to understand the cut from blurred, pixelated footage to smooth and focused images as a switch from one medium to the other. In addition, the tale of Mazu is told by way of conventional cinematic narrative strategies which are absent from the video surveillance footage. The gaze of the goddess is for instance "sutured" to the images of boiling surges. This cinematic device—which connects shots to the viewpoint of onscreen characters—returns in the installation when Mazu flies through Pudong's high-rises (people are drowning in Shanghai's high-tech business hub, too).

When the goddess flies through the landscape of Yishan island, however, the images conform to well-known, yet quite disparate instances of contemporary Asian cinematic aesthetics. As Mark Nash has pointed out, the sumptuous images of Mazu suspended over a river, framed by the vertiginous limestone peaks, makes one think that one might be participating in the Taoist aesthetic of a fifth-generation Chinese filmmaker, such as Zhang Yimou. The zip pans through the bamboo forest, on the other hand, can rather be understood as an homage to the prestidigitations of Hong Kong popular cinema and Ang Lee's *Crouching Tiger, Hidden Dragon (*2000) (Nash 2010: 40). The installation's tie to cinema is consolidated all the more by the fact that Mazu is played by a famous film star, Maggie Cheung.

What is more, Julien's installation references Chinese cinema by telling yet another well-known story. For, in addition to the Morecambe Bay tragedy and the Mazu myth, *Ten Thousand Waves* revisits the classic Chinese film *The Goddess* (Wu, 1934). The woman who prostitutes herself in order to support herself and her son in Wu's film, is first depicted in a historic architectural setting in Julien's version of the story. Yet, this old Chinese city turns out to be an old Shanghai film studio. The female protagonist moves through this historic film décor, yet she also ends up in contemporary Chinese interiors. One of these interiors offers the woman of easy virtue a splendid view on Pudong's Jin Mao Tower, in front of which Mazu is suddenly flying by.

The latter's presence connects the fictional character of the prostitute to the drowned immigrants, for whom Mazu as well as the surveillance video camera were looking earlier on in the installation. Mazu's gaze upon the prostitute suggests that the latter is either lost and drowning, just like the cockle-fishers, or that she is somehow related to the victims of the Morecambe Bay tragedy. She might very well be missing her migrant son, like the woman in the installation's sample from the video documentary on Morecambe Bay. By being cinematically sutured to the gaze of a mythical deity, the fictional female character from a classical Chinese film story becomes a contemporary Chinese woman who seems to be affected by a real overseas tragedy in the present. *Ten Thousand Waves* manages to intricately relate as well as blur the boundaries between past and present, home and away, and reality and fiction, through a combination of filmed stories with video footage.

Two media

This combination of cinematic features with forms of video complicates the definition of *Ten Thousand Waves* in terms of its medial character. As the work's images—including the cinematic ones—are stored and projected in high-definition digital video format, the piece is a video installation in technological terms. Yet, should a video installation which so overtly foregrounds cinematic devices, and which moreover includes so many references to film, primarily be defined in terms of video? On the other hand, it seems inaccurate to understand Julien's piece—which is not only video in a technological sense, but which also looks like video in so many formal respects—as principally film(ic).

Most discussions of *Ten Thousand Waves* circumvent the relation between film and video in the installation by ignoring one of the two media. Notably, institutions of contemporary visual art which exhibit the installation emphasize the medium which operates most prevailingly within the field of art, that is, video. In press releases from the Boston Institute for Contemporary Art (ICA) and the Brandhorst Museum in Munich, to name but two, Julien's piece was referred to as a nine-screen *video* installation. However, when the installation is shown or discussed in institutions, exhibitions or articles concerned with film, the medium of video is often left unmentioned. In 2012, *Ten Thousand Waves* was, for instance, shown in an exhibition entitled *Expanded Cinema* at Amsterdam's Filmmuseum EYE. The museum's exhibition leaflets and captions referred to Julien's piece as a *film* installation. To give one more example here: in an article which aims to outline the installation's cinematic predecessors, Nash refers to *Ten Thousand Waves* as a multi-channel film, or even more simply, as a film.

These definitions of *Ten Thousand Waves* in terms of one single medium are limiting, because the complexity of the installation cannot be fully seen, appreciated, analyzed, or understood without acknowledging the fact that the piece contains both cinematic and "videomatic" elements. The meanings, effects, and affects that are generated by the installation largely depend on the difference between video forms and film features within the piece, as well as on the interplay between the features of these different media. In Julien's installation, the two media for example offer the viewer different, yet complementary ways of relating to the problems of China's impoverished working class.

Although definitions which group *Ten Thousand Waves* under expanded cinema or classify it as video installation art are both justifiable, the installation's psychological and physical effects, as well as the critical reflections on (among other things) migration which the artwork gives rise to, can be grasped more fully when the difference between video and film is not overlooked or ignored. This not only goes for *Ten Thousand Waves*. Many contemporary moving image objects are, on the one hand, ruled by (a group of) elements which derive in the first place from the field of film, and, on the other hand, by features which are more typical of the video medium. This mixture of the cinematic and the videomatic is most prevalent in museum pieces such as Julien's, yet it is also common in contemporary narrative fiction films—both mainstream and so called art-house films. In addition, the combination of film and video forms functions in the ubiquitous moving images which surround us outside of the museum, art gallery, or film theater today. It infuses home movies, videos on the Internet, commercials on TV, and clips on cellphones.

Medium specificity revisited

In order to study the combinations of film and video within contemporary cultural objects, an analysis of their intermedial relationship may seem an obvious starting point. When it comes to *Ten Thousand Waves*, definitions of the piece as a "multi-media work" or "post-cinematic video installation" (Julien's own description) appear to be suitable onsets to such analyses, as they take the medial plurality of the installation into account. Moreover, the above-mentioned definitions are only two instances in a wide range of possibilities. For, in spite of the fact that the multi-medial character of installations like Julien's is often left unmentioned, contemporary (new) media theory offers a wide range of terms by which interrelations between media can be defined and conceptualized.

In addition to prefixes and adjectives such as inter-, mixed, multi-, or hybrid media, (new) media scholars such as Noel Carroll (1996), Jay David Bolter and Richard Grusin (1999), Steven Maras and David Sutton (2000), Lars Elleström (2010), and Jens Schröter (2011) have conceptualized the relationship between media in terms such as aping, imitation, convergence, remediation, hyper-mediation, repurposing, re-forming and refashioning, transition, bundling, absorption, combination, integration, transformation, and so on. Most of these notions are applied in concord with the theoretical conclusion that it is no longer possible to detect pure media in the contemporary digital age. Today, all media are entangled in processes of remediating or repurposing another's forms, which leaves us with nothing but intermedial cultural objects. The once dominant, modernist idea that artistic media have their own, autonomous, unique essence, is highly problematized by these objects in which media are so overtly involved in imitating and refashioning each other. Any claims at medium specificity are impeded by the ubiquitous intermedial and mixed media artworks.

Although I do not disagree with such a characterization of today's situation, and take the wide variety of notions such as remediation and hypermediacy as helpful tools in analyzing the relationships between media, I argue that the starting point of an investigation into intermedial interactions should be the concept of medium specificity instead of the many notions which define forms of intermediality. The problem is, as Elleström also remarks, that intermediality has tended to be discussed without clarification of what a medium actually is (2010: 11). Nevertheless, an investigation into relationships between or even convergence of, different media still starts out with the presupposition of different, distinguishable media. Steven Maras and David Sutton rightly point out in their article entitled "Medium Specificity Re-visited" (2000) that theorists who deal with intermedial relationships often critique and problematize essentialist notions of the medium through concepts such as refashioning and remediation. Yet this method often merely delays and defers the question of essentialism. In their critical discussion of Bolter and Grusin's medium theory, Maras and Sutton aptly remark on the former's methodology that: "Their approach is based around acts of refashioning that ultimately problematise the essence of a medium, but at the outset of each act the predecessors of that medium [...] stand more or less fully formed" (2000: 108). Thus, models of intermediality which supposedly demonstrate the end of medium specificity, are often implicitly based on an originary ground on which media do have essences, are fixed, and achieve a final form.[1]

The fact that many influential theories of intermediality are unable to circumvent the essentialist notions of medium specificity which they wish to defy, does not mean, of course, that we should return to these seemingly inescapable, persistent essentialist ideas on medium specificity. Yet, it is nevertheless imperative to ask what mediality means when we discuss intermediality. In order to investigate what happens between media, it first needs to be clear how these media are (to be) understood. The rightful conclusion that essentialist ideas on medium specificity are rendered untenable by today's mixed, multi-, and intermedia, too often overshadows the question of *what* is being mixed, expanded, remediated, refashioned, converged or combined. Maras and Sutton are right to state that, when faced, for example, with a definition of multimedia that incorporates "video, text and graphics" it is simply a useful question to ask: "what do you mean by video?"(2000: 112).

In this study I ask the questions "what is meant by video?" and "what is meant by film?" How are these two media (to be) understood? Can film and video be defined as distinct, specific media, and if so, how? I argue that in this era of mixed moving media, it is vital to ask such questions precisely and especially on the media of video and film.

From a technological point of view, however, it no longer makes sense to differentiate between film and video. Upon its arrival in the 1960s, video started out as an analogue electronic medium which clearly differed from film. In its initial phase, it was only able to produce grainy black-and-white footage. Its magnetic tape, moreover, could not easily be edited and was prone to electronic distortion. In addition, video footage could only be watched on a TV monitor. Hence, the early low-quality video images did not look like film, and could, moreover, not be looked at in the same viewing set-up as back-lit film projections. However, the formal and technological properties and abilities of the video medium evolved rapidly. The differences between film and video became less distinct with the arrival of video projectors, the development of video editing equipment, as well as the improvement in video image quality.

One could even argue that my objects of research—the media of film and video—disappeared while I was preparing and writing this book. When I initiated my first research on the two media in 2006, the difference between the media of film and video was still a noticeable technological fact. Although both media had already been taken up in the process of digitalization, and hence came to share important aspects of their technological support, neither analogue nor digital video images were able to meet the high image quality of analogue film footage. When narrative fiction films were screened in digital video formats, members of the audience would often complain that the images didn't look as good, as bright, as sharp or as smooth as "real" film. Today, such a perceptible difference between film and video images is no longer a technological necessity.

Yet, in spite of the fact that technological differences between the two media have largely been bridged, distinctions between film and video are still ubiquitously perceptible—for instance in works like *Ten Thousand Waves*. This demonstrates that the difference between video and film is made rather than given; it is repeatedly shown, (re-)produced and applied by visual objects and artworks. In addition, the distinction is made by spectators, who (sometimes only subconsciously) recognize and thereby respond to the difference between film and video features in the process of viewing and reading moving images. As opposed to the idea that intermediality is to be understood as a bridge between medial differences (Elleström 2010: 12), the films and videos I study demonstrate that in many cases, the distinction between two media can form a persistent yet productive gap in intermedial objects.

Defining video and film as two distinct media first of all begs for a definition of medium specificity which does not solely rely on the given technological, material components of a medium. How can the constantly mixing, merging, and rapidly evolving media of film and video be defined as distinct media when the technological differences between them have become almost superfluous? What is more, how can film and video be defined as distinct, specific media without reverting to essentialist notions of medium specificity?

A Voyage on the North Sea

My search for a nonessentialist definition of medium specificity starts with *A Voyage on the North Sea* (1999). In this pamphlet-sized book, art historian Rosalind Krauss aims to distance the notion of the specific medium from its unfortunately loaded meaning. From the 1960s onwards, Krauss explains, a definition of the medium as mere physical object, in all its reductiveness and drive towards reification, has become common currency in the art world. The word "medium" has been pervasively "Greenbergized," as Krauss rightly states. The ideas of the late art historian on the relationship between the history of art and medium specificity have been highly influential.

In his well-known essay "Modernist Painting" (1961), Clement Greenberg depicts the history of art as a continuous development in which the different arts—such as painting, sculpture, architecture, and literature—gradually sought to discover their own unique, exclusive qualities. Within this process, which reached its highpoint in the period of modernism, it became perfectly clear that "the unique and proper area of competence of each art coincided with all that was unique to the nature of its medium," according to Greenberg (102). During modernism, he claims, works of art approached the boundaries of their own medium in order to determine each medium's unchanging essence. According to Greenberg, this fixed and autonomous essence of every medium could eventually be reduced to a single, unique property of its material, technical support.

In line with many of the aforementioned new media theorists such as Bolter and Grusin, Krauss argues that Greenberg's essentialist ideas have first and foremost been superseded by the fact that intermediality is now ubiquitous. According to Krauss, contemporary art exists in the era of the "post-medium condition." For, since the 1970s, it has become especially difficult to divide the visual arts into specific media. In contrast to the modernist arts described by Clement Greenberg, recent artistic practices do not set great store by the distinction between media. The traditional media into which art was long subdivided are made subordinate to a whole range of expressive means that artists have at their disposal. Since the 1970s, all kinds of techniques are mixed within artworks, with no possibility left to define them as pure media. Medium purity is no longer a goal, and in many works of art it is even determinedly undermined. Through this, the concept of medium specificity seems to have become superfluous.

In addition to her observations on contemporary artistic practices, Krauss argues that the concept of medium specificity is no longer tenable in theoretical terms either. Poststructuralist ideas in particular have contributed to the fact that the idea of a pure, autonomous medium has become a mere fiction:

> From the theory of grammatology to that of the paragon, Jacques Derrida built demonstration after demonstration to show that the idea of an interior set apart from, or uncontaminated by, an exterior was a chimera, a metaphysical fiction. [...] That nothing could be constituted as pure interiority or self-identity, that this purity was always already invaded by an outside, indeed, could itself only be constituted through the very introjection of that outside, was the argument to scuttle the supposed autonomy of the aesthetic experience, or the possible purity of an artistic medium. The self-identical was revealed to us, and thus dissolved to, the self-different.
>
> Krauss 1999: 32

After the poststructuralist deconstruction of the self-contained medium, the opinion that media have a specific essence can no longer be sustained.

Nevertheless, the notion of medium in itself is retained by Krauss. After explicitly distancing herself from Greenberg's views, she replaces his essentialist ideas with another definition of medium specificity: "the specificity of mediums, even modernist ones, must be understood as differential, self-differing, and thus as a layering of conventions never simply collapsed into the physicality of their support" (1999: 53). According to Krauss, a medium is to be seen as a layered structure that is constantly being repeated. This structure is not given; it is made and composed out of the physical support plus a set of rules and conventions. These conventions determine how the expressive possibilities offered by the technical support of a medium are delimited or applied.

One of the most important benefits of Krauss' definition is that it opposes the temporal fixity of Greenberg's notion of the medium. In Krauss' model, a medium's specificity is never complete; media are always caught up in the process of differing from themselves. Instead of understanding media as static entities, Krauss defines them as changeable and differing structures. Secondly, she rewrites the concept's meaning by adding a layer to the medium's technological or physical base in her definition. Whereas Greenberg located a medium's specificity purely in the materiality of its support, Krauss argues that the specificity of media is built out of conventions, too. The word "built" in the previous sentence already points to the third way in which Krauss' definition differs from Greenberg's. Krauss emphasizes that a medium's specificity is a construction, which disables an understanding of medium specificity as an autonomous, given essence.

Since Krauss stresses that media are not given units, but that they are built and made, the medium specificity of which she speaks depends on medium specification. The difference between the terms "medium specificity" and "medium specification" is important. Medium specification indicates that media *are being* specified, while medium specificity rather indicates what *is* specific about media. In contrast to Greenberg, Krauss holds the opinion that media do not have absolute and fixed specificities, but that their specificities are made, and hence, that medium specificity is established through specification.

When it comes to medium specification, Krauss mostly focuses on the production of conventions. A technology or material becomes a specific medium as soon as it is repeatedly being used according to a specific set of conventions. The structure of conventions defines how and which possibilities of a certain physical support are applied. Such a conventional structure is a kind of grammar; a coherent set of rules which is iterated each time a technology is used. In her writings on medium specificity, Krauss particularly discusses how artists invent sets of conventions, and consequently produce specific media.[2] Hence, she pays most attention to the senders; to the ones who apply a certain technology or material according to a specific set of conventions in order to (re)produce something—information, sound, image, text, art.

However, Krauss' definition of the medium implicitly implicates another party. Like grammar, the rules of the medium are not mainly applied (and hence produced) by those who utter messages or produce objects with a certain technological or physical support. Conventions are also to be understood by the audience, by the receivers of medial objects, if a medium (or language, for that matter) is to be recognized as such. Often, recognition is something of an understatement, for the conventions which specify a medium are equally *produced* by the spectators of media. It is illuminating, in this regard, to speak of multiple layers rather than one layer of conventions. For, quite apart (but not entirely so) from the actual conventionalized applications of a technology, medium specificity comes into being by sets of conventions which determine how a medium is *seen*. The specification or definition of a medium depends on conventional notions/ideas on what a medium "is." The governing opinions or expectations about the possibilities of a medium are just as important for a medium's specification as the way in which these possibilities are used in practice. A canvas painted totally ultramarine would for instance not have been considered as a painting two hundred years ago. Nowadays, such a canvas meets our expectations of what painting is and what it can do.

My investigation into the media of film and video relies heavily on the idea that historically and socially relative conventional opinions on what a medium "is" shape medium specification. Although I will focus on some of the (ever-changing) technological differences between film and video, and moreover aim to map out the most distinct conventions which shape the specific dominant applications of each medium's technology, my study also comprises comparisons and analyses of the most dominant reflections on film and video. I hold that the distinct specific features of film and video can only be defined by also studying definitions of the media. Reflections on the two media do not only describe, but also (co- and re)produce the specificity of film and video. Following art historian David Green (2005), I take the view that media are to a large extent simply what we think they are. And what we think they are, moreover, very much depends on dominant reflections on what they are. The reflections I study are mostly theoretical texts. However, the distinction between reflections and applications is not always clear cut; many of the visual objects I analyze can be understood as self-reflexive reflections on the specificity of their medium or media. Such objects specify and produce the media with which they are produced in more than one way.

This brings me to yet another way in which medium specificity is produced according to Krauss' definition of the concept. The art historian defines a medium's specificity as differential, indicating that a medium's specificity is in part determined by differences from other media. Remarkably, this idea of differential specificity was not unknown to Clement Greenberg, who claimed that the specificity of a medium can be determined by comparison to other media. The unique essence of a medium, Greenberg argued, lies in that characteristic by which it differs from all other media. However, Greenberg basically undermines his own idea of autonomous media by acknowledging the importance of difference to a medium's specificity. This was also noted by Schröter, who wrote that: "the definition of the 'specific character' of a medium requires the differential demarcation from other media; the terms for other media are paradoxically absolutely necessary for every 'purist' and 'essentialist' definition [...]" (2011: 5).[3] In other words, if medium specificity is dependent on differences with other media, a medium cannot be regarded as an autonomous, isolated unit. It is specified by other media.

The differences between media can be considered of importance without adopting Greenberg's opinion that the unchanging essence of media can be determined on the basis of this difference. A medium can, among other things, be specified because it can do things other media cannot. However, such unique qualities are temporary. As soon as the unique possibilities of a medium are equaled or imitated by means of technological development or an alteration of medial conventions, the specification of the existing medium changes.[4]

In addition, medium specification doesn't necessarily imply the demarcation or recovering of a medium's unique essence. Although media can only be distinguished by way of the differences between them, these differences do not always point to unique properties or capabilities. Analogue film, for instance, shares its photochemical base with the medium of photography. Yet, it distinguishes itself from photography by producing moving instead of still images. This capacity to produce moving images, however, is not unique to film: it is also a capability of the video medium. The latter medium, however, doesn't rely on a photochemical process for the production of its images. Within this web of differences and similarities between lens-based media, no single property is unique to film. Yet the latter medium's position within the web of intermedial relations, the precise ways in which it differs from as well as resembles other media, *is* unique, *is* specific. Hence, I argue that media are specified by mutual differences from as well as specific similarities with other media. I take the differentiality in Krauss' definition of medium specificity as a term which suggests or refers to the comparison of different media, rather than a notion which solely focuses on differences. Following this train of thought, the act of defining a medium's specificity can in part be understood as a process of mapping the differences and similarities between media, rather than the disclosure of a medium's single, unique essence.

The idea of differential specificity indicates the direction of my investigation into the media of film and video. By way of comparing and contrasting the differences and similarities between the two media, I aim to map out the layers of their related and similar, yet specific structures; that is, parts and sections of their specific structure. It is not possible to outline all media which constitute the specificity of film and video by way of differences and similarities, or to provide a historical overview of all forms and functions, specifications, and applications of film and video over the past decades in one study. However, it is possible to locate times and places where film and video met, crossed paths, altered each other's course. In spite of a wide array of existing terms for all kinds and forms of intermediality to choose from, this book does not set out to classify or name all the different intermedial interactions between film and video. Instead, it highlights those discourses, contexts, functions, forms, and objects in which the two media have specified, or still specify each other most strongly—and studies these processes of specification. It points out which—often already changed or neutralized—differences and similarities between the media have led to the forms of film and video which we have and see today. As I will demonstrate, the two media have thoroughly altered and influenced each other's specificity over the last decades. This strong mutual influence is not so much the result of differences, but is mostly caused by the fact that in many ways they are so alike.

The above shows that, although the primary aim of this research is to gain understanding in contemporary intermedial objects which combine film and video features, it necessarily comprises media-archaeological components. Yet, in some ways, these media-archaeological passages should rather be defined as media-theory archaeological analyses; for, as media specificity depends on medium specification, the related histories of film and video are histories of related medium specifications. As explained previously, media are specified both in practice and by theory. When it comes to the media of film and video, there has been much cross-over between medial practices and theoretical specifications. As I will demonstrate, the medium of video has not only influenced the specificity of film through video practices which, for instance, have taken over some of film's dominant applications, but also via the medium specifications which film theory forms. The arrival of video made film theorists sensitive to some of the abilities of cinema. Abilities, that is, which had not yet been widely noted before video images brought them fully into sight. In this way, video managed to shed a new light on film, which was consequently viewed differently.

On the other hand, film theory can provide insight into the specificity of video. Film-theoretical concepts have proven to be either elucidating or useless in the analysis of video works. Either way, in the absence of a coherent field of video studies, film-theoretical ideas have guided, and still guide, the specification of video as a medium. Therefore, the notion of differential specificity which forms the basis of this study goes hand in hand with differential specification—the latter involving both visual objects and theoretical texts. How do theoretical specifications of film relate to specifications of video? In what way do reflections on video differ from thoughts about film? How do ideas on film affect the use and understanding of the video medium? How have video works influenced film theory, and hence film?

What is more, interestingly, the idea of differential specificity shows that the answer to my initial questions (How can film and video be defined as distinct, specific media? How are these two media to be understood?) can be sought in the intermedial objects of which I aim to gain a better understanding by way of investigating those questions on the specificity, or rather, the specification of film and video. If media are fundamentally specified by their mutual differences and similarities, then this process of specification can be presumed to be visible and active in visual objects in which film and video images are placed in, over, or after one another. All in all, analyses of the intermedial relations in mixed film/video objects require insight into general specifications of the two media. Yet, the intermedial objects which I study in this book each constitute contributions to these specifications of film and video as well, and therefore need to be approached with the question of how film and video are specified by and within the specific intermedial piece.

Traveling forward, expanding the voyage

It is remarkable that Krauss does not embrace intermedial artworks in her writings on differential medium specificity, of which *A Voyage of the North Sea* is the most comprehensive. As film and video scholar Ji-Hoon Kim has noted, there is no reason why intermedial artworks contradict Krauss' medium theory. Yet, in contrast to her predilection for obsolete media, she excludes intermedia or mixed media from the outset (Kim 2009: 121). In fact, Krauss condemns the international fashion for installation and intermedial work with the argument that, in this trend, "art finds itself complicit with a globalization of the image in the service of capital" (Krauss 1999: 56). However, Krauss' idea of differential specificity is sustained and carried out precisely by the intermedia works which she despises. As Kim puts it, Krauss' criticism on intermedial artworks "brackets out any potential for investigating the relationship that makes the 'differential specificity' of a medium, such as film, become dramatized and altered by other new media [. . .]" (2009: 121).

Kim rightly concludes that the fact that differential specificity is not intrinsic to Krauss' privileged artworks makes clear that her thesis on medium specificity is still anchored in a belief in the uniqueness and singularity of the means of expression that is part of the modernist argument on medium specificity that she intends to renew (Kim 2009: 121). Such implicit, unintended recourses to essentialism can be discovered in more than one way in Krauss' medium-theoretical work. Thus, although her definition of medium specificity forms the starting point of my research, I will discuss the problems and shortcomings of Krauss' thesis throughout this study. In each of the following four parts, I propose a supplement to her definition which can obviate the recurrent "pull" of essentialism. These supplements will be provided in the form of existing concepts (e.g., the field, discourse) with which Krauss' definition is compared and expanded.

My expansion of the notion of the medium partly follows theorists such as Lars Elleström and Maras and Sutton, who have proposed valuable categories (called modalities and nodes, respectively) by which many features and aspects of media can be mapped, hence leading to outlines of the medium as a more complex configuration than Krauss' two-layered structure. However, instead of pinpointing "the essential cornerstones of all media," as Elleström (2010: 15) sets out to do, I propose a comparative approach to the concept that questions both essential cores and cornerstones. In a sense, my examination of the concept of the medium resembles my differential investigation of film's and video's specificity: by mapping the differences and similarities between concepts, and studying the (possible) interrelation between them, the different sides and boundaries of the concept of the medium will be probed.

The first supplement to Krauss' definition can already be found in the common denominator of the four parts of this book, each of which is structured around an effect of the two media on their users. Krauss diverts attention from the essentialist question of what a medium is by focusing on the question of how a medium is produced. To Krauss' question of how a medium is made and specified, I add the question of what a medium does. What are the (distinct and/or similar) performative effects of film and video? How do the two media affect their viewers? How do they relate their users? Which positions do they enable, preclude or create for the subject? The four parts of this book are organized around four effects which surface most pervasively in specifications of film and video. Those four effects, moreover, form a suitable ground for comparison, as the most notable differences and similarities between film and video are tied to them.

In Part I, I compare the way in which film and video each produce reality effects, yet in different ways. Some of the most famous discussions of film's specificity circle around the medium's inherent realism. Video has, however, altered the way in which the relation between film and reality can be understood, as the technology of the video medium relates video images differently to referents in reality than film does. What is more, although film and video both produce a reality effect, their impression on the viewer is slightly different. In addition, the conventional devices by which film and video produce their respective reality effects are disparate. Intermedial video artworks and films often combine the reality effect producing devices of both film and video. What is the effect of such double, yet different, reality effects in one visual object? In two close readings of *Benny's Video* (Haneke 1992) and *Family Viewing* (Egoyan 1987), I analyze how the videomatic reality effect enhances the cinematic one, while the two films in turn constantly specify the video images they show as "real." In addition, the specific (yet conventional) relation between video images and reality turns out to offer new narrative possibilities to fiction films.

The comparison of the reality effects of film and video leads to some questions on the concept of medium specificity. Krauss' definition proves to have its shortcomings, as it cannot account for the fact that film and video each have many, sometimes even opposing abilities and characteristics at the same time. In Part I, I therefore suggest expanding Krauss' definition with a term which spatializes Krauss' predominantly temporal term, namely, George Baker's notion of the "field".

In Part II, I study the ways in which film and video each affect the viewer's sense of being a physical body in time and space. Why is the medium of film usually theorized as a medium which produces a disembodied viewer; a viewer who forgets her own bodily presence in time and space? Why has video, on the other hand, been defined as a haptic, embodying medium? In order to answer these questions, I turn to Jean-Louis Baudry's influential film-theoretical concept of the *dispositif*. Not only has this concept formed the basis of the discourses of so-called apparatus theorists, who more than anyone have produced the dominant view that the film spectator is a disembodied one, it is also a very useful concept in explaining why video often functions as an embodying rather than a disembodying medium. What is more, the intermedial cinematic video installations by David Claerbout and Douglas Gordon which I will discuss in this part combine some of the most typical disembodying and embodying qualities of film and video, most of which concern features of the media's *dispositifs*; features such as the spatial viewing set-up of their technologies, the spatial and architectural features of the viewing room, (institutional) viewing conventions, as well as the position of the spectator.

In Part III, I frame film and video within society. In addition to the fact that the concept of the medium in general necessitates attention to the social field, this field is especially important to an investigation of film and video. First of all, video came into being in a decade in which medium theory (as formulated by, most prominently, Marshall McLuhan) centered on the idea that media produce social structures. Many early video practices relate to this dominant, influential idea. The technological determinism which is expressed by these theoretical texts and objects gives rise to new questions on Krauss' definition of medium specificity. The concept will be redefined in this part by way of Raymond Williams' ideas on so-called soft determination.

Out of all the domains within which the two media operate (culture, politics, art, etc.) the social field can be said to point out the internal differentiation of the two media the most. When film and video are framed by their operation within the social field, the specificity of the two media turns out to be fraught with contradictions. In addition to these internal contradictions, film and video overlap, differ, and oppose each other in the social field. Besides theoretical texts which specify the social effects of film and video, I analyze how the different social meanings, functions and effects of the two media are (further) exposed as well as applied in intermedial artworks by video artists Lynn Hershman and Sadie Benning.

The positive and sometimes even utopian specifications of film and video which are discussed in Part III have dominant negative counterparts. In addition to texts and objects which emphasize the specific ability of film and video to produce stable subject positions within (democratic, emancipated, utopian) social structures, many practical and theoretical works specify the two lens-based media as cold, objectifying media which hurt and obstruct, rather than aid or create the subject. Although some of the dystopian views of film and video are discussed in Part III, I zoom in on these other sides of film's and video's respective "Janus heads" in Part IV, which deals with the violent features of the two media. As the violent impact of film and video can hardly be considered separately from harmful social discourses, I investigate how the concept of the medium relates to Foucault's notion of "discourse."[5]

What is more, the violent features of film and video cannot be understood without taking the common ancestor of the lens-based media into account, that is, photography. A triangulation with photography will provide insight into the specific ways in which film and video are each able to hurt their users, most notably the subjects in front of the lens. Such triangulation with another medium is not unique to Part IV; mapping the differential specificity of the two media vis-à-vis each other necessarily involves comparing the ways in which the two media relate similarly or differently to other, closely related media. In the first part, literature and literary theory will bring out some of the specific qualities of film and video. In Part II, art-historical ideas on painting, theater, and sculpture are brought to bear on film and video. The medium of television will mostly play an important part in Part III. The influence of the computer, finally, runs through all four parts. The question of how digitalization has (or hasn't) altered the applications and possibilities which are specific to analogue film and video will be addressed throughout this study.

Near the end of Part IV, the Janus heads of film and video are turned again—by films and videos themselves. In the final chapter of Part IV, I will compare the different ways in which feminist films and videos work to oppose the misogynist traits of traditional narrative cinema. Whereas feminist films radically disengage themselves from classical film conventions, intermedial video works such as *Phoenix Tapes* (1999) by artist duo Matthias Müller and Christoph Girardet, and *Approximations* (2000–2001) by Johanna Householder and b.h. Yael form critical reflections on misogynist film conventions by mimicking or sampling scenes from classical narrative films. These videomatic strategies of mimicking and sampling will bring me back to *Ten Thousand Waves* in the conclusion, where I will demonstrate how my differential mapping of film and video can form a guide through the blurry, swirling waves of intermedial film/video works.

PART I
THE REALITY EFFECT

INTRODUCTION: FROM REAL TO REEL IN *BENNY'S VIDEO*

Did *you* film that?

Mm-hmm.

What was it like, with the pig? I mean, have you ever seen a corpse before, for real?

No. You?

No.

It was only a pig. I once saw a program on TV about the special effects they use in actions films. All ketchup and plastic. Looks real though.[1]

Michael Haneke's narrative fiction film *Benny's Video* (1992) starts with moving video images. It is mainly because of their poor quality that the medium of these images can be discerned. Their texture is marked by the square grain which is typical of video images. The graininess of the surface is especially visible in dark areas of the images, where pixels have dropped out and have left small white squares and lines. Primary colors within the images, especially reds, look pale and unsaturated. Skin tones are covered with an unnatural faint blue shimmer.

Besides the fact that the image quality of the footage is low, it is rather poorly recorded as well. Clearly recorded with a handheld camera, the images shudder and shake. All camera movements in the unedited material are fast and abrupt, as are the zoom movements. The disorienting effect of these amateurish traits diminishes, though, when the camera zooms in on a pig that was first dragged out of a dark sty by a couple of people. Surrounded by a small crowd and a barking dog, the squealing animal is pushed to the ground. First its large bluish pink body fills the image frame, then the camera zooms in on the pig's head, through which a bullet is shot with a gun for slaughtering cattle. Pale red blood starts to flow, while the pig starts to spasm.

These movements stop, however. The image of the dying pig is brought to a standstill, then partially rewound, and subsequently replayed in slow-motion. The scene ends with an abrupt change into "snow"—the noise of an untuned television. On the one hand, these actions affirm that the medium of the shown footage is video. They bring out typical formal features and technical possibilities of the medium, such as the possibility of pausing or rewinding a videotape on a VCR, and the characteristic horizontal flickering scan lines which cross the video image when those possibilities are used.

On the other hand, the operations of pausing, rewinding, and playing the videotape in slow motion indicate the fact that the videotape is actually embedded in another medium, namely film. The actions direct the spectator's attention to the diegesis of Haneke's narrative fiction film because they imply another spectator; someone who is looking at and controlling the movement of the video images at the same time. In other words, the manipulations and interruptions of the moving video point to a viewer who is using the remote control. This active spectator turns out to exist inside the world created by the narrative film which follows the video. The film's fourteen-year-old protagonist named Benny is shown to repeatedly scrutinize the images of the dying pig by operating the remote control.

Because Benny's actions with the remote control are both visible within the video scene and in the subsequent narrative film, they function as the most important link between the two parts—the video and the film. Moreover, as the pausing, rewinding, and slowing down of the moving video images already implicitly refer to a viewer/actor which the film will make explicit later on, they motivate and soften the abrupt transition between the shaky, coarse-grained, unedited video material and the filmed part which consists of steady shots and the smooth, well-edited images of a high-quality film production. Another aspect which relates the video segment to the narrative film is the fact that two of the people in the small crowd around the suffering pig are introduced later on in the film as Benny's parents. What is more, Benny is not only shown to be the diegetic viewer of the video, he also turns out to be the producer of it. All in all, the bond between the video clip and the narrative film is tightened in many ways as the film proceeds. As it turns out, the moving images of the dying pig do not simply precede the cinematic narrative; they are embedded in the film's diegesis.

However, although the transition from video images to film images is quite smooth because the relationship between the shown video material and the film story soon becomes clear, the switch from video to film does not come about entirely without a hitch. The transition remains complicated because the video recording and the narrative film each produce a reality effect, yet in a different way. In other words, the video and the film both evoke the impression that what they represent is reality, but the characteristics or strategies by which this impression is evoked are dissimilar. Put briefly, the video images produce the impression of showing reality through features which can best be characterized as flaws or imperfections, such as blurriness and color distortion. The reality effect of the film scenes, on the other hand, depends entirely on the flawlessness and seeming transparency of the material. What is more, the reality effects produced by the video and those of the film images give rise to a different sort and extent of belief. The viewer's belief in the world shown by the video is, for instance, likely to be more profound than the viewer's belief in the filmed world. In this part, I will further pinpoint the reality effects of film and video by looking into films and videos in which the two media are combined. Alongside *Benny's Video*, the main corpus of investigation includes the film *Family Viewing* (Atom Egoyan 1987) and *Battles of Troy* (2005), a video documentary by Krassimir Terziev.

The apparent recurrence of the same two reality effects of video and film in a large number of works makes it reasonable to assume that the effects are related to the specificity of video and film. But how can an effect such as the reality effect exactly relate to a medium's specificity, which I defined in the introduction as a layered structure which consists of a physical support and a number of conventions? How do the typical reality effects of film and video which recur in films and videos relate to specific technological possibilities and conventional applications of the two media? As will become clear below, answering this question will not only further delineate the specificity of film and video, but will also lead to a redefinition of the concept of medium specificity itself.

CHAPTER 1
REALITY EFFECTS: LITERATURE, FILM, AND VIDEO

In "The Reality Effect" (1982), Roland Barthes attempts to discover the significance of seemingly insignificant parts in realist novels; the useless details and superfluous descriptions to which structural analysis—"occupied as it is with separating out and systematizing the main articulations of narrative" (135)—can assign no functional value within the narrative. The detailed descriptions are insignificant in that they seem to be detached from the semiotic structure of the narrative. They do not, for instance, constitute an indication of characterization or atmosphere. Nor can they be said to have a classical rhetorical function, for the realist descriptions do not comply with the demands of plausibility and possibility which governed classical discourse.

To rush to the conclusion of Barthes' text before discussing the argument leading up to it, the detailed descriptions produce a reality effect. These "residues of functional analyses" seem to "denote what is commonly called 'concrete reality' (casual movements, transitory attitudes, insignificant objects, redundant words)" (1982: 38). Instead of depicting the plausible, possible, and general (i.e. the *vraisemblable*), detailed descriptions in realist texts appear to give a naked account of what is or was. The apparent interest of realist narratives in referential reality—including all its particularities—seems to resist being given a meaning. First, the detailed descriptions do not *mean* anything; they do not stand for anything other than themselves, they just *are*. Secondly, they seem to resist meaning because, as Barthes explains, reference to concrete reality is brandished as a weapon against meaning by the ideology of our time, "as if there were some indisputable law that what is truly alive could not signify—and vice versa" (139).

In order to further examine the seeming resistance of realist texts to meaning, Barthes turns to Ferdinand de Saussure's ideas on the sign. According to de Saussure, the category of the referent is not indispensable for the functioning of language; communication can occur through signifiers and signifieds alone. If language is to be studied effectively, de Saussure argues, the referents of signs can best be placed in brackets. With this idea in mind, Barthes notes that realist texts do not place such brackets at all. Instead, they seem to attempt to draw in the referent. As concrete details and descriptions in realist novels do not have a clear meaning or function within the structure of the narrative, they seem to be pure encounters between signifiers and referents. With that, the signified appears to be bypassed, or rather, to be expelled from the sign. *Seem*, that is, because such an encounter between signifier and referent at the expense of the signified would imply an impossible alteration of the sign. It is rather an illusion which is evoked by realist texts—the referential illusion, as Barthes calls it. The fact is that the details do not really denote reality directly, they rather signify reality by connotation. As Barthes explains:

> The truth behind this illusion is this: eliminated from the realist utterance as a signified of denotation, the "real" slips back in as a signified of connotation; at the very moment these details are supposed to denote reality directly, all they do, tacitly, is signify it. Flaubert's barometer, Michelet's little door, say, in the last analysis, only this: we are the real. It is this category of the real, and not its various contents, which is being signified; in other words, the very absence of the signified, to the advantage of the referent, standing alone, becomes the true signifier of realism. A reality effect is produced, which is the basis for that unavowed "vraisemblance" which forms the aesthetic of all standard works of modernity.
>
> 1982: 16

Precisely because the insignificant details in realist texts evoke the referential illusion—the illusion that the signified is expelled from the sign and that signifiers collide with their referent—they signify the category of the real: "the absence of the signified, to the advantage of the referent [. . .] becomes the true signifier of realism" (1982: 16). In other words, the insignificance of details becomes a signifier whose signified is the category of the real. This process is, however, marked by Barthes as the truth *behind* the referential illusion. The connotations "we are the real" or "this is reality" are not recognizable as signifieds, nor is the category of the real. Instead, realist texts seems to have hauled in the referent; to refer to referential reality directly. Reality thus seems to be denoted directly by realist texts while it is in fact signified.

Expanding "The Reality Effect"

In "The Reality Effect," Roland Barthes focuses solely on literary texts. In order to gain understanding of the reality effects in—among others—Haneke's film *Benny's Video* with the help of Barthes' ideas, it is necessary to consider how these ideas would function outside of the scope of literary texts alone. More specifically, how does Barthes' theory apply to the media of film and video?[1] Can the reality effect Barthes identifies in literary texts be produced in a similar fashion by film(s) and video(s)? Can the device of detailed descriptions, which Barthes points out as being responsible for the reality effect of literary texts, also function in films and videos?

The differences between detailed representations by literature on the one hand and film on the other, have been explored by theorists studying the adaptation from novel to film, such as Seymour Chatman and Robert Stam. One of the lessons that can be drawn from adaptation studies is that detailed depictions by film and video cannot simply be regarded as the visual equivalent of detailed descriptions in literary texts. The first reason for this is that, whereas many aspects can still remain undetermined in detailed literary descriptions, the details shown in film and video images are inevitably specific. Films and videos possess an "excessive particularity, a plentitude of visual details aptly called [. . .] 'over-specification'" (Chatman 1980: 126). Moreover, whereas the selection among the number of details evoked is determined and limited in a literary text, the number of details in a film or video representation is indeterminate (125).[2] Comparative studies such as Chatman's therefore define film images as over-detailed, over-specified, and excessively particular.

Another reason for which the detailed depictions by film and video cannot be regarded as the visual equivalent of detailed descriptions in literary texts is that the depictions are less likely to halt the narrative timeline of a film or video. For although film and video mostly possess a plenitude of visual details, the movement of the images does not always allow the viewer time to dwell on this plenitude, and to notice each and every detail. Films can place some emphasis on certain details through techniques such as framing, zooming or focusing—techniques which can signify that certain details are significant. Yet a large measure of superfluous detail is an inevitable characteristic of film and video images. Although the details depicted by film and video do not hold the temporal progress of the narrative (if any), they have an important thing in common with the details in realist literature: they are largely insignificant.

Overflowing with superfluous detail, film and video might be expected to outshine literature in creating reality effects. Yet, although the excess detail certainly contributes to the strong reality effects that film and video are able to produce, it is not the most important source of these effects. Rather, one of the most important sources of the reality effects of the two lens-based media lies in the source of the excess detail itself: the technological and chemical ways in which analogue film and video images are produced.

Both film and video images are brought about by rays of light that pass through the lens of a camera; rays of light, moreover, which are generated or reflected into the camera by objects that are present in front of the recording device. In film cameras, the light is projected onto the light-sensitive celluloid filmstrip which passes by the shutter. The light beam imprints discrete, rectangular images onto the transparent filmstrip, which only become visible (and projectable) as positive images after a chemical development process. In video cameras, the visual information which the rays of light contain is transformed into an electronic signal by a cathode ray tube or by a light-sensitive CCD-chip. This electronic signal can subsequently be sent through wires and be broadcast immediately by devices which are able to translate the electronic signal back into a luminous image (e.g., a TV or the video camera itself). The electronic signal can however also be stored on magnetic videotape, on which magnetic particles can be magnetized by and in proportion to the electronic signal.[3] Unlike film stock, magnetic tape doesn't show discrete images; the visual information is stored continuously on the length of the tape.

As these processes of image production are to a large degree automatic, the registration of details can hardly be prevented. All objects which appear in front of the lens of a film or video camera will leave their imprint on the resulting images. However, the reality effect of film and video does not so much depend on the detail itself. It rather lies in the fact that the images are caused by what they show; they are traces of objects which were once present in front of the lens. Both film and video images can be understood as indexes; signs which refer to something on the basis of contiguity or continuity. Film and video images in the first place work as an index by contiguity: they are physically caused by their referents, indicating physical proximity, even touch. Yet the temporal aspect of continuity is not entirely absent from this, for although the cause of the image (its referent) can lie in the past, image and object must once have been in the same moment. Roland Barthes argues that photographs (indexical images which come into being by the same photochemical process as film images) prove that something was once there, at that place, at that time, in front of the photo camera. Hence his famous claim that the essence of photographs, their *noeme*, is the "that has been" (2000: 77).

One of the remarkable things of indexical signs is that they are able to provide the past objects of which they are a trace with physical presence. "The object is made present to the addressee," Mary-Ann Doane explains in one of her discussions of indexicality (2007: 133). In her "Notes on the Index," Krauss defines indexes as "marks or traces of a particular cause, and this cause is the thing to which they refer, the object they signify" (1986: 198). The intriguing effect of the index, Krauss explains, is caused by time, which provides the past (by definition transient and ungraspable) with an existential and physical presence. In Krauss' account, the indexical sign appears to carry physical traces of its physically and temporally absent cause with itself in the present. This idea points to a remarkable similarity between the effect of superfluous literary descriptions and the index: the referent seems to be "hauled into" the sign. For although Krauss writes that indexes signify objects, the objects she refers to are not so much the signifieds, but the referents of the index. The close alliance of the indexical sign with the physical world seems to bypass signification. Like descriptive realist texts, indexes seem to be pure encounters between signifiers and referents. With that, the signified appears to be expelled from the sign. It is telling in this regard that Barthes has argued that a photograph "is never distinguished from its referent (from what it represents), or at least it is not *immediately* or *generally* distinguished from its referent. [. . .] It is as if the photograph carries the referent with itself" (2000: 5, emphasis in original).

The ability of the index to make its past cause and referent present is sustained by the movement of film and video images. Although film images, like photographs, necessarily show something that actually was in front of the lens at the time of shooting, the pastness of their referent is overruled by the movement of the filmed images. Both photographs and film images signal "there it is" as well as "that has been" at the same time; yet, the "there it is" tends to dominate in film. Christian Metz has argued that the essence of film should indeed be defined as "there it is," because film literally presents objects and persons from the past in the present (1974: 41). For, Metz explains, movement cannot be represented, it is always real, happening now. The distinction between the material characteristics of an object and its representation—which is still more or less evident in photography—dissolves when it comes to movement, according to Metz. He therefore invokes the linguistic notion of an "index of actualization" to name this particular quality of film.

Although video images, like film images, have the capacity to reanimate past objects in the present through movement, the indexical contiguity between video footage and its referents is slightly less straightforward than the physical causal relationship between film images and the objects they show. Analogue video images are certainly caused by objects in front of the lens, yet the videotape is not touched by the rays of light that these objects directed into the camera. The physical spatial contact between video image and referent is therefore less direct than the contact between film and filmed object.

In a temporal respect, however, the video image can be much closer to its referent than the analogue film image. Precisely because of the fact that video cameras translate light into electricity, video images can be broadcast instantaneously at the moment of recording. This "electronic continuousness," as John Belton (1996: 65) calls it, ensures that—in spite of the tube or chip between light and tape—video images are directly caused by referents in reality. For the temporal simultaneity of the object and its video image ensures the status of the image as an immediate trace of reality.

Thomas Y. Levin has aptly defined live video images as "temporal indexes" (2002). Unlike analogue film images, their indexicality is not predominantly based on spatial contiguity. It is rather motivated by temporal continuity as well as temporal presence; image and referent exist together, touch each other, in the now of both recording and broadcasting. Therefore, the video image is an even stronger "index of actualization" than the film image. For, unlike film's actualization, the deictic "here it is" of live video images does not go hand in hand with a "that has been." Instead, they unequivocally proclaim: "here it is, now!"

The indexicality of analogue film and video—which is grounded in their technological, physical support—gives the images of both lens-based media a documentary status, a veracity which can produce a reality effect. However, the reality effect of film and video images is not solely caused by the indexicality of the images. For although the status of film and video images as indexical traces might be understood as a technological fact, the rhetorical reality effect of this indexicality on the viewer can only arise when it is recognized by the viewer—when it is known, or seen, by the spectator. As I will demonstrate, film and video images relate to their indexical status differently when producing a reality effect. Video images produce a reality effect by way of formal features that signify veracity, documentary, and authenticity. Through formal devices, video images produce a reality effect by pointing out their indexical status. Therefore the sign, the index, first has to become signified in order for video's reality effect to come about.

CHAPTER 2
DEVICES IN VIDEO

(Re)turning to (Benny's) Video

The opening video in Haneke's *Benny's Video* can be of help in defining the formal devices by which videos create an impression of reality for their viewer. Benny's video fragment of the dying pig looks real because it has the appearance of an amateurish documentary—but which characteristics cause this appearance? To begin with, the video looks documentary and amateurish because of the wobbliness of the images, as well as the sudden, disorienting moves the camera makes. Those features indicate that the camera is hand-held—which is common in documentary video. Moreover, they point out that the recording device is held by inexperienced and clumsy hands—which justifies the addition of the adjective "amateurish." Many more characteristics contribute to the nonprofessional character of the video. The filmed objects are, for example, not always brought into focus properly, and the zooms are too rapid. In addition, the tape is unedited and ends abruptly.

Next to the features signaling the inadequacy of the producer's skills, the video fragment in *Benny's Video* is marked as an amateurish documentary by characteristics that reveal the poor quality of the video equipment itself, such as the grainy texture of the images, the "drop-out" of pixels, and the pale, unnatural colors. Other features indicating the inferiority of the video material are, for instance, the flickering wavelike patterns which move upwards over the image surface and the seeming luminosity of many light areas within the images. The visible low contrast ratio and low image quality of the fragment enhances the video's amateurish appearance because cheap, low quality video equipment is mostly designed for, and used by, nonprofessionals.[1]

All of these seemingly haphazard flaws and technical imperfections together produce a reality effect. This may seem slightly counterintuitive. For what this group of flaws and imperfections first of all draws attention to is the fact that the video images are not transparent registrations of reality. The pixel drop-out, flickering, graininess, luminous spots, wobbling, and blurriness all show that the video distorts and shapes the reality it depicts because the tape is a limited object that is produced by a human subject. The materiality of the medium is made visible by the imperfections, and the surface of the images is shown to be opaque. Nevertheless, the flaws lend the video an air of truthfulness and credibility. They all function as what German art historian Tom Holert (2004) has called "signs of authenticity"; they are understood as indications (signifiers, one might say) of the reliability and veracity of the video recording they are part of.

The fact that we read certain features as markers of veracity is a matter of convention; it is something we have learned. However, the meaning of the formal flaws is not entirely arbitrary. The exposure of the physicality of electronic video images might obliterate any sense of transparent visual access to the represented world, yet it does contribute to their status (and effect) as an index. The video flaws ensure that the footage is physically linked to reality. For, by pointing out its materiality, the ephemeral medium of video, the perceptible images of which exist only in the transient form of projected light, is established as a material ground on which the natural world can leave a physical imprint. Some of the imperfections are in fact already such an imprint. The camera movements that are visible in Benny's images, refer indexically to the cameraman. They hence reveal that the images are man-made, but they also show that the video functions as an index. As indexes, the camera wobbles suggest that the video footage might work as an index in its entirety. They are indexes of indexicality, so to speak.

What is more, the fact that the viewer's access to this world is limited by the low quality of the video footage further enhances the status of the video as a veracious trace of reality. In line with Didi-Huberman, Mary Ann Doane has pointed out that the index resists iconicity (2007: 135). The less iconic or mimetic a trace is, the greater its authenticity, and the more its indexical value is guaranteed. This can in part be explained by the fact that indexes, as traces, are caused by contact with their referent. In a discussion on the indexical value of a formless stain on the shroud of Turin, Didi-Huberman puts it as follows:

> The effacement of all figuration in this trace is itself the guarantee of a link, of *authenticity*; if there is no figuration it is because contact has taken place. The noniconic, nonmimetic nature of the stain guarantees its indexical value. [...] The absence of figuration therefore serves as proof of existence. Contact having occurred, figuration would appear false. And the signifying opaqueness itself reinforces the *it was* of an object [...].
>
> Didi-Huberman in Doane 2007: 135

Naturally, the video images in *Benny's Video* are not completely nonfigural or noniconic. In general, video images are hardly ever completely abstract or nonmimetic. Yet, Didi-Huberman's reasoning shows that insofar as the video signal does seem distorted with mimetic shortcomings, this doesn't necessarily obstruct the viewer's impression that the images present reality. It rather produces a reality effect by authenticating the video as a veracious trace of reality. The "signifying opaqueness" which Didi-Huberman mentions in this respect, plays an important part in the effect of the amateurism which is signaled by the video flaws in the opening clip of *Benny's Video.*

The conventional association of many of the abovementioned video flaws (hand-held movements, absence of editing, poor lighting) with amateurism, further contributes to the establishment of video as index. As indexes are direct traces of physical objects, they seem to bypass signification. They refer to their referents in a deictic way, and as such, make their referents present in the here and now. But other than "there!," indexes do not assert anything (Peirce 1932: 226). They have no other meaning. For this reason, indexes have been defined as "uncoded messages," or "hollowed-out signs" (Didi-Huberman 1984, Krauss 1986, Doane 2007).The idea of amateurism sustains the indexicality of video footage, because amateurism indicates that the producer is unskilled. Which in turn suggests that the footage is probably uncoded; it is taped by someone who merely knew how to press the record button, loosely holding the camera while it automatically recorded.

As most amateur videos, *Benny's Video* is not entirely uncoded or hollowed out in this respect, though. The framing and the zoom movements in the opening video can be understood as a form of signification; they indicate that the pig is somehow intriguing or important. However, the amateurish look of the footage still sufficiently guarantees that the recorded material isn't imperceptibly adapted, highly coded or thoroughly manipulated. Hence, the video's imperfections and anti-iconic distortions function as signifiers whose meaning is: "there is no meaning here." As signifiers, the flaws ensure that the video will be read as hollowed-out sign which refers directly to reality: "there!"

Intermezzo: growing conventions

The features I have pointed out as "reality-effect producing" in the video fragment that *Benny's Video* starts out with, are very common video characteristics. However, they are not inevitable features of every video: since the 1980s, the technique of video is sophisticated enough to avoid or highly diminish most of the discussed flaws. This means that those imperfections are not necessarily haphazard characteristics which happen to function as signifiers of authenticity; they are artifices which can deliberately be applied in order to achieve a desired effect. Rather than random imperfections, the formal features in question serve as rhetorical devices which produce a reality effect.

The reality effect of inferior image quality has, moreover, grown stronger over time. For the formal "flaws" of low quality video have not always functioned as a sign of amateurism—the suggestion of which can create a reality impression today. Video wasn't associated with amateurism in the first decade after the arrival of the first so-called Portapak video camera in 1967, as it was mainly used by artists in its initial period. Moreover, in this early period, all videos were of a relatively poor quality; features such as graininess and blurriness were the rule rather than the exception. After that, the technique of video improved so that variations in quality arose. The lower region became available to a large group of people as home video equipment, while artists and other professionals could have recourse to video of a higher standard. Only then did features of poor video quality become a sign of amateurism within video.

Although the production of a reality effect is clearly tied to the technical evolution of the medium in the case of video, the fact that certain characteristics became producers of a reality impression while they didn't spark off such an impression before implies an alteration in cultural and social conventions as well. In order for a reality effect to be caused by formal features signaling amateurism, it first had to be common for the medium to be used by amateurs. Both the widespread non-professional usage of the medium and the public familiarity with this usage within culture and society had to develop before the association of video with amateurism could arise at all. Moreover, viewers had to learn to read certain features as signs of amateurism, a matter which is very much based on convention. To put it in Peircean terms; some imperfections function as symbols which mean "amateurism," and because of that, these symbols sustain the status of video as an authentic, direct, and uncoded indexical trace of reality.

The conventional aspect of these formal features functioning as symbols indicates that the production of the reality effect depends, in part, on the viewer.[2] Barthes' structuralist text on the reality effect doesn't explicitly focus on the position of the reader or viewer. In Barthes' account, it is the realist *text* which produces an effect. Following poststructuralist views on meaning production (e.g., Culler 1981, Casetti 1983) I would say, however, that in order for a reality effect to be created, the viewer of an image has to recognize, interpret, and understand certain features as signifiers signifying "this is real" or "this is a veracious, authentic trace of reality"—if only by connotation or via a chain of other signifiers and associations. The latter meaning does not come into being without a—historically, culturally, and socially situated—viewer/reader who activates or co-produces it together with the object on view by choosing and applying certain conventions in reading the image or text.[3] Thus, the reality effect is at the same time an effect *on* the viewer produced by certain devices in a text or image, and an effect originating *in* the viewer which is partially produced by the viewer (on) herself.

Mobile video

In spite of the relativity, changeability, and conventionality of the reality effect, it is safe to assume that, when it comes to video, the formal features which I described above in relation to *Benny's Video* function as devices which produce a reality effect in (with) most Western viewers. That is, they have done so approximately from around the 1980s until today. However, for a while, low-quality video image features such as graininess and color distortion were in danger of developing from indications of amateurish documentary into signs of obsolescence. The reason for this was that in the past decade, high-quality video equipment became more and more available to the general public. Therefore, it became less common for amateur videos to look as qualitatively deficient as in *Benny's Video*. Moreover, because of the improved user-friendliness of the equipment, many amateur flaws such as shaky or unfocused images were automatically resolved or diminished by the technique. Even though features of poor quality could (and can) still be deployed as devices, their reality effect started to diminish because the rapid technological development of nonprofessional home video equipment had started to weaken the link between imperfect video images and amateurish documentary.

The arrival of video cameras built into cellphones, however, strengthened this link again. The quality of videos resulting from this application of the medium is often lower than of amateur videos produced in the 1980s and 1990s. Like those, cellphone videos are marked by image features such as graininess, contrast and color distortion, unsteadiness, blurriness, and pixel drop-out. Moreover, video cameras on phones are clearly designed for nonprofessional use; they can be used by anyone who knows how to handle a cellphone. And since many cellphones currently produced have a built-in camera, video cameras are nowadays used by almost anyone who owns a GSM device. The ubiquity of the recognizable—usually rather short—cellphone video fragments on the Internet demonstrates this, and moreover shows how familiar we are today with shaky, relatively low-quality video fragments which mostly show trivial or everyday events, recorded by ordinary people documenting pieces of their daily lives.

That these short and shaky cellphone videos produce a reality effect is well demonstrated by Krassimir Terziev's video documentary *Battles of Troy* (2005). In his documentary, the artist exposes how a large group of Bulgarian men were hired to act out the battles of the Trojan War in Wolfgang Petersen's Hollywood blockbuster *Troy* (2004), starring Brad Pitt as Achilles and Orlando Bloom as Paris. Unlike these star actors, however, the Bulgarian extras were grossly underpaid and had to work overtime in health-threatening circumstances. In order for the rather startling exposures this film production makes to come across, the video documentary has to convince us as viewers of its own truthfulness. One of the most important ways in which this is achieved is the use of cellphone videos within the work.

Although the documentary is shot on video, most fragments cannot clearly be recognized as such because they are recorded with high-standard equipment. This has created video images which approach—yet not quite reach—the quality of the film images from *Troy* which the piece sometimes shows. In these well-lit, professionally edited, high-resolution video fragments we mostly see the Bulgarian extras in Sofia as they are interviewed on their experiences in the Mexican desert where the battles of *Troy* were filmed. Alongside the stories of the extras themselves, additional information on the large film production and the undervalued role of the Bulgarian men in it is provided by some colored graphs, informational texts and quotes by the film producers appearing on screen, and an anonymous commentator. Besides providing information, all of these sources—from the interviewees' subjective eyewitness reports to the more objective and scientific-looking graphs—have the rhetorical function of convincing the viewer of the documentary's truthfulness.

The information sources are ultimately able to successfully carry out this function, however, because they are authenticated by the GSM video fragments which appear throughout the documentary. These video images show the film-set of *Troy* on a vast beach adjoining the desert, usually with some of the Bulgarian extras in it, and sometimes with actor Brad Pitt standing in the distance. Apart from the famous actor and a pair of injured legs, nothing sensational is shown in the uneventful videos of the dusty sand plains. In fact, the recordings are too short, shaky and blurred to reveal much of the situation of the Bulgarians during the shooting of the Hollywood film without the additional verbal explanations of the extras. Yet, they do produce a reality effect which affects the credibility of the entire documentary.

The devices which create a reality effect in *Troy* are similar to the ones I pointed out in *Benny's Video.* When it comes to the production of the reality effect, the only substantial difference with the video in Haneke's film is that the videos in Terziev's work are noticeably recorded with cellphones. In the case of *Battles of Troy*, the recognition of the video recording device enforces the reality effect of the fragments. A few conclusions precede this enforcement, though. For a start, the discernible use of a cellphone as video camera confirms what can also already be suspected on the basis of the recorded images themselves, namely that the videos must have been filmed by the extras in-between their activities. Filmed, that is, with a piece of equipment they could have at hand on the set because it could be hidden from view in their large armor costumes: a cellphone.

The fact that the videos are recorded by the extras themselves, then, implies that the images present us with a direct, almost secret and exclusive inside view on the unglamorous and unspectacular sides of a blockbuster film set. This contributes to the reality effect of the cellphone fragments, because the idea that subjects who were really involved in the situation have surreptitiously documented what usually remains unseen makes it easier to believe that the video images represent a past reality.

In addition, the fact that the videos were recorded on the spot from the Bulgarians' point of view as insiders not only fosters belief in the truthfulness of the cellphone recordings, it also proves that the Bulgarian extras were actually there, on that particular spot in the Mexican desert. The heightened impression that the cellphone video fragments show reality as it really was—and thus not some digitally manipulated version of it—sustains their function as evidence. This is important, because when conceived as evidence of the Bulgarian's presence on the film set of *Troy*, the truthfulness of the whole documentary is confirmed by the short and grainy video clips. All written information and graphs presented in the documentary on the role of the extras in the production of *Troy*, as well as the memories and experiences recounted by the Bulgarian men themselves, are much easier to believe because as viewers we seem to be provided with visual access to the film-production site by way of a pixelated peek through the eyes of the extras.

Family Viewing

Alongside the amateurish documentary video—recorded with either a conventional camera or with a cellphone—a couple of related genres have to be mentioned in which the devices of "flaws and deficiencies" are often deployed as well. In the preceding paragraphs, I mentioned "documentary" a few times in relation to the devices without "amateurish" as an adjective. The reason for this is that the discussed devices are often used by professional documentary producers. Unlike Terziev, who edited short amateur documentary videos, including their technical flaws, into his own smoothly recorded video material, many artists, journalists, and reporters use the devices in the material they produce themselves when creating a video documentary. Even though such documentaries can mostly be recognized as being more professional products than, for instance, the amateurish videotape of a teenage kid with morbid fascinations, the association with amateurism is still made by those works, with the known effect as a result.

Another genre in which the devices play an important part is the home video. In fact, home videos can be understood as a subcategory of amateur documentary video. They are produced by people who use their video camera (often solely) to document their family life.[4] Besides uneventful episodes from daily life, important highlights and milestones are captured on tape or memory card. As home videos are in general filmed with handheld, low-quality video cameras, reality-effect producing features such as shaky images or color distortion are usually commonplace in these videos. In addition, the specific, limited subject matter of home videos can initiate the production of a reality effect. Subjects such as birthday parties, marriages, or newly walking toddlers immediately make clear that a video is a home video. And like the general genre of documentary of which the home video is a specific sub-genre, an important connotation of the genre of the home video is "this is reality."

A common denominator of all the previously discussed video genres is that the producer or camera operator is apparent through the formal traces I call "clumsy" flaws, such as hand-held effects or rapid zoom movements. In home videos, the producer of the recording is often all the more apparent by the filmed people smiling, speaking or waving directly into the camera. Such responses are directed at the person behind the recording device—generally a family member who is a part of what is being recorded.

In Atom Egoyan's film *Family Viewing*, many home video clips are shown which refer to the cameraman both by the clumsy flaws and by the overt responses of the filmed people. At first sight these video fragments mainly contrast with the filmed material in which they are embedded, for in the filmed parts no signs or traces of the material's production are overtly visible. As the film proceeds, however, it turns out that the home videos also contrast with several other video recordings which are shown throughout the film. The contrast is produced by the fact that, unlike the home movies and similar to the filmed parts in *Family Viewing*, these rather static video fragments seem to lack a producer. Previously, I explained how many of the features which expose the producer of a videotape produce a reality effect in video. In the static video fragments in Egoyan's film, though, a reality effect seems to be created precisely by the fact that no trace of a person handling the camera can be discerned. In order to understand why this is the case, and which formal devices contribute to this reality impression, it is necessary to further analyze the fragments in question.

Static shots and surveillance

In fact, two sorts of static images without a noticeable creator can be discerned in *Family Viewing.* First of all, there are images filmed from the corner of a bedroom with a double bed in it. On this bed, the video images show Stan and Sandra, the father and stepmother of the film's adolescent protagonist, Van. The couple remain in front of the lens, while the camera records both the sexual acts they perform together, as well as their failed approaches to each other. Although the images show that the camera clearly has an effect on the two people on view—an arousing effect on Stan and an embarrassing effect on Sandra—they in turn do not have any effect on the camera. The only influence the couple exerts on the recording equipment is that they turn the device on and off. Otherwise, the camera automatically and continually records, with no change in its position on a tripod in the corner of the room. In the shown images recorded by the camera, no changes in focus or zoom movements can be seen. The camera never turns, swerves or shakes. In all, the video fragments seem to be cool and detached registrations of a camera that has objectively and disinterestedly captured whatever appeared in front of the lens, with no visible influence of a human subject on the recording.

In these static video fragments in *Family Viewing*, the straightforwardness or truthfulness of the images is not guaranteed by the cameraman's lack of recording skills (as in *Benny's Video*), nor by his or her unique insider's position (as in Terziev's documentary), but by his or her apparent absence. This absence of a human producer implies that the footage is produced entirely automatically by the video camera, seemingly ungoverned by any sort of intentional agency. The impression which is thus raised is that "this is reality," automatically captured as it appeared in front of the lens, with no possible distorting or manipulative interference of a person pointing the camera, adjusting the focus, meddling with the lighting, and so on. Image features such as a continuously static image frame, the absence of editing, unchanging contrast, the absence of zoom movements and an unvarying focus and depth of field all function as indications of the absence of a camera operator. Therefore, they can be understood as devices which contribute to the production of a reality effect—especially when combined.

In addition to *Family Viewing*, Haneke's *Benny's Video* also shows how a reality effect can be produced by video in different ways. As I demonstrated earlier, the film's opening video produces a reality effect because of its amateurish look. The fact that we can see Benny's amateurish hands in the footage creates a reality impression. However, Haneke's film also contains video footage which produces a reality effect precisely because Benny no longer holds the camera. Later on in the film, protagonist Benny no longer acts out his fascination with death from behind and with his video camera, but in front of it. Suddenly, he is physically visible in a video fragment. The static viewpoint of the camera and the unmoving image frame indicate that the recording camera is now placed on a tripod. Image features such as unchanging focus and the absence of close-ups confirm that Benny no longer has his hands on the camera. Instead, the video images show how he uses his hands to operate another device. With a cattle gun familiar from the opening video, he shoots the young female friend with whom he has first watched and discussed the fragment of the dying pig. The girl dies, but only after drawn-out minutes of agony in which Benny shoots her twice again. During these minutes, the static video camera films only parts of the shocking event. Parts, that is, because there is no camera operator. No one points the lens at Benny in order to keep the murder in full view. In general, video image features which suggest automatic recording on a tripod sustain the indexical character of the footage because, like features of amateurism, they declare that the images are uncoded. When suspenseful or shocking events such as murder are framed in a seemingly arbitrary way which obstructs the viewer's visual access to the place of action, the indexicality of the images is emphasized all the more. For, whereas Benny's framing of the dying pig slightly shaped the meaning of the images, the static footage of "half a murder" attaches no meaning at all to what it records. That is, it only signifies, like the aforementioned flaws, that the video-as-sign is void of meaning; that reality has imprinted itself directly onto or into the video.

Alongside the static video images in *Family Viewing* and *Benny's Video*, a second kind of video footage can be found in Egoyan's film in which the camera doesn't move and seemingly records without the guiding intervention of a camera operator. Like the static video images, these images are also characterized by a lack of zoom movement, contrast adjustment, and variation in focus. There is, however, one important additional, distinguishing feature which characterizes this video footage: it is filmed from a high angle. Because of this, the fragments can immediately be understood as video surveillance footage, as it is usual for surveillance cameras to be placed in a high position in order to be out of view and out of reach.

The association of the shown fragments with video surveillance produces a reality effect for two reasons. First, surveillance cameras are as a rule not held or operated by a human agent. If they do something besides recording, such as moving or focusing, this is usually the result of movement detectors within the device. An exception to the rule is surveillance cameras which can be controlled from a distance. Although this diminishes the status of the resulting video footage as recordings produced by an entirely automated device, it hardly undermines the association of surveillance video with the objective and disinterested registration of reality. The general purpose for which surveillance video is deployed is for the objective and truthful registration of reality, as well as the conventional expectation most Western people have of the genre. As Thomas Y. Levin puts it: "When one sees what one takes to be a surveillance image, one does not usually ask if it is 'real' (this is simply assumed) but instead attempts to establish whether 'the real' that is being captured by the camera is being recorded or is [...] a closed-circuit 'real time' feed" (2002: 585). Moreover, when video images are "live," their indexicality becomes temporal.

Media theorist John Belton has argued that the possibility for instantaneous broadcast is so specific to the medium of video that the medium is by convention strongly associated with a real time feed. As a result, Belton claims, the possibility that "it could be live" always infuses the way in which we look at video images (Belton 1996: 68). Their potential temporal indexicality is always at work for the viewer, so to speak. However, it goes without saying that some video genres are more commonly known to often rely on live broadcasting than others. Surveillance is of course one of these genres, another example is television news reportage. Whereas surveillance footage produces a reality effect through a combination of static, automatic recording and (the possibility) of instant feed, the documentary genre of the TV news reportage often produces a reality effect through a combination of live broadcast with devices such as hand-held effects and graininess.

CHAPTER 3
DEVICES IN FILM

Although analogue film is unable to produce "live" images, many of the formal devices which I discussed in the previous chapter on video can technically be applied in film footage as well. In fact, they have been quite widely applied in the past, and are not completely absent from more contemporary cinematic practices. However, whereas devices such as hand-held movements, graininess, color distortion, and the absence of editing are some of the most dominant reality-effect producing devices within the medium of video, they are marginal devices in film. In addition, they are less effective as reality-effect producing devices *when* they appear in film. I will turn to the marginality of these formal features in film later on. First, it is necessary to outline the most common ways in which film produces a reality effect. The most dominant cinematic devices for creating a reality effect are applied in the most dominant application of the medium: the production of narrative fiction film.

From setting to surface

The most obvious difference between video and film in producing reality effects is very much implicated in the mentioned difference between the genres in which a reality effect is produced by each medium. To put it very bluntly, the genres in which video produces a reality effect show something "real," while the genre in which film creates a reality effect shows things that are "not real." Nuancing this statement has to begin with the remark that apart from the actual "realness" of what is shown, all genres in question are able to produce a reality effect and hence convince the viewer that what they show is real. Yet, the video genres I mentioned, such as home movies, surveillance video and news reportage, all show something which is "real" in that the shown events are not staged and the filmed people are not acting.[1] The events shown in narrative fiction film, on the other hand, are as a rule staged, and the people appearing in them are usually acting.

Therefore, in order to produce a reality effect, narrative fiction films need devices which remain unused in the documentary genres of video. As a reality impression cannot easily be evoked when the staging and acting are visible within a film, the cinematic devices are in the first place aimed at hiding the fact that a narrative fiction film is staged and play-acted. Some of the most important devices in hiding the staging and acting are almost too obvious to describe. These include the device of good play-acting; acting which does not look like acting.[2] Good casting furthermore contributes to hiding "staginess," for the performance of actors can only come across as natural behavior when they fit the role they are playing—if only physically.

Similar to the devices of good acting and good casting, good staging helps to hide the constructed nature of a film. Good staging, however, includes many facets: the setting has to look natural and appropriate to the shown scenes, the right props have to be in the right places at the right time, as do the right actors. Moreover, costumes have be appropriate to the characters in their historical and social context, special effects must be convincing, extras have to be mobilized when their presence can enhance the credibility of a scene. In addition, all these factors and many more aspects which the *mise-en-scène* of a film involves, have to be geared to one another and to the overarching narrative of the film in order for the depicted scenes to look as real as possible.

It is striking that some of the most important devices by which a reality impression is created by video and film are almost complete opposites. In Haneke's *Benny's Video*, this oppositeness first surfaces through the stark contrast between the formal features of the opening video and the subsequent film fragments. Compared with Benny's video of the dying pig, the film fragments look remarkably smooth and transparent. No color distortion, graininess, pixelation, flickering or throbbing can be discerned in the film images. A similar contrast arises in *Family Viewing*, in which coarse-grained home videos alternate with filmed material of a much higher resolution.

The difference in image quality between video and film, which becomes visible in the two films, is not so much the fixed result of the media's technical supports. Like the features of low quality which produce a reality effect in video, the impeccability of film images is not technically inevitable. For the most part, it is a controllable and adaptable factor which can be deployed in order to produce (or evade) a certain effect. One of the effects which is produced by the seeming transparency of the film images in for instance *Benny's Video*, is a reality effect of a different kind. This effect comes about because the transparency of the images seems to grant the spectator direct visual access to the depicted scenes. Through this illusion of unmediated visual access, the impression arises that what is seen is reality. After all, no signs of artificiality, materiality or mediation are apparent on the image surface. The perfect view hence provided seems to be similar to a glance through a clear window onto the outside world.

The reality effect as it is produced by the medium of film almost entirely coheres with—and depends on—the spectator's illusion of unmediated visual access to the world on view. The creation of the illusion of visual access simultaneously evokes a reality impression in the viewer. In order for the illusion of visual access to be produced and maintained, it is important that the film spectator is provided with a sense of a stable overview—even mastery—over the depicted world. Christian Metz (1976), Stephen Heath (1981), Bordwell, Staiger, and Thompson (1985), and Laura Marks (2002), among others, have noted in this respect that conventional narrative films aim to retain the illusion of stable overview which is created by the linear, monocular perspective which the cinematic medium automatically produces in its images. In addition to the fact that linear perspectival images are by convention considered realistic by Western viewers, they also create a single stable viewing position from which the illusionistic space is fully visible to the viewer. However, as the film camera moves, or scenes are cut, the vanishing point keeps shifting on the screen: there is no stable viewing position for the viewer to look from. Yet, classical narrative fiction films deploy a range of devices which sustain and "repair" the illusion of visual access and overview in the film spectator, creating what is sometimes called a form of "seamless realism" (see for instance Hayward 2000). With the help of *Benny's Video* and *Family Viewing*, I will demonstrate how conventional narrative films solve moments of instability and repair or hide their seams and gaps.

Before pointing out these devices, however, it is interesting to note that the production of a reality effect by film hinges more strongly on the denial of the medium's materiality through devices such as a smooth image surface, than on the connotation that "this is reality" of the applied devices. In video, on the other hand, the reality-effect producing devices do signify "this is reality"—or rather: "this is a veracious trace of reality." Moreover, in the case of video, the illusion of unmediated access is often undermined when a reality effect is produced, because many of the devices which create a reality effect within this medium expose rather than hide the physical character of the representation so as to define the video image as an index. Conventional narrative films, on the other hand, mostly work to make the viewer forget that she is watching a representation at all.

Conventionally constructed surveyability

In order to further define the reality-effect producing devices which function in film, the differences between video and film as noted in Haneke's and Egoyan's films serve as a suitable starting point. Besides the most obvious difference in image quality, another dissimilarity between the opening video and subsequent filmed sequences in *Benny's Video* lies in the visibility of the producer. Whereas the presence of a person handling the camera could be discerned in the opening video through, for instance, hand-held effects and brusque zoom movements, the film fragments do not show the hand of the camera operator in such an overt way. All images are filmed in a steady, stable way. Whenever the camera turns, pans, or zooms, these movements proceed slowly—unlike in the opening video—and therefore draw little attention to themselves.

However, although the interferences and actions of a camera operator aren't exactly emphasized in the filmed parts, they aren't completely absent either. After all, the camera *does* turn, pan, and zoom. Therefore, in *Family Viewing*, a contrast quickly becomes apparent between on the one hand the filmed parts which are abundant with camera swerves and cuts, and on the other hand the static, unedited surveillance video footage or the bedroom videos recorded on a tripod. A similar contrast arises in *Benny's Video* when we, as viewers, witness Benny's crime through the "staring" lens of his video camera. Compared to these video fragments, the film footage looks quite labored and constructed. Thus, the filmed parts in both *Benny's Video* and *Family Viewing* differ both from the video fragments which produce a reality effect by overtly drawing attention to the acts of their producer as well as from the video footage which creates this effect by looking entirely untouched by human hands.

Yet, the middle position those narrative film parts occupy between the two kinds of video recordings with regard to the visibility of a creative, interfering agent, sustains the creation of a reality effect because this position enables the film to evoke an illusion of overview in the observer—an illusion which goes hand in hand with a reality impression. Some acts which are visible within the filmed material—such as cuts and zoom movements—reveal that the film is a construction. Yet, this revelation is for an important part overruled by the fact that most of the interventions in the film material make the represented world visually accessible to the spectator of the film. Successive shots from different angles do for instance map out the spaces in which the characters exist. A sense of overview is also provided when the camera slowly scans a space. Together with possibilities offered by close-ups and establishing shots, these devices can give the spectator the best possible viewpoint at each moment of a scene, and are able to give an overview of one space in a more all-embracing way than one single, static image could ever provide.

In order to give the viewer an impression of a stable overview and visual access instead of the possible feeling of disorientation which can also be caused by these operations, some rules are followed in classical narrative films. Continuity cinema is another appropriate and widely applied term for this type of film, as the rules which are followed are aimed at creating and maintaining the illusion in the viewer that space and time each form a continuum in the film—in spite of the fact that only fragments of those illusionistic continuums are shown on screen. Although *Benny's Video* and *Family Viewing* aren't exactly classic examples of classical narrative film, they do follow many of the conventional rules deriving from this tradition. One rule which is, for instance, followed by the two films, is that camera movements, especially turns, mustn't proceed too quickly or be too abrupt. Other important rules which are never disobeyed in Haneke's or Egoyan's film are that the camera must not cross the 180-degree line, and that a so-called master shot of a space must be given when the space and the scene unfolding in it are also mapped out by medium or close-up shots from different angles. These formal strategies make sure that the represented space remains surveyable and understandable for the viewer. Another condition which has to be fulfilled in order to attain the impression of spatial overview is a clear relation between the different shots of a single space.

As Stephen Heath has pointed out, shots mapping out a space are related to each other in narrative cinema by character looks: "the role of the character look has been fundamental for the welding of spatial unity" (1981: 44). The look of characters can join or stitch different shots together when eyeline matches are created through the principle of shot/reverse shot: if one shot shows a character looking in a certain direction, and the next shot shows a certain object or space, the suggestion is evoked that the character is looking at whatever is present in the second shot. Sometimes, this second shot can even be understood as coinciding with the exact viewpoint of the character, or in other words, as a point-of-view shot. Such shots suggestively related by character looks create spatial continuity because the spatial position of the looking character and the spatial position of the things he or she looks at are connected by the direction of the look itself, which appears to cross the space between them rectilinearly. In addition, according to Heath, the voices of characters can function as an equivalent of their looks. For, like looks, utterances are aimed at something (or someone) which the next shot can bring into view.

Two other factors bind the shots together in narrative cinema, however. First, a narrative is needed in order to sustain and explain the relationship between shots, most of all because the looks and voices of the characters can only construct meaningful relationships between shots because those characters are related by and embedded in a narrative which clarifies their nonspatial relationships.[3] Secondly, the shots are related by the spectator, who is familiar with cinematic conventions and therefore knows how spaces are mapped out by narrative film by way of successive shots. In the end, the link between shots and the space they, so to speak, build together can only be seen by a viewer who understands how the relationship between these shots is established through character looks or voices.

Although the illusion of visual access and overview which classical narrative film instills in the viewer mostly concerns an impression of overview of the cinematic illusionistic space, the way time proceeds needs to be just as clear as the spatial layout of the world represented by a film in order for the viewer's illusion of overview to be maintained. This means that the fabula of the film's narrative has to be easily reconstructable.[4] In the case of *Benny's Video*, in which all events are shown in chronological order without very long inexplicable time lapses between the different shots and scenes, such a reconstruction is fairly easy. At first sight, *Family Viewing* forms more of a challenge in this respect, as the story involves flashbacks and repetitions. However, in the end, the plot of the film makes those deviations from a chronologically ordered narration understandable, and the linearly progressing time of the fabula can relatively easily be reconstructed.

The progression of time in conventional narrative fiction films is just as much ordered and constructed by subsequent shots as the spatial layout is. Like the spatial relations between shots, the temporal ones are created by two factors: a consistent overarching narrative and a viewer who is familiar with the conventional ways in which different shots are used in narrative films to order—and mostly condense—the story. Because of the importance of the first factor in making the fragmented cinematic representation of both time and space cohesive, narrativity can be understood as a filmic reality-effect producing device in itself. The temporal and spatial cohesiveness and relatedness which a narrative can create between successive shots and scenes reinforces the viewer's illusion of visual access to and overview of the world on view, the illusion on which the most typical cinematic reality effect is primarily based.

That narrativity is an indispensable factor to the production of a reality effect by film is well demonstrated in Krassimir Terziev's video work *A Movie* (2004). Although *A Movie* is technically a video, it cannot immediately be recognized as such. At first sight, the video looks like a movie. Many devices by which film creates a reality effect are present in this "movie." Its images are of a high quality and therefore look smooth and transparent. The groups of people who appear in the streets of a small medieval looking village are dressed in historical costumes which, on the face of it, seem to match the ancient village. What is more, the streets and the characters in them are represented by stable shots which succeed each other at a steady pace. These shots, moreover, consist of both close-ups of the characters, medium close-ups in which small groups of people are shown, and establishing shots from a high angle which provide an overview of entire streets. However, no narrative unfolds. Except for people strolling and talking, nothing really happens in the streets, and no events can be discerned. Because a narrative is lacking, the spatial and temporal relationship between the successive shots remain unclear. As a result, the diegesis depicted on screen is not cohesive. Because it looks so fragmented and constructed, the viewer is not provided with an illusion of visual access and overview, and a reality effect fails to materialize.

Although narrativity is thus indispensable to the creation of a reality effect in film, the fact that a story is told is hidden by film which produces a reality effect. The reason for this is that a narrating character in the film would point out its constructed character, which needs to remain hidden in order for film to create its reality effect. The act of narration is covered up by the narrative of classical fiction films by keeping all signs of a narrating agent out of sight. So, although a story *is* told in narrative films, which implies both a (first person) narrating agency and an addressee (a second person), the traces of enunciation—the structure of an "I" addressing a "you"—are obliterated in traditional narrative films. Film theorists who have studied film along the lines of Emile Benveniste's enunciation theory have therefore concluded that traditional films are as a rule presented as a *histoire*, not as a *discours*. In the latter, narration is exposed as an act that is carried out by a narrating agency, while in the former, the story seems to tell itself for no narrating "I" can be discerned in it. As films are told by an unseen, external narrator, they seem to tell themselves.

As opposed to narrativity, the second "shot-binding factor" mentioned above—the viewer's familiarity with the conventions of narrative film—cannot be understood as a reality-effect producing device of film, as it is a characteristic that rather belongs to the viewer. However, the familiarity of the viewer with conventions is a prerequisite to the production of a reality effect by narrative fiction film, which again goes to show that the reality effect is just as much an effect *of* as *on* the viewer. Not only is the familiarity in question important for the connections between shots to arise, and for the reconstruction of space and time to be possible, it also makes the filmic reality-effect producing devices less visible as such, as artificial devices. Most viewers have become so used to the conventional manner in which classical narrative films represent and build a spatially and temporally coherent story world that it has become difficult to still notice the representational and constructed character of the object—the film—on view.

However, as I will explain in the next chapter, the viewer's belief in cinematically depicted scenes as real is still slightly restrained and reserved, especially compared to the belief which is put in the realness of video when this medium produces a reality effect.

CHAPTER 4
SLIDING SCALES

Degrees of belief

When the ways in which video and film create a reality effect are compared, it is not only striking that the two media produce the effect in question by entirely different means, but it is also remarkable that although both media are able to produce a reality effect, in the end they give rise to different degrees of belief in the representation. The overall impression that "this is reality" may be produced by both media, yet the extent to which we as viewers truly believe that what is shown is real differs.

In *Benny's Video* this difference becomes perceptible when the opening video switches to film. Not only have the devices by which a reality effect is produced suddenly changed; the viewer's belief in the realness of the depicted scenes has changed too. It has, more particularly, diminished. The slaughtering of the pig in the video fragment, as well as the reactions of the people surrounding the suffering animal, were hard to conceive as staged or play-acted. When the same people appearing in the opening video are shown in scenes of suffering in the following narrative film, however, most viewers will now recognize the represented people as actors and the depicted events as staged—in spite of the fact that the acts and events look very convincing and real. For although the filmed part in *Benny's Video* on the one hand produces a reality effect through its seemingly unmediated, direct way of representation, this mode of representation—which includes many reality-effect producing devices—reveals that the film is a narrative *fiction* film as it is a mode of representation typical of this genre. Ironically, many of the devices which produce a reality effect in film at the same time diminish it. Not only because they can be recognized as artifice, but also because they are characteristics by which the genre of narrative fiction film can be recognized.

Previously, I explained how the reality effect of video is often sustained by the connotation of the video genres in which this effect is usually produced. With narrative fiction film, the recognition of the genre works counterproductively when it comes to the creation of a reality effect. For, instead of signifying "this is reality" by connotation, the genre of narrative fiction film rather signifies "this is an imaginary, fictional story" and "this is a construction" by connotation. Those meanings clearly oppose the functioning of the reality-effect producing devices deployed in classical narrative films that hide this constructed nature, and work to conceal the fact that the scenes on view are staged and acted.

Therefore, when devices such as a smooth image surface, steady camera movements and clear transitions between shots are used in a film, they serve both as producers of a reality effect and as markers revealing the genre of the representation. The viewers to whom a reality impression is given by the devices will in all probability also recognize the genre of the film through the devices. Because of this recognition, they will always remain slightly aware of the fact that what the film shows is not real but constructed, that the story it tells is imaginary, that the shown events are staged, and that the shown people are actors playing their roles.

Narrative fiction films will therefore hardly ever be completely believed as a truthful representation of reality by viewers who are familiar with the genre. No matter how real and accessible the represented world looks, viewers will at some level still recognize its artificiality. As the familiarity is present in most contemporary viewers, narrative fiction films are usually not believed as truthful representations of reality. Compared with this, the belief in the veracity of videos tends to be much more profound. When videos produce a reality effect, the shown people, events and actions are believed to be much more real than the play-acting characters and staged happenings appearing in narrative fiction films. In order to examine the subtle differences of belief in film and video more closely, it is first necessary to further define the degrees of belief to which film gives rise.

When fiction films create a reality effect, the weakest form of belief they produce in the viewer can best be defined in a negative way, that is, by emphasizing not so much the presence of belief but the absence of disbelief in the spectator. As Samuel Coleridge has explained with regard to poems, some works do not so much invite belief but merely require the reader to suspend her disbelief for the moment. For stronger forms of belief in the reality shown by fiction films, however, "pretending to believe" is a more appropriate characterization. The idea that spectators can pretend to believe in the truthfulness of a representation was introduced by Kendall L. Walton and further developed in relation to realist literature by Lilian Furst. For Walton, this stance of pretending to believe is part of the games of make-believe that have to be played in order to appreciate fiction. Readers of fiction, he argues, "do not believe in the existence of fictional characters. Appreciation involves playing games of make-believe, and as part of these games appreciators *pretend* to believe in characters" (1980: 2).

Both Walton and Furst consider the pretense of belief in the first place as an act carried out by the reader/spectator. As mentioned above, Walton describes it as an operation through which the reader/spectator plays games of make-believe. Furst in addition designates pretending to believe as "the recipient's performance" (1995: 37). An important observation made by both scholars, however, is that the viewer isn't an entirely independent agent when it comes to the pretense of belief. First of all, Furst points out how readers have been culturally conditioned to call on their imaginative capacities under certain circumstances (29). Walton's remark that we as readers have "a *habit* of playing along with fictions" (3, emphasis added) further sustains the idea that the act of pretending to believe is often ordained by convention.

Walton's remark contains a second reason for which the viewer isn't an entirely independent agent in the game of make-believe. For the idea that readers have a habit of playing *along* with fiction implies that the game of make believe is also played—and perhaps even prompted by the works in which the viewer pretends to believe. That the text also does something is recognized by Furst as well, who states that readers accede to an invitation made by the text when they (pretend to) believe in them: "the crucial transition into belief [. . .] is made as we accede to the invitation to invest credence in the fiction through our readiness to pretend" (1995: 31).

Besides the fact that pretending to believe is not always an act which the viewer performs entirely voluntary or independently, she is not always completely aware of the fact that she is pretending to believe. Furst states that, on one level, readers can be so engrossed in the pretense of belief that they forget their belief is only pretended, while on another level maintaining awareness that they are in fact engaging in a pretense. The two positions are not mutually exclusive, according to Furst (1995: 34). In order to explain this, she refers to an example Walton provides when he argues in line with Furst that readers both know and don't know that they are participants in a game of make-believe:

> In order to make his point, Walton introduces the figure of Charles, who goes to see a horror movie, and whose heart rate and blood pressure rise as he watches the green slime ooze out toward him, threatening to engulf him. Charles "loses hold of reality" and *momentarily* takes the slime to be real and really fears it, even though he knows perfectly well that he is sitting in a movie theatre [. . .].
>
> 1995: 34

It is striking that Furst and Walton use film as an example to illustrate their argument on the double position readers can simultaneously hold towards the veracity of a work, not only in light of my own previous remarks on the belief in film as always slightly reserved and restrained, but also because a similar argument has been developed specifically on film by adherents of the so-called apparatus theory, such as Jean-Louis Baudry and Christian Metz. The latter has compared the film viewer with a dreamer who knows that he is dreaming. Although a dreamer does not so much pretend to believe, Metz' analogy corresponds to Furst's and Walton's ideas in that it implies the same double position of believing yet not believing completely, of being aware of the fact that something is not real, while at the same time experiencing and reacting to it as though it is real.

According to Metz (1982), film is the preeminent medium for inducing this double awareness in the spectator because, in the dominant application of the narrative fiction film, it is able to produce a reality impression unlike any other medium. Similar to dreams, films can present worlds which do not comply with the logic of everyday reality. Yet, because of the strong reality impression which the medium is able to create, the viewer is willing to invest belief in what she sees, even when knowing it isn't real and perhaps even couldn't be real. The fetishist formula which therefore applies specifically to the medium of film according to the French film theorist, somewhat resembles the "performance of pretense" Furst expounded: "I know very well that [. . .] (what I see isn't real), but all the same [. . .] (I believe in the film)."

Although the viewer's belief in videos which produce a reality effect is not entirely unrestrained or naïve, it isn't profoundly characterized by the double position of belief and nonbelief which is produced by film. Belief in the truthfulness of videos does not have to be pretended, because the depicted scenes aren't understood as imaginary or staged to begin with. However, some disbelief is held by most video viewers, albeit a mild form. Whereas the initial disbelief of the film viewer can only be suspended or partially and momentarily suppressed by pretending to believe, mild disbelief holds just a small and secondary position toward the viewer's belief in the veracity of videos which produce a reality effect.

This mild disbelief can function as a critical tool by which a too naïve mode of looking is prevented, and it is often adopted automatically by contemporary viewers. For in this digital era in which images can be manipulated or created from scratch in a trice, most spectators have learned to hold some suspicion about the veracity of images. Moreover, as the electronic signal of analogue video images is more susceptible to manipulation and distortion than projected analogue film images are, the viewer's wariness of distortion might be stronger in the case of video images.[1] I would say that rather than pretending to believe, the viewer of videos pretends slight disbelief in order to remain on the alert for image manipulation and simulation. The formula Metz ascribed to film, then, can be redesigned for videos which produce a reality effect as follows: "I know that [. . .] (what I see is real), yet I pretend that [. . .] (I do not believe in the video entirely)."

As the suspicion about the veracity of images is a culturally conditioned attitude of most contemporary, "digitally literate" viewers, the pretense of disbelief in videos is as much a conventional act as the pretense of belief in fiction films, which is prompted by "our habit of playing along with fiction"—as Walton pointed out. However, besides the acquired character of a critical attitude towards images, videos themselves often invite the pretense of mild disbelief. They do so, for instance, by showing that they are not entirely undistorted or objective representations of reality, and therefore should not be believed entirely or too eagerly as true and transparent. However, such urges towards mild disbelief not only lead to mild disbelief in the viewer, they can also conversely contribute to the viewer's belief in the representation. They lend a video an air of what can be called self-reflexive honesty; an air which only incites more instead of less belief in the viewer. Thus, video's invitations to disbelief can in the end result in belief.

As video looks more real than film when both media produce a reality effect in their own typical ways, and the viewer's belief in the truthfulness of videos is as a rule more profound than the belief in films, it is possible to conclude that the medium of video is able to produce a stronger or more intense reality effect than film. Without casting aside this idea of a subtle difference between the intensity of the reality effects of film and video, it is useful to consider whether the reality effects produced by the two media also differ in kind instead of only in strength and degree.

Kinds of reality

Whereas the subtle difference in intensity of the media's reality effects concerns the intensity of the effect, a difference in kind—although not an absolute one—can be found by focusing on the reality part of the reality effect. A question to be asked when the impression that "this is reality" is raised by video or film is: "which reality?" When posing this question while watching *Benny's Video*, the answer would be that the reality which seems to be represented by the opening video is referential reality. The reality on view really is or was, or so we are inclined to believe as viewers. The film part of *Benny's Video*, however, does not give rise to the belief that what it shows is reality as it really is or was. Instead of producing the illusion that referential reality is denoted, the narrative film rather creates the impression that it depicts a certain reality. It seems to show a world which looks real but is nevertheless known to be a fictional and constructed reality in which imaginary events take place, not to be mistaken with the (daily, historical) reality.

The answers found in Haneke's film to the question "which reality?" are representative of the two answers that will come up when posing this question with regard to the reality effect of video and film. The kind of reality video mostly seems to represent is *referential* reality, while film as a rule convincingly shows *a* reality when it produces a reality effect. The latter reality is a constructed world which looks real in its own right, quite apart from the referential reality we as viewers (believe we) live in. The reality effects the two media produce can thus be said to differ in that the realities they seem to depict are different kinds of realities. My proposal is to call the reality effect produced by video a referential-reality effect, and the reality effect created by film a constructed-reality effect. The added adjectives, then, do not so much concern the effect but the reality.

The difference between the referential-reality effect and the constructed-reality effect should not be understood as an absolute difference for two reasons. First, the difference in kinds of reality implies a difference in the degree of the effect. This has to do with the fact that the referential reality we (believe we) live in is still likely to be conceived as more real than the imaginary, fictional realities constructed within a discourse.[2] Hence, when a representation produces an impression that "this is reality," this reality is conceived of as more real when it is understood as referential reality than when it is understood as a constructed reality. In the latter case, disbelief will have to be suspended, or belief will be pretended. When the represented reality is understood as referential reality, though, the viewer's belief in the represented reality will in all probability be plain or only slightly reserved.

Thus, the strength of the reality effect and of the belief it gives rise to are related to the kind of reality a representation seems to depict. The more a work produces the impression that the reality it represents is an imaginary, fictional, and constructed one, the weaker the reality effect and the viewer's belief in the veracity of the representation are. Conversely, the reality effect of a representation is stronger when it convinces the viewer of the fact that it depicts "the" instead of "a" reality. Bearing in mind again that the adjectives "referential" and "constructed" concern the reality rather than the effect, it is possible to say that the referential-reality effect is more intense and stronger than the constructed-reality effect. The previously drawn conclusion that the medium of video is able to produce a stronger or more intense reality effect than film therefore still holds, as the former medium usually produces a referential-reality effect while the latter in general produces a constructed-reality effect.

Secondly, the difference between the two reality effects is not absolute because representations hardly ever create the impression that they only refer to referential reality, or show an entirely imaginary world. The referential-reality effect and the constructed-reality effect should rather be understood as opposite ends of a sliding scale. Between those ends, many subtle and comparative differences exist, because the status of the depicted reality is never entirely unambiguously referential or imaginary. The many possible combinations, mixtures and shades between the two ends are as varied and complex as the degrees, calibers, and combinations of belief in the veracity of a representation.

Although I stated previously that video produces a referential-reality effect while film creates a constructed-reality effect, the reality effects produced by the two media are hardly ever purely referential or constructed. Video rather produces a reality effect which is predominantly (yet almost never completely) referential, and film creates a reality effect which is mainly (but not entirely) constructed. The reality effect produced by single works is hardly ever entirely referential or constructed either. Not the reality effect of the filmed parts in *Benny's Video*, nor the reality effect created by the home video footage in *Family Viewing*, nor the one produced by the realist novels Barthes discusses—none occupies the far ends of the "reality effect scale." They are all positioned somewhere in between.

The filmed parts of Haneke's work show particularly well how an intermediary position can be occupied on the scale in question. For although those filmed parts predominantly create a constructed-reality effect, not many of the film's characteristics truly obstruct a referential illusion. Alongside the fact that, as mentioned previously, visual access to the world on view seems direct and transparent, a referential-reality effect is not impossible because the world Benny and his parents inhabit could be real. For although some events in the lives of these seemingly ordinary bourgeois family members are quite extraordinary, the film does not transgress the boundaries of what is possible within reality according to general West-European views.[3] The ontology represented by the film does not greatly differ from the one most of the film's viewers believe they live in. In addition, some of the towns and places shown and named in the film really exist; for instance Austria's capital Vienna and its Stephansplatz, the Egyptian town Hurghada and the nearby pyramids.

So, although the narrative film part of *Benny's Video* creates a story world which looks real in its own right but which can also be recognized as imaginary, referential reality does sometimes seem to slip in. In other words, a referential-reality effect is not completely absent from the film, but the constructed-reality effect predominates. The latter reality effect can, however, predominate more strongly than it does in *Benny's Video*. Think of fairy tales or horror movies in which creatures or events are depicted which do not exist or could not have occurred in reality as the viewer understands it. In these cases, the words or images do not have (or could not have) referents outside of the (visual) text. They rather compose an enclosed world which is clearly separated from referential reality. As the represented enclosed world is an ontology which differs strongly from the ontology the reader resides in, it can easily be understood as constructed, fictional, and imaginary. If a reality effect is produced by such works depicting an ontology which strongly differs from the reader's, it is an effect which approaches the "constructed-reality end" of the reality effect scale. Conversely, the "referential-reality end" of the scale is approached by works which represent an ontology which seems similar to the reader's or viewer's world. The more the depicted ontology resembles the ontology of the reader, the more easily it can be understood as referential reality.

Strikingly, the realist narratives Barthes discusses in "The Reality Effect" do not necessarily occupy the referential reality pole of the reality effect scale. This is striking because the reality effect as Barthes defines it is a referential-reality effect; it concerns the impression that referential reality is denoted directly by the text. However, although the realist texts Barthes mentions create the impression that they refer to referential reality in some respects, the novels equally construct contained, fictional story worlds which seem real in their own right. Those worlds can nevertheless still be recognized as fictional and imaginary, especially when the stories appear in the form of a novel. Like the narrative fiction film, the genre of the novel is counterproductive to the construction of a referential-reality effect; it is by convention associated with imaginary and constructed worlds instead of with the documentary registration of reality.

However, the recognition of the worlds depicted by realist texts as constructed and fictional is historically relative, and with that, their reality effect is so too. When realist narratives first appeared, they were often published as serials in newspapers, and the typical realist mode of writing had not yet become a style common to narrative fiction. The constructed, fictional character of the realist stories was therefore often overlooked by nineteenth-century readers. Instead, the texts caused a predominantly referential-reality effect. This is well illustrated by an anecdote on Louis Couperus' *Eline Vere* (1887–1888), a novel which was first published as a serial in a local Dutch newspaper. When the episode in which the fictional character dies appeared in this newspaper, people riding the tram in the writer's home town whispered to each other: "Have you heard? Eline is dead."

CHAPTER 5
MEDIUM SPECIFICITY AND THE REALITY EFFECT

The first chapter of this part ended with the assertion that the media of film and video do not only produce a reality effect automatically because of the chemical and technical ways they each record objects in front of the lens. For, as can be seen in recent films and videos such as *Benny's Video*, *Family Viewing* and *Battles of Troy*, the two media also produce a reality effect through other devices. My discussion of these devices has shown that the devices which are generally used in videos in order to create the effect in question differ from the ones which are commonly applied in films.

The adjectives and adverbs used above, such as common, general, mostly, and usually, indicate that is customary for video and film to produce a reality effect by means of certain conventional devices, and to produce a reality effect of a certain degree and kind. Many of the reality-effect producing devices of video can however be applied in film, too. In fact, devices which point out the indexicality of the medium were once quite common in some applications of the cinematic medium. Many home movies shot on film, as well as films produced within famous cinematic documentary strands such as *direct cinema* and *cinéma verité*, were characterized by many of the formal devices which now typify video practices. However, when video arrived, it slowly took over the making of documentaries, home movies, and other amateur productions. As the medium was cheaper and its camera easier to handle than film's, it simply became more attractive for many practitioners within these domains to use video instead of film. Hence, many formal cinematic devices which were applied within these genres to signal authenticity and indexicality, were adopted, adapted, and expanded within video practices. They became more typical to the latter medium over time.

However, the arrival of video not only changed the specificity of film by taking over some of its genres. The video-specific characteristic of instant broadcast very much altered the way in which film was specified. Previously, I explained that film images always refer to something that has been because, as opposed to video images, film images cannot be shown as soon as they are recorded. Interestingly, this characteristic of film was not discerned as a distinct quality of the medium before video was invented. For a long time, film's specificity was mostly determined in comparison to photography. And compared to photography, the most specific features of film seemed to be the liveliness and continuous movement of its images, both signaling presentness, not pastness. The deictic reference of film images was defined solely in the way which is now featured as a video-specific form of indexicality: saying "now!" Only when video arrived did film's reference to the past became more apparent. Compared to this new medium and its capability of instantaneous broadcast, film suddenly began to resemble the medium from which it was usually distinguished, and moreover in a respect on the basis of which it was distinguished from this medium: the "that has been" of photography.

Video's immediacy, its temporal indexicality, as well as the dominance of its typically referential reality effect have altered the identity of film in one more respect. Compared to the relatively strong, referential reality effect which video images are able to produce, the constructed-reality effect of narrative fiction film has become less strong. Compared to the raw and immediate indexicality of video, the smooth realism of narrative fiction films looks constructed. Although aimed at hiding the mediated and material character of the medium, film's reality-effect producing devices tend to appear slightly contrived in comparison with video. As Belton has put it well: "video has subtly redefined film as mediated reality" (1996: 86). This redefinition cuts both ways, though: video is only able to establish itself as more real in relation to film.

In the digital age, the indexical nature of film and video is waning—to put it mildly. When we look at moving images today, they might be digital ones. In fact, they probably are just that. This obliterates any certainty concerning their relation to a profilmic reality. Not only are digital images very susceptible to image manipulation through computer software, they can be "painted" from scratch with computer software too. The pixels of computer generated images (CGI) are not in any way caused by rays of light reflecting into a camera. In sum, film and video images have lost their technological status as indexical traces. However, video has not lost its status as *temporal* index. The only images which can still (more or less) be trusted as authentic, veracious representations of reality are what we call "live" images. In the digital age, this temporal indexicality turns out to be important to the specification of the cinematic medium.

First of all, as Thomas Y. Levin has pointed out in his "Rhetoric of the Temporal Index" (2002), since the 1990s, many narrative films have incorporated video footage in their narrative structure (e.g., *Wag the Dog* 1997, *The Truman Show* 1998, *Sliver* 1993). All of these films show video images: surveillance videos, video reportages on television, and webcam videos. What the video clips have in common is that they belong to genres which are associated with instantaneous feed. This live aspect is, moreover, affirmed by the narrative structure of the films which incorporate the clips. In addition, some films do not merely contain video clips—they are presented in video form alone, without an overarching film framework to embed them. Mike Figgis' remarkable narrative film *Time Code* (2000) is, for instance, told in its entirety through the quadruple split screen of a video surveillance monitor.

Levin explains this widespread use in light of cinema's digitalization. For although narrative fiction films never emphasized the indexical nature of their analogue medium, this indexicality was so widely known that it nevertheless had a rhetorical reality effect without being signified within films. The disappearance of the indexical, material link between film images and their referents must therefore be compensated in narrative fictions films. Levin argues that "by adopting the rhetorics of real-time broadcast, [. . .] cinema has displaced an impoverished spatial rhetoric of photo-chemical indexicality with a thoroughly contemporary, and equally semiotically 'motivated' rhetoric of *temporal indexicality*" (2002: 592). The indexical rhetoric of cinema's pre-digital photo-chemical past thus survives in the digital age, albeit now re-cast in the form of the temporal indexicality of the real-time video image (592).

It is remarkable that influential contemporary theoretical specifications of the cinematic medium also redefine the cinematic in the digital age around a form of indexicality which comes close to video's temporal indexicality. In "The Indexical and the Concept of Medium Specificity" (2007), Mary Ann Doane argues that the digitalization of film does not mean that the specificity of the medium can no longer be structured around the concept of indexicality. Although the idea of index as trace no longer applies to digital film images, the definition of the index as deixis is very much applicable to film, Doane suggests. Pepita Hesselberth, who takes up Doane's suggestion to rethink cinematic indexicality as deixis rather than trace in her *Cinematic Chronotopes: Here, Now, Me*, puts it as follows: "The difference is temporal: trace connects to the past; deixis to the present" (2014: 9).

Adding the field

My discussion of the ways in which video and film each produce their most dominant reality effect, as well as the overview of the manner in which the two media have specified each other in this respect, confirm Krauss' definition of medium specificity in several ways. First, the fact that media produce their respective reality effects through formal devices demonstrates that their specificity is indeed not merely a technological matter. For although the devices in question spring from (and point back to) the material, technological base of film and video, they are nevertheless avoidable conventional artifices. Secondly, the fact that the specific identities of film and video in relation to their most typical reality effect have so thoroughly changed and developed over the years clearly supports Krauss' idea that the specificity of media is always changing. Moreover, in the case of film, the changes in question didn't come from "within": the identity of film changed with the arrival of video. Certain abilities and formal features were no longer unique to film. In addition, the functions of the medium altered as video largely took over its application in certain genres. This influence of video on the specification of film is in line with Krauss' idea that the specificity of media is differential.

This notion of differentiality leaves us with some questions concerning the reality effects of film and video, however. Although Krauss has stated that the specific structure of media is an agglomerate one, consisting of many components, the idea of differentiality can still be understood as a suggestion that the specificity of media lies solely in those things by which it differs from all other media: in one or more unique characteristics or abilities.[1] And although she defines the structure of the medium as ever changing, her temporal model does not rule out the possibility that at some point, the unique abilities of the medium can temporarily be pinpointed, and that the specificity of the medium is then fixed at that specific moment and those unique features. These implicit suggestions do not only imply a return to Greenberg's essentialist understanding of the medium—they do not apply to film and video when it comes to their reality effects.

Although it is surely possible to pin down some unique technological abilities of film or video at a certain point in time (think, for instance, of closed-circuit video), these unique features do not explain many of the other notable differences between the two media in light of the reality effect. For, as opposed to unique features, these differences mostly lie in what I would call typicalities and commonalities. It is, for instance, more typical for video than for film to signify the indexicality of its images. Film, on the other hand, more commonly produces a reality effect by hiding the materiality of its support. It is, moreover, specific to film that it more commonly produces a reality this way, just as it is specific to video to predominantly produce a reality effect in another way. Moreover, we can call the typical devices of film specific because, through their common appearance in film, we have come to recognize them as specifically cinematic aspects. This also goes for the videomatic devices I discussed. It is through the typicality of certain features that the two media are specified and differentiated from each other. However, none of this relies on unique, inevitable technological features. It is mostly a conventional distinction. Film and video are very well able to imitate or adopt each other's reality-effect producing devices, yet they do so in the margins of their more dominant applications.

This brings me to another important aspect of medium specificity which Krauss' definition cannot account for. Media do not necessarily (or hardly ever) form a continuous, homogeneous unity. Most media can do one thing, as well as another. Their technological abilities as well as conventional layers can be contradictory and conflicting. And within all their different abilities, conventions, and applications, some forms dominate. How can these matters of heterogeneity and dominance within the medium be reflected in a definition of medium specificity? Or, to put it differently, which concept can guide our analysis of the complexity of the aggregate condition of media? These questions can be said to be particularly pressing in relation to film and video, both of which exist in many forms. In particular, video's heterogeneity has been stressed by theorists. Krauss, for instance, has called the medium "hydra-headed, existing in endlessly diverse forms" (1999: 31). In his seminal work *Videography*, Sean Cubitt chose to speak in the plural form of video *media* in order to point out that "there is no essential form of video, nothing to which one can point out as primal source or goal of video" (1993: xv). Video media, Cubitt states, "can only be understood as the product, the site and the source of multiple contradictions, lived out in multiple practices [. . .]" (3).[2]

In order to account for such a multiplicity of contradictions, I propose to add a concept to Krauss' definition of the medium which she once coined in a discussion of sculpture, and which has been further defined in relation to medium specificity by art historian George Baker (a one-time student of Krauss). In "Photography's Expanded Field," Baker conceptualizes the medium as a field of possibilities, "consisting of multiple sets of oppositions and conjugations, rather than any singular operation" (2005: 124).

In some respects, Baker's ideas are clearly imbued by those of Krauss. Like Krauss, Baker insists on the fact that a medium's specificity is a culturally composed structure. The expressive and formal possibilities of a medium are not dependent on its sheer technological demise, Baker states. In fact, he almost completely rules out the importance of a medium's technical support to its specificity. Moreover, Baker surmises, a medium's field can change without losing its delineation as specific field. Yet, his argument differs from Krauss' in one crucial way. Although Krauss acknowledges the composed, aggregative, changeable, and differing nature of a medium's specificity, she still speaks of media as singular entities. In her eyes, a medium is constructed out of one technical support plus one set of conventions. Baker's model of the medium takes into account that a medium consists of many opposing sets of possibilities at the same time.

In addition to the fact that the spatial notion of the field makes it easier to envisage the internal differentiation of a medium, it also provides us with a way to envisage the relationship between similar media such as film and video. When media share possibilities, their fields overlap. Such overlaps do not mean that the fields as such lose their specificity, however. Following Baker's idea of the field, the ever-changing specificity of media can be said not to lie in their unique capabilities, but in their unique composition of several—sometimes opposing—sets of possibilities.

Another important component of Baker's medium theory is the so-called field of operation. Being fields of expressive and formal possibilities themselves, media also have the possibility to operate within one or several particular fields, realms, or domains, according to Baker. Moreover, he designates such fields as *cultural* fields. The field of operation of a medium, then, could be understood as the cultural field(s) within which media can operate without losing or altering their specificity. However, the term "operation" can, in my eyes, also be conceived of as "application," in order to stress that media do not act on their own account, but are used within certain fields. The domains Baker names as cultural fields are varied; from art to documentary, from archive to science fiction. Apparently, quite disparate matters can be conceived of as cultural fields. Some of them, such as art, are institutionalized domains. Others, such as science fiction, are fields demarcated as genres.

In light of medium specificity, however, such disparity does not matter much. Baker's notion of field of operation is relevant because the operation of media is often restricted to certain domains, be they institutions, genres, modes of entertainment, or culturally delineated spaces. A medium's field of operation is part of a medium's specificity, because it is part of a medium's field of possibilities. Thus, it is a field within a field. A medium's field of operation designates a medium's possibilities with regard to the cultural places and domains within which it can operate. The specificity of television, for instance, is in part determined by its often-applied possibility to operate within the culturally delineated space of the living room. Another example is the specific possibility of painting to operate within the domain of art. Its application in the realm of documentary is however hardly imaginable. If the medium were to be used as documentary, its specificity would have to be reconsidered.

When it comes to the reality effects of film and video, it is possible to say that their respective reality effects are produced by a specific set of their possibilities within one or more of their fields of operation. In the case of film, that medium's most typical reality effect is produced within its most dominant field of operation: the genre of the narrative fiction film. Baker's notion of fields of operation is not only relevant with regard to the reality effects of film and video, it is useful in mapping out the fields of film and video in general. The medium of video is characterized by a couple of very disparate fields of operation. One the one hand, it operates within documentary and amateur genres, and on the other hand, it is widely applied within the field of "high art." Although documentary and art are fields of operation for film too, the latter medium is mostly characterized by one very dominant field of operation/application: the genre of the narrative fiction film.

This dominant application of film can be said to overshadow that medium's entire field of possibilities. For, as for instance Roger Odin has argued, all nondominant uses of a medium are linked to the dominant mode, just as "what is written in the margins of a text bears a relation [...] to this text, to the large corpus to which it is linked, on which it depends, on which it is commenting or which it is refuting by means of notes and arguments" (1995: 221). Film's dominant application as a narrative medium not only shapes other applications of the medium; it is also a deciding factor in theoretical specifications of the medium. Christian Metz, for example, has designated narrative fiction film (or as he also calls it: diegetic film) as the positive pole of film to which the majority corresponds, and with respect to which the rest can be defined (1982: 39).

However, media can also be each other's field of operation. This brings me back to the reality effect. In the previous chapter, I discussed Levin's observation that many contemporary films adopt reality-effect producing video clips in their narrative structure. In doing so, narrative fiction films become a field of operation for video and its medium-specific, or medium-typical reality effect. In the following chapter, I will study how this affects the reality effects of both film and video. As will become clear, the rhetorical impact of video's reality effect on the reality effect of film is not as unidirectional as Levin leads us to suspect.

CHAPTER 6
INTERACTION: BETWEEN REALITY EFFECTS

In the works I have discussed so far, the combination of video and film within the single object of a video or film made differences visible between the reality effects of the two media. In that sense, the two are enabled to specify each other with regard to the reality effect within and by the films and videos in question. The relationship between the two media in the works discussed is, however, a lot more complicated than that. For in *Benny's Video*, *Family Viewing* and *Battles of Troy*, video and film do not remain separated units between which the only form of interaction—mutual specification—is caused by the fact that their neat juxtaposition exposes differences between their respective reality effects. In these works, as well as in a number of other films and videos that I will mention below, mutual specification occurs between film and video because they interfere with each other's reality effects in ways which go beyond exposing difference alone. The two media, for instance, sustain, enhance, question, or diminish each other's reality effect, become part of each other's reality-effect producing devices, alter the reality effect of the other medium by way of their own devices, or use the reality effect of the other medium to sustain their own reality effect. These and other forms of intermedial interaction concerning the reality effect will be the topic of this chapter.

Any form of interaction between media which influences reality effects or which affects the reality-effect producing devices is automatically of influence on the specificity of the two media. On the one hand, when video fragments in a film enhance the constructed-reality effect specific of (the) film, the medium of video sustains the conventional specificity of film. When, on the other hand, video diminishes film's reality effect, or makes this effect more referential than constructed, the medium of film is respecified by video because video shows that film can produce a reality effect which is not understood as specific to it.

I have argued before that video and film each have their specific reality effects, that their reality effects are produced through medium-specific devices, and that the specificity of these effects and devices comes into being through differences with the effects and devices of other media. All three of these assumptions are, however, more or less questioned by the works under discussion. The films and videos in question first of all show that although particular reality effects are specific to film and video, their specificity with regard to the reality effect can easily be altered or respecified by the other medium. Secondly, the forms of interaction in the case studies demonstrate that the creation of a reality effect by film and video not only depends on their own specific devices. Finally, the specificity of their reality effects or of their devices is shown to depend not solely on *differences* with other media. The works in question reveal that the reality effects of film and video can depend very much on *interaction* (and not only in the sense of specification through difference) between film and video.

Film's video

The first object by which I will study forms of interaction between film, video, and their reality effects is the film which has reappeared as an object of study throughout Part I: Haneke's *Benny's Video.* As the following analysis will show, the influence of film on the reality effect of video is equivocal, and so is the influence of video on the reality effect of film.

In *Benny's Video*, interaction between film and video first arises when the filmed material which follows the film's opening video is recognized as narrative fiction film. The filmed material can be recognized as narrative fiction film pretty quickly, because many of the genre's representational conventions are followed. The camera work is, for instance, carried out calmly and with steady precision, the 180-degree line is not crossed, spaces are mapped out by clearly related successive shots, and a sense of overview is further sustained by a number of establishing shots of the spaces in which the protagonists reside. Although a reality effect is created by these devices because they give rise to an illusion of overview and visual access to the depicted world, they also enable the recognition of the genre of narrative fiction film. Through that, they make clear that the world on view is a constructed and imaginary reality.

This recognition influences the reality effect of the opening video, albeit retroactively. As pointed out previously, the opening video of the dying pig produces a referential-reality effect; it invites the viewer to believe that it represents referential reality. This referential-reality effect is however diminished by the subsequent narrative fiction film once this film is recognized as a narrative fiction film, because important aspects of the reality depicted by the video return in the staged and acted out world shown by the film. The reality effect of the video weakens once the place it shows can be understood as a film set, and once the people surrounding the dying pig can in retrospect be recognized as actors. Their slightly shocked and awkward expressions when they witness the dying pig can in hindsight be read as play-acted emotions. Even the event of the pig's slaughter can now be assumed to be performed for the sake of the film. In sum, the (referential) reality effect of the video diminishes because the narrative fiction film makes clear that the reality depicted by the video is not referential reality but the imaginary reality constructed by the fiction film.

Video proving film

Although the narrative film diminishes the reality effect of the opening video, this video at first temporarily enhances the reality effect of the film. When the people shown in the opening video appear in the filmed material, it is impossible to immediately recognize them as actors. Nor can the dialogue and events which subsequently take place at once be understood as acted and staged. One of the reasons for this is that the filmed material has to be recognized as narrative fiction film before the world on view can be considered as a fictional and constructed one. A second reason is that the reality effect produced by the preceding video has invited the viewer to read the images referentially, and to believe in their truthfulness with little effort. Once the film sets in, these modes of reading and believing cannot be cast off straightaway. Because of that, the behavior of the characters, as well as the setting and the portrayed events in which they play a part, initially look as real and unstaged as the people, places, and events in the opening video. This impression only lasts until the film is recognized as a narrative fiction film. The referential-reality impression evoked by the video does, however, postpone the moment at which this recognition takes place.

Once the narrative of *Benny's Video* has started to unfold, video fragments keep appearing in the filmed material. Like the opening video, most of these fragments are recorded by protagonist Benny, who almost constantly uses the medium of video. If he is not watching, editing, borrowing, or discussing videos, he is producing them by filming the world around him with one of his video cameras. As the video recordings which succeed Benny's opening video are clearly embedded in the fiction film, they are not able to produce a referential-reality effect as strong as the one produced by the opening video before the narrative film had set in.

Yet, the video fragments do still produce a reality effect which is more referential and therefore stronger than the constructed-reality effect created by the narrative film. Because of specific video devices—such as graininess and color distortion, a wobbly image frame indicating amateurism or the opposite static "stare" typical of surveillance video—the video fragments give the impression that the reality they depict is referential reality, and hence not an imaginary world of make believe. Although, as viewers, we remain aware of the fact that the world shown by the video fragments is actually the imaginary world constructed by the film, the referential-reality effect produced by video cannot be entirely suppressed by this awareness. When the imaginary world constructed by the narrative film is shown using video images, it looks more real than when it is shown using film.

The referential-reality effect created by the video fragments enhances the reality effect of the entire film. The film's diegesis not only looks more real when it is shown by video, the film world looks more real throughout the entire film because parts of it are represented by video. The video representations seem to prove that the world shown by the film is not a constructed reality, but referential reality—even though some awareness of the constructed nature of the film world remains. In *Benny's Video*, video can be said to function as a medium which authenticates the reality shown by the fiction film.

This function is mostly noticeable when it comes to events and situations in the film which are in need of authentication. The rather ordinary holiday Benny and his mother spend in Egypt does not have to be shown by video footage in order to be credible. The foregoing event of Benny shooting and killing his young female friend with a cattle gun, in contrast, is in need of some validation by video in order to be believable. Immediately after Benny has shot the girl for the first time, the view of the murder scene is no longer presented by film. It is only through video images that the viewer can see how the injured girl collapses and drops on the floor, and how her dead body lies in a pool of blood after Benny has shot her twice more.

These horrific video images demonstrate that the scenes in which the murder is shown do not merely represent the fantasy of the death-obsessed protagonist. They also make it difficult to understand the crime as staged and acted. For, through reality-effect producing devices such as the absence of operations like zoom movements, cuts, and camera swerves, and the presence of flaws such as color distortion and pixel drop-out, the video creates the illusion that it provides an objective, documentary view of reality—in this case the reality of a girl being murdered by a teenage boy. If Benny's cruel act and its bloody consequences were not shown by both film and video images, but by film images alone, the viewer's awareness of the scene being staged would probably have been stronger. Without the referential-reality impression evoked by the video material, the impression evoked in the viewer by the film images might then resemble the remark Benny's makes in conversation with his victim on special effects in films: "All ketchup and plastic. Looks real though."

The contributing and counteracting narrator

Many of the scenes and events shown by video fragments in *Benny's Video* contribute to the film's narrative, not least because some are shown by video images alone. The video fragments which represent things not depicted by film images as well, are often indispensable to the cohesiveness and comprehensibility of the narrative. The plot of the film would be incomplete without the video images which show how Benny's parents are arrested by the police. Because of the importance of video footage to the unfolding of the film story, it can be argued that the medium of video is an embedded narrator in the film. The strong referential-reality effect video produces through its specific devices, moreover, makes the medium a reliable narrator which is easily trusted. Through this air of reliability and trustworthiness video is not only able to contribute to the narrative told by the unseen, external narrator of the film, but also to confirm it. What is more, as a narrator, video contributes *to* and is embedded *in* one of the most important devices by which film creates its reality effect: narrativity. Thus, in *Benny's Video*, the medium of video—including many of its specific reality-effect producing devices—is a sustaining part of one of film's specific reality-effect producing devices. And because the device of narrativity is specific to film, video can even be said to become part of the specificity of film by contributing to the film's narrative.

However, although video contributes to one of film's reality-effect producing devices as a narrator, the medium of video in its capacity as internal narrator also frustrates an important way through which (the) film produces a reality effect. The reality effect of film is mostly caused by evoking an illusion in the viewer of overview and visual access to the depicted world. The video fragments in *Benny's Video* shatter this illusion. First of all, the video images do not look as transparent and smooth as the film images. Instead, the video material shows its opaqueness and materiality in many ways. Secondly, the video images do not always provide the viewer with a complete overview of scenes. Events which are important within the narrative of the film are often only partially visible when they are presented in video. This is the case in the scene where Benny murders the girl. Although the falling body and corpse of the young woman are brought in to view, her prolonged suffering and death take place just outside of the video frame. When such charged events are kept from full view, video does not provide the viewer with the illusion of unmediated visual access to the film's diegesis, but rather bluntly withholds this access from the viewer.

Hence, the peculiar thing is that, in *Benny's Video*, the illusion of transparency and visual access which is specific and indispensable to the way film creates a reality effect is undermined by video through some of the specific devices by which video creates a reality effect. The coarse-grained, slightly flickering image surface of the video images undermines the impression of transparency which is important to the reality effect of film. Yet, the graininess and unsteadiness of the images are devices which produce a reality effect in video.

What is more, when important scenes are out of shot in the video parts of Haneke's film, the camera isn't deliberately turned away from the scene. The camera just doesn't move at all, it keeps "staring" in one direction without turning, zooming or focusing. These features of motionlessness and passivity reveal that the video camera is not operated by a human agent, but is left on a tripod or adjusted on the wall in order to record automatically. Within video, such features therefore function as reality-effect producing devices. In *Benny's Video*, however, they also counter the way in which the narrative film creates a reality effect. For because of those specific video devices, video is a trustworthy yet imprecise image narrator that keeps significant parts of the story world from view, thereby obstructing the viewer's illusion of visual access on which the reality effect of film relies.

Exposing video

Besides being a narrator, video can also function as an actor within the narrative of the film. The video fragments in *Benny's Video* tell parts of the cinematic story, yet they also influence the course of events as it unfolds within this story. The video recording of Benny's crime, for instance, proves to his parents that he is really the murderer of the girl whose body is hidden in the family's apartment. This proof prompts the father and mother to cover up the crime. Video also functions as an actor when Benny has his parents arrested on the basis of a fragment of one of his videos. In the fragment, the two poised adults calmly make the shocking decision to dispose of the body by cutting it into pieces and flushing it down the toilet.

Previously, I stated that in Haneke's film, video often authenticates the constructed film world. Because of the referential-effect video creates, the medium seems to prove that the film world is real. However, video does not solely owe its function as evidence and authentication within the film to the strong reality effect it is able to create. The medium also functions as such because the narrative film designates video as a medium which shows the truth. The film does so by having video function as an actor that influences the course of events because it shows reality, reveals the truth or proves that things really happened. By assigning this function within the story to video, the narrative fiction film confirms and sustains the referential-reality effect which video also produces through its own devices.

It is worth noting that as in *Benny's Video*, video often has the function of the truth-revealing actor in contemporary narrative films. A good example is a more recent film by Michael Haneke, *Caché* (2005). In this film, anonymous videotapes sent to protagonist Georges subtly expose painful aspects of Georges' childhood that he has long kept hidden. Video also often has the function of an actor that exposes, reveals, and proves in narrative films more strongly related to mainstream Hollywood cinema than Haneke's European art-house films. In M. Night Shyamalan's *The Sixth Sense* (1999), for instance, a videotape found in the room of a recently deceased girl reveals that the child was poisoned by her own mother. Video surveillance recordings of robberies frequently affect the course of events in fiction films, because as incriminating proof such recordings have to be kept out of the hands of the police by the wrongdoers—which leads to problems and conflict in, for instance, the Hughes brothers' *Menace II Society* (1993)—or because the recordings initiate a police chase, as in *Thelma and Louise* (Scott 1991). The frequent recurrence of video as a truth-bringing actor in narrative fiction films is important because, by repeatedly assigning this function to video, films specify video. Through repetition, the exposure of the truth by video is turned into an act which is conventional to the medium. And as a convention, it becomes part of video's structure of specificity.

Benny's Video, as well as many of the films discussed here, in part allot the function of truth-exposing actor to video by the way in which the film characters understand and use the medium. Benny's parents only accept that Benny has murdered a girl when they witness the crime on video, because they believe that video shows the truth. In addition, the parents are arrested because the police believe that Benny's video of his parents discussing the disposal of the body proves they must have murdered the girl. Haneke's film in addition shows that video can be understood as a medium which shows reality by the way in which the film's protagonist uses the medium.

For Benny, video is an epistemological tool. This goes somewhat against the grain of the specification of video as an indexical medium (including the self-reflexive ones in videos), for as discussed previously, the index is mostly defined as a sign which doesn't tell or show anything about its referent, but rather just points at it. Benny, however, videotapes whatever fascinates him, in order to be able to take a closer look at it later on. By playing videotaped fragments on a VCR, he scrutinizes events ranging from parties to death in the hope of learning more about it. The young boy seems to consider video as a medium by which more can be seen and discovered about reality than by eyesight alone.[1] The way in which reality is shown by video appeals so much to Benny that he even prefers to look through the window of his bedroom window using a video camera instead of his own eyes. One of Benny's video cameras constantly records the outside world through a thin gap between closed curtains, while the footage is shown in real time on a television screen. The medium truly serves the protagonist's desire to fathom certain aspects of reality by some of the options video offers its viewer when recorded material is played on a VCR. The options of pausing, rewinding, fast-forwarding, and playing moving video images in slow motion enable Benny to see events repeatedly, faster, and longer than would be possible with his own eyes.[2]

Because Haneke's film integrates video as a truth-revealing actor within its narrative structure, and because *Benny's Video* moreover has its protagonist demonstrate how video can be used as a medium through which reality can be seen and known better than using human eyes alone, it can be argued that narrative film sustains the referential-reality effect of video. On the other hand, film can also be said to offer a warning against the reality effect of video. The reality effect of video is shown to be so strong that it easily entices its viewers into believing that the medium shows the truth about things and events (as accepted by the police) and that it can provide an insightful view on reality (as Benny believes). However, in Haneke's film, video is shown to be inadequate when it comes to these assumptions. The film, moreover, shows how false assumptions raised by video's reality effect can have grave consequences. As mentioned, Benny's parents are arrested after the police have seen a video fragment in which the father and mother plan to get rid of the girl's dead body. Some videotaped parts of the conversation are however edited out of the video footage by Benny before he hands the tape over to the police. In these omitted parts, the parents provide each other with reasons for covering up their son's crime. Without these parts of the conversation, Benny's guilt remains undisclosed by the video. While in fact it only shows a part of the truth, the video now seems to reveal that the parents have committed the murder.

What is more, the falseness of the assumptions video gives rise to through its strong reality effect can even be said to lie at the basis of Benny's crime. The young boy expects that video can provide him with an insightful view on reality, and he constantly attempts to study the subject which fascinates him most by watching videos. After a while, however, Benny finds out that the high hopes which the medium of video had raised in him are vain. For in the end, he doesn't really get to know, experience, and especially not to see death by studying videos. In order "to see what it's like," he has to kill a girl and watch her die with his own eyes—which is also the explanation he gives when his parents ask him why he has committed the crime.

Features casting doubt

In Atom Egoyan's *Family Viewing*, the medium of video first appears within filmed material in the form of surveillance video fragments. Sometimes, these fragments are of a young woman named Aline, who is shown working as a telephone operator. A video image shows the entrance to her office from a high angle. After that, Aline ends a telephone conversation in a film shot. A few moments later, she leaves her office through the door which is kept under surveillance by video. In this sequence, film and video enhance each other's reality effect reciprocally; the order in which they influence each other cannot be determined. On the one hand, the film images sustain the belief that the surveillance video images are live, for there is no delay between the filmed actions of the character and her whereabouts on video. The possibility that the video images are live enhances their reality effect because, as explained previously, liveness precludes postproduction through which images can be manipulated. On the other hand, the presumed liveness of the images enhances the reality effect of the film, because when the video images are broadcast in real time, the film images which show the same situation must be live as well. This in turn enhances the reality effect of the filmed pieces for the same reason that the idea of live broadcasting enhances the reality effect of the video images.

A second way in which video appears within the filmed material is in the form of clips of home video footage. The function of these pieces of footage within the narrative film will be discussed later. First, I will focus on a third way in which video is part of the narrative film. Besides the fragments of surveillance and home video footage, the video medium is embedded in the filmed material of *Family Viewing* in a form other than as a well-defined part with a beginning, an end, and a certain length. Instead of video *fragments*, single video *features* sometimes "enter" the filmed material, without a clear-cut switch from film images to video images taking place.

In a filmed scene where protagonist Van is having breakfast with his father and stepmother, it becomes noticeable that they all have a weird bluish complexion. Upon closer inspection, all objects within the image look rather pale and blue. This color distortion can be recognized as typical of video. Another typical video feature which at times becomes temporarily visible within the film is the seeming luminosity of lighter parts within the images. When Van's stepmother Sandra is wearing a white outfit in a rather dim room, it seems as if she is somewhat glowing in the dark. What is more, on the surface of some film images the square grain which is typical of video can sometimes be detected. In addition, features such as pixel drop-out and flickering patterns which are common in low-quality videos can be seen to briefly emerge in several film images of *Family Viewing*. Video suddenly appears in the film during a scene in which Van and Sandra move towards each other on a couch, when their movements suddenly freeze. Within the image, a horizontal flickering line of black-and-white dots and stripes becomes visible—a line which can immediately be recognized as the scan line which crosses the screen when a videotape is paused.

Apart from this scan line, all features of video which appear within the filmed footage of *Family Viewing* are devices by which a reality effect is created in video. When they emerge separately and outside of a video context within the filmed material of Egoyan's movie, however, they do not produce this effect. The reason for this is that the fact that certain features function as reality-effect producing devices can be medium-specific. It is specific for video that features such as color distortion and pixel drop-out function as devices which produce a reality effect within the medium. The same features do not function in the same way when they appear in the other medium: film. What is more, the features do not just lack the ability to create a reality effect when they invade the film images; they even diminish the reality effect as it is produced by the film images.

The reality of the narrative film fragments in *Family Viewing* is produced by devices specific to film—smooth images of a high resolution and a high quality, steady and composed camerawork, clearly related successive shots which map out space and organize time. The illusion of transparency, overview and direct visual access these devices produce, is however canceled out when the above-mentioned features traverse the film footage as those features attract attention to the materiality of the images. When the smoothness of the film images is temporarily replaced by a granular video look, the image surface no longer seems transparent. The color distortion and pixel drop-out further point out the opaqueness and imperfection of the representation. The paused image with the scan line further reveals the constructed, recorded character of the moving images.

However, at certain points in the film, the video features do create a reality effect. This is the case when the characteristics so strongly dominate the film material that they raise doubt as to the medium of the images on view. When the images on view look a little bluish, but still look like film in all other respects, the medium of the images isn't radically called into question. When the film images simultaneously look bluish, luminous, and grainy, they resemble video images in so many ways that one has to wonder if the film images still really are *film* images. What is more, the sudden video-like interventions in the moving film images, such as pausing and rewinding with the appearance of typical video scan lines on the image surface, raise the question of whether the material which predominantly looks like film might not even be video. For how could a film reel be paused like a videotape?

When doubt as to the medium of the images on view is raised, the video features do start to function as devices which create a reality effect. The mere possibility that they are embedded in video instead of in film provides them with a referential-reality effect. Instead of undermining the illusion of visual access to the imaginary film world, and diminishing the constructed-reality effect of the film, they now seem to make this world look less imaginary—an impression which enhances the reality effect of the representation.

Nevertheless, the referential-reality effect of the features is not only caused by the medium in which they are or seem to be embedded, it also depends on the viewer. The idea that cinematic-seeming scenes in *Family Viewing* might not be depicted by film but by video gives rise to a different conventional mode of reading. When they appear in film, the video features are usually not interpreted by the viewer as signs which indicate that the representation is authentic, documentary, and truthful. Instead, they are by convention understood as such when they are part of video. Thus, the video features invading the filmed material in *Family Viewing* only turn into reality-effect producing devices once they have created the impression that the medium of the representation is probably video. For only then will the viewer read the features as signs indicating the reliability and trustworthiness of the representation as a document of referential reality.

The outstripping narrator

As in *Benny's Video*, the medium of video functions as an internal narrator in *Family Viewing*. Many important events in the film's narrative are told only by video. The burial of Aline's mother, for instance, is only shown by video images, and as viewers we can only witness the sexual contact between Sandra and Van's father Stan through video recordings. An important difference between video's functioning as a narrator in Haneke's and Egoyan's films, however, is that in *Benny's Video*, video often denies the viewer visual access to important parts of the film scenes, whereas video in *Family Viewing* does evoke an impression of visual access in the viewer. Through this, the medium of video contributes to the reality effect of the narrative film in *Family Viewing*. In Egoyan's film, the medium of video evokes an impression of visual access in the viewer by revealing things which are secretive and/or shameful and which are therefore supposed to remain hidden from view—at least from public view. The videotaped sexual escapades of Sandra and Stan are, for instance, a rather private matter. They are also experienced as slightly shameful and humiliating by Sandra, who sometimes even casts an embarrassed look towards the automatically recording video camera in the couple's bedroom. When video images show the burial of Aline's mother it also shows a quite secretive event. Aline's mother is quietly and surreptitiously buried by Van, who has tricked the authorities into believing that the dead woman is his own grandmother. In doing so, he is able to release his real grandmother from the nursing home without getting in trouble with his father. Another secretive and shameful act which is shown by video is Aline's performance as an escort girl.

Because most of the hidden acts and situations which are shown by video in *Family Viewing* are shown by video alone, the medium does not merely contribute to the reality effect of film by sustaining the cinematic illusion of visual access. Video even seems to outstrip film when it comes to providing the viewer with (the illusion of) visual access to the depicted reality. For in Egoyan's film, video has access to scenes which film does not view. In classical narrative films, the film viewer is provided with an illusion of overview and access with the help of an external and unseen, yet omniscient narrator who shows everything in the best and clearest way possible and who has access to all relevant scenes and events. The external filmic narrator of *Family Viewing*, however, is by default compared to its embedded internal video narrator, who has more access to relevant scenes and events than the external narrator. Therefore, in *Family Viewing*, video surpasses the medium of film in creating a reality effect in a specifically cinematic way: by providing the viewer with an illusion of unlimited visual access.

Although video contributes to the reality effect of film as a narrator in *Family Viewing*, and even outstrips film in creating this effect in a specifically filmic way, the medium of video not only acts out an influence on film by contributing to or outstripping specific aspects of the cinematic medium; it has to be kept in mind that video as a narrator is embedded in the narrative of the film's external narrator. It is film that allots the role of supreme narrator to video. By having video as a narrator surpassing the cinematic narrator in providing the viewer with visual access to the story world, the film portrays video as a medium which can provide visual access to reality like no other medium because it penetrates and exposes parts of reality which usually remain hidden from view.[3] Therefore, video not only contributes to the reality effect of film, film also sustains the reality effect of video in *Family Viewing*.

The double illusion of visual access

By allotting video the role of an internal narrator and focalizor whose abilities in showing and revealing reality are outstanding, the narrative film sustains both the reality effect of video and its own reality effect. By handing over the capacities of omniscience and visual access from the external filmic narrator to video as an embedded, internal narrator, the narrative film succeeds in providing the viewer with an even stronger illusion of visual access—an illusion which subsequently enhances the reality effect of the film. In order to explain this, it is necessary to add something to my previous remark that an unseen, external narrator contributes to the reality effect of a narrative fiction film. An internal narrator and/or focalizor is just as indispensable to a film's reality effect as an external one.

As Kaja Silverman has pointed out in her discussion of "suture" in cinema, the film viewer craves to know whose (literal) point of view is represented by certain images, in other words; to whose viewpoint shown images can be attributed. One of the reasons for this craving is that an observer whose view is represented by film images can serve as a stand-in for the viewer within the story. The viewer's impression of looking through the eyes of a character in the film can contribute just as much to the illusion of visual access to the world on view—an illusion which is so important to the reality effect of film—as the omniscient and objective survey provided by an external narrator. Images which are sutured to an internal and possibly confined and subjective point of view can thus contribute just as much to the reality effect of narrative film as unsutured shots which can be only be attributed to the presumably objective, externally focalized view of an external, unseen narrator/focalizor. The former have the ability to provide the viewer with the illusion of visual access to the film world because they can evoke the impression that the film world can be entered by the viewer. The latter provide the viewer with the illusion of visual access and overview because they present an omniscient survey on the story world which cannot be shared by any internal character.

By using video as an internal narrator, *Family Viewing* combines some of the reality effect enhancing characteristics of both an external, unseen narrator and an internal narrator/focalizor. Like the conventional external narrator of classical narrative film, video as a narrator seems to have access to all spaces and events in the narrative. The fact that video as an internal narrator does have access to all spaces and events in the film can be explained by the fact that it is common for video cameras to be positioned anywhere. Because of this, it makes sense that *video* images show Van's parents making love in their bedroom, Aline walking through a hotel corridor, or Van running through the garden as a little boy. In all cases, it is not unlikely for a video camera to be present at that moment, in that space within the film's diegesis. The presence of the video camera is sometimes even made explicit in Egoyan's film when images which are visibly produced *by* a video camera are followed by images *of* a video camera. Another important characteristic which video shares with the conventional external narrator is the seeming objectivity of its outlook. As the video images in *Family Viewing* can be attributed to the viewpoint of a technical device instead of the subjective perspective of a character, video's internal point of view is as objective as that of the external narrator in conventional narrative fiction films.

The fact that the video images in *Family Viewing* can be attributed to the literal viewpoint of devices which are (often visibly) present within the film's diegesis, implies that the viewer's need for suture is satisfied when it comes to these images. For, the video images can be sutured to the intra-diegetic "look" of the video cameras. Although the viewer's identification with the devices might be complicated as the cameras are not human subjects, the film spectator is offered a physical standpoint within the film world in which she can imagine herself, and through whose "eyes" she seems to look. The advantage of this viewpoint over the viewpoint of characters is that it offers greater overview and has seemingly unlimited access to the film world. Therefore, *Family Viewing* offers the film viewer a double illusion of visual access to the depicted world: first of all with the illusion of being positioned within the film world as an eye (or actually, a lens), and secondly with the illusion of having visual access to every facet of this film world *as* this seemingly all-seeing and ubiquitous eye.

More vision(s)

Two films worth briefly mentioning here are *Fight Club* (Fincher 1999) and *Red Road* (Arnold 2006), because these films both resemble and differ from *Family Viewing* in interesting ways. Although the conventionally presumed objectivity of the external narrator is shared with the internal view provided by the video cameras in *Family Viewing*, the objectivity of the external narrator is not undermined in that film. Both the external and internal narrator/focalizor seem to show the reality of the film objectively, that is, unaffected by the subjective vision of the characters. In *Fight Club*, however, video as an internal narrator and focalizor exposes that the external cinematic narrator isn't as objective as is presumed by convention. In the film, protagonist Jack is often shown by the external narrator to be in the company of a second character, Tyler. However, when a fight between the two men is presented by way of internally focalized surveillance video images instead of by the external narrator, Jack is shown to be beating up himself. Apparently, the external narrator is not as objective as expected, for it has conformed to Jack's distorted vision by depicting his imaginary friend (Verstraten 2006: 112–113). In *Fight Club*, video appears to function as the only narrator which shows the reality of the film as it really is.

As in *Family Viewing*, video is depicted as a medium which has seemingly unlimited access to reality in *Red Road*. However, in Arnold's film, this ability is not shown by the way video functions as an internal narrator, but by the possibilities the medium offers to the film's protagonist, Jacky. Through video, Jacky seems to have unlimited visual access to the world; "the world" in this case being the living environment of the female protagonist, who lives and works in Glasgow as a CCTV operator. It is Jacky's job to study live surveillance video footage all day long, in order to alert the police when anything suspicious is perceived on screen. One day, a man appears on one of Jacky's monitors who once destroyed her life. In the following weeks, she follows the moves he makes, in real time, through video. If the man leaves the area covered by Jackie's monitors, she turns to the monitors of a colleague. And if she misses any of his actions in real time, Jacky turns to the videotaped versions of the live footage. By the way in which Jacky uses the surveillance video footage, the film shows how video is a medium that can instantly provide visual access to all corners of a city, at any time.

Family Viewing through video

Like *Benny's Video*, *Family Viewing* can be said to specify the capacity of video with regard to showing reality in part by the way in which the protagonist of the narrative film uses and understands the medium. Both films have a protagonist who makes abundant use of video equipment, yet there are slight differences between the ways in which Benny and Van understand the medium. Benny mainly uses video as a tool by which he can see and know reality. For him, it is important that video can show things in ways they cannot be perceived by human eyes. For Van, on the other hand, it is more important that video is able to show things exactly as they are or were in reality. He sometimes ignores the representational and material character of video recordings. Seeing things on video is the same for Van as seeing them in reality. Watching an event on video even equals "being there" for the adolescent boy. This becomes apparent when he gives Aline a video of her mother's funeral. Aline hasn't attended the funeral because Van secretly buried the old woman as his own grandmother while Aline was out of town, working as an escort. When Van gives her a tape of the event, she is understandably astonished. Van, however, acts as though seeing the funeral on tape is the same as attending in person. The point for him is that Aline can witness the funeral. When she angrily remarks that she can only watch it on a television screen instead of in reality now, Van doesn't really seem to understand the problem: "You're just not in the mood right now, but when you are you can play it. Any time you want."

A similarity between the ways in which Benny and Van use video is that like Benny, Van uses the medium to get to know reality. The reality Van tries to get to know by way of video recordings is the past reality of his childhood, of which he has few memories and which is moreover a subject Van cannot discuss with his father. As Van's mother left Van and his father a while ago, the past is too painful to talk about. For Van, however, it is important to get to know his past. So when he finds out that his father is erasing videotapes of Van's childhood, he secretly secures and watches the tapes. These recordings seem to satisfy his desire to get in touch with his own past, and with his missing mother who appears on the tapes.

Whereas Benny's expectations with regard to the capabilities of video are shown to be too high by the narrative film, Van's idea that video can bring one in contact with a past reality is confirmed by the film on a formal level. It is, moreover, confirmed by the film through a specific cinematic form of representation, the shot/reverse shot pattern by which images are sutured to a character's looks. This form of representation usually contributes to the creation of a reality effect in narrative films, because it creates an overview of the depicted space. In *Family Viewing*, the shot/reverse shot pattern is applied so as to show that the past represented by video can be very real and present.

The final scene of the film shows how Van and his family members meet in the hall of an old people's home. Images of them now, in the hall, are alternated with video images of the past in which younger versions of all family members are visible. The video images and film images succeed each other in such a way that images from the past are sutured to the characters in the hall of the home, and vice versa. A video close up of little Van looking at something outside of the image frame is followed by an establishing shot of the hall in which his mother and grandmother are sitting next to each other. When Van's mother explicitly turns her head to point outside the image frame, this film image is followed by a video image of Van's mother without the grey hair she has in the preceding film image.

Through these shot/reverse shot sequences, the young Van seems to look at his mother and grandmother sitting in a space about fifteen years later. Likewise, it is suggested that Van's mother is looking directly at a younger version of herself. Besides these examples, a number of other shot/reverse shot sequences combine film images of "now" with video images of "then." Because of that, it seems as if all family members are looking at past and present versions of each other and themselves. Thus, the film suggests that the young videotaped versions and the older, present-time versions of the characters are close to each other in space, although we know that they are separated from each other in time. The family is viewing through time, through video. *And* through film, as the temporally remote characters are seemingly brought into (visual) contact and physical proximity by a typically cinematic mode of representation.

In this part, I discussed how film and video can have an effect on the viewer, and how these medium specific effects can form the basis for different forms of intermedial interaction between film in video. In the following part, the relationship between the two media and their respective spectators is taken one step further. Instead of exploring how film and video can have an effect *on* the viewing subject, the next part explores the idea that the viewing subject can be understood as an effect *of* the two media. That is, film and video each produce subjective positions for their respective spectators in medium-specific ways. As I will argue with help if the concept of *dispositif*, (dis)embodied viewing positions can be understood as an integral part of a medium's specificity.

PART II
(DIS)EMBODIMENT

INTRODUCTION

"People!" The voice of a young Polish man echoes through a large, dilapidated stadium. "People!" he screams again, this time even louder. No one responds, for apart from some kids on the field, the Decennial Stadium in Warsaw is empty. Counter-shots to the close-ups of the young man's face show that he is talking to rows of empty benches, overgrown with weeds. So who is this speaker calling? Who is he addressing? The orator features in Yael Bartana's short film *Mary Koszmary* (2007). Together with two other short films, *Mur i wieża* (2009) and *Zamach* (2011), it forms an installation entitled *. . . and Europe will be Stunned: The Polish Trilogy*, which tells the (fictional) story of the Jewish Renaissance Movement in Poland (JRMiP) that pleads for the return of 3.3 million Jews to Poland. This is precisely what the young founder of the movement calls for in his political speech. The people he is addressing are *his* people: Polish Jews, who have fled the country due to strong anti-Semitism. As a consequence, the addressees of the speech are not present in the Polish stadium where Slawomir Sierakowski is speaking.

The audiences who *do* listen to the plea for a new Jewish Movement are located elsewhere. Not in Warsaw's old stadium, but in art galleries where Bartana's film is screened. Seated at museum benches, or standing in the room, the visitor can behold the man's filmed image as he talks. Glances into the camera, moreover, suggest that Sierakowski is looking back at the viewer. Although the old-fashioned glasses of the man suggest he belongs to the past, his glances into the camera tie him to the present. The present of the museum visitor, that is.

Although *Mary Koszmary* ("Nightmare") is called a film by the artist, the way it relates to the spectator is uncinematic in several respects. Not only is the "breach" of the fourth wall unconventional in traditional narrative cinema—which usually strictly separates the space of the viewer from the film world—Bartana's film does not tell a story with a beginning or an end either. The message of Sierakowski's address can be grasped within minutes at any time during the film projection. In addition, the short film is presented in looped form. This means that the visitor can come in and leave the room whenever she wants, as the movie itself does not set limits to the film show. Besides entering and leaving, the viewer has to make another physical decision: to look at the moving images while standing still, walking around, or sitting down on one of the few benches. By explicitly addressing the spectator, and offering the possibility to make bodily choices while (and in the process of) watching, *Mary Koszmary* makes the viewer aware of the position of her own body in time and space.

Such an embodied mode of looking is usually associated more strongly with video than with film. Many video artworks tend to engulf, surround or address their viewers in a physical way. Because of that, they incite a mode of looking which involves not merely the eyes, but the whole body. The dominance of embodying effects in the field of video art has led art historians and media theorists to investigate the physically affective, tactile, or so-called haptic qualities of the medium in general. Laura Marks (1998) and Margaret Morse (1990), among others, have pointed out that—in comparison with media such as film, photography, painting, and traditional sculpture—video in particular has a propensity for appealing to the spectator's whole body.

The theoretical and artistic attention to the embodying qualities of the video medium stand in contrast to the way in which the medium of film has traditionally been theorized. Instead of giving rise to an embodied viewer, film is generally regarded as a medium that produces a disembodied spectator. Film theory dealing with cinematic spectatorship has been highly influenced by Christian Metz' psychoanalytic model of film viewing, which posits the film viewer as a detached, immobile voyeur. This voyeur is a disembodied entity who experiences the film on view with his eyes and ears only. The rest of the viewer's body is left idle and ignored, for conventional film screenings do not make us more aware of our bodies (as video installations tend to do) but instead aspire to the loss of self-consciousness, which is necessary for the viewer to lose herself in the fictional narrative film world on screen. For this reason, Richard Rushton considers the bold claim that "the act of watching a film does not require one to have a body" (2002: 112). Stephen Heath, to give one more example here, asserts that the ideal of classical cinema remains that of photographic vision, in the sense of a detached eye free of the body (1981: 32).

Although these embodied and disembodied modes of looking have been theorized as fairly distinct medium-specific modes of spectatorship, many contemporary artistic film and video practices disobey this distinction. Conventional cinematic modes of disembodied spectatorship are mixed with video-like features that give rise to embodied spectatorship. This also goes for Bartana's *The Polish Trilogy.* The first film in the video installation, *Mary Koszmary,* stimulates an embodied way of looking. However, when the viewer of this first film moves her body to the next room of the exhibition space, she will become a disembodied voyeur by the installation's second film, *Mur i wieża* ("Wall and Tower"). As this film does have narrative plot development, and moreover has a longer duration than *Mary Koszmary,* it prompts the viewer to sit down and follow the story from beginning to end. The movie shows how a large group of people comes to the Polish capital. At the former site of the Warsaw ghetto, they built a kibbutz, separated from the surrounding community by a high wall. In contrast to the narrator in *Mary Koszmary,* the characters in *Mur i wieża* do not look into the lens. The viewer is invited to identify with them, but is not directly addressed by them. The spectator's position in the space in front of the screen is therefore not signaled by the film. Hence, the screen world is a closed-off space, just like the kibbutz the walls of which start to fill the image frame. The viewer can only enter the narrative film space by leaving her embodied self momentarily behind and "becoming" through identification one of the depicted Jews.

The alternation between embodied and disembodied viewing positions which is subtly created by Bartana's piece highly influences the meaning of the installation, as well as its political effect. First, the viewer of the piece is hailed by Sierakowski to join the Jewish Renaissance Movement in Poland. The set-up of the installation forces the embodied spectator to answer his call, or at least mimic the journey to Warsaw's former ghetto which Sierakowski so forcefully proposes. For, by walking from one museum room to the next, the installation's visitor moves to another moment and another place in the story of *The Polish Trilogy.* Like the Jews who are supposed to come to Warsaw after the young intellectual's speech, the wandering viewing subject of the piece travels forward in the fabula's time, to another place.

This other place is the next museum room, but also another narrative place. These two spaces seem to merge when the beholder is positioned facing an image which shows how one person after the next enters the large square in Warsaw, while one museum visitor after another trickles into the second exhibition space. However, the story world also rapidly closes itself off at this point, as the moving images appear to follow the dominant conventions of classical narrative cinema, and the visitor is prompted by the set-up of the room to sit down for a while. The spectator, who by now is a disembodied entity, has to make a decision at this point. For although she has physically mimicked the journey to Warsaw, she can now only gain access to the story world in the kibbutz through identification with the Jewish characters who live there. Because of the switch from embodied to disembodied spectatorship, this process of identification is not an automatic, unconscious process. When the film space overtly closes itself off from the exhibition space, from the space of the viewer, the spectator is faced with a choice. This is what *The Polish Trilogy* then asks: Are you with us? Or against us? Are you in? Or out? Can you identify with these returning settlers? Or will you be stunned, and remain on the other side of the kibbutz' walls, with the other shocked Europeans?

The viewer of intermedial pieces like Bartana's is positioned somewhere in between different media forms as well as between several modes of embodied and disembodied looking. As my analysis of *The Polish Trilogy* shows, it is important to ask how that "in-betweenness" shapes the viewing experience. (How) does the combination of medium-specific cinematic and "videomatic" forms of (dis)embodied looking produce meaning in relation to the images on view? In addition, the combination of viewing positions gives rise to questions on medium specificity. How do modes of looking affect the way in which a viewer determines the medium of moving images? At what point can the viewer read them as cinematic, and when are they understood as video footage? Can we still recognize video and film as different media in the intermedial pieces in question at all, or does the specificity of the two media dissolve in the mix of several modes of looking?

In this part I will look into these questions by studying several intermedial video installations and films which, like Bartana's piece, combine different viewing positions. Works by Douglas Gordon and David Claerbout function as analytical reflections on the difference between cinematic and videomatic ways of looking, that are able to expose which medium-related conditions are decisive in the production of (dis)embodied modes of viewing. Yet, in order to see how (and if) these conditions are indeed medium-related, it is necessary to further unravel and outline the different ways in which video and film can be—and have been—related to the spectator's body. My starting point will be the film-theoretical concept of the *dispositif.* Not only does this concept, which was coined by Jean-Louis Baudry in 1978, lie at the basis of the most influential film theoretical ideas on cinematic spectatorship, it is also extremely relevant with regard to the first question of this investigation into the interaction between medium specificity and modes of looking must address: how can the viewing situation be related to the concept of the medium?

CHAPTER 7
DISPOSITIF: AN EXPANDED LAYERED STRUCTURE

French film scholars Jean-Louis Baudry and Christian Metz were of the opinion that films bring the film viewer in a state which is close to dreaming and hallucination. According to Baudry, this dreamlike state of the film viewer is not so much the result of the discursive organization or "film language" of the moving images projected on screen, but rather of cinema's *dispositif*, which involves aspects of the projection as such. Put briefly, Baudry defined cinema's *dispositif* as a particular set of film technologies (the camera, moviola, projector, theatre), as well as specific conditions of the projection (such as a darkened room, a hidden projector, and an immobile spectator).

It is important to distinguish *dispositif* from the term "apparatus," the latter generally applied as the English equivalent of the French term. As scholars such as Judith Mayne (1993) and Frank Kessler (2006) have noted, this usual English translation of *dispositif* is rather unfortunate. First of all, the word "apparatus" does not render the idea of a specific arrangement or tendency (*disposition*), which the French term implies (Kessler 2006: 60). Secondly, the single term "apparatus" has been used to translate two distinct concepts in Baudry's writings, namely "*appareil de base*" as well as "*dispositif*." In an essay titled "Le dispositif" (1975), Baudry explains that "*appareil*" refers to all the components necessary to both the production and the projection of a film, whereas "*dispositif*" is more limited, referring solely to "projection and which includes the subject to whom the projection is addressed" (Baudry in Mayne 2002: 47).[1]

Although the concept of the *dispositif* refers to a limited part of cinema's *appareil*, the most important merits of the concept lie precisely in what it adds to a mechanical understanding of the medium—that is, to the medium of film as well as to the concept of "medium" in general. Without ignoring the technological aspects of a medium, the concept enables us to consider how aspects which do not belong to a medium's technological base are nevertheless part of what a medium is and does. Factors such as the architecture of the viewing room or the presence of seats for the spectator are not a part of the material support or *appareil de base* of film. Yet, such seemingly external, nontechnological factors influence the specific ways in which a medium produces a viewing position. The concept of *dispositif* suggests that these factors, as well as the specific viewing position they create, are included in the medium.

Comparing concepts

Baudry's notion of the *dispositif* is not entirely incongruous with Krauss' definition of medium specificity as a structure which consists of a technological base plus a layer of conventions. The conventional, nontechnological layer of the *dispositif* was particularly emphasized by film theorist Jean-Louis Comolli who—unlike Baudry—explicitly stated that cinema is "not essentially the camera, the film, the projector" and "not merely a combination of instruments, apparatuses, techniques" (1980: 122). Nevertheless, many of the factors which Baudry assigned as components of cinema's *dispositif* operate on the verge of material prerequisites to a film screening on the one hand, and cultural conventions which further shape the viewer's position in relation to the movie on the other.

Take, for instance, the hidden projector which Baudry pointed out as being a part of cinema's *dispositif*. The projector itself is a vital technological part of a film projection. The fact that it is hidden during a film screening, though, is not a matter of technological necessity. It is rather through convention that the camera is kept out of sight. This cultural convention, then, is just a much a part of cinema's *dispositif* as the machine beaming film's moving images onto the white screen, as it shapes how the film spectator relates to the film on view.

Another example is the seated, immobile position of the film spectator. On the one hand, this position can be understood as a material necessity to the visibility of a movie. If spectators were to stand upright or walk around, they might cast shadows onto the screen, and block the sight or divert the attention of other viewers, which would disturb the film show. On the other hand, walking around and casting shadows onto the screen *is* completely acceptable and even an important part of watching video installation artworks, which are hardly ever presented in rooms lined with seats. This points out that the seated, immobile position which the film spectator is supposed to take up is, first and foremost, a conventional part of cinema's *dispositif*.

The conventions of mobile or immobile spectatorship are not only part of the *dispositif*, but also of the broader cultural, institutional places in which the respective *dispositifs* operate. The "viewing rules" of the museum prescribe a quiet, meandering, yet attentive mode of viewing, while the cinema is related to the convention of the immobile, silently seated viewer. The cultural place of the living room, to give one other example, does permit distracted and fragmented ways of looking (at the TV or PC). The fact that cultural and institutional fields in which media operate inscribe their conventions onto a medium's *dispositif(s)* shows that the viewing room is not merely part of the *dispositif* in the sense of a geometrical, material space. It should also be understood as an institutional, cultural place.

Although Baudry's *dispositif* and Krauss' idea of the medium as a layered structure have the combination of technological and conventional aspects in common, the two notions differ in one important respect. Baudry excludes the formal features of the projected films themselves from cinema's *dispositif*. He does not consider the characteristics of the film on screen to be part of the projection situation, because the cuts and compositions we see in a film are the result of operations carried out during the production of the movie.[2] Krauss, on the other hand, focuses particularly on the conventionality of discursive patterns within (groups of) media objects. Although she is not oblivious to the interrelation between media objects and the contexts in which they are exhibited and viewed, her definition of a medium's conventional layer in terms of "expressive possibilities," "traditional forms," and "grammar" diverts attention to the aesthetic and formal properties of the media objects themselves.

When Krauss applies her own concept of the medium, the viewing context and the position of the beholder in that context are part of her analysis, but not of the medium she analyzes. In an article on James Coleman ("Reinventing the Medium," 1999), she mentions how the dark rooms in which the Irish artist exhibits luminous slide projections set up a relationship with cinema. Yet, Krauss does not regard this room, nor the viewing situation which the room creates, as part of the structure of Coleman's (reinvented) medium. This structure is rather located in the material support of a slide sequence, together with the compositional grammar (derived from the photo novel) which is applied in the projected images. Through the reiteration of these particular compositional conventions, Coleman is able to derive his own specific medium from the material conditions of the slideshow's technical support.

In the case of Krauss' analysis of Coleman's work, an exclusion of the projection space and the spectator's position from the structure of the medium under discussion has some notable disadvantages. Most importantly, it obscures the complex, heterogeneous intermedial character of Coleman's invented medium. Moreover, it implicitly promotes a return to the idea of medium specificity as an autonomous material unity—an idea which Krauss fiercely refutes in *A Voyage of the North Sea* (1999).

At first sight, however, Krauss seems to acknowledge the intermedial and conventional structure of Coleman's newly invented medium of slide projection. Not only does she mention how the projection situation of a darkened room resembles cinema, she also construes the composition of Coleman's images in relation to classical narrative films. As the groups of depicted characters in the projected images face neither each other nor the viewer, but instead stare at undefined points outside of the frame which are never rendered visible, Krauss considers Coleman's still compositions a refusal and subversion of cinematic suture (1999: 301). Whereas point-of-view editing in narrative films causes the viewer to become visually and psychologically woven—or sutured—into the fabric of the film, Coleman's slide projections produce a completely externalized viewer. This viewer cannot lose herself imaginatively in the depth of the depicted world. She remains firmly grounded in front of an impenetrable flat image plane.

Krauss' analysis of the viewer's positioning does not mean that she is discussing the medium's *dispositif*, though. For, in Krauss' argument, the externalization of the viewing subject is not part of Coleman's medium: it is precisely through the externalization of the viewing subject that Coleman's slide projections establish themselves as a medium; that is, as a material, physical medium. For, in the eyes of Krauss, the refusal to suture allows Coleman to confront and underscore the planarity of his medium. It forms a reflexive acknowledgement of the flatness of the image plane; of the impossibility of the visual field to deliver its promise of either realism or authenticity (Krauss 1999: 301).

It appears that, in "Reinventing the Medium," the (re)invention of the medium not only depends on the inscription of a material base with conventions, but also on quite the opposite move: a return to modernist exposure of the support's materiality. Krauss' attention to the intermedial references of Coleman's installations does not obviate this subtle return to a Greenbergian understanding of the medium. For although slide projections in dark spaces refer to film and resemble the cinematic projection situation in important respects, Krauss emphasizes how they ultimately subvert and reject the cinematic medium. Slide projections are a-cinematic, they are *not* film. Film is excluded from Coleman's allegedly pure new medium.

The concept of *dispositif* could have precluded Krauss' implicit retrogression to thinking of the medium in terms of autonomy, unity or purity, because Baudry's notion adds aspects to the structure of the medium which are—in Krauss' and other media theories—excluded from it in order to posit the specific medium as an autonomous material entity. Coleman's compositional grammar does indeed confront the viewer with the flatness of the image plane, and with the impenetrability of the screen. It produces an embodied mode of looking, for the viewer is reminded of her body being in front of the screen. The concept of *dispositif* shows that such a visual exclusion of the viewer from the depicted image world does not automatically imply that the medium is a closed material entity, though. For the idea of the *dispositif* allows us to think of a specific viewing position as a part of the medium.

When it comes to Coleman's work, the French film-theoretical concept can also be helpful in underlining the intermedial character of the slide projections. The darkened projection rooms in which the images are shown highlight a relationship with cinema. In addition to the fact that the rooms are necessarily darkened, they also resemble cinema halls because they often have soft, carpeted floors, and sometimes contain comfortable chairs.[3] Moreover, the slides are projected on the scale of a small cinema screen. If these components are regarded as features of a medium's *dispositif*, it is possible to argue that the *dispositif* of Coleman's medium contains some of the most typical features of (classical) cinema's *dispositif* (which I will outline more extensively later on). Therefore, Coleman's medium can be regarded as a hybrid and heterogeneous one. Its *dispositif* is produced out of components which are characteristic of film, while its material base as well as its aesthetic conventions are to a large degree photographic.

Yet, the aesthetic conventions of Coleman's medium are quite dissimilar to cinematic ones. As Krauss pointed out, they are derived from the photo novel as well as the theater, and clearly refuse the strategy of cinematic suture. This makes Coleman's invented medium not only a hybrid, but also an internally contradictory one—it is filmic in some respects, and blatantly a-cinematic in others. For Krauss—who does not include aspects of the *dispositif* into the medium's structure—it is mainly the refusal of cinema that counts. In her essay, the relationship between Coleman's medium and other media principally serves to outline the pure specificity of the new medium, which is not film, not photography, not theater, etc. I would, on the other hand, argue that Coleman's medium is not film, not photography, and not theater in some respects, but that it simultaneously *is* film, photography, and theater in many others. And, it is exactly this complicated, contradictory mixture of media which establishes Coleman's medium as unique and specific.

Mixing, expanding, multiplying

The unwanted propensity towards essentialism in Krauss' analysis of Coleman's projections demonstrate that her definition of the medium as a layered structure can benefit from adding components of the *dispositif* to this structure. At the same time, Baudry's definition of *dispositif* can be complemented by the aesthetic conventions which play a dominant part in Krauss' layered structure of a medium's specificity. Although Krauss does not include the spectator's position in her definition of the medium, her discussion of Coleman's compositions show very well how formal and aesthetic image features (co-)produce a certain viewing position.

This has also been noted within the disciplinary field from which the concept of *dispositif* originated. Film philosopher Noël Carroll, for instance, critically remarks that Baudry is not particularly interested in "the content of the images or the stories of particular films or even particular kinds of films," but only in "a network which includes the screen, the spectator, and the projector [...] the projection situation itself, irrespective of what is being screened" (2004: 224–225). The importance of what is being screened to the positioning of the viewer within the network of the projection situation has been demonstrated by film theorists such as Laura Mulvey and Raymond Bellour, who have extensively analyzed the way in which narrative film forms, styles, and narrative structures produce a specific type of viewing subject. When these formal aspects are also taken into account as part of the *dispositif*, the interrelated components of a medium's *dispositif* can be summarized as follows:

- the material technological components of a medium which are applied at the moment of exhibiting, showing, or projecting a medium object (screen, canvas, projector, monitor etc.);
- the architectural and interior design of the exhibition space (including lighting, furniture, the hiddenness or exposure of the above-mentioned technological parts, the position of objects in space etc.);
- the cultural and institutional meanings and conventions of the place of exhibition;
- formal, aesthetic, stylistic, narrative, and discursive features of the shown objects or images;
- a certain viewing position, stimulated by the above conditions.

In this part I will work with this outline of the *dispositif* to study the intermedial relationship between film and video in objects which mix embodied and disembodied viewing positions, by combining medium-specific components of film's and video's *dispositif*.[4] Before discussing the respective *dispositifs* of film and video, though, some further defining remarks have to be made on the methodological concept in question.

First of all, the concept of *dispositif* is not always suitable for investigating intermediality or medium specificity. Although the notion is helpful in illuminating how a work of art or medium object relates to its spatial surroundings as well as its audience, not every medium can be said to have a specific *dispositif*. Or, to put it differently: the specificity of media is not always related to a single *dispositif*. This is mainly a matter of historically, culturally, and socially relative dominance. The field of some media is, at some points in history, in certain societies, dominated by a specific *dispositif*. In such case one particular configuration of technology, space, form, and viewing position becomes so widespread and well-known that it will eventually be regarded as wholly specific to and characteristic of the medium in question. Other possible *dispositifs* of the medium become so marginal that they are, so to speak, pushed towards or even over the boundaries of a medium's field. When one particular *dispositif* dominates a medium's field, deviations from the dominant *dispositif* will appear to put the specificity of the medium into question.

Film is one of the best examples in this regard, as it has a very specific, dominant *dispositif* (which is why it is not surprising that the concept was first coined by film theorists). Film projections which differ in one or more respects from cinema's dominant *dispositif* often bring into question their status as film. When film cannot be viewed from a seated position, it promptly becomes questionable whether the shown object still *is* a film. In Anthony McCall's solid light films, for example, the spectator can walk through and around differently shaped light beams emanating from film projectors. Moreover, these (visible) projectors project celluloid tapes which determine the size and shape of the light beams. Technically speaking, the medium of McCall's works is film. Yet, the way in which they can be viewed is so unlike film's dominant *dispositif* that they can hardly be understood as film. This different viewing position makes manifest a characteristic of film which is invisible from a seated position facing the screen, that is, the alleged solidity of film's light beam. Through this, film seems to turn into another medium; sculpture. Although I would say that these deviations from cinema's dominant *dispositif* should still be regarded as parts of film's heterogeneous field of possibilities—in fact, they bear that out—it is telling that McCall's installations are labeled with terms such as expanded cinema and paracinema, or are discussed under the heading of "Film beyond its Limits" (Baker 2006).[5]

The field of some media is not dominated by one single *dispositif* at all. Then, the plurality of *dispositifs* which is latent in each medium is not overruled by one specific configuration. In the case of photography, for instance, it is difficult to point out one typical medium-specific *dispositif*. Photographs can be looked at while standing in front of them, or while holding them, they can be glued to a lamppost or be printed in a newspaper, placed in a spacious light museum room or within the dark inside of a personal locker, and in all these cases, they will still be photographs. Because none of these variations alter the "photographness" of the images in question, it is possible to conclude that photography does not have a *dispositif* which is so characteristic to the medium that deviations from it would affect the medium's specificity, expand photography's field or push it beyond its limits.

Besides the plurality of a medium's *dispositif*, the plurality of the viewers should be pointed out. An important point of critique on the concept in question has been that real spectators play no part in the *dispositif*. The position of the subject of a medium's *dispositif* is a construction, an effect of the interrelation between technological and conventional medium-specific forms of address. Although, in Baudry's opinion, cinema's *dispositif* produces a viewing subject as an active center and origin of meaning, the actual, real spectators do not have any agency vis-à-vis this powerful (and highly ideological) structure; they are subjected to the transcendental viewing position theatrical films create for them.

Although this part in the first place discusses the implied spectator which is created by the two media of film and video, the real viewer is taken into account as well in the analyses that follow. In spite of the fact that the way a real spectator can view a piece is affected and delimited by (physical) properties of the *dispositif*, I hold that this real viewer does have considerable agency. She can make choices in the way she views and interprets the (visual) text, and can either work with or against the viewing position or mode of looking an object assigns to her.[6] When texts and images are read or viewed, an ongoing interactive process takes place between what the text programs as/for the reader and how the real reader or viewer responds to this. However, in order to avoid confusion between the (nevertheless related) implied and real viewer I will mostly refer to the constructed spectator in the *dispositif* in terms of a "viewing position" or "mode of looking," whereas the words "spectator" and "viewer" will be reserved for the general real viewer.[7]

CHAPTER 8
(DIS)EMBODYING *DISPOSITIFS*

What does looking with one's body entail exactly? What does it mean to look in a disembodied way? Which aspects of a medium's *dispositif* can be said to stimulate an embodied or disembodied mode of looking? Put briefly, a disembodied spectator looks in a way which involves mainly sight, while an embodied spectator participates with his or her whole body in the process of looking. This difference between embodied and disembodied looking is a subtle one, however, and at the outer ends of the sliding scale, pure forms of embodied or disembodied looking do not exist. It is impossible to ever look completely without the body. As Vivian Sobchack stated: "Our vision is always already 'fleshed out'" (2004: 60). Not only are our eyes physically attached to rest of our bodies; also, our visual perception influences other bodily sensations and vice versa.

At the same time, the idea of beholding an object with the whole body is something of a chimera. Although recent theories on embodied spectatorship (e.g., Williams 1991, Barker 2009) have convincingly argued that our skin, musculature, glands, and viscera can play a part in the act of perception, we do not use all our bodily parts and functions in equal measure when we behold an object. Depending on the circumstances and the object on view, some senses and body parts are more involved in the act of perception than others.

This is also how the difference between embodied and disembodied looking is best understood: disembodied looking relies most heavily on the eyes, whereas embodied looking involves other parts of the body as well. In addition, the difference between embodied and disembodied looking often has more to do with a psychological state of awareness than with actual physical participation or bodily processes. As will become clear below, the phrase "embodied looking" is frequently used to indicate a viewer who is thoroughly conscious of her own presence as a spectator at a certain time and place, and moreover, of the fact that her own act of looking takes up time and space. Disembodied looking, on the other hand, describes an act of perception during which the viewer forgets herself, including her body and its physical position in time and space.[1]

The distinction between embodied and disembodied modes of looking can be further explained by some concepts corresponding to (dis)embodied looking. Art historian Norman Bryson (1983) introduced the notions of the gaze and the glance as two modes of looking at a painting, the former term indicating a disembodied, the latter an embodied look. The gaze, Bryson argues, reduces the body of the spectator to one single point, one eye. It is a disengaged mode of looking in which the viewer is unaware of her own position as a viewer, or of her bodily participation in the process of viewing. Viewing is not even a process in the case of the gaze. It is placed outside duration, leaving the time of the act of viewing unacknowledged. In addition, the gaze is a static mode of looking for it does not move or linger over the object in vision. The glance, on the other hand, is an involved mode of looking in which the viewer is aware of her own bodily engagement in the process of looking. Furthermore, the glance is a mode of looking in which, unlike the gaze, viewing is acknowledged as a practice which takes up time. Moreover, the glance is a look that moves; it scans and wanders over the image surface.

Bryson further distinguishes the gaze and the glance by the way in which they relate to what they behold. The gaze objectifies or seizes the contemplated object, it masters what it beholds. Moreover, the gaze is a mode of viewing which does not distinguish between model and figure in representation, between what is real and what is represented. The object in vision is not regarded as something which is made, and hence, the work of representation is not taken into account by the gaze. As mentioned previously, the glance is an involved look in which the viewer is aware of the participation in the process of looking. And because of this awareness, the glance does not deny the work of representation. As Bal explains in her discussion of Bryson's notion of the glance: "The awareness of one's own engagement in the act of looking entails the awareness that what one sees is a representation, not an objective reality, not the 'real thing'" (1991: 142).

In a discussion of modes of looking stimulated by different media, Laura Marks introduces two modes of looking which—as she indicates herself—strongly resemble Bryson's notions of the gaze and the glance; optical and haptical looking. "Optical visuality," Marks writes, "requires distance and a centre, the viewer acting like a pinhole camera" (2002: xvi). Haptical looking, on the other hand, bubbles up to the surface to interact with another surface. Like the glance, the haptical mode of looking is aware of the representational status of the object in vision, as it interacts with it as "another surface." Moreover, as with the difference between Bryson's gaze and glance, the static optical mode of looking is not a process, while the mobile haptical look does take up time.

Yet, Marks' notions can be distinguished from Bryson's through the former's specific emphasis on surface. Because the haptical look "clings" to the surface of representations by focusing on details and by lingering over the object, Marks compares haptical looking to touch. Touch as a mode of looking indicates an involvement of the whole body of the spectator, especially the skin. Moreover, touch also implies closeness and interaction between *two* bodies or two skins, which is why haptical looking involves an embodied viewer responding to the object in vision as another body, and to its surface as another skin (Marks 2002: 4). Optical looking, on the other hand, does not linger over or press against the surface, it remains immobile, detached, and distant instead. This "distance between beholder and object allows the beholder to imaginatively project him/herself into the object" (5). Thus, while haptic looking tends to rest on the surface of its object, optical looking "plunges into depth" (5).

Although the (dis)embodied modes of looking which Bryson and Marks define can be adopted or rejected by the viewer, they are very much prompted by the objects on view. If we return to the concept of *dispositif* for a moment, it is possible to say that the two theorists mainly focus on one of the *dispositif's* four components, namely the formal and stylistic aspects of the viewed object. Bryson, to begin with, argues that the gaze is a mode of looking which is encouraged by realist representations, that is to say, representations which look transparent. This transparency is effected by effacing the traces of the labor of representation. In the case of painting, for instance, the labor of representation is removed when no brush strokes are visible on the painted canvas.

A similar argument is provided by Marks, who states that optical looking is stimulated by images with smooth surfaces. However, in Marks' writings, smoothness is not only understood as the result of hiding the labor of representation in the sense of manual production. Lens-based images can also be called "smooth" when they are fine-grained, or have a high resolution. This is effected by the quality of some of the technological and chemical parts of the apparatus (most notably the light-sensitive emulsion, or the digital sensor), rather than by the invisibility of the producer's hands in the final image(s). Moreover, as Marks points out, smoothness not only hides the production process but also conceals the materiality of the object itself, as for instance the smoothness of high resolution film images hides the materiality of the celluloid.

Since both the gaze and the optical look are modes of viewing which entail a sense of access to the depth of the image, it is obvious that those modes of disembodied looking are also stimulated by pictures that depict illusionistic space. According to both Marks and Bryson, a disembodied mode of looking is especially produced by images in which the principles of linear perspective are used. Not only does space depicted according to the rules of linear perspective look very real in the eyes of many viewers, linear perspective also produces a static and single viewpoint outside of the image through its vanishing point inside the image. Any spectator adopting this viewpoint becomes a disembodied viewer; immobile, distant, reduced to a single eye. Moreover, as the illusionistic space is fully available to view from the stable single viewpoint which linear perspective creates, the disembodied spectator of perspectival images has a sense of visual mastery over the space in vision.

An embodied mode of looking is stimulated by images which are in many respects quite the opposite of the ones discussed above. Instead of smooth surfaces, objects which give rise to the glance or the haptical look have rough, coarse, textured, blurry, scratched or granular surfaces. In this way, images which invite embodied viewing do show the work of representation and/or their materiality. Moreover, they do not instill a feeling of visual mastery in their spectator; haptic looking "depends on *limited visibility* and the viewer's lack of mastery over the image," according to Marks (2002: 5, emphasis added). This limited visibility can also be caused by close-ups which make the depicted forms or figures unrecognizable. Also, coarse surfaces and close-ups often obstruct depth of vision, which Marks points out as another characteristic of haptic images (i.e., images which give rise to haptic looking). Unlike linear perspective images, haptic images lack an immobile outside point of reference. They draw attention to the two-dimensional plane of the surface itself.

Here, now/there, then

A slightly different, yet also valuable approach to the production of disembodied and embodied modes of looking is provided by Margaret Morse in her piece on video installation art called "The Body, the Image, and the Space-in-Between" (1990). Instead of focusing on what images depict or what their surface looks like—as Marks and Bryson mostly do—Morse bases her ideas on a distinction between art forms. In doing so, she accentuates other aspects of the *dispositif* than Marks and Bryson. The status of the space of representation (or of exhibition, projection) is of central importance to Morse, who analyzes this space of representation in relation to represented space as well as time.

Another difference between Morse's theory and the previous approaches I discussed is that the actual physical position and (im)mobility of the viewer are involved in Morse's conceptualization of spectatorship. The notions of closeness and distance, movement and static centeredness which Bryson and Marks, respectively, attach to the glance, the gaze, the haptic and the optic look, do not necessarily denote the actual physical position or mobility of the spectator. While her eyes wander over the image's surface, the haptic film viewer can sit motionless at a fair distance from the screen.[2] In Morse's essay, on the other hand, (dis)embodied looking relies very much on the way in which the beholder's body moves (or doesn't move) through the space of projection or exhibition. Because of that, embodied looking does not mean "looking as-if touching," "viewing as-if wandering around" or "watching as-if being close to the contemplated object." From Morse's perspective, the "as-ifs" in the previous sentence can be replaced with "while."

According to Morse, disembodied looking is mostly produced by the so-called "proscenium arts." Embodied modes of viewing, on the other hand, are created by art forms which Morse has termed "presentational arts." The main reason for proscenium arts inviting a disembodied mode of looking is that they represent "things apart from us, using language as a window to another world" (1990: 156). In doing so, they form a division between what they represent and the "here" and "now" which the spectator bodily occupies:

> In the proscenium arts, the spectator is carefully divided from the field to be contemplated. The machinery that creates the vision of another world is largely hidden, allowing the immobilized spectator to sink into an impression of its reality with horror and delight but without danger from the world on view. The proscenium of the theatre, and its most ideal expression, the fourth wall, as well as the screen of film divide the here and now of the spectator from the elsewhere and elsewhen beyond with varying degrees of absoluteness.
>
> 1990: 156

Presentational arts, on the other hand, do not divide the spectator from a represented "not here" and "not now." Morse explains the effect of the proscenium's absence by comparing presentational arts to theater: "It is as if the audience were free to cross the proscenium and wander about on stage, contemplating the actor's makeup and props, able to change point of view [...], seeing both the process of creating another world and—more dimly than before—the represented world itself" (158). In some cases, however, presentational arts do not even represent another world. For, as the term indicates, presentational arts are not so much representations as presentations. Interactive works, closed-circuit videos, performance art, site-specific artworks and installation art are practically always presentational, according to Morse, as they all share a common denominator: they all implicate a real time and/or a real space, rather than referring to another time or space. Closed-circuit video is for instance grounded in real time and real space in that the technique enables images of a space to be recorded and relayed simultaneously and in the same space, exploring the fit between images of a space and the space itself in a live and ongoing fashion. Installation art not only occupies an actual space, it also *is* a real space that can be occupied by the spectator. As Morse explains, the room in which an installation is installed is "the *ground* over which a conceptual, figural, embodied and temporalized space that is the installation breaks" (154).

The important effect of the "here and nowness" (as Morse calls it) of these artworks is that the spectator exists *with* them instead of apart from them (1990: 155). For the beholder necessarily occupies the same time and space that these artworks so explicitly do. Performances which are addressed directly and explicitly to the spectator turn the spectator into a "you," a partner inhabiting the same world; a partner who, moreover, has the capacity to physically influence and respond to events.[3,4] Likewise, the beholder of a video installation needs to do something in order to behold the piece; namely to enter it and to choose a trajectory through its spatial construction. She is indeed inside the piece as its experiential subject, not by identification, but in body. According to Morse, the visitor can actually be said to perform an installation by being in it, experiencing it, and choosing a unique trajectory so that each time a work is perceived differently (Morse 1990: 158).[5]

The viewer of closed-circuit video also figures inside the work, yet in a slightly different way. As the spectator's whereabouts in the exhibition space are video-taped and simultaneously relayed on screen, she is no longer just the one who looks, but also a figure in the work that is looked at. Although these closed-circuit video installations duplicate the viewing space as they create a represented space out of the space of representation, and create a double position for the viewer who becomes both the observing and observed, the represented world on screen cannot be considered apart from its close relation to the one in front of the screen. Unlike proscenium works of art, closed-circuit video installations do not refer to a completely other world; it is not the "there" and "then," but the "here" and "now" which is depicted. This embodies the viewer, who is forced to reflect on her physical position "here" and "now" in front of the screen, as it is simultaneously shown live *on* screen.

In sum, the viewer's position in time and space is implicated by artworks which directly address the spectator, artworks that offer the viewer the possibility to act out an influence on them, artworks that require the viewer to move around and respond to them, or artworks which offer the viewer a role or position in them. By being implicated as present in time and space, the viewer is automatically implicated as an embodied spectator, for it is in her body that the beholder is present in real time and actual space. This embodiment is enhanced all the more when an artwork overtly responds to the physical presence or movement of the spectator's body, or when an artwork clearly calls for the spectator to act or participate physically. It goes without saying that the acts of physically co-producing or participating in an artwork embody the viewer.

On the one hand, the concept of *dispositif* can be useful in naming the relationship between the characteristics which Morse points out in her essay. Her discussion of presentational art forms can be understood as a discussion of similar *dispositifs*. The *dispositifs* of presentational art forms have in common that their spectator is an indispensable embodied, mobile performer of the object, that the viewing space and time are part of the produced object, and that the (technological) processes which are involved in the act of creation are not hidden from sight.

On the other hand, these presentational art forms can shed a new light on the concept of *dispositif* itself. First of all, when it comes to presentational art forms, it is no longer possible to distinguish the contemplated object from, or within, the *dispositif*. Whereas the viewed object in Baudry's theory is but one part of the *dispositif*, the presentational piece of art cannot be seen as a distinct object, somewhere in space, with a viewer in front of it. This space, the viewer, as well as the time of viewing, are implicated by the presentational artwork to such an extent that the *dispositif* itself is the object, is the piece of art.

In addition to this conflation of the object with the *dispositif*, presentational art forms "rewrite" the concept somewhat by merging production and reception. Baudry aimed to apply the notion of *dispositif* to aspects related to the space and time of film projection only. Aspects of an object's production were not to be counted as parts of the *dispositif*. This separation is tenable in the case of classical cinema, yet does not hold when it comes to the art forms which Morse has termed presentational; for, next to the fact that presentational art forms show how represented worlds should not always be understood as another place and another time, presentational *dispositifs* also point out that the production process does not always primarily belong to a there and then. In presentational works of art, the acts of creation and production enter into the here and now of the viewer. In part, they do so through the viewer, who gets to carry out physical acts of co-production.

This inclusion of the production process in the site of presentation/reception does not render Baudry's concept insignificant. It merely points out that the viewing situation (which is the central denotation of *dispositif*) is not necessarily a spatio-temporal vacuum which remains untouched by spatio-temporal dimensions of the production process. Moreover, as presentational art forms do not separate the viewing context from a represented world, the spatio-temporal characteristics of such a represented world (if any) cannot be seen apart from the here and now of the viewing situation either. In sum, presentational art forms point out that, instead of adverting to the production process as well as represented worlds as (or to) other "theres" and "thens," we should consider the possibility that they infuse the space and time of the arrangement we call *dispositif*.

CHAPTER 9
FILM'S DISEMBODYING *DISPOSITIF*: AN EFFECT OF AN EFFECT

... il est la proie de l'impression, d'une impression de réalité.

Jean-Louis Baudry (1978: 30)

In *L'Effet cinéma* (1978), Baudry compares cinema's *dispositif* to the cave pictured by narrator Socrates in Plato's *Politeia*. Like the prisoners in Plato's well-known allegory, Baudry argues, spectators of the cinema are lured into believing that the images they are watching on screen in a darkened hall are reality. As in Plato's account, this illusion is not depicted as an innocent one by Baudry: it victimizes the film viewer, who is the "prey of an impression, of *an impression of reality*" (1978: 30–31, translated by the author).

For Baudry, this victimization of the spectator mainly concerns an ideological form of oppression. The film viewer is not presented with an "objective reality," with an "open and indeterminate horizon," but is instead forced to believe in an ideologically homogeneous image of reality where heterogeneity, difference, openness, and indetermination are eliminated. Film's *dispositif* produces an illusion of continuity from discontinuous elements. Therefore, Baudry states, "We could say that film [...] lives on the denial of difference. Difference is necessary for it to live, but it lives on its negation" (1986a: 290). The victim of this illusion willingly accedes to this denial of difference, because cinema caters to a deeply rooted desire, that is, the desire to return to "a mode of relating to reality which could be defined as enveloping and in which the separation between one's body and the exterior is not well defined" (1986b: 315). This leads Baudry to the conclusion that cinema, like dreams, seems to correspond to a form of regression, an (artificial) hallucinatory psychosis (1986b: 315).[1]

Baudry's psychoanalytical interpretation of film's *dispositif*, as well as the ideological consequences he ascribes to it, have been widely criticized (mainly for being too "sweeping," Mayne 2002: 55). Yet, in spite of these justified critiques, Baudry's outline of cinema's *dispositif* is of paramount importance because of its dominance. First of all, the traditional cinematic viewing set-up which Baudry first defined as *dispositif* has for a long time dominated cinematic practices, which iterated this traditional configuration when films were projected. I am using a past tense here, though, for the classical cinematic viewing configuration in a darkened cinema hall on which Baudry's concept is based has lost its monopoly due to viewing set-ups which are nowadays produced by electronic media and digital mobile screens.

However, besides a material, technological construction, the traditional *dispositif* is just as much a theoretical idea that has highly influenced thinking on film. It functions as a "horizon of expectations," as well as a framework through which we determine the medium of moving images. Raymond Bellour speaks of a "more or less collective experience" and a "special memory experience" in this regard, when he poses the hypothesis that cinema's traditional *dispositif* (in short, a film projected in a cinema, in the dark, according to an unalterably precise screening procedure) remains the condition from which every other viewing situation more or less departs (Bellour 2013: 206).

In addition to the fact that Baudry's writings have been influential, they cannot be ignored here because they point to an effect of film's (dominant) *dispositif* which is most relevant to the subject of this part: the disembodiment of the film viewer. As mentioned earlier, Baudry holds that film's reality effect complies with a desire to eliminate the distinction between perception and representation, as well as between one's body and the exterior. When it comes to film, the latter can be regarded as an effect of the former: when film's reality effect makes us forget that we are watching a representation, we are prone to forget the distinction between our own body and the film (as a body, that is, as a physical object). Instead, we imagine ourselves into the reality shown on screen, and momentarily forget our own actual physical existence in front of that screen.

Therefore, in this part, I read Baudry's remark that the film spectator is prey to the impression of reality not in the first place as a metaphorical reference to the ideological subjugation of the viewing subject to the cinematic illusion. Instead of discussing this presumed ideological victimization of the viewer further, I focus on the disembodiment which the more literal meaning of "being prey" indicates. As will be demonstrated below, this disembodiment can be understood as an effect of an effect: it is the (by-) product *and* a prerequisite of the reality effect which the many components of cinema's dominant *dispositif* pursue.

Blotting out the body: splitting worlds

The disembodiment of the film spectator relies on two operations of cinema's traditional *dispositif* which, at first sight, seem slightly contradictory. On the one hand, the disembodiment of the film viewer is caused by the fact that film is, as Morse also pointed out, a proscenium art form. The film screen separates the beholder's here and now from the space and time of the story world which is depicted on that screen. On the other hand, the disembodiment of the spectator depends on the negation of this separation, of the impenetrability of the screen. Most components of film's dominant *dispositif* contribute to hiding the fact that the screen is a screen, and that the film world which appears on it is a manufactured, projected representation. This does not mean, however, that the worlds in front and on or "in" the screen become related or merged: the here and now of the viewer's position is rather brushed aside. It is left unacknowledged, unemphasized, and is meant to be forgotten as much as possible by the viewer in order for her to sink into the illusionistic film world.

Before turning to the disembodying effects of this negation of the distinction between the viewer's spatiotemporal position and the represented world, let me first discuss the separation itself. It is obvious that the flat screen on which films are projected forms an indisputable physical boundary between the viewer and the represented world "behind" the screen. As Richard Serra remarks on film:

> When someone uses a slow dolly with a camera, or progressively moves into a foreshortened space, it still seems to me that you are dealing with an illusion on a flat plane you can't enter into. The way it is understood denies the progressive movement of your body in time. It's from a fixed viewpoint.
>
> Serra in Weyergraf, 1980: 96

However, although screens cannot be entered by the body, they do not always form a rigid boundary between the viewer's physical position in time and space on the one hand, and a world on view on the other. The temporal distinction between the worlds "on" and "off" screen can be bridged. When the images which are projected or broadcast on a screen are live, the screen no longer provides visual access to an "elsewhen." While the photographic base of analogue film ensures that film images on celluloid always refer to something "that has been," this temporal distance is no longer ensured by cinema's chemical-technological base in the digital age (although the signs of postproduction which characterize most narrative fiction films, such as cutting and editing, still point out that *if* digital film images have an indexical relation to referent—as opposed to being painted out of pixels—this referent must lie in the past).

The separation of the represented space on screen and the space of representation in front of that screen is harder to bridge. Even if projected images show the projection room (the viewer's "here") itself, the illusionistic space on screen remains a physically inaccessible represented space. This boundary of physical inaccessibility can seemingly be perforated by *dispositifs* which allow the viewer to feature in the images on view, or affect them physically through possibilities of interaction. Whereas such possibilities of small "perforations" into the screen space are common in video *dispositifs*, they are not utilized in cinema's dominant *dispositif*. Besides a lack of influence, not much physical activity is required from the film viewer either. In this regard, it is not surprising that Metz has called the viewer of film "a great eye and ear" (1982: 48).

The conventions of narrative fiction films sustain the viewing situation that is produced by other components of the *dispositif's* set-up, as the "fourth wall" is not breached by characters and the traces of enunciation are obliterated in classical narrative films. The viewer is not addressed, and remains an unacknowledged entity.

Another reason for which narrative films—and not necessarily just the traditional or classical ones—give rise to a disembodied mode of looking has to do with the fact that the duration of the viewing experience is dictated by the length of the projected film. The convention that the film viewer watches a movie from beginning to end is enforced by an architectural component of cinema's traditional *dispositif*: in the traditional theatrical situation, cinema halls are entered and exited through the same doors. Unlike some projection rooms in museums or art galleries, the cinematic projection room is not a passageway to other rooms. In addition, the entrance/exit doors of cinema halls are closed during a film show, which further discourages visitors of the cinema to run in and out. Thus, although sitting down to watch a movie and getting up to leave the room after the end are both physical acts, they are not really active choices that would draw attention to the spectator's own body. Compare this with viewing a looped video which goes on and on forever, and is moreover shown in a room that is connected to a string of other exhibition spaces. In such case, it is left up to the viewer to decide how long to stand and watch, and when to move on. This mode of looking requires more conscious physical performances by the viewer, and hence produces more awareness of viewing as a bodily act.

Other components of film's traditional *dispositif* that contribute to the spectator's obliviousness to her physical position in the viewing room are the darkness of the room and the suppression of the ambient sounds by curtains and carpets that deaden the sounds which are inevitably produced by the audience—even in spite of the social convention to be quiet during a film show. Both components work to draw a spectator's attention away from the viewing room itself, and hence enforce the viewer's attention to the represented film world. The *dispositif's* suppression of the world in front of the screen stimulates the disembodied film viewer to take the fictional diegesis which is visible on screen as the (one and only) real world. In order for this reality effect to come about, the representational character of the world on screen needs to be disguised. For this reason, it is not only the projector that is hidden in cinema's dominant *dispositif* so as to hide the mechanical on-the-spot realization of the illuminated moving images on screen; sound players and speakers are hardly ever visible from the viewpoint of the spectator either.[2]

The disguise of the representational character of projected fiction films is, however, most of all carried out through formal properties of the film images—most of which I have identified in the previous part on the reality effect. To a remarkable extent, some of the most prominent reality-effect producing devices can simultaneously be pointed out as causes for disembodiment. Smoothness and linear perspective are, for instance, specific cinematic image qualities which create a reality effect, yet these two qualities have simultaneously been indicated by Bryson and Marks as image features which produce a disembodied gaze or optical look, as they suggest the eye is able to plunge into the depth of the image, mastering what it sees.

As discussed in the previous part, the film viewer's sense of stable overview and mastery over the depicted world is threatened by a film's succession of shots, as well as its camera movements. These cinematic properties are potentially disruptive to the optic gaze, as the represented space can become fragmented or ungraspable through cuts and camera turns. There are two ways in which this instability can be settled. First, Baudry, Metz, and other adherents of the so-called apparatus theory have argued that although the film spectator is not capable of taking up the exact (an often shifting) viewpoint constructed by the linear perspective images of film, the filmic apparatus does offer two singular, unified points with which the viewer can identify, namely, the camera and the projector. Secondly, the three related conventional cinematic aspects of continuity editing, suture, and narrativity together relate cinema's moving images in such a way that traditional film provides its spectator with the best possible viewpoint at each moment of the action, and is in addition able to give an overview of one space in a more all-embracing way than any single, static image could ever present. The strategy of suture is, moreover, especially important in this regard, because it invites the spectator to imaginatively occupy the place a character occupies within the film, and to look with the character from a position inside the film's illusionistic space.

Richard Rushton has pointed out, however, that we don't necessarily have to identify with a character in order to enter the film as an other. In one of his critical reflections on Metz' film theory, he defines the disembodiment of the film viewer in terms of becoming an imaginary body. Rushton proposes that we enter the film with, or rather as, this imaginary body:

> As a spectator of the cinema, I am encouraged to forget the existence of myself in its bodily form. At the cinema, the antagonism between the "real" existence of my body and the "imaginary" existence of my mirror image recedes. My body itself becomes an imaginary entity, a body conceived in terms of an eye (and an ear) that can travel vicariously through the imaginary world of film, where it becomes an anonymous and all-seeing inhabitant.
>
> 2002: 112

Rushton's idea of the body as an imaginary entity is especially relevant when it is related to the previously discussed ability of cinema's *dispositif* to simultaneously create and hide a strict division between the on and offscreen world. By referring to Metz' comparison of cinema and theater, Rushton explains how cinema's reality effect depends on the unreality of film; on the fact that everything in the cinema (I would say cinema's entire *dispositif*), including the spectator's body, is raised to the level of the imaginary:

> The space that my body occupies in the theatre is the same space as that is occupied by the stage—and actors—the space of the theatre is "too real" to offer a strong impression of reality. Hence, at the theatre, there is a confusion between the imaginary space of the theatrical representation that I am trying to conjure

> and the necessary interference my body and its materiality bring to this representation [. . .]. In the cinema, on the other hand, everything is raised to the level of the imaginary so that any contradiction between the space that my body occupies and that which the other world of filmic representation occupies no longer bears weight. There is no longer a situation in which a self is confused with or opposed to an other, for it is already as imaginary other that the spectator enters the imaginary representation of the film.
>
> 2002: 113

When we follow Rushton's interpretation of Metz' reflections on narrative fiction film, we can conclude that cinema's traditional *dispositif* eliminates the space of the spectator—including her actual body within that space—because the proscenium division between the space of the audience and the narrative space of the film is so very strong in the cinema.

CHAPTER 10
OTHER VIEWS ON FILM VIEWING

The traditional, dominant *dispositif* of cinema has been questioned in many ways. The critical discussions of the *dispositif* can roughly be divided into two kinds. First, the disembodiment of the film viewer in film's dominant *dispositif* has been disputed. Secondly, doubt has been thrown on the dominance of the traditional *dispositif* itself. The first line of approach basically centers around one question: does the film viewer really "lose" or forget her body during a film show? One of many answers to this question has been formulated by Richard Rushton. He argues that "while watching film, the spectator does not lose the awareness of his/her body for the *entire* duration of a film" (2002: 114). It is more likely, Rushton writes, that one has such "out of body experiences" at those rare moments when "there is a synergy between what is presented on the screen and what is amenable to the most convincing levels of the spectator's belief" (114). However, these are the moments to which the classical narrative cinema aspired, and still aspires, according to Rushton.

Whereas Rushton's argument can lead to the conclusion that, although the disembodying effect of film only comes about every so often, it is nevertheless aspired to by each part of cinema's traditional *dispositif*, other theorists have pointed out how the traditional *dispositif* is not a homogeneous, unidirectional composition. This is because classical narrative fiction films, which are often theorized as the viewed object within cinema's *dispositif*, frequently contain components which work against the *dispositif's* predominant tendency to disembody its viewer. Laura Marks and Mary Ann Doane have, for instance, pointed out how the commonly applied cinematic form of the close-up draws attention to the viewer's body. Marks explains this embodying effect mostly as a result of the fact that close-ups tend to "chop up" the objects they bring into view. Such denial of an entire object or shape can make it difficult to interpret visually. At those moments, a haptic mode of looking takes over in order to make sense of the image. What is more, close-ups discourage a disembodied, optic mode of looking because the effect of monocular perspective almost entirely disappears in shots which were taken at a close range. The vanishing point is hard to detect in close-ups. As a result, the images look blatantly flat; they do not invite the viewer to visually plunge into the image.

Mary Ann Doane, in addition, has pointed out that the close-up puts forth matters of detail and scale. The close-up has a double status: in the space of narrative, the depicted object is a small detail, whereas in the space of the viewer, it momentarily constitutes itself as an enormous autonomous totality, the only thing to be seen. These matters of scale and detail which the close-up puts forth necessarily draw (theoretical) attention to the spectatorial space and the viewer's body within it. For, as Doane puts it; "scale as a concept in general can only be understood through its reference to the human body" (2003: 18).

In her writings on the close-up, Doane pays particular attention to the way in which theoretical reflections on the close-up counteract the dominance of the traditional *dispositif* as a theoretical construction. According to Doane, theoretical celebrations of the close-up as an autonomous entity by film scholars such as Béla Balázs, Gilles Deleuze, and Jean Epstein, should be understood as an attempt to salvage spectatorial space, to reaffirm its existence and its relevance in the face of the closed, seamless space of film, and to reassert the corporeality of the classically disembodied spectator (2003: 18).

In addition to theories which point out the embodying qualities of certain moments or formal features within traditional narrative cinema, Linda Williams (1991) has demonstrated how particular cinematic genres oppose the disembodying effect of the traditional *dispositif* because they create a strong physical reaction in the film viewer. In the so-called "body genres" of pornography, horror, and melodrama, the body is displayed in sensational ways. These genres respectively portray the sensational body spectacles of orgasm, violence and terror, and weeping. While watching these spectacles, Williams argues, the body of the viewer is caught up in an almost involuntary mimicry of the emotion or sensation on screen.

Williams' theory points out that the process of character identification through which the film viewer is enabled to enter the film as a disembodied eye, can have a strong embodying effect when it creates (involuntary) physical reactions.[1] I would contend that this potentially embodying effect of the viewer's identification with an on-screen character is most prominent in, but not exclusive to body genres which produce mimicry, however. It is, for instance, possible to weep or cringe because one identifies with a character who is going through a psychological ordeal that is not physically displayed.

Williams' use of the concept of mimicry has been taken up and stretched somewhat by film theorist Jennifer Barker, who applies it as a much wider model for film spectatorship. Like Doane, Barker is interested in theoretical alternatives to the strict distinction between the viewer's world and the film world which Baudry's influential delineation of cinema's *dispositif* insists on. She proposes to understand both spectator and film as bodies; bodies, moreover, which take up similar structures of perception and expression, and are therefore involved in a mimetic relationship. Many film forms and rhythms mimic the pulses and movements of human bodies, while spectators' bodily responses to film mimic film itself. When the camera dives under a bridge in a chase movie, the spectator will be inclined to duck, too. However, even when we don't actually copy the movements on film with our body, we feel whip pans, long takes, and tracking shots in our muscles because our bodies have made similar movements. Our responses to film's body, Barker states, are a case of kinaesthetic memory (2009: 75).

When film and viewer are envisaged as co-constituted, related, embodied entities, the border between them can no longer be described in rigid terms. In Barker's theory, the material contact between viewer and viewed is less a hard edge or a solid barrier than a liminal space:

> Watching a film, we are certainly not *in* the film, but we are not entirely *outside* it either. We exist and move and feel in that space of contact where our surfaces mingle and our musculatures entangle. [...] This sense of fleshy, muscular, visceral contact seriously undermines the rigidity of the opposition between viewer and film.
>
> 2009: 13

One of the problematic points in Barker's argument is that, in order to distance herself from traditional film theories related to Baudry's *dispositif*, she claims that the mimetic relationship between viewer and film does not involve, as Baudry and Metz have it, the spectator's identification with parts of the cinematic apparatus. To me, the process of mimicry that she describes *does* seem to concern this form of identification. Yet, this does not undermine her argument; in fact, it makes her ideas all the more effective as deconstructions of the traditional understanding of film viewing as a disembodied act. It shows that when the viewer in cinema's dominant, traditional *dispositif* adopts the disembodied subject position of an all-seeing eye in the film world by identifying with the camera and/or projector, she nevertheless feels this position with her actual body which is sitting in front of the screen. Due to what Barker terms "kinaesthetic memory" and "bodily empathy," the film spectator can imagine how it would feel to physically occupy that position, or carry out those movements in space.

In this regard, it is telling that Rushton argued that the spectator enters into the film as an imaginary body, as opposed to the disembodied eye which is so often mentioned in the traditional film theories which he discusses. An imaginary body can only be imagined by someone with a body, *with* that real body. Moreover, when the monocular position of the camera/projector is occupied by the viewer's imaginary body, this is felt with her real body in the space in front of the screen, which can hence not be forgotten or eliminated. The embodied film viewer is indeed not entirely in, or entirely outside the film, but rather resides in the liminal "space of betweenness" (Barker 2009: 12).

In addition to theories such as Barker's which provide theoretical alternatives to the idea of the dominant *dispositif*, in order to show that it isn't the only or the right model with which to consider cinematic spectatorship, many scholars have questioned the dominance of the traditional *dispositif* by pointing out that it doesn't dominate or hasn't always dominated cinematic practices. Following scholars such as Tom Gunning (1990) and Antonia Lant (1995), Frank Kessler (2006, 2007) has convincingly discussed how the field of film was once dominated by an entirely different *dispositif*. In the era of early cinema, films were very much oriented towards their audience. Actors would for instance look and smirk into the camera, while carrying out physical slapstick which spurred bodily reactions in the viewers. In the words of Gunning, who has coined the term "cinema of attractions" for these film practices, this form of cinema was "willing to rupture a self-enclosed fictional world for a chance to solicit the attention of the spectator" (Gunning 1990: 57). Unlike the viewer in cinema's most dominant, well-known *dispositif*, the embodied viewer in this early *dispositif* was not bound into the space of film, but rather placed vis-à-vis a space where spectacular attractions were being displayed (Kessler 2006).

In addition to the *dispositif* of the cinema of attractions, Parante and de Carvalho point out two other cinematic *dispositifs* which differ strongly from the traditional cinematic viewing configuration. Although the *dispositifs* in question never completely overpowered the dominance of the traditional *dispositif*, they took firm root within the field of film in specific historical periods. The first alternative *dispositif* is the so-called film practice of "expanded cinema," which flourished in the 1960s. Works of expanded cinema are best described as multimedia happenings which operate on the verge of cinema, theater, and performance. The works in question ask viewers to participate in an experience which has its own preestablished duration, although chance and surprise can be part of the experience (Parente and de Carvalho 2008: 49). In *The Exploding Plastic Inevitable* (1966), for instance, Andy Warhol combined film projections with a music performance by the Velvet Underground, accompanied by a group of dancers, and the simultaneous flickering of revolving slide projectors, strobe lights, and moving colored spotlights. The film images were projected onto the playing band, while the bodies of the dancing audience got caught up in overwhelming surroundings filled with light and sound.

The second *dispositif* which Parente and de Carvalho identify is the "cinema of exhibition" or "artists' film." This term applies to films which are shown in museums and galleries, often in a multi-screen, spatial set-up. The fixed duration of both the traditional *dispositif*, the cinema of attractions, and the *dispositif* of expanded cinema, no longer applies to the cinema of exhibition. Its conditions of reception imply an elasticity of time, allowing viewers to follow their own trajectory, to participate in an experience unique to them alone (Parente and de Carvalho 2008: 50). The viewing position which is created by these works of art is clearly an embodied one. Artists working in this genre are Philippe Parreno, David Claerbout, Douglas Gordon, Isaac Julien, Eija-Liisa Athila, Aernout Mik, Sam-Taylor Wood, and Stan Douglas, to name only a few.

Both the *dispositif* of expanded cinema and the *dispositif* of the cinema of exhibition rely heavily on intermedial relationships, which reconfirms my claim that the dominant *dispositif* of film has become so typical and specific to it, that most deviations from the norm will necessarily operate on the boundary between film and other media. When it comes to the practices which Parente and de Carvalho describe as "cinema of exhibition," this other medium is video. Many of the characteristics by which the *dispositif* of the cinema of exhibition deviates from cinema's traditional viewing set-up are derived from video installation art. In fact, the material support of pieces termed cinema of exhibition by Parente, de Carvalho and other film theorists, is actually video technology. The intermedial character of the installations in question is so strong that a definition which would count them within the field of video, such as "cinematic video art," would be just as adequate as "cinema of exhibition" or "artists' film."[2]

In addition to these artistic explorations of cinema's dominant *dispositif*, the viewing configuration of the traditional narrative fiction film has also been reformed by the video medium outside of the artistic domain. First, video technology has moved films outside of the film theater to the inside of the living room, where movies are now watched in a (home) video *dispositif* which does not meet the parameters of immersive spectatorship that are set by cinema's conventional viewing situation. Secondly, digital video technology has subsequently transported both film and video outside of the living room, into public space. Today, movies can be watched anywhere on small mobile screens. This allows the film spectator to leave the traditional cinematic *dispositif* far behind, and instead combine and alternate the act of film viewing with, for instance, a jog around the park, a bus ride to the mall, and a conversation with friends.[3]

Not only have the *dispositifs* of contemporary cinematic *objects* been influenced and reshaped through the medium of video, the *theoretical* attention to the embodying, haptic and tactile qualities of the cinematic medium which I outlined above, can just as well be ascribed to the medium of video. The embodied spectatorship which theorists aim to formulate with regard to film is effortlessly and overtly created by the medium of video. Unencumbered by a single dominant *dispositif* that represses embodied spectatorship, the plural *dispositifs* of video are each characterized by the fact that they create an embodied viewer. It is not far-fetched to presume that the embodying characteristics which are so prominently present in video's *dispositifs* have taught us to look at moving images—even the most conventional cinematic ones—while paying attention to our body. Laura Marks, for instance, first wrote an essay on haptic video before she addressed the haptic moments in narrative fiction films. The strong embodying qualities of the video medium seem to have enabled theorists to discover the more covert haptic characteristics of film, and to consequently rethink as well as oppose the dominance of the traditional cinematic *dispositif*. With Marks' essay on haptic video as an important guide, I will further discuss the embodying qualities of video's *dispositifs* next.

CHAPTER 11
SURFACES AND SCREENS: VIDEO'S EMBODYING *DISPOSITIFS*

> *I can feel my body. I am lying in a dark space. I can feel my body lying here. I am awake. I feel my breathing, in and out, quiet and regular. I can feel my breathing. I move my body. [. . .] I imagine my body. I imagine my body in this dark space. The space is like a large black cloud of soft cotton, silent and weightless. A soft black mass slowly pressing in around my body. I can feel it slowly pressing in around my body. Pressing in around me. Everything is closing down. Closing down around my body.*

The soft voice rapidly whispering these lines is barely audible. At first, the repetition of the word "body" is mainly heard. The indiscernibility of the spoken words also applies to the coarse video images which accompany the murmuring voice. These images are projected on four large screens which form a square that can be entered through four narrow openings on the installation's corners. The grainy projections show colored structures in which recognizable objects occasionally appear. However, the succession of hardly moving shots of, for instance, a glass bowl, a façade or a field of flowers do not appear to have any obvious meaningful relationship with each other. In addition, these apparently random representations of things often slowly turn dark or out of focus, which means the visibility of the depicted objects is constantly tarnished. In all cases, the images can be defined as flat and impenetrable, either because they are too dark or blurred to show depth of field, or because the close-ups or long shots of flat surfaces lack the single vanishing point of Renaissance perspective.

Because of the flatness of the images the viewer entering the piece is likely to feel physically enclosed by the installation's screens. The initial unintelligibility of the surrounding sounds and images in the black museum room heightens the spectator's senses. What do I hear? What am I looking at? How should I turn my head in order to catch as many words of the whispered monologue as possible? How fast do I have to turn my body in order not to miss what is visible at my back when I am looking at the screen in front of me? Should I try to get further removed from the obscure images, or get even closer to them in order to discover more detail?

Then, all at once, the soft sounds turn into cringingly loud noises, and the slow images suddenly show frantic camera movements which turn the vaguely displayed objects into an even less discernible whirl of video pixels. This unexpected change from slowness and stillness to loud visual and auditory noise can only be experienced as a jolt to the body. It makes one jump, or cringe. It gives rise to the urge to cover one's ears and look for the nearest exit in order to flee from the installation's violent outburst. Then, before the square of images can actually be left by the spectator, stillness and silence return as suddenly as they were broken. Slow images of flat surfaces reappear on the four projection screens. The soft voice resumes its hasty murmuring monologue: "I can feel my body, I am lying in a dark space, I can feel my body lying here. [. . .]"

The title of Bill Viola's video piece *The Stopping Mind* (1990) may suggest that the installation's alternation between slow- and fast-moving images, as well as soft and loud sounds, represents faltering thought processes. The effect of Viola's famous piece on its viewers, however, has little to do with the meaning the title attaches to the video installation. For *The Stopping Mind* first and foremost moves the body.

What is more, Viola's piece displays a self-reflexive awareness of its physical effect on the beholder. For the murmuring voice which, in part, causes the embodied mode of looking in the installation's visitor, describes the installation's effect while producing it. The monologue expresses the experience of feeling (with) the body. This is precisely the experience to which Viola's piece gives rise. If the alternation between stillness and loud chaos isn't enough for the installation's visitor to become highly aware of her own bodily movements and sensations, the strongly reiterating word "body" in the hypnotic monologue will ultimately draw the visitor's attention to her own physical being-there, in a confined dark space between illuminated screens.

Viola's installation is a paradigmatic example of a video piece which fully employs the embodying qualities of the video medium. As such, it brings an effect to the fore which can be ascribed to a large range of video artwork that have been produced in recent decades. During the process of production, video is not a haptic medium because—unlike analogue film stock—it cannot be manually altered.[1] Within the context of the viewing process, however, video *can* be characterized as a tactile, embodying medium. For within the viewing set-up, many videos have an embodying effect on their beholder. This relationship between video art and the spectator's body has not only been explored and exploited by artists such as Viola; it has been noted by media theorists as well.

The embodying qualities of video are not grouped in one medium-specific viewing configuration. Unlike film, the medium of video does not have a single dominant *dispositif.* Yvonne Spielmann has emphasized the open structure of video in this regard. Not only can the signal be generated in various ways (externally through a light impulse but also internally through a broadcast signal generator, in addition the electronic video and audio signal are interchangeable), the signal process can also be altered multiply and modularly with various devices (synthesizer, scan processor, keyer, field switcher), by which several sources can be integrated (2008: 134). What is more, Spielmann continues, "the output of video does not depend on a particular setting: video appears on the monitor of the processors, just as it does on the television screen and in big-screen projection" (134). This leads Spielmann to concede that video's structure "does not possess any fixed dispositive" (134).

Although Spielman is right in pointing out the multiplicity and openness of video configurations, I would say that the medium has produced several specific *dispositifs* that can be outlined, even if they are as ever-changing and heterogeneous as the medium itself. None of these dispositifs overshadows the others. What the most characteristic video *dispositifs* have in common, however, is that they stimulate embodied modes of looking—albeit in different ways. Also, two cultural places play a predominant part in video's viewing configurations, namely the museum and the family home. Videos are watched most frequently in one of these places. The cultural, social, and institutional conventions of the museum (or art gallery) and the living room instigate the embodied mode of looking which so many other components of the video medium solicit as well. For, as mentioned previously, the museum is related to the convention of wandering spectatorship, while the living room prevents the viewer from becoming a disembodied, immersed entity, as it brings (and allows) social interaction and everyday domestic distractions into the viewing situation.

Although some of video's embodying qualities originate from the early stages of its technological support, most of these qualities have become specific to the medium by convention, while other technological possibilities and properties are left unutilized or underemphasized. Like film images, video images are always linear perspective images. Moreover, like film, video can be used as a narrative medium. However, within the field of video, the possibility of telling stories is not as dominant as it is within the field of film. Hence, the conventions, narrative techniques, and compositional strategies that have become so prominent in classical narrative films are not so frequently applied in videos. This also makes the strategies and techniques by which narrative films tend to construct a disembodied viewing position relatively unfamiliar to video. So, in spite of the fact that video images are perspectival, the supreme viewing position created by linear perspective is—unlike in cinema's dominant *dispositif*—not sustained by most forms of video.

Some technical and formal possibilities of video—possibilities which are not necessarily unique to the medium—have repeatedly been used by artists, with the result that some of these technical possibilities have become specific characteristic properties of the medium. The loop, for instance, has become a characteristic feature of video art. In "The Temporalities of Video," Christine Ross designates the loop as one of video's key mechanisms in addressing the viewer through time, and as one of its most important modes of presentation (2006: 98). However, the loop is not so much a unique technical possibility of video, for film fragments or sound-recordings can be looped as well. It has rather become a hallmark of video through the excessive use of loops by video artists (98).

As mentioned previously, looped videos produce an embodied mode of looking because they allow the spectator to begin or start looking at any preferred moment. As Ross explains, loops consist of short scenes, but the potentially endless repetition of these short fragments can lead to an extension of time, or to endless duration. Because of this combination of relatively short fragments with endless continuing repetition, loops do not force the viewer to a halt for a fixed period of time—as narrative films do—but instead leave the spectator relatively mobile and free. Looped videos allow the spectator to come in at any time and leave at any preferred moment (Sharp 1976: 253). Therefore, it is ultimately the spectator who must decide how long to stand to watch, and when to move on. This requires conscious activity by the viewer, and makes her aware of the fact that looking is a time-consuming, bodily act.

The extended duration and repetition often created by loops can in themselves be regarded as two of video's main characteristics. Again, prolongation and repetition have chiefly become typical of video through the use of the medium, that is, by convention and not by the unique possibilities or limitations of its technical support. Although the prolongation can in part be explained by the fact that editing was next to impossible in video's early phase, it was embraced and continued when it was no longer an inevitable consequence of technological limitations. When the medium was taken up by artists in the 1970s, they regarded video as "a unique means to disrupt dominant conventionalities of time, notably acceleration and temporal linearity" (Ross 2006: 83). Hence, for technological, artistic, aesthetic, and ideological reasons, videos were made in which time seemed to be extended, endless, and slow instead of fast and condensed. Repetition contributed to this prolongation, and moreover disrupted linearity. In addition, acceleration was countered—and extended time was expressed—by videos depicting uneventful actions with no beginning and no end, often shown in real, unedited time. That these applications have become characteristic to video over time, is suggested by the fact that repetition and uneventful prolongation can still be perceived in many contemporary videos—for instance in those by David Claerbout which I will discuss later on.

How does this prolongation affect the spectator? According to Ross, extended time increases "the spectator's sensorial and attentional faculties, so that one might liberate oneself from the habit of viewing objects as we see them" (2006: 84). In addition, Ross notes that "expanded time became [. . .] an aesthetic strategy that could problematize the opticality of the image" (84). This intensification of the spectator's sensorial and attentional faculties, and the problematization of the opticality of the image, relates to the ideas of Marks and Bryson, who argued that disembodied modes of looking have no duration, but are rather placed outside of time. Images that express extended time do not give rise to an optical mode of looking. For, as not much happens in them, they test the patience and attention of the viewer. Once looking becomes boring, or when no end or change is in sight, the (real, unaccelerated) time the act of looking takes up suddenly becomes noticeable. Moreover, like the loop, uneventful prolongation offers the spectator the possibility to choose her own viewing length, which compels the viewer to consider how much time should be spent looking, and hence evokes the awareness that perception takes up time. In sum, extended time is time that "weighs on the body," as Graig Uhlin (2010: 21) puts it, for exaggerated duration and uneventfulness eventually direct the viewer's attention to the position of her own body in time.[2]

Another aspect of video's *dispositifs* which produces a viewer who is aware of her own position in time is the medium's technological capability of instantaneous broadcast. Video images can be recorded, transmitted through a cable and be broadcast at the same instant, with no delay due to development or transportation. First, this possibility further enhances video's characteristics of endless continuation and prolongation. For if no storage is needed, the duration of video is not limited by tape length. As long as the electricity supply is uninterrupted, the broadcast of video images can go on forever.

Secondly, the technical possibility of instantaneous broadcast enables video to produce live, real-time representations of events which are absent in place. This "liveness" diminishes the temporal division of the screen world and the world of the viewer, for both come to inhabit the same "now." When again taking into consideration Morse's opinion that images which share the time and space in which they exist with their spectator produce an embodied spectator, then live video images can certainly be understood as producing such a spectator. As video artist Dan Graham puts it: "Video is a present-time medium. Its images can be simultaneous with its perception by/of an audience. The time/space it represents is continuous, unbroken and congruent with that of real time, which is the shared time of its perceivers" (1979: 62). The word "of" in Graham's phrase "its perception by/of an audience" also indicates the possibility of closed-circuit video, which stems from the medium's capability of instantaneous broadcast. Closed-circuit video as a *dispositif* contributes to the embodiment of the spectator when images of the viewer are simultaneously recorded and broadcast within one space, with the result that the spectator figures in the images she perceives.

Closely related to video's ability of instantaneous broadcast and closed-circuit transmission is the medium's aptitude for interactivity. Because a video signal is electronic, devices which can convert touch, sound, light, temperature, or movement into an electronic signal that can be connected to the medium, and influence its signal. Hence, the open structure of video that Spielmann pointed out enables video images to respond to the physical presence of the spectator. For instance, sound-sensitive sensors can detect the presence of the spectator by the sound of her footsteps, and video images can then immediately respond to the signal from the sensor. Another example is that the spectator can press buttons or touch screens in order to alter the video image. In all cases, the response of the image to spectator's body and/or actions carried out with this body result in the embodiment of the spectator. For, indeed, the reaction of the image to the spectator's body acknowledges the presence of the spectator as a body, which makes the spectator aware of this body as well.

In relation to the electronic medium's aptitude for interactivity, Marks has pointed out that the electronic and digital manipulability of video is a source for haptic visuality, regardless of the interactive component. Video images and sounds can easily be distorted by way of magnets, electronic devices such as synthesizers, keyers, scan processors and amplifiers, or, in the digital age, computers. Marks writes:

> The tactile quality of the video image is most apparent in the work of video makers who experiment with the disappearance and transformation of the image due to digital and other effects. Electronic effects such as pixellation can render the object indistinct while drawing attention to the act of perception of textures.
>
> 1998: 30

Viola's installation described earlier is a good example of the effects Marks describes. The whirl of pixels and noises which now and then appears so suddenly in *The Stopping Mind* is the result of electronic manipulation. Not only does this manipulation lead to embodied viewing because it renders the depicted objects invisible; it also creates a storm of rapidly moving colored squares which is physically overwhelming, even threatening.

Another aspect Marks regards as an intrinsic quality of video, and one of its most important sources of tactility, is its contrast ratio. In her essay "Video Haptics and Erotics" (1998), Marks point out that video's contrast ratio of 30:1 is approximately one-tenth of 16mm or 35mm film. In addition, the resolution of analogue video is at the most one-tenth of the resolution of 35mm film images. However, these "insufficiently visual" qualities—as Marks terms them—have improved tremendously since Marks wrote her essay in 1998. Today, the contrast ratio of digital video equals the contrasts between darkness and brightness that can be captured by analogue film images. Digital video images, in addition, can reach such a high definition nowadays that they are used for projection in cinemas, and go under the name of digital cinema when they represent a (fictional) narrative in the viewing setting of the movie theater. Although even the most advanced Ultra High Definition digital video format (8k UHD) is not yet able to match the resolution of analogue 70mm IMAX film, the resolution of HD video images has reached such a high level that the difference between video and film is no longer perceptible.[3]

How has this improvement in image quality affected the specific embodying quality of the medium? First of all, the fact that cinematic-looking high image quality is technically possible for video nowadays, does not mean that all video images automatically now have such a high quality. The most common video cameras for home use still do not produce images which look like film. Secondly, a low contrast ratio and low resolution are still features we recognize as typical of video today. When we see images in which a bright spot in a dark image (such as an open door at the back of a dark interior) brightens the whole image because of low contrast ratio, or when pixelation is visible on an image surface due to low resolution, we recognize these as video images. Moreover, the shortcomings of analogue video are still deliberately applied by artists who are interested in their aesthetic and affective appeal. The low image quality of video footage has thus become a conventional, rather than a technologically inherent feature of the medium. It is reasonable to conclude that the tactile features of low resolution and low contrast have become less dominant since these characteristics are no longer technologically inevitable. In this sense, the hapticity of the video medium has waned since the quality of its images has improved.

However, while video has lost some of its automatically haptic image features, it has gained embodying abilities because of developments in other areas of its apparatus (I am using it in the sense of *appareil de base* here). Video projectors were developed in the 1980s. This added new possibilities to video's *dispositifs*. Before the advent of the video projector, video was always viewed in configurations which necessarily included one or more TV monitors. In its first decades, the video image was tied to, and limited by, the small size and bulkiness of the TV. With the advent of the video projector, video images could suddenly be much larger, and appear on any surface. In addition to the video *dispositifs* in which the viewer looks into the light source of the cathode ray tube, the medium of video was now expanded with *dispositifs* in which the viewer looks at a back-lit projection on a flat surface in front of her.

The video projector offers video the possibility of copying cinema's traditional viewing set-up. Yet, although cinema's viewing situation is frequently imitated by video projectors, one of the most prevalent applications of the video projector differs markedly from cinema's traditional *dispositif.* The video projector was taken into the museum by video artists, who had already applied the (bulky) TV monitor in sculptural ways within this context.[4] As a result, the spatial set-up of multi-screen video installations became one of video's new, specific *dispositifs*. Unlike the proscenium *dispositif* of narrative film projection, the *dispositif* of multi-screen video installation art functions as a presentational art form which addresses and envelops its embodied viewer in the "here" and "now."

CHAPTER 12
IN BETWEEN: THREE INTERMEDIAL INSTALLATIONS

Many contemporary art forms which make use of moving image material combine embodying and disembodying strategies; some of which can be understood as more specific to video, while others are more typical of film. Put somewhat simply, films tend to disembody their viewer, whereas video is disposed to the production of an embodied mode of looking. However, many media theorists have rightly argued that this distinction is not clear-cut: recent video images can be just as optic as film, and film is quite capable of affecting its viewer physically—both in manners which resemble and which differ from video's embodying strategies.

On the one hand, the video and film pieces I will analyze below confirm the idea that the disembodying qualities of film and the embodying characteristics of video are by no means essential and unique to the two media in question. Through intricately hybrid or double *dispositifs*, the films and video installations by Douglas Gordon and David Claerbout produce moments and spaces in which film images have haptic qualities, video produces optic looking, cinema seems to turn into a presentational art form, and the video installation momentarily functions as a proscenium medium. In sum, the most typical (dis)embodying effects of film and video appear "switched" in these works of art. As a consequence, the works by Gordon and Claerbout give rise to questions on medium specificity. Are film and video still film and video when they are shown to be able to copy each other's most characteristic (dis)embodying effects? And how should the medium of the images on view be determined or specified if the traditional *dispositifs* of film and video seem to have become disconnected from the two media?

On the other hand, the switch is never complete; the most traditional, dominant and typical *dispositifs* of film and video remain active in the works in question. In Gordon's *k.364*, the hapticity of film images is, for instance, countered by some of the most prominent disembodying aspects of cinema's traditional *dispositif*. In Claerbout's *American Car* the embodying effect of the video installation depends on the spectator's familiarity with some of the narrative film conventions that sustain cinema's dominant *dispositif*. *Bordeaux Piece*, in addition, shows how cinema's traditional *dispositif* can be invaded and altered by video-specific forms of time, yet simultaneously presents the presentational video *dispositif* and the proscenium film *dispositif* as fairly distinct and decisive set-ups. In sum, all three film/video pieces (partially) transgress the conventional (dis)embodying *dispositifs* of film and video. Yet they show that these transgressions cannot be understood without paying attention to the common, more traditional (ideas of) medium-specific *dispositifs* on which the transgressions themselves often depend; that is, the respectively disembodying and embodying *dispositifs* of film and video. In my view, the objects in question self-reflexively explore the double move which implicitly marks many moving image productions today—they both move away from, and back to the dominant, conventional viewing set-ups of film and video.

Two journeys: *k.364*

Douglas Gordon's documentary *k.364* brings us back to the journey with which this part started out: a journey to Warsaw. Whereas this movement to Poland's capital was prompted by the fierce call of a fictional movement in Yael Bartana's *The Polish Trilogy*, Gordon's *k.364: A Journey by Train* portrays two Israeli musicians, both in their thirties, who travel to Warsaw in order to perform a concert. The two musicians, violist Avri Levitan and violinist Roi Shiloah, board a train in Berlin which first takes them to Poznan. In this Polish town, they rehearse Mozart's *Sinfonia Concertante in E-Flat Major, K.364* with the Amadeus chamber orchestra. After the rehearsal, Avri and Roi continue their journey by train to Warsaw, where they perform the piece with the orchestra in the city's majestic Philharmonic Concert Hall. As both musicians are from Polish Jewish families, the journey brings them to a country from which their parents had fled due to World War II. This is, unsurprisingly, one of the topics they discuss during the trip.

The way the musicians and their stories come across to the spectator, however, very much depends on the two distinct *dispositifs* of the piece. From the same high-resolution video footage, Douglas has produced two versions of *k.364*, each of which has its own particular viewing configuration. One of the versions is best defined as a movie. This movie version has a narrative character, and was shown in movie theaters as a conventional documentary film with a set beginning and ending. The other version is a multi-screen installation with two large mirrors, which was exhibited in museums. In this version, the film material is projected in looped form, on two large screens placed adjacently at an angle of 90 degrees in the middle of a spacious museum room.

The double *dispositif* of *k.364* is not unique in Gordon's oeuvre. In 2006, for instance, he produced the film *Zidane* together with Philippe Parenno (who is known for his multi-screen narrative films, and was also involved in the creation of *k.364*). *Zidane* portrays soccer superstar Zinedine Zidane during one match. Instead of following the ball, the seventeen cameras of Gordon and Parenno focus solely on the player for the duration of one game (Real Madrid vs. Villareal in the spring of 2005). In the resulting single screen documentary film, the footage of Zidane from seventeen different angles has been edited into a linear movie, in which we see how he communicates with other players, constantly scans the pitch with his eyes, alternates between moments of activity and moments of recuperation, and is finally sent off because of a brawl. Although some of the most exciting or suspenseful moments are repeated in the film (as they usually are in TV coverage of sports games), most cuts from one shot to the next also involve a movement forward in time.

In the installation version of *Zidane* the spatial set-up with seventeen TV monitors creates a different temporal organization between shots. Instead of showing one moment after another, each monitor shows the same moment within the game; yet each image was filmed from a different angle by one of the seventeen cameras. So, when Zidane makes a run to the ball, one monitor provides an establishing shot of the situation, the next one shows the soccer player's concentrated face in close-up, the third shows the star in medium-close-up, and so on. As a spectator, you cannot watch the screens of all monitors at the same time, however, for they are scattered on the floor of a large museum gallery, each facing in a different direction—like the players on the pitch. This leads to the paradoxical situation that the spatial arrangement of the *dispositif* both limits and expands the viewer's sense of visual access to the game.

On the one hand, the spectator cannot see all of the images on the monitors at once. Although most positions in the museum room offer a view of about five screens at a time, the seventeen screens cannot be watched simultaneously. Thus, in order to see the entire group of monitors, the viewer has to move around in order to look at groups of TV screens one after another. As an embodied spectator, she then creates her own unique "montage" by walking through the installation. As Ursula Frohne (2008) has put it; "perception turns into participation" when the fundamental lack of visibility caused by the impossibility of viewing a video work in its entirety becomes a challenge for the observer (Frohne 2008: 357).[1]

On the other hand, the multiplicity of screens provides several perspectives on one and the same moment. It shows something which cannot be shown by a single screen projection, nor by one pair of human eyes alone. As such, the installation simultaneously gives rise to an extraordinary sense of overview, insight and visual access to the depicted scenes. Hence, the video set-up with multiple monitors creates both an embodied presentational mode of looking which is typical of video, but also seems to form a continuation of the aspiration towards the illusion of unlimited visual access, which is attributed to cinema's traditional *dispositif.*

Like *Zidane, k.364* wavers between limited and expanded visibility. Its *dispositifs* stimulate both optic and haptic visuality, and give rise to several modes of embodied and disembodied looking. The difference between *Zidane* and *k.364* is that whereas the movie version of *Zidane* is mostly a conventional optic piece, both the installation version and the film version of *k.364* combine haptic and optic moments—albeit in distinct ways, and with different results. Therefore, a comparison of the two versions of *k.364* can provide insight into the possibilities and limitations of the cinematic and "videomatic" *dispositifs* when it comes to the production of (dis)embodied modes of looking.

One of the most striking features of *k.364*, in both its film and installation version, is the alternation between extremely sharp close-ups, and out-of-focus images which are either very dark or have an overexposed look. In the first half of the narrative, Roi is for instance hardly ever filmed directly. Gordon points his camera at the train window on which the musician's reflection appears against the outside darkness. The transparent, vague outline of his face almost disappears into the dark landscape which rapidly passes in the background of the traveling passenger. These painterly shots are interspersed by detailed close-ups of the musician's hands, filmed while he is playing the violin. In these well-lit images it is almost possible to discern every pore in the skin of the violinist's hands.

Needless to say, the first type of image can be understood as optic cinematic ones because of their smoothness and sharpness, whereas the second type is reminiscent of haptic blurred video images with a low contrast ratio. However, the sharp extreme close-ups are not solely optic; in spite of their high resolution, perfect depth of field, and balanced lighting, they instill a sense of limited visibility in the beholder, as they dissect the depicted subject. Moreover, as mentioned previously, close-ups give rise to questions of scale which can only be deliberated in relation to the spectator's body. In sum, both the sharp and blurred images in *k.364* tend to invite more strongly an embodied, rather than a disembodied, mode of looking.

The limited visual access is further enforced by the fact that the montage of both the movie and the video projections do not follow the rules of continuity editing. The extreme close-ups of Avri and Roi—which focus especially of their hands and faces—are, for instance, hardly ever preceded or followed by medium-close ups or establishing shots. For this reason, it remains unclear how the two protagonists are seated in the train, how they are positioned in relation to each other in the carriage they presumably share, and what the interior and exterior of the train look like. The same goes for the rehearsal of Mozart's *Sinfonia*. Having arrived in Podzan, Avri and Roi join the Amadeus Chamber Orchestra with which they will perform *k.364* in Warsaw. When they enter the rehearsal room, we see that they greet the orchestra by nodding, smiling, and shaking some hands. However, the film and video never show whom they greet: with the exception of the conductor, the members of the orchestra as well as the room in which they reside remain invisible to the spectator. The camera only pictures the two musicians.

This brings me to a second aspect of continuity editing which is lacking in *k.364*; the close-ups of the musicians' faces are never sutured to another shot. In addition to the fact that it remains visible how the musicians are positioned in the space of the train or rehearsal room, we do not get to see what they are looking at. In the first half of the film, the camera switches back and forth between close-ups of Roi and Avri. The close-ups are only occasionally undercut by rather vague images of swimming girls, the railway which recedes into a dark landscape, as well as abstract black images interspersed with yellow dots. Although the last two shots may be interpreted as views from the train by night, it remains uncertain if they represent a character's point of view, as the musicians are never shown while looking outside a train window.

The only scene in *k.364* which does provide the viewer with some sense of overview is the start of the concert in Warsaw's Concert Hall. Before the music comes in, a shot of the large seated audience, the orchestra, and a shot of Avri and Roy on stage, rapidly succeed each other. However, the sense of stability which this spatial mapping may have instilled in the viewer, is undermined in the film version. Images of the playing Roi transgress the 180-degree line; the violinist is shown alternately from the left and the right side, which is highly disorienting to the film viewer.

All in all, both the film and the video versions of *k.364* are dominated by embodying qualities. Neither the cinematic piece, nor the video installation, allows the spectator to visually "plunge" into the represented world, as visibility and overview are constantly thwarted by formal characteristics of the moving images. This observation could lead to the provisional conclusion that Gordon's piece demonstrates how film and video are both able to produce an embodied viewer, irrespective of their *dispositifs*. For even though the movie version of *k.364* was screened in a conventional way, in traditional theaters, its embodying effects hold sway. However, as I will demonstrate below, the traditional *dispositif* of the cinematic version is more prevalent than first thought.

Disembodied listening

When *k.364* is viewed in a movie theater, the opening credits of the film form the concise onset of a story. The subtitle of *k.364* reveals that the movie will depict "A journey by train, from Berlin, to Poznan to Warsaw." In addition, the opening credits let us know who is undertaking the journey by stating that the film features: "Avri Levitan: The Violist." and "Roi Shiloah: The Violinist." The expectation of story development which is raised by the opening credits is further enhanced by the *dispositif* itself, as the traditional viewing situation in the cinema room tends to provide a view on traditional narrative movies.

When the film starts, the initial bare outlines of a story on two musicians who travel from Germany to Poland is hardly expanded into a more comprehensive narrative. The haptic, blurred images which succeed each other in Gordon's *k.364* are hard to interpret. In addition, it is hard to decide on the temporal and spatial relationship between the images as well as the characters they depict due to the absence of continuity editing techniques. However, after a while, the movie starts to conform to the expectation which its opening credits and *dispositif* have awakened. The story of two musicians in a train starts to unroll when the violinist and the violist, who have known each other since childhood, begin to tell stories themselves.

In the cinema, the stories told by Avri and Roi are comprehensible, whereas the viewer of video installation must do her best to catch snippets of their spoken sentences. This difference is first caused by some distinct aspects of the two different *dispositifs*, namely the acoustics as well as institutional conventions related to the halls in which the movie and installation are screened. In both the cinematic and the installation versions of *k.364*, the voices of the musicians are soft. In addition, the two men are not always intelligible because they speak English with a Hebrew accent. However, in carpeted cinema halls with silently seated viewers, the attentive spectator can catch the remarks and anecdotes of the musicians. In spacious museum galleries, where the footsteps of visitors echo through the room together with the musicians' spoken words, the viewer of the installation fails to understand most of the stories.

In addition, the audibility of the musicians' stories is diminished all the more in the installation because its two screens are each accompanied by their own soundtrack. As a result, the spoken words are often drowned out by another soundtrack playing simultaneously. When Roi talks about his mother, for instance, the image of his face is juxtaposed with a shot of a receding railway on the other screen. His words, then, can hardly be heard over the sounds of the train which come with the image of the railway. A final reason why the stories of Avri and Roi do not come across very well in the video installation is that the video version is shorter than the cinematic one. In order to keep the wandering museum-goer's attention, the feature film length has been cut to fifty minutes in the installation. As a consequence, the video piece contains less visual and less auditory material.

In the film, one of the first spoken remarks is uttered by Avri. The violist explains that even though he doesn't have a "Holocaust complex or anything," he cannot look at the woods outside of the train window without imagining how cold it must have been out there, in wintertime, during the night. His remark points out that he must be Jewish, and that hence, the train journey to Poland is an emotionally charged one. The journey turns out to be all the more meaningful to the two musicians when it becomes clear that they are of Polish-Jewish descent. Roi explains how his mother and her family fled the country during World War II, through the cold dark woods to which Avri also referred. Thus, the two Jewish musicians are not only traveling to a country which held some of Europe's most infamous concentration camps, they are also returning to the motherland of their parents. Although they have never lived there, Roi explains how the country is somehow familiar, even though he grew up in Israel. He recognizes words and dishes when he visits Poland. Without knowing the meanings or names, he identifies them as the sounds and flavors of his childhood.

These stories place the journey by train in a grand historical narrative. In addition, they tell us more about the relation between the two protagonists of the story. The fellow musicians share a homeland, as well as their mother's homeland. As the stories proceed, it turns out that the two musicians have known each other since they were children. They went to the same high school, and served in the Israeli army together, where they played in a string quartet. Some funny anecdotes about this period make the two friends laugh out loud.

When the narrative character of the film settles, the haptic, embodying qualities of the film's moving images diminish. Through the narrative, the images become more intelligible. The images of the dark woods outside are, for instance, invested with meaning through Avri's and Roi's accounts. Likewise, the inexplicable close-up images of girls in a pool can now be identified as girls in *Poznan's* swimming pool, which—as Avri points out—is a remarkable place because it used to be a synagogue. Today, it still looks like a synagogue, but it "smells like a swimming pool," the violist adds. Although anecdotes like this do not abrogate the visual haziness of the many out-of-focus close-ups, they do counterbalance their embodying effect. For, as Marks explains, haptic looking often sets in when we can't make sense of images with the eyes. In the film version of *k.364*, the sense of the moving images no longer has to be looked for with the viewer's whole body when it is sufficiently provided by the narrative unfolding through the protagonists' anecdotes.

Likewise, the narrative character of the movie neutralizes the embodying effect of its absence of point-of-view shots, since the close-ups of Avri and Roi are hardly ever sutured to shots which can be interpreted as their point of view. Their spoken remarks and anecdotes to some extent solve this absence of suture, because the images which surround shots of their faces often show the things they are talking about, such as the woods or the pool. Although they are not looking at these things while they talk, the images attach themselves to their point of view because their stories prove that they have once been looking at the woods outside, or the pool in Poznan. More importantly, however, the soundtrack reveals that the musicians are looking at each other while they talk, even though the montage of the images does not confirm this. When Avri is talking, we either see a close-up of Roi's face, or we hear him respond to his friend with words or laughter. This also works the other way around—when Roi is uttering words, we know these words are heard by Avri, who is either depicted listening or whose responding voice can be heard. In sum, the two friends clearly listen and respond to each other's words.

This interaction proceeds all the more impressively when the musicians rehearse, and later on, perform Mozart's piece together. Gordon's film meticulously depicts how the violist and the violinist listen to each other while looking at each other. The previously provided narrative information on the long-standing friendship between the two men, moreover, enhances the visibility of the intimate and concentrated auditory interaction between them. Each of the isolated close-ups of one of the two male faces now appears to be sutured to the other musician, albeit in a way that is not predominantly visual. When Roi's face is shown, we don't get to see what he is looking at. Yet, we can always hear who he is listening to, or who is listening to him: Avri—who is either talking (back), laughing or playing the viola. As a viewer, you are therefore not invited to identify with these musicians in a conventional cinematic way, by being able to look through their eyes. Instead, the film prompts the spectator to identify with the musicians *as* musicians. For, through an auditory form of suture, Gordon's film allows the beholder to enter the film's diegesis as—above all—an ear.

Two bows

The video installation version of *k.364* enhances the embodying effect of the piece's haptic images in many ways. As the two large, double-sided projection screens of the installation are placed at an angle of 90 degrees in the middle of a room, the spectator has to move through the room in order to see the installation from all sides. In addition, the viewer is made aware of her own physical presence in the viewing space by the two large mirrors which are attached to opposite walls of the exhibition space. Besides the fact that the mirrors reflect the spectator's body, they also make the proportions of the installation in relation to the viewer's body more visible. Whereas the spectator in a cinematic *dispositif* can only roughly estimate the scale of close-ups in relation to her body, the viewer of Gordon's installation can actually see how small her body is compared to the detailed close-ups of the musicians which appear on the tall screens.

What is more, the mirrors cut up, multiply, reframe, and refract the projected images. In doing so, they both enhance the visibility of the installation by offering additional perspectives onto the projected images, *and* diminish its visibility as they preclude the possibility of viewing the piece at once in its entirety from one fixed viewing position. As Pepita Hesselberth (2014) has noted with regard to multi-screen exhibitions, "the out-of-the-corner-of-one's eye perception of either a detail of an image or an entire other screen pulls the visitor's perception out of the perspectival grid" (49). In Gordon's installation, this embodying loss of the single stable viewing point of lens-based images, which can be ascribed to all multi-screen installations is all the more enhanced and complicated by the addition of mirrors, which multiply the vanishing points of the two projected images in disorienting ways.

In spite of, or perhaps precisely because of the addition of mirrors, the installation version of *k.364* conforms to common outlines of video's *dispositifs*, as it confirms the idea that the *dispositifs* of the video medium tend to produce an embodied spectator. However, despite—or again because of—all its video-specific qualities, the *dispositif* of Gordon's installation allows the piece to do something cinematic. Whereas the cinematic version of *k.364* lacks visual suture, the video installation *does* produce a cinematic form of visual "stitching," yet in a videomatic, embodying way. In the installation piece, the close-ups of the musicians' faces are juxtaposed with images on the other screen. In the film, it never becomes clear what their staring eyes are looking at. In the video installation, the looks of the musicians traverse the space between the screens formed by the angle of 90 degrees, and fall onto the other screen. In this way, Roi's eyes are looking at moving images of train tracks on the opposing screen when he talks about his Polish-Jewish mother, and Avri's look rests upon shots of the outside scenery when he is reflecting on the coldness out there. The image on the other projection screen is therefore not so much sutured to the point of view of the characters by convention, but because the protagonists are looking quite literally at the images in question during the projection.

It is important that the looks of the musicians travel through the real space of the viewer before falling upon the other projection screen. In this way, the illusionistic space of the projection space infuses the actual space of representation between the two screens. Such an extension of the illusionistic represented space within the viewer's space is in a more general sense one of the most prominent ways in which video's installational *dispositif* has expanded cinema's traditional *dispositif*. It returns in other forms, and with diverse effects, in the installations by David Claerbout which will be addressed later on in this chapter. In Gordon's installation, the transgression of the proscenium is especially interesting because it not only transgresses the traditional cinematic division between the on-screen and offscreen "real" world, but also returns to a cinematic form, absorbing the viewer into the represented on-screen world.

Let me explain this by addressing the installation's depiction of the concert in Warsaw. While the violist and violinist are playing Mozart's *Sinfonia* with the orchestra, one of the projection screens shows Avri and Roi as they were filmed from the right side of the stage, while the other projection screen shows an opposing view of the two musicians, from the left side of the stage. These sideways camera standpoints thus do not show us the two musicians as they face the audience in the music hall; not frontally, standing next to each other, but in profile, standing behind each other. Although both musicians are visible off and on within the image frames of both projections, the right-hand camera has focused mainly on Avri, whereas the left-hand camera catches Roi's face most of the time. As a result, whereas the musicians are positioned shoulder to shoulder on stage, they seem to be facing each other in the juxtaposed projection screens of the video installation. In the museum room, their glances at the audience in the concert hall now seem to be directed at each other.

However, while playing in the concert hall, Avri and Roi often turn their eyes away from the audience in order to look at, and listen to, each other. However, when the two musicians turn their heads in order to face each other on stage, they no longer face each other in the spatial set up of *k.364*'s two screens. Instead, their eyes are cast outside of the screen, into the space of the viewer that has already been cast as a part of the illusionistic space.

The viewer of the installation, who was already under the impression of being simultaneously in the real museum space and the represented space of the images, is now visually addressed in turn by both musicians. When their glances break the so-called fourth wall and rest upon the spectator, however, the spectator is not primarily addressed as herself—a museum visitor—nor as member of the concert audience. The viewer is addressed as one of the musicians; she alternately stands in for each of them. For she is addressed by the look which Avri casts at Roi, and catches the glance which Roi directs towards Avri. As in cinema's classical *dispositif*, the viewer of Gordon's installation is invited to identify with the characters on screen by being enabled to look through their eyes. Yet, in the case of *k.364*, this invitation is created through an uncinematic, embodying breach of the proscenium, by which the spectator is allowed to look through the eyes of an on-screen character by being looked at as if *being* one of the on-screen characters.

The double screen set-up which creates such an intricate viewing position in the installation version, is at some point copied by the cinematic version of *k.364*. When the violist and violinist enter Warsaw's concert hall, the elongated cinema screen splits in two. That is, it shows the two images that are also projected at the installation's double screens, yet within one flat cinema screen. Although the movie is shown to partially imitate a common formal feature of video installation art, the split screen is limited by the conventional single screen of cinema's *dispositif*: the two images cannot face each other on the single flat screen of a movie theater. As a result, the two musicians never catch each other's eye, nor are they able to address the spectator as an inhabitant of the represented space. Hence, the fourth wall remains intact in the film version. The film viewer remains a physically excluded and unacknowledged entity outside of the film world.

When the concert and with that, the film, have come to an end, the two musicians take a bow. In the split screen of the cinema version, Roi and Avri blend into one large black arced figured during the film's final shots. For in the split screens, they bow towards each other until their bodies meet. They visually become one in the middle of the cinema screen, at the adjacent boundaries of the two images within the one flat film projection. The two fusing dark figures resemble the closing curtains of the theater; they signal the end of the show and close off the illusionistic space from the eyes of the spectator.

In the video installation, the same shots of bending bodies produce a different effect. First of all, the bowing musicians never meet at the edges of the two frames, as the two large projection screens of the installation are not entirely adjacent: there is a small opening between them. In addition, the spatial set-up of the two screens turn the bows into gestures which, just like the musicians' glances, extend from the illusionistic space into the exhibition space. Therefore, in the installation *dispositif*, the violist and the violinist not only bow towards each other, they also seem to form an arch over the viewer. This enveloping gesture made by two large blown-up bodies on screen can even be physically threatening to the beholder. As a consequence, she may be inclined to slightly duck away from the large approaching figures. And by that mimicking move, she will once again become like one of the musicians.

Being in *American Car*

Waiting for action

David Claerbout's video installation *American Car* (2004) consists of two large-screen video projections, exhibited in two adjacent rooms. The first projection shows two men in a parked car, the second depicts a car in a vast landscape. Whereas the two images could very well be understood as shots from a classical narrative fiction film, the overall piece is unlike film because of important deviations from cinema's dominant *dispositif*. The spatial, double-folded form of the installation, for instance, is unlike the single screen on which films are usually projected. More importantly, the way in which the two images are positioned in space requires the spectator to walk through the rooms in order to see the entire piece. This spatial set-up of cinematic shots, which creates an embodied mode of looking, diminishes the filmic character of the images. Incorporated and taken apart in the *dispositif* of the multi-screen video installation, these film shots can just as well be specified as video images.

However, the ways in which Claerbout's artwork affects the spectator, and the ways in which the spectator in turn determines the medium of *American Car,* are much more complicated than this brief outline would lead one to suspect. The video installation can never completely be distinguished from film; both the media of video and film can be perceived while looking at *American Car.* Moreover, the ways in which the viewer is positioned by the piece changes from cinematic to videomatic and back again when the installation's route through the two rooms is followed. As I will demonstrate, this route through two rooms is a route through media. For *American Car* not only leads its spectator from film to video images, but also brings the viewer inside the space of film, through video.[2]

At first sight, only the first projection of *American Car* is visible. When entering the dark room in which it is projected, the viewer cannot see into the next room. Therefore, the spectator does not suspect the presence of the second projection of *American Car.* This influences the perception of the first one. As I have mentioned previously, the image of two men sitting in a car can easily be associated with a scene from a narrative film; two detectives patiently staking out a location. So, when walking into the first room, the first impression of the viewer is likely to be determined by this resemblance of the depicted scene to the Hollywood cliché. Although the projection is shown in a dark museum gallery instead of a cinema, and although there are no seats to sit on, the strong familiarity of the scene is enough for the spectator to assume that he or she has entered in the middle of a narrative film. Having missed the preceding story, the reason why the two detectives are sitting in the car will not be completely clear. However, by waiting patiently, as the detectives do, you might find out who or what they are waiting for. Something will happen eventually, for the stake-out is usually a prelude to dramatic action. At least, this is what you, as a spectator familiar with conventional narrative cinema, are likely to expect. And as long as this expectation persists, the video image looks like film.

The expectation does not persist, however, because it slowly becomes clear that nothing will happen. Except for some minimal movements preventing them from seeming to be statues, the two men remain seated in the same position, while rain keeps pouring down the windshield of their car. Suddenly, the flat impenetrability of the images becomes more apparent. As the two men remain silent and practically immobile, the viewer is likely to search for narrative clues in their background. Perhaps something is going on outside of the car? Perhaps we could get a glimpse of action if we peer outside through the window, just like the detectives. However, the windshield can hardly be penetrated with the eyes, as it is almost constantly covered with pouring rain. The viewer's optic film look, which expects to plunge into the depths of the representation, is thus halted by the image. Not so much by the quality of the image surface—as is often the case with video—but by the opaqueness of a surface which is depicted by the smooth projection. The chances of gaining visual access to the story world do not seem entirely nil at this point, however. For the viewer can still wait for the rain to stop, or for a shot which will show the outside of the car. However, the probability of these changes diminishes as the viewing process continues. After a few minutes, the period of time after which something would certainly have happened in a narrative fiction film—if only the appearance of a different shot—has passed.

In fact, nothing will happen for hours, because the projection shows a looped fragment. Because of the invisibility of the loop, the scene has an endless duration. Moreover, the uneventfulness of the scene, which becomes apparent after having watched a while, contributes to the sense that time is extended in *American Car*. The loop, endless duration, uneventfulness, prolongation, all these aspects are—as we have seen—characteristic of video. And not only are these aspects likely to be recognized by the viewer as characteristic features of video, they also have an effect on the viewer that can be recognized as typical to video's main *dispositifs*.

As soon as it has become clear that nothing is going to happen in the first projection in *American Car*, it is also obvious to assume that nothing has happened before either. As a spectator, you haven't missed a previous piece of the story; there simply is no story with a beginning or an end. Apparently, you can come in and leave at any time without missing anything. And as I argued earlier, such a possibility gives rise to an embodied mode of looking, for it leaves the choice of the viewing duration to the spectator. This compels the spectator to consider the amount of time spent on looking, and hence evokes the awareness that perception takes up time. In addition, once it slowly dawns on the spectator that nothing will happen, waiting can suddenly turn into boredom, which again leads to the awareness that viewing is a slow and time-consuming process, and moreover that an active choice to physically leave the room has to be made.

Once this decision is made by the viewer, she will be invited by the piece to an even more embodied mode of looking. Besides the fact that walking out of the room is a physical act, the spectator is also enticed into an embodied viewing mode by the trajectory which leads to the next room. For in order to leave through the door opening in the wall on your left side, you have to approach the projection screen first, as the opening is close to the projection surface. This inevitable approach undermines the possibility of keeping the distance from the projection surface which is needed to have an overview of the whole image, an overview which sustained the sense of mastery which is so closely connected to disembodied, optic looking.[3]

So when you, as a spectator, are forced to move close to the projection, the overview you might have had is lost, and more importantly, the image no longer looks smooth when viewed at a close range. The flatness and impenetrability of the windshield now become visible characteristics of the image surface itself. For, whereas the high resolution of the image provides its surface with a smooth, transparent look when it is looked at from at a distance, this same surface looks grainy and pixelated when seen from close up. As the distance between the viewer and the image surface diminishes, the materiality of the image becomes perceptible. Together, these aspects give rise to the embodied kind of visuality which was already given an initial impetus by the rainy windshield. The mode of visuality, that is, which Marks terms haptic, and Bryson indicates as the gaze; a mode of looking which acknowledges the representational status of the object on view and which therefore relates to the image as another surface.

Haptic looking is not merely stimulated, but almost enforced by *American Car.* Marks describes the haptic look as a look which presses up to the surface of an image, for instance by focusing on its details or by lingering over its surface. Thus, the pressing up to the surface does not have to be taken literally. Yet, in the case of *American Car,* it is something which the spectator physically needs to do in order to comply with the installation's *dispositif.* The spatial arrangement of the installation insists on the viewer's bodily movement from room to room, from screen to screen. Without following this path, the spectator cannot see the entire piece. Hence, when looking at *American Car*, closeness to the image surface is not attained by focusing on details. Instead, focusing on details becomes inevitable by having to move close to the image surface. Therefore, in this case, haptic looking is not primarily the cause, but rather the *result* of embodied, kinaesthetic spectatorship.

The act of focusing on details might only be brief, though, as it happens in the process of walking to the door in order to leave the room. Yet, it is important that between the moment at which the spectator of *American Car* begins to realize that the perceived image is uneventful, and the moment at which she sees the graininess of the image before leaving the first exposition room, *American Car* looks more like video than like film. This is because both the extended uneventfulness and the graininess of the projection—even though the latter aspect is only perceptible from close range—are more characteristic of video than of film. However, upon entering the next room, a strong association with the medium of film is reinstated.

Looking, being looked at, and looking at yourself being looked at

The successive film shot which so obviously didn't appear in *American Car*'s projection shown in the first room, seems to be present in the next room. There are two reasons why the image of the car in a landscape can be understood as the shot which would succeed the one of the two men in a narrative film. First of all, as mentioned previously, one of the rules applied in classical narrative fiction film is that a master shot (or establishing shot) of a space must be given when the space and the scene unfolding in it are also mapped out by medium or close-up shots from different angles. The reason for this is that, in order for the spectator to maintain a sense of overview, it needs to be clear how everything which is shown is positioned within the represented space. Thus, in a narrative film, the medium close-up shot of the two men in a car would have had preceding or succeeding establishing shots showing where and how the car of the two men is situated in space. The image of a car in a landscape can therefore be understood as such an establishing shot.

In addition to the rule that medium shots of characters are preceded or followed by an establishing shot which defines their position in space, it is of course customary in classical narrative films to suture images of characters to point-of-view shots. In particular, close-ups of characters who are explicitly looking at something are likely to be preceded, or mostly followed, by a shot which shows us what he or she is looking at. If such a shot clearly corresponds with a character's viewpoint its status as point-of-view shot is clear. Since the two men in the first image of *American Car* so insistently stare at a fixed point outside of their vehicle, the second image can also be understood as a point-of-view shot instead of an establishing shot.

Interestingly, the possibility that the men *in* the car are looking *at* a car is furthermore sustained by the way in which the two flat projections are positioned in relation to each other in the two rooms. Ignoring the space between them for now, the first projection is square to the second projection. This fact becomes relevant in relation to the depiction in the first image. The two men sitting in the car are shown from the back, yet their heads are turned to the left, which is therefore also the direction in which they are looking. Following the direction of their looks, the second flat projection surface is positioned precisely in front of them. Whereas a narrative film which is shown within a traditional viewing set-up can only suggest that a shot shows what the characters are looking at, the *dispositif* of the video installation enables a spatial arrangement in which the characters in *American Car* are actually looking at the shot which shows what they are looking at. That is, if it is assumed that the image of the car shows us their point of view.

Both possibilities for understanding *American Car*'s second image—as an establishing shot or as point-of-view shot—can be considered. And although the effect of the overall piece depends on how the second image is understood, both options have the following two effects on the spectator. First, the viewer who perceives the work is looked at by the characters. Secondly, the viewer seems to become part of the illusionistic space which is mapped out by the film shots.

If the second image is understood as an establishing shot, and hence as showing the car in which the two men are sitting, the spectator is looked at by the men in the car in the second image. Because the left side of the car is shown in the second projection, and the men in the car were shown peering out of the left front window of the car in the first image, they must be looking straight at the viewer who is standing in the second room. If the two images of *American Car* were to succeed each other in a narrative film, the spectator would probably not have a very strong impression of being watched. As neither the men in the car nor their gazes are perceptible in the second shot, the characters' looks can only be supposed to point in the direction of the viewer. Moreover, in a narrative film, it would soon become clear which event or character from inside the film's diegesis the detectives are waiting for. This does not become clear in *American Car*, however, for as in the first image, nothing happens in the second one either. The question which was raised by *American Car*'s first projection—who or what are the two detectives observing?—can therefore only be answered with: the viewer.

If we regard the second image as a point-of-view shot, the viewer is also looked at by the two men, but this time from out of the first projection. For as we have seen, shots suggestively related by character looks create spatial continuity, since the spatial position of the looking character and the spatial position of the things he or she looks at are connected by the direction of the look itself, which appears to cross the space between them rectilinearly. The space which is crossed by such a look in narrative films is an illusionistic space within the film, a space in or behind the film screen. In *American Car*, however, the look of the two characters also seems to cross the real space of the exhibition rooms if the second image is understood as their point of view. For, as explained previously, the two men quite literally look at the image of the landscape (possibly) representing their viewpoint because of the spatial arrangement of the two projections. Therefore, if it is assumed that the second projection shows what the two men are looking at, then the viewer who is looking at the car in the landscape is standing physically in the men's field of vision, within the illusionistic film space.

Hence, as in *k.364*, the proscenium is breached by Claerbout's installation, as the real space of the exposition room seems to simultaneously be the illusionistic space between the two men in the car, and the car in the landscape. Even if the second image is not understood as a point-of-view shot, the real space between the images would stand in relation to the illusionistic space that is mapped out by the camera's shift from the inside to the outside of the car. Walking from one image to the next can then be experienced as a trajectory in a direction opposite to that traversed by the camera.[4] Thus, as a whole, *American Car* occupies an actual three dimensional space, for the space between the two projections is not vacant; it is enclosed by the two related images. However, the way in which the images are related causes the illusionistic space within the images to expand into the real space of the exposition rooms. Consequently, the viewer is physically positioned within both the real space occupied by the work, *and* within the illusionistic space of the images which expands into this real space. It goes without saying that this position offered to the viewer gives rise to an embodied mode of looking. For it is in bodily form that the spectator can stand and walk through the spaces occupied and formed by *American Car.*

However, this embodying effect is not a given when it comes to video installations in which the illusionistic space "breaks over" the ground of the exhibition space, as Morse would put it. In some instances, the actual space can lose its concreteness, and the viewer can lose her awareness of being in a museum or gallery space. In other words, the presentational art form of the multi-screen video installation can produce a reality effect which is so strong that it eliminates the real space and produces a disembodied spectator. For even though she is physically present between the screens, and has to move her body in order to behold the surrounding screens, the viewer of a multi-screen installation can still become so engrossed in the story world that she momentarily forgets her own bodily position in the exhibition space. At such moments, the three-dimensionality of the video installation appears to come close to the potential which Bazin saw in cinema; to depict the profilmic world as real as reality. In its ultimate, most complete form, "total cinema" would be able to imitate, replicate and reproduce allegedly objective reality without the hindrance of material limitations or artificial interventions such as cuts and camera swerves—the latter being absent from *American Car*, and extremely limited in many other installations which apply this particular video *dispositif* in relation to narrative cinema.[5]

However, most of the time, multi-screen installations that produce an illusionistic space which covers the exhibition space leave some room for the actual exhibition space itself. They give rise to the impression of being in two places at once; within the space of representation as well as the represented space. In this sense, the multi-screen *dispositif* resembles the older video *dispositif* of the live feedback set-up, in which the viewer features in both the represented and viewing space. The difference is, of course, that the viewer of multi-screen installations usually isn't split in two; she doesn't look at herself within the screen world. *American Car* forms an interesting exception to this rule, though. For in Claerbout's installation, the spectator can be said to be looking at herself. After all, sharing the point of view with a character when looking at a point-of-view shot invites the viewer to imaginatively occupy the place the character occupies within his/her diegesis.

Therefore, when looking at *American Car*, the viewer can both be standing in the room while being looked at by the two men, and simultaneously be with the men in the car in order to look at herself. The cinematic identification process by which the film spectator is supposed to enter the film as a disembodied entity, now becomes an act which leads the spectator back to her own embodied existence between the screens. She is persuaded to imagine looking at herself standing in the room while looking. Naturally, this imaginative act only contributes to the spectator's awareness of her own body, the position of this body in space, and the fact that this body is present at the time of looking.

Yet, even without this process of identification by which the viewer looks at herself looking, the fact that the spectator is looked at by the men in the car is in itself sufficient to produce an embodied mode of looking. For, when the spectator is looked at by the characters in a representation, this can be understood as visual address which turns the viewer into a "you," a partner inhabiting the same world. It acknowledges the physical presence of the spectator, and breaks through the division between the time and space of the representation and the time and space the spectator resides in.[6]

In addition, in *American Car*, the spectator's physical presence is not only acknowledged by the fact that the characters are looking at her. Because it is raining in the projection showing the two men in the car, and it has just stopped raining in the image showing the car in a *wet* landscape, some time has past between the two "shots."[7] In this respect, *American Car* differs from *Zidane* and *k.364*, in which multiple screens represent the same moment. Through a subtle and short lapse of time, Claerbout's installation seems to take into account that it takes time for the viewer to move from one room to the next. In other words, the slight change between the two images acknowledges the physical presence and action of the viewer. Finally, the ambiguity of *American Car*'s second image can in itself be said to contribute to the embodiment of the spectator. For, when it comes to the embodying effects of the video work, it doesn't really matter whether this second image is understood as an establishing shot or a point-of-view shot. In both cases, the spectator is looked at and seemingly positioned in illusionistic space. However, how the second image is understood affects how the spectator is looked at, and how the viewer's movement through real space relates to the illusionistic space mapped out by the two "shots." The gazes which are directed towards the viewer can come from different directions, either from the first or the second projection. And the trajectory she takes through real space is either congruous with the direction in which the gazes of the characters cross an illusionistic space, or is opposed to the camera's course through an illusionistic space. These multiple possibilities are not necessarily mutually exclusive, however. The viewer does not have to regard the second image as either an establishing shot or a point-of-view shot; she can consider both options at the same time or alternately while beholding the video work. This would imply that looks can come from every direction—perhaps even simultaneously—and that the illusionistic space between the images is constructed in two different ways. The complication caused by these double possibilities only contributes to the viewer's awareness of her own body in space, for she has to actively consider—and perhaps decide over and over again—which space she is in, and how she is looked at.

Questioning the medium

In sum, *American Car* clearly produces an embodied spectator through aspects which are more typical of video's *dispositifs* than film's dominant viewing conditions. The uneventfulness which incites the spectator to action, and the spatial construction of two related projections in which the spectator is positioned, are both aspects which have become characteristic of video artworks because these expressive and formal possibilities enabled by the medium's support have excessively been applied—the latter mainly in video installation art. Moreover, although *American Car* refers to film, it deviates from some of the most important conventions of the dominant cinematic *dispositif.* First, characters looking at the viewer—as those in *American Car* do indirectly—are an anomaly in classical narrative films. Actors in such films do not look into the camera so as to keep the film's diegesis closed off from the world outside the screen. This already indicates the main reason for which *American Car* differs strongly from film: it does not keep the world represented on screen closed off from the one in front of it.

A connection between the diegesis on screen and the one in front of it is, however, not only caused by the characters' looks being directed at the viewer. The breach of the division between them is far more radical, because the illusionistic space represented in the images seems to extend into the real space in front of them by the spatial positioning of the projections. With this, *American Car* differs from classical narrative film and the convention belonging to this dominant application of the filmic medium of representing a contained diegesis. The ostensible extension of illusionistic space into real space differs from film in a wider sense, because film is regarded as a proscenium art. Even if the film spectator is addressed by characters on screen, the illusionistic space represented by film can never be entered physically by the beholder. And although the viewer of *American Car* still cannot enter into the space *on* the flat surface of the projections, she does seem to enter into the illusionistic space which is suggested between them.

American Car, then, looks like video in important respects, and very much unlike film in others. A conclusion which can be drawn is that although the video work refers to film, its medium is overtly video. In addition, it can be argued that the effect of the work on the spectator is mostly enabled by features typical of video, which again shows that this is actually the medium of the work. Any initial doubt as to the medium of *American Car* could now be regarded as settled. This rash conclusion, however, doesn't account for the work's reference to film. Should this reference to film be regarded as superfluous? And moreover, are the work's overt differences from film irrelevant?

Both these questions can be answered in the negative. As I argue below, the medium of film cannot be excluded from the work as unimportant for three reasons. First, because the reference to film does to a large extent enable the embodied mode of looking which is produced by the overall piece. Secondly, because the strong association with film upholds doubt on whether—in spite of all the differences—the medium of the work might nevertheless be film. Finally, because *American Car* gives rise to a reflection on the specificity of film.

The association with classical narrative fiction film has an important function in the embodiment of the spectator throughout the viewing process. Earlier, I explained how the viewer is eventually invited to an embodied mode of looking by the extended uneventfulness in *American Car*'s first projection. The process leading up to the spectator's awareness of the fact that viewing takes time—waiting for the action to start, doubting if it will ever start, getting impatient or bored, and then realizing that no action will ever start—depends to a large extent on the familiarity of the depicted scene. For the viewer's expectation that something is about to happen, and her willingness to wait for it in spite of the fact that the scene is uneventful from the beginning, depends on the resemblance of the scene to a recognizable situation in narrative fiction films.

What is more, the fact that both of the projections are regarded as film shots once the spectator has entered the second room affects the manner in which the two images can be related by the viewer. The fact that the viewer can have the impression of being looked at, or can have the sense of entering the illusionistic space mapped out by shots, is wholly dependent on familiarity with the way in which successive shots map out a space in narrative fiction films. The spatial construction of two related screens—which is a customary form of the medium of video—is in itself not enough to evoke the impression that the illusionistic space of the images extends into real space. This impression only arises when the two projections are related to each other *as* film shots. Therefore, the association with the conventions of narrative fiction film is needed throughout the viewing process in order for the abovementioned effects to arise.

Besides the fact that the association with film is needed for these effects, the association with film evoked by the video work is likely to be determinative of the way the spectator perceives the medium of the work. Previously, I claimed that almost every aspect of a work which produces an embodied mode of looking, as well as the production of an embodied mode of looking itself, are characteristic of video, and that the medium of *American Car* can therefore be understood as video. However, although the abovementioned aspects—including the production of an embodied mode of looking—can be taken into account as characteristic of video, they are not completely decisive in determining the medium of *American Car.* Because the work's reference to film is so prominent, the impression of walking through a space mapped out by film shots is likely to prevail in most viewers. Yet, the video installation differs from film in many respects. These differences, however, do not necessarily lead to the conclusion that the medium of *American Car* then must be video. They rather lead to the question of whether the medium of the work can possibly be film.

Previously, I have argued that the specificity of a medium consists of both a technical support and a set of conventions, both of which are determinative for the medium's specific field of possibilities. The conventions of which a medium consists determine which possibilities offered by a medium's technical support are used, and thereby become specific to the medium (i.e., part of the medium's field of possibilities). This counts for both video and film; many of their characteristic possibilities have become typical of them because they are repeatedly used. Similarly, many of the possibilities that the technical supports of film and video offer remain unused by convention, and are therefore not part of their field.

The most important aspects through which *American Car* produces an embodied spectator—extended uneventfulness and the spatial construction of the two screens—are conventional characteristics of the medium of video, as they have become typical through repeated usage. In a technical respect, however, these aspects are not unique to video. The same extended uneventfulness could be expressed with the use of film's technical support, and there is no reason for which two film projections could not be shown in two adjacent rooms. The problem is that those aspects are not by convention specific to film. It would be unusual for a film to show the same uneventful scene for hours on end. And in its typical form, film only exists with one projection screen. Moreover, film mostly does not produce an embodied spectator. Therefore, the question of whether the medium of *American Car* can be film now leads to the following question: is a film still a film if it doesn't meet the conventional limitation of the possibilities which the medium's technical support offers? When it comes to the technical support of film alone, the medium of *American Car* could be film.

The above question is not answered by *American Car.* Rather, it is only posed. However, by just raising the question of whether the video work *could* be film in an unusual form, doing unusual things, *American Car* compels the viewer to consider the technical possibilities of film. In this way, the work might lead to the realization that, technically speaking, film is able to deviate from the form it usually takes, from what and how it normally expresses itself, and even from the mode of looking it generally produces. Moreover, *American Car* can evoke awareness of the fact that the technical support of film is able to equal the characteristic aspects of video which are used in the work. In all, the video installation not only compels the viewer to realize that film is technically able to expand beyond the limits of its conventional *dispositif*, but also that the specificity of both film and video are to a large extent based on conventions, and therefore historically relative.

Video without attractions

Yet, in spite of the fact that *American Car* could technically be film, and can even be understood as *being* film, the actual medium of *American Car* is not film, but video. This is important especially because of the historical relativity of the specificity of the two media. When seen in a historical perspective, it is significant that video is able to show largely unused technical possibilities of film's support.

As mentioned previously, in the history of film, the medium has not always been used for the production of narrative fiction films representing an enclosed diegesis, nor have its viewing conditions always been predominantly ruled by traditional cinematic *dispositifs.* When the medium was newly invented, the so-called cinema of attractions functioned within a *dispositif* that is unlike the traditional *dispositif* of narrative cinema that has become prevalent in later decades. These early films did not represent a contained story world; the characters in them seemed to acknowledge the presence of the viewer. They addressed the spectator and put on a performance in order to entertain her. In addition, the acts represented in those early films—such as pulling funny faces and physical slapstick—call for a bodily response by the spectator. After about 1906, however, the cinema of attractions had to make way for classical narrative cinema, which from then on became the dominant mode of filmmaking. There, the disembodied spectator was, as we know, strictly separated from the world on screen.

In *American Car,* the spectator is in part invited to an embodied mode of looking by a characteristic convention video had acquired through its use when it had just become accessible to artists. In the 1970s, artists used the medium of video to show uneventfulness and prolongation. Importantly, these characteristics of video partly came into being as a reaction to narrative fiction film. The features of uneventfulness and prolongation were meant to counter the accelerated and compressed time which had become common in many narrative fiction films. In Claerbout's video work, the uneventfulness and extended duration of the first projection embodies the spectator by compelling her into action, into making the decision to walk from one room to the next.

American Car stimulates one to realize that the specificity of both video and film are largely conventional. Because of the work's reference to film, the video piece evokes the awareness that the technical support of film is able to function in *dispositifs* which differ in many respects from cinema's dominant viewing configuration. Moreover, in spite of all the video aspects in *American Car*, the work ultimately still looks like film with a twist because the resemblance of the first depicted scene to a conventional narrative film scene is indelible. This twist, then, is clearly provided by video. Therefore, video seems to lend one of its characteristics—uneventful prolongation—to precisely that which this aspect was meant to counter in the eyes of the first video artists; narrative fiction film. Consequently, video exposes the technical possibility of film to produce an embodied spectator. However, the way in which film is shown to be able to do this, is quite unlike the way in which the medium of film once did give rise to an embodied mode of looking. For instead of putting on a performance in order to provoke a reaction in the viewer—as the cinema of attraction films did—*American Car* provokes the viewer into physical action by removing all action from narrative fiction film.

Bordeaux Piece: looking through sound

Bordeaux Piece offers two viewing positions to the spectator. The first is a mobile, upright position which gives rise to an embodied mode of looking. The second is a seated and immobile position which produces a disembodied mode of looking. Both positions and modes of looking resemble the *dispositifs* which are characteristic of video and film respectively. Moreover, *Bordeaux Piece* looks either like video or film, depending on the viewing position from which it is watched. The different *dispositifs* in which the video projection can be watched not only involve different *viewing* positions; both positions also offer a different soundtrack. The soundtrack which accompanies films as well as videos is often forgotten in discussions of the *dispositif*, as the concept has been developed predominantly in theories which focus on vision and visuality. Yet, *Bordeaux Piece* emphasizes that soundtracks are of paramount importance to the ways in which images are, or can be, watched. Moreover, in *Bordeaux Piece*, the fact that the viewing positions can be discerned and recognized as two positions at all wholly depends on sound. As I will argue below, this work forms an important contribution to the discussion on the embodiment of the spectator by exposing the strong influence of sound on viewing. In my discussion of *k.364*, I already discussed how narrative time often depends on the soundtrack which accompanies moving images. *Bordeaux Piece*, in addition, exposes how the soundtrack not only affects the temporality of moving images, but also produces spaces—both within and beyond the image frame.

Embodiment by ambient sound

When first entering the room in which the single large-scale projection is shown, the second viewing position is immediately visible, because a couple of benches are positioned in the middle of the room on which wired headphones lie ready for use. In most circumstances, such a position can easily be understood as the only position from which a video work can be completely perceived, because often the headphones suggest that the soundtrack accompanying the image can only be heard through them. This is not the case with *Bordeaux Piece*, however. For even without putting the headphones on, sound can be heard in the exposition room. Subtle rural ambient sounds such as rustling leaves, chirping crickets, twittering birds, and humming bees fill the exposition space. They can easily be related to the projection on view. For, in the projection, medium close-up images of a villa and three characters in and around it alternate with shots that show how this villa is positioned in a vast and mountainous Mediterranean landscape.

The characters depicted by the projected representation are clearly related; they exchange looks and are involved in inaudible conversations. However, as in the video installation version of *k.364*, no coherent narrative can be discerned in the images without the soundtrack of the dialogue between the characters. It is unclear what is happening between the three figures, or how they are related. In fact, not much seems to be happening at all, for no vivid gestures or dramatic facial expressions are shown. Moreover, no events or changes of situation can be detected. In addition, it remains unclear as to how the successive shots express the passage of time. Time lapses or flashbacks are undetectable; nor is it clear whether or not time progresses at all.

Thus, with no accompanying sound other than ambient sound, the images of the villa and the characters in and around it remain incoherent and hard to interpret. Moreover, the rural sounds draw the beholder's attention away from the villa and the characters, and instead direct it to the landscape in which the villa and the characters are positioned; to the swaying trees on the mountain slopes surrounding the villa, and to the bees and butterflies which sometimes pass through the air. What is more, the ambient sound seems to extend beyond the image frame. For although some of its sources are visible within the image, most of them originate far beyond the space that is visible on screen.

Because the ambient sound indicates a space much larger than the illusionistic space represented within the projection frame, this sound seems to extend the illusionistic space of the vast landscape beyond the limits of the image into the exposition room. This impression is especially evoked by the fact that ambient sound is *all* you can hear; no sounds the source of which lies visibly and solely within the image are audible. Such sounds would perhaps redirect the attention of the spectator to the contained illusionistic space on screen. However, in the absence of sounds with an exclusively on-screen source, the illusionistic space on screen seems to expand into the exposition room through the vastness of the ambient "soundscape." Therefore, like *American Car*, *Bordeaux Piece* provides its beholder with the sense of being simultaneously in real space and in the illusionistic space of the representation. However, whereas *American Car* evokes this impression through a spatial construction of two related projections, *Bordeaux Piece* produces the same effect with only one flat image. It is through sound that the viewer seems to be positioned inside—as opposed to in front of—the space formed by *Bordeaux Piece*, and is thereby invited to an embodied mode of looking.

By demonstrating that ambient sound is able to relate the illusionistic space within an image to the real space in which the viewer of the image resides, *Bordeaux Piece* makes an important contribution to the discussion of the embodiment of the spectator. For although Morse has convincingly argued that the spectator becomes an embodied viewer by being in the same space which an artwork occupies or constructs, her discussion—like many discussions of *dispositifs*—remains mainly confined to the material and visual aspects of art forms. *Bordeaux Piece* proves, however, that sound can be added as an important aspect to producing an embodied spectator by artworks and their spatial viewing set-up. Yet, it is important to note that it isn't the aspect of sound in itself which produces an embodied spectator. It is its combination with images which enables sound to effect a seeming expansion of the illusionistic image space into the real space which the beholder physically occupies.[8]

As noted above, another important effect of the fact that ambient sound is all you can hear in the first *dispositif* of *Bordeaux Piece* is that a coherent story remains indiscernible. This is important because as soon as you, as a spectator, abandon any attempt to reconstruct the story which only *seems* to evolve on screen without ever becoming truly discernible, two important temporal aspects of the video work become more noticeable. For, once it becomes clear that time cannot be extracted from the unreconstructable narrative, it has to be looked for or measured differently by the viewer.

One way in which this can be done is by paying attention to the brightness and color of sunlight, and to the position of the sun within the sky that appears sporadically in the images. After a while, it appears that the intensity of the daylight is slowly changing, and that the position of the sun is shifting as well. The pace at which this process occurs is more or less congruous with the natural pace at which the sun rises and sets again every day. In *Bordeaux Piece* it takes thirteen hours for the sun to rise and set: the average length of a West-European summer day is the length of the video itself.

In addition, by paying attention to such a change or progression in order to measure time, repetition becomes noticeable in *Bordeaux Piece*. Every ten minutes, the same prolonged shot of the landscape is shown. Then, suddenly, one of the characters walks into the frame. From then on, everything is repeated, the same shots succeed each other, and the characters repeat the same minimal gestures and restrained expressions all over again. Because hardly any differences can be detected between the repeated parts, it almost seems as if the video is looped. The position of the sun, however, keeps shifting slowly throughout the fragments.

Both temporal features mentioned above—real, unaccelerated time, and repetition—can be recognized as characteristic of video. Importantly, although ambient sound itself is not a typical feature of video, it is mainly due to the soundtrack that these typical features of video become noticeable. For, when the soundtrack is altered in the second position from which the video work can be watched, these features become less apparent. Which is why *Bordeaux Piece* mainly looks like video from the first viewing/listening position.

Moreover, the real, unaccelerated time which becomes noticeable in *Bordeaux Piece* contributes to the production of an embodied spectator. First, because the real time represented in the work is congruous with the real time in which the spectator resides. Even the time which is indicated by the position of the sun in *Bordeaux Piece* can more or less coincide with the time of day at which the spectator is looking at the work, for the work is often screened for its entire duration, starting at sunrise.[9] Secondly, and more importantly, this represented time can produce an embodied spectator because, if it is assumed that the video runs in real time, it *could* be live, which would only enhance the embodiment of the spectator. It does not really matter if the images are truly broadcast live; the mere suggestion is enough to evoke the impression in the viewer that she physically exists at the same moment as the images.

In sum, the sound which is audible in the first viewing/listening position is not typical of video, yet it does make the work look like video. First, it produces an embodied spectator by enabling the illusionistic space within the image to seemingly expand into the actual exposition room. This production of an embodied spectator can be recognized as typical of video, even if it isn't caused by a feature specific to video in this regard. Secondly, the soundtrack makes temporal features noticeable that are characteristic of video, and therefore lead to the assumption that the medium of *Bordeaux Piece* is video. Thirdly, the discernment of one of these characteristics—real, unaccelerated time—gives further rise to an embodied mode of looking.

Disembodiment by dialogue

Whereas *Bordeaux Piece* looks like video from the first viewing/listening position, it looks like film from the second one, if only because of the viewing position itself. The silent and immobile viewing position which *Bordeaux Piece* offers alongside the more embodied one has become so specific to film that these aspects in themselves lead to the inclination of regarding images on view as cinematic ones. In the second *dispositif*, immobility is quite literally enforced on the spectator. Because the headphones which the viewer is invited to put on are wired, turning one's head in any other direction than the screen is hardly impossible. The well-known comparison of film's *dispositif* to the prisoners in Plato's cave applies unequivocally to the second viewing set-up. "Chained" by the wires of the headphones, the spectator of Claerbout's piece is compelled to look forwards at the projection screen. Moreover, like the prisoners in Plato's cave, she is stimulated by the set-up to accept the projected images as "real."

When viewed from this distant position, the surface of the projected images on view looks incredibly transparent. The sharpness and brightness of the images match the high quality which film images can have. Only closely approaching the screen—which *is* possible from the first mobile viewing position—would bring the materiality, as well as the actual medium, of the image to light: from up close, digital video pixelation can be perceived.[10] However, the second, immobile viewing position obliges the spectator to keep a distance from the screen, and invites her to sink into the represented world with her eyes.

This cinematic invitation into the depicted world is further affirmed when another characteristic of film becomes apparent in this second viewing/listening position, namely narrativity. As opposed to the soundtrack which jointly produced the first *dispositif*, the soundtrack which is audible through the headphones does contain dialogue. Moreover, the ambient sound which dominated the first viewing position is now substantially diminished. Because of the dialogue, the narrative, which could only be guessed at from the first position, now becomes entirely discernible. A story unfolds about the diminishing love of a woman for her husband, and her budding affair with another man. The two men, in addition, are in dispute over a film script which the woman's husband is writing, and which the other man is going to produce. In this respect, among many others, the story in *Bordeaux Piece* resembles Jean Luc Godard's film *Le mépris* (1963). Thus, the video work doesn't just look like a narrative film from the second viewing/listening configuration; it also refers to one.

As soon as the story of *Bordeaux Piece* becomes perceivable (through dialogue) from the second position, the viewing position itself comes to resemble the conventional cinematic *dispositif* even further. The narrative forms an enclosed fictional story. Consequently, the spectator is separated from the time and space on screen. As the rural ambient sounds are diminished, the earlier impression of the illusionistic space expanding into the real space of the spectator is no longer evoked. Instead, because a narrative unfolds through the dialogue, the on-screen foreground space is the space between the three characters. This space between them becomes more apparent for two reasons.

First, because the spatial relations indicated between them through different shots can be reconstructed now that these shots are related through narrative—an effect which could also be noted in the film version of *k.364*. Secondly, because the spatial relations between the characters become invested with meaning through the story, for the emotional, romantic, or discordant relationships which the story exposes between the characters bind the characters through space. Moreover, these emotional and psychological relationships make the spatial distances between the characters—their remoteness or proximity to each other—more significant.[11] In all, in the second *dispositif* of *Bordeaux Piece*, the narrative space between the three characters is activated, while the viewer's space is left unaddressed and untouched by this other, enclosed story world.

Similarly, the time which becomes noticeable through the characters' dialogue excludes the viewer from the video work. For the narrative which emerges turns out to represent a linearly progressing, compressed form of time which is unlike the real time in which the spectator exists. In *Bordeaux Piece*, this compression of time is mainly achieved by time lapses. When one shot succeeds another, a considerable amount of story time has passed. Like the spatial relationships between shots, the temporal relationships between them can only be appreciated because they are explained by the overall narrative on the evolving relationships between the three characters.

However, from the second position, *Bordeaux Piece* only looks completely like film for a limited period. After ten minutes or so, the resemblance to conventional narrative film diminishes because an aspect characteristic of video becomes noticeable. The repetition of the fragment which was visible from the first position also becomes noticeable from the second one. Once the story has ended, it starts all over again. Thus, although the characteristics which make *Bordeaux Piece* look like film from the second viewing/listening position remain unchanged, a video aspect eventually "infiltrates." As a result, the medium of film seems to change (back) somewhat into the medium of video.

One medium, or a medium within a medium

Because the medium of video eventually becomes noticeable from the second position, film can be said to be embedded in the medium of video in *Bordeaux Piece*. This conclusion is further sustained by the fact that the second viewing position, from which *Bordeaux Piece* initially looks like film, is spatially embedded in the first one, from which the work looks like video. For although the two viewing/listening positions can be alternately adopted by the beholder, the first position is automatically taken up by the spectator as soon as she enters the room. Only after having walked through the exposition space while hearing the ambient sounds, can the spectator choose to sit on the bench. In addition, the work's disembodied seated viewing position, which is typical of film's dominant *dispositif*, becomes even more like the embodied viewing position of video in the respect that, as it is embedded in this mobile viewing position, it is presented as an option to the viewer. Because the spectator is required to make a conscious choice between two possible positions, both sitting down and remaining statically seated become necessarily consciously performed physical acts. Furthermore, film seems to be embedded in video because the narrativity which only becomes fully manifest from the second position, is already latently present when the work is perceived from the first position. As the work looks like video from the latter position, the more filmic aspect of narrativity seems to be latently present in the medium of video as well.

The question remains as to whether the medium of the work should be understood as video, or if film is still present in *Bordeaux Piece* as a medium within a medium. On the one hand, video seems to have absorbed the medium of film completely. However, the actual support of the video work is digital video. This can be perceived, as mentioned previously, by looking at the screen from close range. For when doing so, digital video pixelation can be detected. Thus, it is possible to say that the work demonstrates how the medium of (digital) video is able to imitate film. It can copy film's viewing position, equal its narrative capabilities, and meet the high quality of its images. By showing these capabilities, *Bordeaux Piece* exposes the relativity of film's specificity. On the other hand, the medium of *Bordeaux Piece* does not necessarily have to be determined on the basis of its technical support. Moreover, the medium of the work does not necessarily have to be singular. The medium of *Bordeaux Piece* can also be regarded as that which the spectator understands it to be, if only for a moment. A medium is also what we—its beholders—think it is. If the seated, immobile viewing position, as well as the narrative structure visible from this position, are still understood as characteristic of film, they cause the viewer to *see* film, not video. Hence, the *dispositif* decides which medium is seen, regardless of the technological base which has produced that *dispositif.* Following this thread of argument, film just *is* film in *Bordeaux Piece* for as long as the spectator recognizes the work as film from *and because of* the second viewing position. When accepting this conclusion, film exists within *Bordeaux Piece* as a medium within a medium, while both medium-typical *dispositifs* exist within the single artwork.

Both conclusions drawn above are valid, for *Bordeaux Piece* itself does not provide a clear-cut answer to what its medium is. It rather provokes the question as to whether and how it is decided in relation to the two *dispositifs* the installation presents. The artwork in question seems to point out that particular viewing set-ups not only influence the meaning and effect of the images on view, but also their medium. Not only is the viewer offered the possibility to choose and alternate between different *dispositifs*, it is the viewer who potentially relates the viewing configurations to different media, who decides which features count as characteristic and specific of film and video—since what medium is seen depends on what is regarded as typical of which medium.

This part started out with the assumption that media affect the spectator through their medium-specific *dispositifs*. Either by their conventional characteristics or through technical possibilities, the *dispositifs* of film and video produce modes of looking or viewing positions. Following this line of argument, the viewer was theorized to be an effect of the medium. *Bordeaux Piece* shows that the assumption with which this part started out can be reversed. The media of film and video each produce a viewing subject, yet the two media are also an effect of the way in which the viewer beholds projected images. This reciprocal relationship of determination between medium and user will be central to the next part on social structures.

PART III
SOCIAL STRUCTURES

INTRODUCTION: FRAMING THE MEDIUM

"Meaning is context-bound, but context is boundless." This famous phrase by Jonathan Culler is still very apt if the word meaning is replaced with the word medium. Although it would be relevant to pair up the first part of the phrase with its reverse ("Context is medium-bound") in order to consider the reciprocity of the relationship, there is no question that every medium is related to its context. As Culler explains, "there is no limit in principle to what might be included in a context, to what might be shown to be relevant to the object, event, text, speech act or medium in question. Therefore, context is not given but produced; what belongs in a context is determined by interpretative strategies; contexts are just as much an elucidation of events; and the meaning of a context is determined by events" (Culler 1988: xiv). In order to avoid the positivistic "giveness" which is often associated with the context idea, Culler proposes the term framing in place of context. As a verb, this term reminds us that framing is something we do, not something we find.

In this part, I will frame the media of film and video within the social field. I chose the social over many of the other general categories which constitute the context of film and video, such as the cultural, the historical and the political. The social relationships within which the two media will be framed cannot entirely be disentangled from these other aspects or categories. For the social sphere is closely tied to culture, history, and politics, or rather, the social *is* cultural, historical, and political. In addition, the concept of the social has many meanings and connotations. I will use it in a very broad sense to refer to interrelations (through interaction) between human subjects. The notion of the social is often used to refer to the public, as opposed to the private. This usage can be confusing when it comes to, for instance, familial relationships or close friendships, for these relationships are social structures which are often considered to belong predominantly to the private domain. Therefore, I will not use the social as a synonym for the public in this part. However, the contrast between private and public (or between micro and macro levels of social organization) does play an important part in specifications of film and video vis-à-vis the social. It is impossible to frame the frame; no clear-cut impermeable limits can be drawn around the category of the social, nor does it have a stable, singular meaning. Therefore, the (social as a) frame should be understood as a focus for attention, not as an enclosed sphere.

Out of the boundless context of the two media, I have selected the social domain as a particularly relevant frame for film and video for several reasons. For a start, the concept of the medium in general induces an investigation of social relationships. A medium mediates. It is the medium in between. As such, it is not only related to its own (boundless) context; the medium also necessarily relates parts and positions within this context. In Part I, these positions were discussed as spatial and temporal ones. Media are in between moments in time and positions in space; they span temporal and/or spatial distances. However, if the medium is understood as "in between," the question should not only be in between *what*, *where*, and *when*, but also in between *whom*?

The human subjects to whom film and video relate have been discussed in the previous parts. In fact, one of the main points of interest of this book is the reciprocal relationship between the medium and the users of the medium (both the producers and viewers/readers of media objects). However, now that the social field is introduced as a central frame, a slight shift of focus occurs. Instead of studying the relationship between the medium and its users, the relationship that will be analyzed is the one between the medium on the one hand and the social relationships between its users on the other. In other words, the question changes from "how is the medium related to the human subjects who use it?" to "how is the medium related to the relationships between the human subjects who use it?"[1]

In addition to the fact that the concept of the medium in general necessitates attention to the social field, this field is especially important to an investigation of film and video. First, video came into being in the same decade in which medium theory (as formulated by, most prominently, Marshall McLuhan) broached the idea that media produce social structures. Many early video practices relate to this dominant, influential idea. Notably, film is not absent from these activist and idealistic video discourses which deal with medium theory. Within the so-called guerilla videos, important stylistic devices were borrowed from the earlier *cinéma vérité* movement, with the aim of adapting social structures.

Secondly, the social field is a particularly relevant frame for the media of film and video because out of all the fields within which the two media operate, the social field points out most clearly the internal differentiation of the two media. Baker's model of the medium itself being a field of—possibly opposing—possibilities and applications again proves to be very suitable here. Especially when the fields of film and video are framed by their operation within the social field, the specificity of the two media proves to be fraught with contradictions. The abilities and applications of both film and video in relation to social structures are manifold, and they seem to oppose one another.

On the one hand, video is often celebrated for its capacity to create communities and to serve individuals in establishing their social identity. On the other hand, the same medium is often described as antisocial. It is said, among other things, to produce narcissistic subjects who can relate to no one but themselves. Although film produces and blocks social relatedness in its own ways, a similar tension between the social and antisocial can be found within specifications and applications of this medium as well. The cinema has for instance been criticized for its isolating viewing conditions. Yet, like video, film has been applied in emancipatory projects which advocate social collaboration. The tension between socially productive and socially obstructive characteristics of film and video has led to both utopian and dystopian perspectives on each of the two media. Their medium-specific influence on social structures is believed either to uplift or to corrupt future societies.

Moreover, the opposition between the (supposedly) social and antisocial characteristics of film and video is closely interwoven with a contradiction between the more helpful, constructive capacities of the media on the one hand, and their violent effects on the other. The reason for this interwovenness is the fact that the production or obstruction of social relationships by the two media has an effect on human subjects; an effect which is consequently valued as either positive or negative. Most of the time, the production of social relationships by film and video is valued as a positive, peaceable act which helps the subjects in question. When, on the other hand, the two media are specified as technologies or structures which block social interaction, they are often described as aggressors which hurt their users. However, the correspondence between social-helpful and antisocial-hurtful does not hold true in every case. Some of the social structures which are sustained by film and video can function oppressively for specific subjects, whereas certain forms of isolation can be experienced positively as intimate and safe.

To make the matter even more complicated, all the utopian, dystopian, positive and negative specifications of the two media are, in turn, produced under the influence of specific social contexts. Therefore, film and video are just as much structured by the social as is the social by the two media. In this part I aim to further analyze the intricate web of interwoven contradictions within the social fields of operation of film and video, as well as the interrelation between the two media and the social contexts in which and by which they are produced. Which technological and conventional aspects of film and video can account for the diverse ways in which the two media (are believed to) affect social structures? Which specifications of film and video have gained the upper hand in the last decades in this respect? What are the differences and similarities between the ways in which film and video (can) relate to the social field? And finally; how do film and video relate to each other when it comes to their operation in the social field? By "zooming in" on some smaller social subfields in which the two media operate, such as the family, therapy and social activism, I will show how film and video have, among other things, displaced, ignored, and imitated each other's social functions. Close readings of intermedial artworks by Lynn Hershman and Sadie Benning will further expose how the two media specify and apply each other within the social field.

Before looking into film and video, however, it is first necessary to discuss how the concept of the medium in general can be related to social structures. The way in which this relationship has been defined (or ignored, or wished away) by scholars from various disciplines depends on the manner in which the particular medium is envisaged by these theorists in the first place. Ideas on what a medium is or does (or is supposed to be or do) are decisive to the way in which it is regarded in relation to the social field.

CHAPTER 13
THE MEDIUM, THE MEDIA, AND THE SOCIAL

Documentation and production

From Egyptian hieroglyphic registrations of genealogical lineages carved into stone statues, to sound recordings of the South-West African Ovambo Group in the National Anthropological Archive, to a collection of black-and-white portrait photographs which aim to map the social groups in twentieth-century Germany, to digital home videos of family get-togethers stored on the hard-disk of a personal computer—the documentation of social structures is age-old and wide-ranging. In spite of the many disparities within the vast field of documentation, the related practices of documenting, mapping, registering, and recording social data have one thing in common; they aim to preserve the information they record for a relatively extended period of time. Because of this, the documentation of social structures goes hand in hand with a particular understanding of the medium. When it comes to documentary practices, greater emphasis is placed on the storing function of the medium (either self-reflexively or unconsciously) than on its transmitting capacities.

The result of this emphasis is that sole attention is paid to the social relationships between the people *within* the object of representation, that is, to the interrelations between the subjects depicted by, for instance, a photograph, a written text or a painting. The view of the medium as a storage facility sometimes goes hand in hand with the notion of the medium as an epistemological tool. By capturing social relationships, media products offer a chance to study the documented social structures.

When the medium is considered as a transmitter instead of a means of storage, can it more easily be envisaged as a tool which relates human subjects and subject positions both in and outside of the representation? As soon as the transmitting action of the medium is emphasized at the expense of its storing, collecting, and capturing functions, the related capacities of media are quickly brought to the fore, because the process of transmitting compels consideration of the subjects who are involved in the process of using a medium. At the edges of the in-between, a source or sender, and a receiver or addressee can be assumed to reside. The medium is then thought of as a communication technology which enables human beings to get in touch with each other.

Discussion of the concept of the medium as a communication technology which connects human beings remains more common within certain disciplines than it is in others. For some sociologists and medium theorists (e.g., Castells, Williams) the idea that a medium enables communication is so self-evident that they use the word "medium" interchangeably with "communication technology." Their main point of investigation is how media socialize human beings. Art historians, on the other hand, seldom describe media as technologies of communication. They rather think of them as materials, inscribed with or without a layer of conventions, which enable artistic expression. In addition, the embeddedness of the medium within the social field is incompatible with art-historical discourses that attach importance to the autonomy of art and the aesthetic field, and with that, the autonomy of the medium of art. These modernist ideals of autonomy and immanence still seep into contemporary reflections on the medium.

Even Rosalind Krauss, who distances herself so explicitly from modernist ideas on the medium in her reflections on the post-medium condition, has trouble shaking off the ideals of interiority and purity that she wishes to overthrow. In *A Voyage on the North Sea* Krauss uses the word *mediums* as the plural of *medium* in order to avoid confusion with *media*, which she reserves for "technologies of communication indicated by that latter term" (1999: 57). Although Krauss does not explain how *mediums* differ exactly from such technologies of communication, she uses the term to refer to what she also calls *aesthetic* media; media used within the domain of art as a support for artistic expression. For Krauss, the distinction between mediums of art and popular mass media is important, because she believes that when the two are leveled, art is reduced to "a system of pure equivalency by the homogenizing principle of commodification" (15). Within the international fashion of installation and intermedia work, Krauss decides, the aesthetic leeches out into the social field in general, and "art finds itself complicit with a globalization of the image in the service of capital" (56).

Although Krauss is well aware of the fact that the idea of an interior uncontaminated by an exterior (or a medium uncontaminated by its context) is no longer tenable after poststructuralist theory as well as postmodernist art, she still tries to save the domain of art from contamination by its social, capitalist context. Her condemnation of art practices which mix "high" and "low" media has rightly been critiqued as "a poststructuralist reformulation of Greenberg's modernist principles" (Lütticken 2000: 137–138). According to Sven Lütticken, the strict separation of the self-differentiating logic of artistic "mediums" from the homogenizing force of corporate "media" is our newest *Laocoon*. Only instead of defending the essential differences between the arts (Lessing, Greenberg), Krauss defends the barrier between art (including its mediums) and the rest of the world (including its media).

However, in spite of the fact that Krauss' argument can be criticized for its failure to carry through the poststructuralist ideas it seems to hinge on at first, the distinction between aesthetic "mediums" and the technologies of communication we call "media" is not entirely counterintuitive. The conventional function of traditional artistic media such as painting and sculpture clearly differs from popular mass media such as newspapers or television, the latter being associated with the communication of information, while the former serve aesthetic, artistic goals. To put it differently; some media operate almost exclusively within the field of art, while others tend to be applied within the realms of popular (commercial) culture, mass communication, and the social field in general. It is therefore not remarkable in this respect that, unlike art historians, sociologists focus mostly on the media operating predominantly within the general social field of everyday life when they investigate the relation between media and social forms. For them, the mass media—including the media *industry*—are crucial to our understanding of the social world.

The difference between aesthetic and corporate media is, however, conventional and diminishing, rather than rigid and essential. For, contrary to Krauss' wishes, many media operate within both artistic and nonartistic domains. Moreover, it should be questioned whether the acts Krauss tries to bar from her notion of *mediums*—channeling communication, operation within the social field—can ever be completely excluded from any medium. Even the "highest" aesthetic media are never entirely cut off from acts of communication within a social context.

The distinction between aesthetic and popular media, and the exclusion of technologies of communication from the concept of the medium are especially unsuitable when it comes to the two media which are the subject of this study. Both film and video operate within artistic as well as more popular cultural realms. They are considered to be both mediums of art and as mediums of (mass) entertainment, news gathering, and documentation. Although film is, as a rule, not thought of as a technology of communication, its ability to deliver (ideologically charged) messages to an audience has been widely theorized and analyzed. Within the field of video, the capacity to enable communication is even more dominant than in the field of film. Thus, because videotapes are relatively easy to produce, send and play, video has functioned explicitly as a medium of communication in the form of the video letter. Moreover, unlike film, the electronic video medium offers the possibility of live two-way communication. This possibility is utilized in the case of video conferences. In the last decade, the so-called video conversation has become more and more common as video became part of contemporary internet communication software such as Skype and FaceTime.

The medium is the master

Above, I claimed that media produce social relationships. This raises the issues of agency as well as causality. When media are said to co-produce social bonds, is this effect believed to be under the control of human producers, or do media technologies act on their own in this respect? When it comes to the effect of media on social structures in general, the precise cause of this effect is under debate. Where should the influence of media on society be located? A sociological perspective on media usually directs attention first of all to the influence of the content of media products. Sociologists are interested in media as communication technologies which are of influence in the process of socialization; the process whereby we learn and internalize the values, beliefs, and norms of our culture and, in so doing, develop a sense of self as well as a sense of social belonging. Next to social institutions such as the family and the school, or socializing influences such as peers, (mass) media are powerful socializing agents in contemporary society, as they explicitly or implicitly articulate social norms (Croteau and Hoynes 2003: 156).

However, as Croteau and Hoynes point out in *Media/Society*, the sociological significance of media extends beyond the content of media messages. Media do not merely influence *what* individuals learn about their place in society, but also affect *how* they learn and how they interact with each other (Croteau and Hoynes 2003: 18).[1] As soon as emphasis is put on how instead of what media teach their audience, the influence of technological medium-specific characteristics on social circumstances is brought to the fore. Compared to social studies, media studies tend to pay more attention to this influence of medium-specific characteristics.

The idea that the specificity of a medium affects the social relationships between its users is carried to an extreme in media-theoretical discourses that not only ignore the impact of medial messages, but also abandon the idea that media are used intentionally by human subjects. Subsequently, all power is placed in the hands of the medium itself. In this view, the effects which a medium has on society are not shaped by the information it mediates, nor by the way it is applied by its users. Instead, a medium's social and political effects are explained as a direct result of its basic apparatus. This mode of thinking strongly contrasts with the idea of the medium as a transparent vessel. Instead of considering the technological or physical support of a medium as noninfluential and transparent, the technological characteristics of a medium are regarded as the single source and origin of social structures. As James M. Moran states:

> This form of fixed causality [. . .], better known as "technological determinism," constitutes a transhistorical discourse proposing the belief that media technologies not only dictate aesthetics but organize and govern perception and behavior, acting as the sovereign determinant of social formations and human volition.
>
> 2002: 2

One of the most famous and influential media theorists who reasoned according to the logic of technological determinism was of course Marshall McLuhan, who argued that the technological forms in which people communicate entirely dominate the messages they communicate; hence his well-known sound-bite "the medium is the message" (1964: 1). In the eyes of McLuhan, the technological characteristics of media carry a certain logic which shapes the way human beings think, perceive, behave, and live together. Because of this, media create specific societies, worlds, or environments in which people are related in medium-specific ways.

Although McLuhan's ideas are still well-known, his legacy has been severely criticized by many of the media scholars who succeeded him. Their main point of criticism of the McLuhanian discourse of technological determinism is that it leaves little room for human intention or agency. Cultural theorist and media scholar Ron Burnett outlines the problem as follows:

> Subjects, agents, the people who use new technologies are placed in the position of respondents, as if their discourse will *inevitably* be transcended by the technology. A rear guard is then fought with the technology. An effort is made to humanize the machine, although its history is, of course, the result of human intervention and creativity. What is at stake here is the degree to which the machine can be conceptualized as being in the control of humans. The *idea* that the machine is more powerful than the people who created it confers an even greater sense of strength onto the technology.
>
> 1995: 143

An additional flaw Burnett points out in this line of thought is that the technology is transformed into an "autonomous vehicle with a set of formal concerns which are not derived from the pragmatic context into which the technology is placed" (1995: 143).

The medium as social practice

The ideas of Raymond Williams—one of the most explicit debunkers of technological determinism—are in accordance with those of Burnett when it comes to the overvaluation of the power of technology. In *Marxism and Literature* (1977), he critically analyzes how, in McLuhan, "the medium is (metaphysically) the master" (159). Like Burnett, Williams disagrees with such view of the medium as a master which not only determines "the 'content' of what is communicated, but also the social relationships within which the communication takes place" (159).[2] In line with Burnett's belief that media are incorporated into already existing patterns of use and thought, Williams looks at the impact which culture and its social definitions (traditions, institutions, and formations) have on the medium. He maintains that a medium is itself an effect of the social environment wherein it was produced. Any new technique depends on society and is, at a given phase, defined by specific social relationships (Williams 1977: 163). He eventually defines the medium as *social practice*; as "work on a material for a specific purpose within necessary social conditions" (160).

With Williams' definition, the causal relationship that characterized McLuhan's thinking seems to be reversed. Instead of a relationship in which the medium determines society, society now shapes the medium. Society provides the determining context in which the medium is, as it were, carried out by its users. Williams does not provide a detailed explanation of his notion of the medium as social practice, yet his writings on language as a medium provide some explanation. Language can easily be envisaged as a social practice because it is such an important component of our everyday social life; it shapes all our social relationships and we (re)produce it every day in order to communicate with others. In the words of Williams, language, as a medium, is "a socially shared and reciprocal activity, always already embedded in active relationships, within which every move is an activation of what is already shared and reciprocal or may become so" (1977: 133).

Williams' more general remark that the medium is a social practice can be understood in the same vein. Every medium is socially shared; it functions between people. It enables social relationships yet also depends on them too in order to exist. Like language, a medium is not simply there; it comes into being and stays there by being used in a more or less similar way over and over again. The idea that the medium is something which is "done" by and between human beings does not, however, mean that this act lacks physical, material components. The medium itself is acted on or carried out by its users, yet this activity shapes a material into a specific form. The fact that Williams formulates this process as work *on* a material rather than, for instance, work with or by a material, fits in with his opinion that technology itself is not an actor. Moreover, his definition of the medium as a practice, as work on a material for a specific purpose, rewrites the idea that media dominate their passive respondents. It restores human intention to the use of communications technologies.

Williams and his followers have argued that society not only influences the destiny of a medium after the invention of a technology, but also prior to this moment. According to Williams, it is a characteristic of communications technologies that all were foreseen before their crucial components had even been discovered and refined (1974: 13).[3] Even if parts of the invention process depended on fortunate accidents, the discovery and refinement of technologies should be understood as purposeful; they are directed to central social needs and concrete cultural practices.

Williams has identified and rejected two forms of determinism in which the latter fact is ignored: mechanistic and symptomatic determinism. The first form of determinism (related to McLuhanian discourse) advances the claim that media are self-contained technologies distinct from their cultural environment, yet empowered internally to exercise social effectivity. The second strain, symptomatic determinism, adds the corrective to mechanistic determinism that, although communications technologies may be invented as discrete, external phenomena, they inevitably enter into the dominant mode of economic and social production, the institutions of which then act on and with the technology to determine its cultural effects (Moran 2002: 3). However, as Moran correctly notes:

> Although symptomatic causality advances on the mechanistic strain by denying autonomous effectivity outside of social formations, it disregards the way in which technologies have been shaped by institutions at their onset,

> casting media as a neutral base for a variety of cultural uses, whose positive or negative values will be wholly determined by the good and evil forces that shape them.
>
> 2002: 3

Many theorists who—like Williams and Moran—refute symptomatic determinism, underline Moran's remark that technology is not a neutral base which was invented and developed independently of a social, cultural, and historical environment. Jennifer Slack states in her study *Communications Technologies and Society* (1984) that it is impossible to generalize about "the technology" as the same physical object, identically constituted, in different historical or social configurations. Slack regards any technology as a historical object, the constitution of which is a social, cultural process. Burnett (1995: 172) subscribes to this viewpoint when he argues against the understanding of a new technology as a "found object" which comes into being in a sphere devoid of subjectivity. Subjectivity is involved at all stages—in the process of inventing, using, and understanding a technology—"and there are no peripheral moments when technology takes on a life of its own" (148).

In this light, it is remarkable that both Williams and adherents of his ideas see the term medium as interchangeable with the terms technology or communication technology. For, at first sight, this seems to be incompatible with some of the most important aspects of Williams' discourse; namely the emphasis on human intention in the development and use of media, the belief that a medium is a social practice, and the idea that a medium is determined by its social, cultural, and historical context. When Williams' conceptualization of the medium is compared to Krauss' definition of the medium as a differential structure consisting of a technical support plus a set of conventions, Williams' theory seems to be in line with Krauss' ideas. Like Krauss, he believes a medium is in part produced by the (conventional) way in which it is used, and that a medium's specificity depends on its social, cultural, and historical context. Moreover, both theorists claim that a medium is more than a bare, autonomous, physical or technological support. So how can Williams and his followers nevertheless refer to "medium" as "technology"?

An important difference between Krauss' medium theory and Williams' discourse, is that in the former, technology can be still be imagined as a bare neutral base, while in the latter, technology is always an historical, social, and cultural construct. For Krauss, technology only becomes a medium when conventions are added to a technological support when it is used and appropriated in a context. For Williams, however, technology itself is always already inscribed by and within such conventions. In his opinion, Krauss' definition would fall under the category of symptomatic determinism, as it stipulates that technology is a physical object which can exist untouched by a social, cultural, and historical environment. Technology as understood by Williams is comparable with the way Krauss defines the medium in that both are regarded as related to and intertwined with social, cultural, and historical context. The difference is that Krauss' medium can consist of two successive parts (first technology, then cultural and social conventions), while Williams' technology cannot be seen apart from, or anterior to, the cultural and social aspects by which it is shaped. Hence, Williams' technology is a "Kraussian" medium from the onset.

While closely following Williams in a study on the specificity of home video, James Moran adds to Williams' theory that a medium's technological base can be thought of as a set of discursive codes:

> [...] rather than identify a medium according to its ontological purity, predetermined effects, and material apparatus, we must instead rethink a medium's technological base as constituted in hybridity, as an effect of social and cultural determinations, and as a set of discursive codes to apprehend its historical rather than essential specificity.
>
> 2002: 16

Moran's proposal to think of the medium as a set of discursive codes is similar to the opinion of art historian David Green mentioned in the introduction; namely his claim that "a medium is what we think it is" (2005: 23). Medium specificity can be understood as the result of medium *specification*, meaning that descriptions, perceptions, and interpretations of a medium—instead of its material, ontological essence—decide what a medium is. The importance of Moran's comment is that it proposes considering the technological base of a medium as a discursive construct. For even theorists who—like Rosalind Krauss—support the notion of medium specificity as a conventional structure produced through practice and in discourse, often still consider the material support of a medium as an autonomous object on which conventional applications or imaginary conceits about the medium are constructed.

When we see Krauss' definition of the medium in light of Williams' and Moran's writings, it becomes clear that Krauss' theory once again does not manage to escape the Greenbergian discourse of an essential, pure specificity which she so desperately wants to overturn. For, at the basis of the medium, she still presumes a pure, uncultured, extra-discursive, material object. This object can be "dressed up" with conventions in order to be (re)invented as a medium.

However, although Williams' and Moran's contextualization of technology admirably overcomes essentialist and determinist notions of the medium, their ideas also raise the question of whether the material aspects of a medium can and should now be taken into consideration at all to grasp the effects of a medium. Williams has defined the medium as work on a material; but doesn't the material have an effect on those who work on it? Can the impact of the physical aspects of a technology still be taken into account at all, or should the medium now be understood as an immaterial, imaginary construct the effects of which are entirely in human hands and heads?

Convergence or reciprocity

Some theorists who follow Williams' idea that technology is interrelated to its social context, would respond to these questions with the assertion that the impact of a medium's material properties on society cannot be taken into account. The reason for this is not so much the belief that technology is an entirely immaterial, imaginary construct, but the belief that technology can never exist apart from the way it is imagined or interpreted within its social context. Ron Burnett finds the idea of reciprocity or exchange between human society and the physical properties of a technology problematic because it would imply a separation of technology and society. And such separation is unacceptable when one adheres to the idea that "technology *per se* has no identity, no space within which 'it' can play out a role without the process of interpretation attached to the exchange" (Burnett 1995: 148).

Therefore, according to Burnett, (media) machines cannot be separated from the social context within which they are anthropomorphized. The idea of reciprocity between society and medium relies on a distinction between the two, and therefore reinstates the ontological status of the machine. Moreover, for Burnett, reciprocity confers continuity on a situation which does not have to be framed by any sort of linkage—because there is no separateness. In a similar move, sociologist Manuel Castells has claimed that society cannot be said to determine technology, or technology to determine society, because "technology *is* society" (1996: 5).

An even more radical view on the intertwining of media and society was formulated by philosopher Jean Baudrillard, who is well known for his opinion that we now live in a hyperreal world consisting entirely of simulacra; empty signs that do not have referents in (a) reality, but which refer only to themselves. Within his system of simulacra, meaning and value are completely absent. This absence of meaning has consequences for the status of the medium. Without meaning, the information mediated by media is empty and superfluous. For Baudrillard, the contents or messages of media have been neutralized. In line with McLuhan, he states that, in the postmodern era of simulation and simulacra, the medium has indeed become the message. Yet, without a message, the medium implodes into the real:

> Without a message, the medium also falls into the indefinite state characteristic of all our great systems of judgment and value. [...] *Finally, the medium is the message not only signifies the end of the message, but also the end of the medium.* There are no more media in the literal sense of the word (I'm speaking particularly of electronic mass media)—that is, of a mediating power between one reality and another, between one state of the real and another. Neither in content, nor in form. Strictly, this is what implosion signifies. [...] It is useless to dream of revolution through content, useless to dream of a revelation through form, because the medium and the real are now in a single nebula whose truth is indecipherable.
>
> 1995: 82–83, emphasis added

For Baudrillard, it is impossible to discuss the influence of media on their environment, because media are not simply located in their own hermetically sealed spaces, but dispersed around us, in all forms of experience (Sandoz 2003). As there is no unmediated reality outside of our mediated world, the medium as mediator no longer exists. Not only is there nothing left to mediate (only empty, meaningless signs; simulacra), there is nothing real left to mediate *between* either. What is mediated is only what is simulated and vice versa. Those experiences in life that are explicitly presented as mediated Baudrillard classifies as simply of a higher order of simulation, one which simulates simulating in order to falsely suggest a real or an unmediated system outside of it (Sandoz 2003).

With Baudrillard's claim that the medium has imploded, we seem to have reached the end of medium theory. How to proceed with a theoretical investigation of the relationship between the medium and the social from here? Should the relationship under investigation in this part rather be the one between *simulation* and the social? In spite of what Baudrillard claims, we still think of media as distinct categories. Even if we provisionally follow Baudrillard's opinion that media have ceased to exist because they no longer mediate, but only simulate, media are very much present in our simulated world as an idea (or simulacrum) which we believe to have a basis in reality. Even as purely imaginary objects, media have performative effects and shape our perception of the world. The mere idea that an object is, for instance, a film, influences what you see. It produces a horizon of expectations and creates meanings that—with or without a referent in reality—potentially affect our social, political, and cultural circumstances in a very real way.

In addition, unlike Burnett and Baudrillard, other theorists (including myself) do insist on the necessity of discussing the effects of a medium's physical properties on their environment, in spite of the fact that the technological support of a medium at no time has a stable, ontological essence or autonomous status within its social, historical, and cultural context, and in spite of the possibility that media constitute a hyperreality and are therefore "in a single nebula" (Baudrillard 1995: 83) with the real. As Moran puts it, "to focus on historical relations and (cultural or social) context entirely at the expense of technology [as a physical object], would swing from one extreme pole [technological determinism] to another" (2002: 19). Moran's proposal to see a medium as a discursive construct does not mean that the material, physical base of a medium does not exist or have an effect on a medium's expressive possibilities. He argues that a medium's technology never exists outside of discourse; technology is always already invested with and formed by socially and culturally specific meaning. However, this does not rule out the fact that a medium's technology does exercise material constraints on media practice. Media are not materially transparent or neutral instruments with which every kind of artifact can be produced.

Saying this does not mean that the discursive or contextual framing of that technology is denied, or that is depicted as an autonomous object. The material technological possibilities and impossibilities of a medium are forever involved in a process of change—change which is instigated by social needs and carried out by human subjects. Moreover, the meaning and importance attributed to certain technological possibilities or restrictions of a medium are conventional and thus historically, culturally and socially relative. As I will demonstrate later on, the technological ability of video to simultaneously record and produce images in a live feedback set-up has been interpreted in opposite ways by people with specific social concerns. Therefore, I would agree with Moran—a medium is both a material and a social product. A material and social product which, moreover, can produce material consequences within social fields. But how can the consequences of a medium's material properties on society be discussed without taking the imperatives of technological determinism into account?

Moran has pointed out that Williams' concept of "soft determination" can be of help here. As Moran explains, determination speaks to partial rather than total necessity, in that the materiality of technologies exerts pressures and limits, yet without guarantees (2002: 19–20). In Williams' own words:

> It does not predetermine human action in any unilateral sense, but it does make some courses of action more likely than others, if only because it makes some course of action more difficult than others, and also acknowledges that there are, at any one time, certain absolute, often material, limits to the range of human action. Determination also implies that humans learn from their historical experience in ways which create habits and thus inertia, and in ways which provide warnings against certain courses of action and thus make such actions less likely in the future.
>
> Williams, in Garnham 1990: 6

Moran does not suggest that the material, physical base of a medium does not exist or has no effect on a medium's expressive possibilities. In his analyses, he still takes the materiality of video into account as a factor which both enables and limits the expressive possibilities of the medium. Yet, he argues that it never exists outside of discourse; it is always invested with and formed by social and culturally specific meaning.

In conclusion, I contend that human actions exert pressure on the development and design of material technologies, and the material aspects of media technologies in turn "softly" affect the possibilities and limits of human actions. Neither human subjects nor material technologies have full control over each other in this reciprocal relationship. When it comes to the relationship between social structures and media, the same reciprocity between a medium's materiality and (groups of) human subjects can be presumed. On the one hand, the interests of a certain social group can produce and define a medium, including its technological properties, according to specific social goals. On the other hand, the medium and its physical aspects may produce the form and the possibilities of a social group. The analyses of the relation between film, video, and social structures that follow will therefore take reciprocity into account.

CHAPTER 14
VIDEO: FLOW AND FEEDBACK

Antisocial flow, narcissistic feedback

Socialization is often measured by exposure to media messages. Anyone underexposed to media (and hence to information) is considered to be desocialized or virtually asocial. Baudrillard and other postmodern media critics claim that subjects are not underexposed but rather overexposed to media messages in the postmodern era. One might expect that this abundance of information would create many cohesive social bonds, but according to the French theorist, the opposite is true. Rather, the incessant stream of information in contemporary society leads to an implosion of the social. Although we live in a world where there is more and more information, the media messages and images which surround us have less and less meaning because of the abundance of messages. The waning of meaning through the pressure of information has turned the act of communication into a performance, pursuing the "destructuration" of social formations (Baudrillard 1995: 81):

> Thus information dissolves meaning and dissolves the social, in a sort of nebulous state dedicated not to a surplus of innovation, but, on the contrary, to total entropy. Thus the media are producers not of socialization, but of exactly the opposite, of the implosion of the social in the masses. And this is only the macroscopic extension of the implosion of meaning at the microscopic level of the sign.
>
> Baudrillard 1995: 82

Whereas Baudrillard discusses social entropy as the result of the flow of electronic media messages in general, the electronic medium of video is often theorized as the medium which is most symptomatic of the unremitting flow of information that obstructs intersubjective social relationships in the postmodern era. Frederic Jameson, for instance, attributes the "sign-flow which resists meaning" especially to the medium of video.[1] Jameson first of all identifies an ongoing flux of superficial fragments within the televisual application of video. Broadcast television never stops, the contents of the screen are "streaming before us all day long without interruption" (1991: 69). Jameson recognizes a similar flow in experimental video artworks. Although these artworks have a limited running time, they seem as never-ending as the unremitting stream of television images because of their uneventfulness and incomprehensibility.

For Jameson, the consequence of video's flow is that the distance and separation between viewer and medium disappears. First of all, because the stream of video information is so pervasive, "what used to be called 'critical distance' has become obsolete" (1991: 69). The most obvious solutions to interrupting video's flow, namely simply turning off the television set or walking out of the museum room, do not create any critical distance either, for video images cannot be properly remembered once they are out of view. Jameson claims that video (unlike film) excludes memory; "nothing here haunts the mind or leaves its afterimages in the manner of the great moments of film" (70).

Secondly, the ceaseless flow of video can give rise to intolerable discomfort in its viewers. In the face of the ongoing cycles of serials and commercials, or the seemingly never-ending unchanging or unexciting images of video artworks, spectators can only experience unpleasant sensations such as panic or boredom. For Jameson, video "clamps" its spectator into place by means of its flow. He compares the medium's effect on the viewer with the old chair-like devices with clasps and belts that were supposedly used by the first photographers to keep their subjects immobile. Video's discomforting, excruciating flow freezes its spectators without actual physical restraint.[2] According to the author, "the helpless spectators of video time are then as immobilized and mechanically integrated and neutralized as the older photographic subjects, who became, for a time, part of the technology of the medium" (1991: 73). By turning its spectator into an object, video thus violently absorbs its viewer. In addition, Jameson argues, the authors of video works are dissolved along with the spectator. Naturally, with no subjects left to relate to, video has canceled out the possibility of intersubjective, social contact between its users.

Like Jameson, Rosalind Krauss recognizes a form of inclusion of the video viewer into the medium. According to Krauss, however, the spectator of video is not so much turned into an object by the medium; she is rather caught between two components of the video apparatus, where she is put into a narcissistic relationship with herself from which she cannot escape. In her seminal article "Video: The Aesthetics of Narcissism" (1976), she explains that this narcissistic spell is in the first place caused by a technological set-up which is specific to video; a closed-circuit installation in which a camera records images of the viewing subject, which are then instantly fed back to this subject on a nearby monitor. On this screen, the viewer (who is also the object of representation, the performer, and often the producer) of the installation can look at herself looking at herself. Video functions as a mirror in this particular arrangement of live feedback in a closed circuit.

However, unlike the singular object of the mirror, the video apparatus consists of two components in the case of instant feedback. Anyone who stands in front of the camera as well as the joint monitor is, as it were, held captive between two technical devices. In Krauss' words, "the body is [...] centered between two machines that are the opening and closing of a parenthesis" (1976: 52). Besides the limits imposed by the spatial set-up of the material machines on which the video medium is based, the viewer is also trapped in a temporal way. Because there is hardly any delay between the presence of the subject in front of the lens and the "now" of her image on the monitor, Krauss defines the situation of instant feedback as "the prison of a collapsed present, that is, a present time which is completely severed from a sense of its own past" (53). Stuck in the present, between machines, the viewing (or performing) subject is hardly able to detach herself from the instant feedback provided by the simultaneous reception and transmission of the video images; images of the self. The medium of video encapsulates the self with the self.

Especially in the early years of video's existence, artists have massively applied the medium's ability for instant feedback. First, artists such as Peter Weibel, Stan Douglas, and Bruce Nauman produced installations in which visitors to the art gallery or museum were "closed in" by closed-circuit video formations. In 1973, for instance, Weibel created an installation with the telling title *Observation of the Observation* (1973), in which viewers would be enclosed in a circle of monitors with live feedback of themselves standing in the middle, looking at the monitors. Even more ubiquitous are the video artworks on tape in which artists position themselves within the loop of live video feedback. The medium offered performance artists the ability to record themselves while watching themselves on a monitor. Krauss bases her dismissal of video as a narcissistic practice on *Centers* (1972), a video performance by Vito Acconci in which he used the video monitor as a mirror while pointing directly at his own image for nearly twenty-three minutes:

> As we look at the artist sighting along his outstretched arm and forefinger towards the center of the screen we are watching, what we see is a sustained tautology: a line of sight that begins at Acconci's line of vision and ends at the eyes of his projected double. In that image of self-regard is configured a narcissism so endemic to works of video that I find myself wanting to generalize it as the condition of the entire genre.
>
> Krauss 1976: 52

Such a generalization is accurate in the eyes of Krauss, because even outside of the instant feedback formation many artists seem to use video in order to encapsulate themselves with their own image in different ways. In *Air Time* (1973) Vito Acconci, for instance, addresses his own reflection when he sits in front of an actual mirror. Linda Benghlis has recorded her own face in profile in front of a video monitor which shows an earlier recording of her face, so that she is face to face with herself in *Now* (1973). Apart from a few videos that can be read as a form of critique on the narcissistic enclosure inherent in the medium, Krauss cannot discover self-reflexivity or any other positive, valuable characteristic within these videos. According to her, video offers reflection in the most straightforward way; it reflects on a monitor what appears in front of its lens. This form of reflection is not critical or elucidating; it is reflection without reflexivity. The medium mirrors the artists who record themselves, but does not offer the difference between the represented subject and its representation which is indispensable in order to produce critical insights. The video image of the self may be understood as another, but this would be a classic (narcissist) mistake; it is really just a mirror image of the self. Within the space of video, there is only the self and its duplicate. The world and its conditions are bracketed out by the medium.

Krauss can be criticized for taking two parts from the field of video, and subsequently presenting these as constitutive, or representative, of the whole medium. As James Moran points out, Krauss first grounds the term video in a specific configuration of the medium (live feedback) which she represents as constitutive of the entire medium, including other technological parts and formations of the apparatus as well as its conventional aesthetics. Secondly, she conflates the medium of video with the genre of performance that appropriated it, thereby "reversing historical causality by suggesting that the properties of the video apparatus beg for solipsism, when Acconci, having already staged his narcissism in other venues, incorporated video into his repertoire upon realizing how well it could be adapted to suit his art" (Moran 2002: 10). Moreover, it is confusing that Krauss on the one hand suggests that—as Moran notes—the technical apparatus of the video medium generates a narcissistic state, while she claims on the other hand that the psychological state of narcissism constitutes the medium. Therefore, it is difficult to distinguish whether narcissism should be understood as a property of the artists who work with video or of the medium itself.

In addition to these methodological objections, Krauss' interpretation of video as narcissistic can be directly questioned. Although video is technically able to function as a mirror that splits the subject, Krauss views this ability in the narrow context of the apparatus and moment of live feedback. This context is narrow because the effect of live feedback depends on the larger field in which video operates. As David E. James argues, "the splitting of the subject and its imaginary configuration in the electronic mirror that was so important in early video may and should be negotiated [. . .] in the total televisual environment—broadcast, interactive, cable, surveillance, medical, and so on, with which it is integrated" (1996: 124).

The fact that closed-circuit video formations are not only used in video art installations, but also in surveillance systems (CCTV) determines the way video art installations with live feedback are experienced by their (split) spectator. According to Krauss, the visitor to such installations will be so mesmerized by her own image on the monitor that she is hardly able to escape from the installation's narcissistic grip. I would say, in contrast, that the many viewers who are familiar with the application of video as a surveillance medium will respond to such installations with the question "who is watching me?"[3] For them, seeing their own image on a video monitor does not result in a private, enclosed sphere in which they are alone with themselves. Instead, it indicates the possibility that this privacy is being violated, that someone is watching them without their permission.

The expansion of the context in which live video feedback should be understood also has a temporal component. Many artistic recordings of instant feedback are displayed at a later time. In addition to this, Krauss does not pay attention to the fact that when video artists use live feedback in order to record images of themselves, the resulting art tapes, which are presented only after the moment of taping them in a closed-circuit formation, do not show the set-up of monitor and camera at all. They just show images of the artist looking right into the camera, out of the monitor, at the viewer. So, although Vito Acconci has indeed pointed at his own image on a monitor when he produced *Centers*, this act is invisible to later spectators of the video artwork. Because of that, within the viewing situation, the forefinger of the artist is not visibly pointing at himself; it seems to address the spectator.

By focusing solely on the spatial and temporal context in which Acconci's video, as well as similar videos, were *produced*, Krauss remains unattentive to the relational dimension of the work which is so poignantly present at the moment and in the set-up of viewing. This blindness to the way Acconci's *Centers* relates to the spectator is all the more remarkable when the piece is regarded in light of Acconci's broader corpus of videos and video performances. In many of his works, Acconci explicitly addresses the spectator via the video monitor. In *Theme Song* (1973) the artist approaches the viewer in a seductive, sexual manner. While he is lying on the floor with his face close to the camera, he looks right into the recording device, at the spectator, and says things like "Why don't you come here with me? [...] Look, my body comes around you. Come on, put your body next to mine. I need it, you need it." Unlike Acconci's attempt to create an intimate closeness with the viewer in *Theme Song*, he tried to keep his public at a distance in *Claim* (1971). During this three-hour video performance, Acconci sat in a basement while his image was seen on a monitor in the upstairs gallery. He behaves in a tense and violent way towards the camera, and threatens to kill anyone who tries to enter his space.

These videos do not disprove Krauss' claim that video encapsulates its users, that its apparatus can form an enclosed space in which the recorded subject is stuck. In *Claim*, Acconci clearly stakes out his territory with the help of video. Even in the case of *Theme Song*, he acknowledges that the apparatus of video forms a boundary. The fact that Acconci uses phrases such as "come here" and "come in" indicates that he differentiates between an inside and an outside of video. The artist himself is inside the space of the video apparatus he operates. He also acknowledges the boundary of the medium's interface when, in *Theme Song*, he remarks: "Of course I can't see your face. I have no idea what your face looks like. You could be anybody out there, but there's gotta be somebody watching me. Somebody who wants to come in close to me [...] Come on, I'm all alone [...]"

However, whereas Krauss theorizes video as a prison in which the recorded subject is entirely cut off from the world, Acconci understands the medium as a tool to realize an intimate space with permeable boundaries.[4] On the one hand, video can form an enclosed space in which one can be alone with oneself, act out, talk without restrictions, peer at one's mirror image, etc. Moreover, for Acconci and others, video can also be an intimate space in which one can be close to one or more other people who reside in the same space in front of the video camera—or in the case of live feedback, between the camera and the monitor. In some of his video performances, Acconci is joined in front of the lens by a woman (often this is his partner Kathy Dillon), with whom he relates in a very physical manner. In *Contacts* (1971), a woman holds her hand above parts of his body. Acconci then tries to locate her hand without looking, using body heat.

On the other hand, even though Acconci relates to himself or to another person within an enclosed, intimate video space, his performances are oriented towards an audience. Often, this relationship to a viewer outside the video monitor is explicitly activated when the artist addresses her, even invites her to come into his video space. At other times this orientation is merely present because the videos are exhibited in galleries and museums. Either way, it would be a mistake to understand Acconci's work as entirely solipsistic and narcissistic. It is telling in this regard that the artist speaks of his video work as a practice that seeks to establish a "face-to-face relationship" between himself and the viewer via a monitor perceived as "a middle-ground, a depository for objects—an area where I, off-screen on one side, can hand things over to the viewer, off-screen on the other side" (Acconci in Schneider and Korot 1976: 8–9).[5]

The fact that video artworks relate to an audience even by the simple fact that they are shown in public art institutions such as galleries or museums is important to all the video artworks which, in the vein of Krauss' video theory, can easily be marked as narcissistic. The many artistic video diaries or extended uneventful video performances in which video artists record themselves for as long as the tape runs, were all produced with the aim of making artworks worthy of being shown in public. This aim, or authorial intention, has an important consequence for the temporal seclusion of the recorded subject.

Krauss argued that the subject within a live feedback loop is trapped in a collapsed present. But video artists who record their own image in such a feedback loop are not trapped in their present moment at all; they have a future audience in mind during the production of their tapes—why else record the fed-back images at all? They not only look at their "live" self-image on the monitor in order to see themselves, they also look at their self-image in order to see how future viewers will see them. The camera is often theorized as a stand-in for the absent future audience. In the case of live video feedback, however, it is the subject in front of the lens who should be understood as a stand-in for this spectator to come. Rather than an invitation to narcissism, the closed-circuit set-up offers subjects to do the opposite of narcissistic self-enclosure; to imagine themselves in the position of someone else. As a result, video artists in live closed-circuit set-ups do indeed look at themselves as others, yet this phrase does not—as Krauss has it—merely refer to Narcissus, who mistook his self-image for another. Subjects in live feedback set-ups can view themselves from the position of another; the future viewer of the tape that is being recorded. In identifying with the other(s) who will see the image of the self, the subjects of live video feedback create a difference between themselves looking as other and their self-image. This opens the door to reflexivity.

Relational immediacy, social flexibility

In both theoretical and artistic specifications of the video medium in relation to social structures, the encapsulation of the subject which Jameson and Krauss attribute to the medium is one of the dominant characteristics. However, like Acconci, many people who use video and/or reflect on it view this encapsulation as a positive, socially productive fact. The medium can draw boundaries around one person or a group of people in many ways. Yet the spatial and temporal enclosure which can be created by the medium tends to be permeable and provisional. Moreover, the enclosure is also understood as an intimate haven in which or from which the subject can safely relate to others. Hence, although video's propensity to encapsulate its users has been widely theorized as an ability which creates socially isolated narcissists, the same ability has been understood even more pervasively as a potential that enables social development and the formation of social relationships.

In addition, the video formation of live feedback that Krauss took as a model for video's narcissistic nature, can just as well serve as a model for more positive, even utopian perspectives on the medium in question. For in the closed-circuit formation, a few important socially employable qualities of the medium are highlighted. The medium's immediacy can be discerned within the structure of instant feedback, where images are simultaneously recorded and reproduced. This immediacy has been pointed out as one of the reasons why video can serve to sustain social bonds as well as enforce social change. For the immediate transmission of recorded images enables live communication as well as a rapid dissemination of beliefs. It can bring people close to one another in a temporal respect, as distances can be spanned in a split second by the electronic video signal.

The communicative potential of video becomes even more apparent when its immediacy is coupled with the impression of intimacy and privacy which video is able to create. The possibility to record video images of oneself without the presence of others stimulates openness. It invites the exposure of personal details, visceral sensations, and interior speech. The immediacy of the medium, however, offers a rapid dissolution of such an enclosed, private space between the camera and the subject in front of it, as the recorded images can be disseminated widely and instantly. This immediacy may seem to be at odds with the impression of privacy. However, they can be said to work together in one important respect: they facilitate "intrapsychic communication, abrogating the monadic isolation of the postmodern subject" (Tamblyn 1996: 13). For video invites you to speak your mind, and can subsequently transmit your mind to many others. Tamblyn, Burnett, and Marchessault, among others, have emphasized that video often functions as an effective communication technology that creates useful interrelations and interactions (debates, exchange of experiences) between human subjects. It is remarkable that, for Tamblyn, video has not caused the isolation of the postmodern subject at all (Baudrillard, Jameson); it rather phases this isolation out.

A second characteristic of the live feedback set-up that has come to stand for the medium as a whole in discourses on video's socializing effects is that it offers many positions to its user. A person who produces a closed-circuit video and takes up the position in front of the camera and adjoined monitor is simultaneously the subject who operates the camera, the subject in front of the camera, the represented subject on the monitor, and the viewing subject. In other words, the user of such an installation is both the enunciating and enunciated subject, the sender and the receiver of the video images, both the recording and recorded subject, both viewing and viewed subject. Whereas the specific set-up of live feedback allows a single person to occupy all these positions at once, the medium in general offers its users the flexibility to choose and alternate between these positions.

Alternation between the positions of sender and receiver/viewer doesn't necessarily involve a switch between positions in front or behind the camera, or in front or on screen. For, in addition to the video apparatuses of the (possibly closed-circuit) camera and the TV monitor, the VCR can be seen as a device that enables its users to become a producer and a viewer at the same time. Because of video's rewinding, forwarding, and pausing functions, each video viewer can produce its own object by manipulating video time while watching. For this reason, Siegfried Zielinski has defined the video recorder an "audiovisual time machine" in his book *Audiovisions* (1999).. He writes that the equipment made it possible for its users to intervene manipulatively in the time structures and processes that had been fixed centrally from the user's side. He attaches much social value to this possibility. In societies in which many people were restricted by rigid time regimes due to continual intensification of work processes, such an opportunity to intervene in time formed a pleasant relief from the feeling of being pressed for time—an empowering experience. The contrast with Jameson's view of video as a medium that smothers its viewers by its continual flow couldn't be higher.

In sum, the apparatus of video allows its users flexibility and agency. Users can alternate between viewing, recording, and being recorded. In addition, they can shape the footage at many points during the production and viewing process. This flexibility, moreover, offers reflexivity; in some of the video practices I discuss below, combining and alternating between positions in front of and behind the camera as well as the monitor serve as strategies in investigations into social identity. Together with video's immediacy and its typical form of (intimate) encapsulation, the flexibility and agency the medium offers to its users are key aspects in the way in which video operates within social structures, both on micro and on macro levels. In the following sections

I will first investigate three domains—confession, therapy, and testimony—in which video affects social relationships predominantly on a micro level. After that, I will investigate how video is used as a tool, weapon, or counterspace in practices which aim to affect social structures on a macro level.

Confession, therapy, and testimony

The intimacy to which Acconci and many others attribute the space in front of the video camera forms the basis for three closely related discourses that have become dominant within the field of video: confession, therapy and testimony. In each of these domains, human subjects expose personal information. They confess their secrets and crimes, work through and analyze their traumas and deepest emotions, and narrate painful memories. Video proliferates within each of the three fields. The medium is widely applied as a confessional apparatus, a therapeutic device, and a "witness to witnesses" when recording people who bear testimony. The medium seems to stimulate something which is crucial within these three domains, namely the willingness to open up and tell what is on one's mind.

This outburst of personal stories in front of the video camera not only leads to the question of how video encourages these exposures, but also brings up the issue of intersubjective relationships. Confessants tell their (shameful) truths to a confessor; a figure of authority who judges, punishes, consoles, and grants absolution. Therapy is guided by a therapist, who asks questions, provides insights, analyzes the patient's narration, and restores injured or incomplete subjectivities. Likewise, bearing testimony to serious facts is not carried out in a vacuum, but requires one or more interlocutors who join a witness in a so-called testimonial alliance; a bond of trust that safeguards the fact that the testimony is being heard and is taken seriously. What happens when video enters these scenes? How does it affect or enable the small yet essential social structures on which confession, therapy, and testimony rely? What happens to the relationship between the speaking subject and their interlocutor, addressee or audience when people talk to the video camera?

Video confession

In "Video Confessions" (1996) Michael Renov points out that the confessional discourse is prominent in contemporary video art. He distinguishes between two forms of video confession: first, the form in which the artist invites other people to confess in front of the video camera, usually in the presence of the artist himself, and secondly, the form of video confession in which artists point the camera at themselves in order to make confessions about their personal lives. Examples of the first form of video confession include Maxie Cohen's *Intimate Interviews: Sex in Less Than Two*

Minutes (1984) in which six persons speak directly into the camera about their sex lives, and *Anger* (1986), in which people, as individuals, groups, or couples, speak about the emotion resulting from what has hurt them (they have been slashed, raped, betrayed, and abused) and which has driven them to violent acts themselves. Another well-known example is Gillian Wearing's video series called *Confess All On Video. Don't Worry You Will Be in Disguise. Intrigued? Call Gillian* (1994). In response to an advertisement in *Time Out* magazine, masked people confess in front of Wearing's camera that they have, for instance, betrayed their girlfriend, stolen computer equipment from a school, or like to make obscene phone calls.

The second form of confession, which shows the artist as confessant, was developed by Lynn Hershman, Vanalyne Green, Sadie Benning, Ilene Segalov, Susan Mogul, Skip Sweeney, George Kuchar, and many others. While looking directly into the camera, or providing images of themselves with voice-overs, these artists tell of their most intimate struggles. In *Binge* (1987), Hershman tells of her eating disorder while we see her gaining and losing weight over time. Likewise, Vanalyne Green discusses her bulimia and complicated relationships with men in relation to her childhood with alcoholic parents in *Trick or Drink* (1985). Between 1988 and 1993, Sadie Benning created a series of videos with a PixelVision camera in which she narrates her thoughts, struggles, and experiences as a gay teenager.

According to Renov, the videotaped autobiographical confessions draw more on video's specific technological abilities than the video confessions where artists record the confessions of others instead of their own. In order to point out that the latter form of confession is not unique to video, Renov refers to some of the experiments in direct cinema and *cinéma vérité* with the development of "camera confessions" in the documentary mode. In *Chronique d'un été* (Rouch and Morin 1961), for instance, the filmmakers—one with a background in sociology, the other in anthropology—self-reflexively investigate whether and if so how people can act normal and real in front of the lens. One of the filmmakers, Jean Rouch, later claimed that the camera functions like a psychoanalytic stimulant that lets people do things they wouldn't otherwise do. In an interview, Rouch explains how he discovered that the camera "was not a brake but let's say, to use an automobile term, an accelerator" (Rouch, in Eaton 1979: 51).

Following this line of thought, we can conclude that the presence of any camera, video or film, would stimulate confession. Because it represents a wide potential audience, the camera taps into the exhibitionist desires of those in front of the lens. However, as Rouch remarks, confessions in front of the camera are not always entirely exhibitionistic. According to him, the camera can be understood as both a window which is open to the outside, and a mirror. Without the live presence of an audience, and with the camera operator hidden silently behind the lens, confessions to the film camera miss a directly responding interlocutor. Therefore, they "backfire" at the confessing self.[6]

However, in the case of both filmed and videotaped confessions, the personal exposures by filmed subjects are very often truncated dialogues for as long as they are somehow directed, stimulated or set-up by film or video artists. According to Renov, a crucial break appears when the camera as confessional instrument is taken up by the confessant herself. Again, the camera has not uniquely been used as an autobiographical confessional tool within the field of video. Jonas Mekas, Maya Deren, Stan Brakhage, and many others have produced films in a first-person diaristic style. Yet Renov claims that the medium of video has added something specific to the first-person camera confession. Video has increased the independency and the privacy of the confessant:

> [. . .] even Brakhage's hand-wrought signatures, etched into the emulsion itself, could not free the cineaste from a dependence on large-scale manufacturers who could discontinue stocks (even whole formats) if profit margins sagged. Then, too, there were the vagaries of the local lab to contend with. The development of the Sony portapak in the mid–1960s provided visual artists with a greater possibility for relative autonomy. [. . .] Indeed, the potential for the handcrafting so beloved by 16mm and 8mm enthusiasts has been lost in transition to electronic pixels. In exchange, the independent video maker or home consumer has been relieved of certain mediating contingencies—material and temporal—that separate shooting from viewing, production from exhibition. It is the systematic solipsism and "immediacy" of video [. . .] that suit it so well to the confessional impulse. No technician need see or hear the secrets confided to tape. None but the invited enter the loop of video confession.
>
> 1996: 84

The fact that artists gain full control over their confessions by way of video does not mean that their tapes are not to be seen by others. On the one hand, the video set-up encloses the confessant; on the other hand, the video apparatus links the confessant to this future audience. This combination of complete temporal and spatial separation from an audience, with the potentiality to be heard and seen in the future is the ideal instigator of confessional monologues. In the words of Renov: "The virtual presence of a partner—the imagined other effectuated by the technology—turns out to be a more powerful facilitator of emotion than flesh-and-blood interlocutors. Camera operators, sound booms, cables, and clapper boards are hardly a boon to soul confession" (1996: 89).

Although the technology of video is theorized as an important reason for the ubiquity of video confessions, these technological characteristics of video do not entirely cause or determine the first-person confessional practices as carried out by video artists. The adoption of video as a confessional apparatus has equally been generated by the societies in which the medium exists. First of all, the medium has evolved into a world where the act of confession has become less and less exclusive. Everyone confesses to everyone else over and over again.[7] Secrets are no longer merely made available to professional confessors such as priests and therapists, they are conveyed to mass audiences through mass media such as magazines and television. It is impossible to say how those media, including video itself, are the cause or merely the vehicle of this social transformation.[8] In addition, the artistic video confession can, from a Western perspective, be viewed in a development which starts in the religious organization of medieval society and ends in today's capitalist economy. As Renov explains, the first-person video confession is founded on religious transformations in the sixteenth century, but was ultimately born of late capitalism:

> From a crudely developmental perspective, one could say that first-person video confession has simply built on an evolutionary dynamic in which the public confession initially ordained by medieval church doctrine gave way to a private, one-on-one ritual. Then, in the sixteenth century, Protestantism eliminated the externalization of confession as a face-to-face ritual of reconciliation, fostering a kind of spiritual entrepreneurship. Video preserves and deepens that dynamic of privatization and entrepreneurship. Now, with the help of cameras, video makers can exhume their deepest fears and indiscretions all on their own, and then put their neuroses on display. In a sense, first-person video confession is uniquely suited to its moment. Born of late-stage capitalism, it endows therapeutic practice with exchange value.
>
> 1996: 88–89

In the above, Renov defines the first-person video as a therapeutic practice. Merely telling their story to the camera helps the speaking subjects; they cure themselves by talking. This doesn't require the presence of an interlocutor, or a therapist who analyzes the speaking subject. However, the medium of video as such offers the confessant a form of self-reflexivity because of its flexibility. Although this is not necessarily visible in the texts, the speaking subject can become a critical viewer and analyst of her own tape either during the production period or later on. In her *Electronic Diary*, Lynn Hershman for instance responds to her own footage, which she watches between the sessions in front of the camera during the extended period of time in which she has recorded her tapes. She discusses her dissociation from her own body, which she also experiences when she watches herself on tape.

In addition, as I will show later on with the help of Hershman's *Electronic Diary* as well as Sadie Benning's *It Wasn't Love* (1992), a level of (self-)analysis is often obtained by the confessants in post production. Through editing, voice-overs, inserts, and video effects such as split screens and fade-outs, the artists organize, recreate, interpret, and analyze their own confessions. Hershman, in addition, applies the video-specific techniques of layering and chroma-keying. Whereas the term "layering" refers to several ways by which video images can be combined, for instance through transparency or inserts, chroma-keying specifically involves the replacement of one color within a video image with another video feed. The latter technique is best-known for its application in the "green-screen" room, which is widely applied in advanced modes of digital filmmaking. Today, this form of video layering has become invisible in its most professional digital forms. State-of-the-art computer software as well as the high definition of contemporary video formats have enabled video keying to evolve into a technique which has become indispensable to the creation of spectacular fictional film worlds by way of smooth and seamless, cinematic-looking images. However, unlike contemporary digital narrative feature films, video artworks often display the different layers of video keying. Especially when the technique of video keying was still in its infancy, it led to prominently visible layers. For Hershman, as for many other video artists, video keying and layering serve as rhetorical tools by which meanings can be produced, connections can be made, and relations can be visually analyzed.[9]

Another form of therapeutic analysis and reflection is carried out when the confessors discuss their tapes with a selected audience. Hershman, for instance, showed her footage to close friends while she was working on her diaries. She discusses and processes their reactions in her tapes, thereby allowing her friends to take up the function of a responding substitute therapist. I will return to the work of Benning and Hershman in the last chapter of this part. In order to further analyze the relation of the medium of video to discourses of confession, therapy, and testimony in works such as those of Hershman and Benning, it is first necessary to gain a more general overview of the application of video within the domains of therapy and testimony.

Video therapy

As Hershman's example already indicated, the video medium can have therapeutic value when it is used in a self-reflexive way by one person. However, video's therapeutic effects become more apparent when the medium is, so to speak, shared by several people who interact with each other while recording or watching a video. In the 1980s, video therapy was rife. Therapists used the camera to film (group) therapy sessions, in order to discuss the material with the patients later on. The camera could also be handed over to the patient, who would then record images of problematic situations in everyday life, or speak to the camera in the absence of the therapist.[10] Again, this footage would serve as an object for analysis in later sessions. Today, the video camera is still often used by psychologists and pedagogues in family therapy. Dysfunctional families are placed under video surveillance in their homes, so that the therapist can gain insight into their problems. In addition, this video material can be used to show the family members where they are going wrong. By rewinding, repeating, and pausing the footage, the therapist or educationalist points out pitfalls, and then explains how the family members can improve their familial relationships.

Video can also have a therapeutic effect when it is used between two subjects without the added mediation of a professional therapist. One of the videos that, according to Renov (1996), established the paradigm of interpersonal video therapy is *The Continuing Story of Carel and Ferd* (Ginsberg 1975). Initially, videographer Arthur Ginsberg planned to catch the complicated relationship between a former porn actress (Carel) and a bi-sexual drug addict (Ferd) on tape himself, but the couple took the camera from him in order to videotape each other.[11] Carel and Ferd in turn operate the camera. They alternately pose and answer difficult questions. The lens of the camera puts a boundary between them which provides them with the distance they need in order to talk. They agree to become objects of scrutiny and observation, only because the camera turns and turns. They are each other's object of investigation. The camera creates an objectifying distance, yet it is used to observe the other in close-up. Carel and Ferd film each other at a close range, they peer over each other's skin with the camera and focus on small bodily details and gestures. The ability to enable intrapsychic communication, which Tamblyn attributed to video, seems to be exploited to the fullest here. Carel and Ferd extract each other's deepest thoughts and feelings not just because the camera facilitates personal conversation; they seem to catch each other's lies and truths by using the camera as a so-called kino-eye. The lens reveals what the filmed subjects hide.

In Wendy Clarke's *One on One* series (1991–1994), the camera doesn't reveal because of its extraordinary optical capacities, but because it enables communication between human subjects who will never meet. Clarke, who is a video artist and a psychiatrist, organized her *One on One* project with the aim of bringing inmates in contact with people from the outside through video. She coupled imprisoned criminals with members of an American church community, and consequently provided both parties with a video camera and a VCR. With this equipment, the inmate and the outsider would record and send video messages to each other, and view each other's messages in the privacy of their home or cell. Although Clarke assisted them with the technicalities of video production, she let the correspondence follow its course. The only precondition was that the prisoner and the outsider wouldn't meet in real life during or after their video correspondence. This precondition, in combination with some of the technical possibilities of the video medium, seems to be a perfect recipe for a therapeutic form of interaction between two subjects.

In one of the most famous correspondences from the *One on One* series called *Ken and Louise*, prisoner (Ken) and church member (Louise) rapidly establish a meaningful relationship through the interchange of videotapes. Although they have to get used to the camera at first, they soon start telling and showing things to each other which they have never exposed to anyone else before. Louise, who has a very cheerful appearance, for instance confesses that she actually feels very depressed and lonely. She shows a secret cuddly toy to Ken, analyzes her problematic relationships with men, and confesses that she finds Ken attractive. The tough-looking Ken talks about his vulnerable side and plays songs to Louise. Although Ken and Louise respond to each other's stories all the time, the most important therapeutic effect of the project seems to be that they can expose their own problems to someone who is open and vulnerable in return. Both Ken and Louise note how easily they can open up to someone who is absent at the time of recording, and whom they will never meet outside of Clarke's video project. The fact that the involved subjects will never be physically proximate to each other is vital to their sincerity and openness. In this case, the medium of video sustains therapeutic and confessional interaction between people, because it allows for the exchange of intimate details while some form of physical distance can remain intact.

Video testimony

The genre of testimony overlaps with the therapeutic domain. People who testify have usually witnessed crimes—and sometimes crimes of which they were the victim. Testifying can be a way of coming to grips with the experienced wrongdoings. By putting their trauma into words, witnesses possibly enter into a process of working through their experiences, integrating traumatic events into existing systems of signification or meaning schemes. Geoffrey Hartman has argued that testifying can be helpful to a witness, even if it doesn't solve trauma. In the 1980s, Hartman was an initiator of one of the most famous video testimony projects, the Fortunoff Video Archive for Holocaust Testimonies at Yale University. According to this American literary theorist, one of the core aspects of testimony is its communal dimension. Testimonies are dialogic; people who give testimony are guided by an interviewer who asks questions and, most importantly, listens carefully in order to emphasize that the person who tells the story is important, as well as the story he tells (Hartman 1995: 194). "The interview situation is social in that it recognizes the survivor and acknowledges what has been endured" says Hartman (1995: 195). In his view, "the interviewing process creates an ad hoc community, and whether or not telling the story relieves traumatic stress, that communal dimension is a comfort" (1995: 202).

What is more, a pact is formed within the communities of transmission. The listener adopts the special responsibility of becoming a secondary witness to the memory of the testifying subject. The primary witness depends on the secondary witness to understand the significance of the memory, to extend it in time and space, and to make it public (Assmann 2006: 269). While dependent on an intimate relationship of trust between witness and interviewer, testifying is also an act which is, in the end, oriented towards a larger, public domain. As Hartman points out; "Testimony has both a private dimension, which is confessional and spiritual, and a public aspect, which is political and judicial" (1995: 195).

When testimonies are recorded by a video camera, as is the case with the Holocaust testimonies which are recorded by the Fortunoff archive, both the public and the private dimension of the testimony are affected by the presence of the medium.[12] As video is a medium that can store a lot of visual and auditory information at once; that can store and preserve this information relatively well; that allows easy replay; and can rapidly be disseminated, it is very much suited to disseminate testimonies to a wide public. In addition, testimonies may benefit from the reality effect the medium is able to create through some of its medium-specific conventional artifices. Such a reality effect may sustain a testimony's status as reliable evidence.

However, as Hartman claims, video can also produce an *un*reality effect. For viewers who are acquainted with the wide array of video manipulations and animations which are applied in so many of the contemporary (digital) videos by which we are surrounded on TV and the Internet, it becomes hard to look at video without suspecting manipulation. According to Hartman, young television addicts in particular suffer from a fatal form of suspension, not a suspension of disbelief, but rather a suspension of belief, "which consist in looking at everything live as if it were a reality that could be manipulated" (2000: 4). The video testimonies that were collected by the Fortunoff archive counter this *un*reality effect by using as little artifice as possible; no editing, no dissolves, etc. In the end, such an unedited style is, of course, a reality-effect producing *device* as well. It is a suitable device in light of testimony, though. Other videomatic reality-effect producing devices, such as hand-held camera movements or poor lighting, might detract too much attention from the testifying subject and her story.

In addition, the private domain of testimony is potentially threatened when video enters the community of transmission, because video can produce what some call a cold gaze. The medium is often understood as aggressive, in the sense that it provides an unemotional, unengaged perspective of the subject in front of the lens. It is said to objectify whatever and whoever it captures on tape. For witnesses who are simultaneously victims of the facts they testify to, which is evident in the case of Holocaust survivors, such an objectification is especially problematic. Victims such as Holocaust survivors have been the object of an oppressive gaze which "intended to implant in them a permanent feeling of nakedness and vulnerability" (Hartman 2002: 96). The "imperturbable" video camera (Hartman's word) should not form a reenactment of this gaze.

According to Hartman, the minimal visuality that characterizes the Fortunoff video testimonies not only counters the possible unreality effect of video images, but also works against the cold and objectifying focus of the video camera. During the recording process, the interviewers did not limit the time of the testimony or impose any conditions whatsoever. In addition, the camera's mobility, as well as its visual field, remains restricted to the face and gestures of one person speaking in a particular place, at a particular time. The words of the witnesses do not fade out, or into a cinematic simulacrum of the events being described. In addition, although excerpts of some testimonies have been made available on DVD and online, the archive only stores original recordings which are not edited or adjusted in postproduction. Moreover, the testimonies are not freely delivered to the impersonal market forces of electronic recall and dissemination; the archive guards the spread and accessibility of the survivor statements. In sum, in the case of the Fortunoff video testimonies, the witness' autonomy is maximized, both during the recording of the testimony and in postproduction.

Hartman contrasts this form of video testimony with cinematic documentaries which rely on testifying witnesses, such as Claude Lanzmann's *Shoah* (1985). In comparison to testimonial videos, films tends to apply more artifice. Lanzmann's documentary is heavily edited in postproduction; it combines the stories of the witnesses with shots of present-day locations. Moreover, during the interviews, the director sometimes put witnesses in difficult situations in order to jog their memory as well as their emotions. When one of the survivors speaks without emotion of how he had to cut the hair of fellow inmates, Lanzmann prompts him to cut the hair of a fellow survivor in order to spur his emotions. Many critics have defined Lanzmann's persistent intrusions as a form of exploitation (Bell-Metereau 2011: 426). The reason for this exploitation may lie with an additional factor which possibly affects the autonomy of the witness: the fact that documentaries on celluloid are embedded in the impersonal, commercial film industry. The medium of video is not as strongly related to conventions of editing, and allows its producers greater independence because of its inexpensiveness. Hence, video can more easily be used in a way that does not intrude into the testimony as it is told; it leaves the pace and space of the testimonial act intact.

When video is used in such a nonintrusive, yet attentive way, the medium is anything but cold, according to Hartman (2000: 11). In fact, many scholars as well as witnesses stress that video "re-embodied" those who had been denied their human body image in the camps. It gave "the tortured person back his human form, which was snatched away from him" (Applefeld 1988: 92). In the eyes of Hartman, the medium of video has had a positive effect on the witness testimonies as collected by the Fortunoff archive. In addition, he claims that the positive effect might be reciprocal. Survivor videography has had a potential impact on the medium: within the specific context of Holocaust witness statements, the minimalistic style of the video testimonies has overturned the coldness of the medium, and has turned video's objectifying gaze into an embodying and subjectifying mode of looking.

In addition, it is important to realize that the simple, minimalistic style of the testimonial videos is not merely valuable for the witnesses. From a political and pedagogical perspective, the quality of the gaze which the videos produce is just as important for the viewers as for the testifying subjects. Every viewer of a video testimony, in an ideal situation, becomes a part of the testimonial community. Like the interviewer who is present at the moment of recording, the viewer of the video is supposed to understand the significance of the testimony. Moreover, in a best-case scenario, the viewer adopts the responsibility of the testimonial alliance; namely to extend the narrated memory in time and space (if only by remembering it). If a spectator were to have a cold attitude of disbelief towards the witness they viewed on tape, some of the intended effects of the testimonies on their audience, such as "learning from the past" and "remembering forward," would surely be precluded. In a way, this would also concern the testifying subjects, who have an interest in the reception of their testimony.

Other potential problems which can block the viewers' ability to remember and learn from the horrors of the past are secondary traumatization and so-called compassion fatigue. When viewers, as secondary witnesses, over-identify with the primary witness who testifies, or when they are too heavily shocked by the suffering which is relayed in testimonies, they may not really be able to receive the stories; they will repress them instead. However, the pressure to respond to testimonies with empathy is enormous, and images and stories of human suffering are ubiquitous today. This may lead to a certain numbness; to an inability to feel compassion at all. Both over-identification and compassion fatigue indicate that empathy needs to be managed. The forms in which suffering is represented can play an important role in this respect. Hartman is of the opinion that, when it comes to the genre of survivor testimony, video is well suited to manage the empathy of the viewer. On the one hand, video testimonies reconnect the enormous event of the Holocaust with the concrete voice and face of an individual (Assmann 2006: 272). On the other hand, it does not overload the viewer with visual representations of the narrated story, as is sometimes the case in cinematic renderings of (Holocaust) testimonies. Video in its most minimalist form is able to relay terrible stories in a bearable, and therefore effective way.

Hartman's concern that explicit images of suffering may traumatize or numb the viewer is shared by theorists who focus on *films* that deal with the Holocaust. In *Haunted Images: Film, Ethics, Testimony and the Holocaust* (2008), Libby Saxton for instance wonders if "it is possible that images of atrocity might effectively shield us from the event itself," as she notes Slavoj Žižek's warning that "imaginary images of trauma can work to screen us from the Real rather than allowing us to approach it" (60). However, in spite of these concerns, film scholars do not necessarily share Hartman's belief that, in comparison to video, the cinema is less able to manage the viewer's empathy so that she can really receive what happened.

Siegfried Kracauer has argued that although films often present us with agitating visions, the audience is put at a distance via the camera's lens. This distance allows for a less distorted vision of a potentially disturbing reality. Therefore, Kracauer contends that the cinema "aims at transforming the agitated witness into a conscious observer" (1960: 58). In addition, Saxton argues that films of the Holocaust in particular play a vital role in the process of seeking truthful ways of bearing witness (2008: 122). She does not so much underline Kracauer's belief that the apparatus of film creates a safe and reflective distance from horrific events; instead, she points out that films which deal with the Holocaust often use ellipses and blind spots as a strategy to refer to horrors without showing them explicitly. Through such strategies, films "dose" the empathy and shock to which they give rise. Like video, film is therefore able to tell horrible stories in a bearable manner. Yet films manage to do so in a different way than the video testimonies.

Video against television, video for change

In addition to the confessional and testimonial genres discussed above, video is frequently used for activism. In a large number of activist projects and movements, the medium is posited as a space apart from the dominant social order, or as a tool which can be used in order to reflect on or recreate conventional social roles and structures. For many of these video practices, the term "alternative" does not quite express the overtone. They often have a militant character. Video is viewed as a counterspace, a space for resistance and action, or—when the metaphor of space is left behind—as a weapon. The medium is not just used apart from, but *against* the ruling order.

Video was first used as a "counter-medium" in the United States, after the invention of the Portapak. Artists, social activists, journalists, political groups, and alternative movements all embraced the versatile video camera as a way of bringing about social change. The aggressor that had to be opposed was the presumed cause of dominant social patterns: broadcast television. In contradistinction to Jameson's idea that broadcast television and video are one and the same medium, early video pioneers viewed popular television as video's evil other. With its standardized program structures and aesthetically homogenized offerings, broadcast television was believed to inscribe stereotypes and conformist patterns of behavior into society. Throughout the United States, video collectives were formed with the idea of producing an alternative form of television. Groups with telling names such as Video Free America, People's Video Theater, Global Village, TVTV (Top Value Television), and Videofreex, first screened their guerilla tapes to a small "in-crowd" audience in galleries, lofts, and vans. Later on, in the 1970s, the guerilla television groups could finally broadcast their footage on public television, and reach the masses.[13]

Under the influence of McLuhan's deterministic medium theory, these guerilla video activist believed that in working against broadcast television (a.k.a. "beast television") by invading it with their new medium, they would (at least partially) restore the corrupting impact of commercial TV on society. According to the medium theorist, the medium of television itself did not create the passivity, uniformity, and social homogenization the video guerillas attributed to commercial television. In *Understanding Media* (1964) McLuhan had claimed that in the electronic age of television, uniqueness and diversity can be fostered as never before. In the eyes of the video activists, this potential of the televisual medium had not yet been realized, as the medium was held back by conventional and commercial structures. This had to be countered by way of video, a medium with an even stronger propensity towards uniqueness and diversity, as well as interrelation on a large scale.

Because of the influence of McLuhan's ideas on these widespread video collectives, it is possible to conclude that, in the 1960s and 1970s, video was for a large part a product of medium theory, that is, of theoretical ideas on the nature and effect of media in general, and in particular of medium theory on another medium, television.

For one of the most dominant applications of the new video technology was shaped by theoretical ideas on electronic media. And by gaining a specific field of application, with its own goals and conventions, the technology became a medium.

McLuhan's emphasis on the logic and form of the medium can specifically be recognized in the importance the video makers attached to the formal features and stylistic traits of their tapes. The video guerillas embraced the unpolished formal features of their video footage. The grittiness and lack of sharpness of the black-and-white images, as well as the real-time character of the unedited tapes, were all dictated by the technological characteristics—or in retrospect, the limitations—of the early video machines; yet this rawness was praised as an honest style in contrast with the quick, edited scenes of conventional television (Boyle 1997: 228).

The conscious acceptance of unpolished style and its further elaboration by video guerillas was very much indebted to *cinéma vérité*. In addition to style, the guerilla video collectives followed the *vérité* principle of participatory filmmaking. The video camera was taken into the crowd, in order to view events from within—not from the conventional lofty, "objective" viewpoint of TV cameras positioned to survey an event (Boyle 1997: 228). This relationship with *cinéma vérité* in particular, as well as with film in general, was all the more active because many of the video activists were trained in film and/or had worked within the field of *cinéma vérité* (Paul Goldsmith, Wendy Appel, and Ira Schneider, among others). However, it is important to realize that although the work of video guerillas was clearly influenced by the medium of film, the collectives did not set out to make or recreate film. Their target was television.

In addition to video's "raw" style, the video guerillas regarded the accessibility and mobility of the video medium as sources for social change. Unlike television's predilection for uniformity and conventionality, video's accessible and mobile technology was seen as an opportunity to give a voice to the many different kinds of people in society, and to reach a variety of specific audiences. For instance, in one of TVTV's most famous video documentaries titled *Lord of the Universe* (1974), a young American Guru (Prem Rawat) and his followers are portrayed by mingling camera men at a large public event at the Houston Astrodome called "Millennium '73." However, in addition to the followers, many other voices are heard by the Portapak-carrying documentary makers. Adherents of other belief systems appear in the video, such as a Hare Krishna follower and a born-again Christian who criticizes devotees for "following the devil." In addition, former followers are interviewed about their disillusionment with the Guru's teachings. The method of recording a multitude of opinions from a participatory position is not an exception in contemporary television programs. In the 1970s, however, this form of television making was new. The diversity of the filmed people, moreover, matched the variety of audiences which the documentary eventually managed to reach. The video was first broadcast on WNET, a local noncommercial educational television station. It later reached a national audience when it appeared on 200 stations of national public television. In addition, the documentary was included in an exhibition on video art at the Whitney Museum of American art.

Guerilla collectives such as TVTV held the opinion that by "de-centralizing" television, video would broadcast as well as "narrow-cast" a democracy of ideas, opinions, and cultural expressions—made both by and for the people—on cable television. These ideas, opinions, and cultural expressions could so easily be mediated by video because of the lightweight video camera. As Lili Berko explains:

> The most revolutionary aspect of the porta-pak was its mobility. Through the porta-pak, television production was not locked into a studio and the confines of the codes of such a mediated experience. [. . .] Video soon became the vehicle through which the social world could be documented, the vehicle which would record the voices and the images of the Newark riots, or a Mardi Gras celebration; as such it proclaimed the public sphere to be its own.
>
> Berko in Tamblyn 1996: 292

As Berko's lines point out, McLuhan's message that the medium is the message wasn't completely taken to heart by the activist video makers. Although the basic characteristics of the medium were expected to make a lot of difference, the message—or content—of their videos was important to the guerilla activists too. Berko's remarks that the social world was *documented*, while the voices and images of the public sphere were *recorded* slightly understate the actions of the video guerillas, however. As Deirdre Boyle explains, the goal of street tapes was to create an "interactive information loop" with the subjects they recorded (1997: 8). In order to contest the one-way communication model of network television, people who were filmed were given authority over the video material with regard to dissemination. In addition, some collectives, such as *The People's Video Theater*, would invite the people they interviewed that day back to their lofts in the evening, in order to watch and discuss the tapes. Video's specific possibility of feedback formed the conceptual and technological basis for these social practices. However, in contrast with the previously discussed video art performances by Acconci and others, the video collectives did not investigate feedback within the confines of an artist's studio or the art gallery. Instead, it was applied in the streets as a tool for communication, dialogue, mediation, and reflection by anyone, between anyone.

In the course of a few decades, guerilla television has been absorbed by mainstream television.[14] Popular television has adopted many of the stylistic traits of the guerilla videos. Participatory video reports (often with a slightly humorous undertone—also a hallmark of the guerillas) are not uncommon in contemporary television programs. The video guerillas' strong belief in the social possibilities of the medium are not so much present in most of these TV shows. This belief has, however, survived in another contemporary discourse; the discourse of community video. Throughout the world, projects are initiated by community workers, video makers, developmental aid bodies, and political groups, in which video equipment is installed within small, marginal communities—ranging from groups of homeless children to declining tribes to besieged minorities. The donated cameras often come with instructions; handbooks are written in which the application of the camera as a tool for social change is explained.[15]

One of the main assumptions of community video projects is empowerment. The common denominator of the involved communities is that they are either dominated or threatened by larger, more powerful social groups. Video is employed as a way to counter this domination and disempowerment. With a clear reference to the slogan "power to the people," community video projects often make use of the phrase "camera to the people." Comparable to the guerillas' view on video, the contemporary video projects regard video as an interactive, user-defined, "horizontal" medium. As Burnett puts it: "Aside from the conventional bow to the hegemonic influences of mass media, there is the key thought of liberation from control, the opening of hitherto closed spaces of experience, and the unveiling of different ways of thinking" (1996: 288). The resulting sense is "that people, once empowered in the use of the medium, will gain a new understanding of their own viewpoints on the world, if not their politics" (1996: 288). In addition, the video medium can empower marginal groups by documenting their suffering. Video projects such as the global cooperation WITNESS project ("See it, film it, change it") and the Palestinian B'TSelem project arrange equipment, know-how and a network for oppressed people who suffer from violence. They are invited to shoot back at their perpetrator(s) with a video camera.

These video applications are characterized by a strong belief in the epistemological and pedagogical power of the medium. Through the documentation of social realities, the truth on (oppressive) social structures is revealed to the video viewers, who gain knowledge and insight from the tapes. In addition to the epistemological and pedagogical effects of the video medium, it is remarkable that the medium-specific domains of confession, testimony, and therapy also reappear in the activist and utopian video projects. Video is used to offer individuals a chance to speak their minds, bear witness to crimes, and to heal subjects and their interrelations with others. However, unlike most of the video projects I discussed before (artists' diaries, couples' therapy, the Fortunoff video archive) video activists are less concerned with the benefit and well-being of one or a few individuals. Instead, they place most emphasis on the interests of the community.

In the field of video, the utopian, idealistic expectations of video—which the video guerillas of the 1970s have passed on to the contemporary community projects—are dominant but not monopolistic. They form the other end of the views on video with which this chapter started: the definitions of video as an isolating, antisocial medium. Both poles represent extremes, and can be criticized for precisely that. On the one hand, critics of postmodernism pushed the matter quite far when they claimed that the video user is cut off from the real world by empty, meaningless video images. On the other hand, the medium is put in too bright a light if it is believed to automatically grant a voice and a "piece" of power to all the different people who inhabit the "global village."

However, instead of evaluating the accuracy of these specifications of video in relation to the social, it is more interesting to consider social explanations or causes for these particular specifications. The theories and practices which blame video for their corrupting effect on society, or which praise the medium for its ability to change social structures for the better, are all born of worries about or discontent with the present state of society, or contemporary developments within particular social formations. The negative evaluation of video by critics of postmodernism should be seen in light of their displeasure with postmodern society (and a simplistic view of postmodernism). The possibilities which video activists saw—and still see—in video can, for instance, be seen in light of their worries about a loss of social differentiation within large, hegemonic societies or the globalized world. In addition, in the 1970s, video was taken up as a revolutionary tool in a world which was already full of social revolutions and protests. In all of these cases, video can be said to have co-produced social developments (leading to postmodernism, globalization, revolutions, and so on), yet the theorizations and applications of the medium were *also* shaped by social developments which were already going on. As Sean Cubitt has put it well: "video is both a symptom of the societies in which it has emerged and is being used, and a tool in their further development" (1993: xvii).

CHAPTER 15
FILM: PRIVATE/PRODUCTION

One of the most prominent social functions of the medium of film should probably be sought in conversations on film. Talking about film can function as a "social lubricant," it enables us to get to know someone by exchanging thoughts about a subject which is familiar to almost anyone: narrative cinema. As Thomas Elsaesser (2000) puts it:

> The popular mainstream film has become a kind of "lingua franca", a common language besides English, which enables young—or not so young—people to communicate, share experiences, and get to know each other. By talking about film, we discover each other's likes and dislikes, each other's sense of humor, and particular outlook on life. Not least because someone's reaction to a film is something personal, intimate even, and at the same time often tends to create a feeling of "belonging."
>
> 9, author's translation

As Elsaesser points out, films are more than a leisure activity in which we look at a story of people who partake in entertaining, interesting or dangerous activities. Today, films have become "a space, a surrounding, a cultural frame of reference, and an experience shared by many" (2000: 9, author's translation). As cinema is a subject we can all relate to, films enable social bonding. In addition to this social effect of popular mainstream cinema, it is important to note the socially binding effect of, frankly, unpopular or less popular films. For, besides a "lingua franca," film also forms languages which are not known, understood, or appreciated by everyone. The "sense of belonging" which, according to Elsaesser, can be produced by conversations about popular mainstream films, might even be stronger when it comes to the social effect of more marginal cinematic genres or films. The less known or the less widely appreciated a specific genre, director, or film is, the stronger the feelings of solidarity and "belonging" among members of its audience. People immediately bond when they turn out to like the same kind of cult movies, unknown upcoming director, undervalued national cinema, obscure, ill-defined genre, or that one film that everyone should have seen but no one has ever heard of, except for those few people.

In the previous chapter, I discussed how video is theorized as an alternative space in which subjects can freely experiment, perform and speak their mind—while being safely apart from and often in opposition to the ruling dominant social order. The space in question, however, mostly concerns the illusionistic, represented space of the video image. When it comes to film, the alternative space is formed in front of the image, too; the space of the audience becomes the alternative space where one can freely speak one's mind, and freely depart from mainstream preferences. The act of simply liking certain cult movies or unknown genres can be a form of resistance to the dominant (aesthetic as well as social) order. In one of the most militant, activist applications of cinema I will discuss below—the so-called Third Cinema—this idea of the viewing space as a space of resistance plays an especially important part.

First, however, I will turn to another film genre that has had an enormous impact on the production of a social order: the home movie. It goes without saying that this genre is incommensurable with Third Cinema in many respects, for it does not serve activist or emancipatory ideals in any way—quite the opposite, one might say; home movies have produced and sustained rather than opposed and attacked the dominant social order. However, besides their impact on social structures, Third Cinema and the home movie have one thing in common: both forms of film are particularly important in relation to video. Not only can the two genres bring some notable differences and similarities between film and video to light; both applications of the filmic medium have been largely succeeded or taken over by video. It is for this reason that my discussion of film's social effects (which are manifold) will focus most specifically on the genre of the home movie, as well as the activist Third Cinema movement. I will compare both of these applications of film to video practices. My discussion of the home movie's production of social structures starts with an effect that seems adverse to social bonding: isolation.

Reel families

According to McLuhan, the "Reel World" is part of the Gutenberg Galaxy. Film is linked to the technology of print, he claims, because it is the business of both writer and filmmaker to transfer the reader and viewer from one world, his own, to another, the world created by typography and film (1964: 311). Whereas the viewer of video has been said to turn into an object because of the boring ongoing flow of its meaningless images (*dixit* Jameson), the novel reader and the film viewer sit in silent psychological solitude while they are mesmerized by the world produced by the book or film. Although I would say that this social and psychological isolation of the film viewer is also due to social and cultural conventions which dictate that films are viewed in silence, McLuhan rightly points out that this solitary viewing mode has been enforced by a technological factor as well. When sound was added to the silent moving images, the audience had to be quiet in order to understand the plot.

The idea that film isolates can also be found in theoretical reflections on the family, one of the smallest social structures in which film has played an important part. As Patricia Zimmerman (1995: 145) wrote, amateur film married the nuclear family in the 1950s, after the standardization of 16mm during World War II. The photographic and mass-market press set out to market amateur film as a hobby as well as a commodity for nuclear families (1995: 113). These marketing strategies capitalized on capitalism. The economic boom within Western capitalist societies after World War II increased leisure time and disposable income. In addition, the nuclear family and the home became central, idealized social structures within post-war societies. The popularity of the home movie can be regarded as the outcome of these social developments.

Although born from its social context, the home movie in turn reinforced the ideology of the nuclear, patriarchal family. In the words of Zimmerman "home movies preserved and evoked a residual social formation of families as important cultural and social agents through idealizing, indeed worshipping its cloistered interactions" (1995: 133). Besides their conventional focus on moments which show a family's togetherness, happiness and generational continuity—such as birthdays, weddings, vacations, and family feasts—home movies can be said to aggrandize the representation of the family through the application of professional film techniques.

These techniques mostly concern film style. As Zimmerman explains, the home movie is dominated and restricted by Hollywood's continuity style. Especially in its initial stages, the practice of amateur filmmaking within the domestic sphere was regarded as "a consumer practice zone for perfecting Hollywood pictorial composition and narrative techniques" (Zimmerman 1995: 145). Many directives for the production of home movies explained the visual grammar and story-telling logic of Hollywood to the public, counseled them in Hollywood-like special effects, and propagated the creation of a coherent story within each family film. In the early 1960s, this idea of the home movie as a controlled narrative in which the family often staged tableaux, was challenged by adherents of more spontaneous, mobile mode of filmmaking in which the camera operator moved around with a hand-held camera. However, even this more spontaneous mode of filmmaking was dominated by the Hollywood continuity style, in that the pursuit of comprehensible narrative organization was never completely given up. In addition, adherents of both the mobile and the more controlled form of home movie production pursued the same goal: to create the illusion of reality. According to Zimmerman, the reality effect of home movies institutionalized the nuclear happy family as a natural construct. Moreover, as the father was the primary filmmaker, the home movie preserved the ideology of the patriarch in total control of the family (1995: 134). Yet, as all family members participated in the preparation, the production, and the reception of the home movie, the genre can be said to have sustained the togetherness of the family.

This performative effect of the home movie seems at odds with my initial assertion that home movies are related to the idea that the medium of film isolates its users. In the case of home movies, the medium seems to establish the opposite; it integrates individuals into a cohesive family structure. However, the isolating effect Zimmerman addresses concerns not so much the relationship between individual family members, but between the family and its social context. As an essentially private activity cloistered within the home, the production of home movies reinforces the separation between the private sphere of the family and the public sphere. By glorifying the solitary activities of the private home, the genre presents the family as an autonomous unit without any connections to larger social structures. Zimmerman laments this disconnection of the home movie from its social context because she believes that amateur filmmaking in general can have radical, critical potential. The genre of the home movie—with its predicates of togetherness and familialism—"colonized" the practice of amateur film production in the 1950s, marginalizing filmmaking as a hobby to fill up leisure time and as a retreat from social and political participation (Zimmerman 1995: 146).

The exclusion of the political, social, and historical context from home movies can become poignantly visible in art films which add this context to home movies, for instance through voice-overs, written texts, or additional visual material. One of the best examples in this regard is the film *The Maelstrom* (1997) by Hungarian filmmaker Péter Forgács. In this film, Forgács has reedited archival home movie material. Most of the found footage the filmmaker appropriated was originally produced in the 1940s by two different families. The first, primary source is the Dutch-Jewish family Peereboom; the second one is the family of Arthur Seyss-Inquart, who represented Hitler in the Netherlands during World War II. This major political and historical event, however, is completely invisible in the personal family clips of the two very disparate families. However, the story of World War II has been added to the home movie clips by Forgács, who uses voice-overs and written texts in order to explain how the families and their images are related to the unfolding of World War II in the Netherlands. This external information doesn't make the political context perceptible within the images, though. For, in spite of the fact that we learn that the Peerebooms are a Jewish family who suffer under the Nazi regime, their home movies do not show this repression in any way. The fact that even the grand history of World War II does not interfere at all with the cheerful, cozy atmosphere of the home footage, proves how strong the boundary between the family film and the family's social and political context really is. Even when the Peerebooms are packing to be deported to Auschwitz, the home movie manages to portray the situation as a domestic scene.[1,2]

Whereas Zimmerman finds fault with the genre of the home movie because its ideology of the nuclear family excludes the social and the political, many critics and artists have focused primarily on the aspects of the family itself that are excluded by the ideological character of the genre. As Michelle Citron (1989) has demonstrated, the sides of family life that are *not* shown in home movies are often more interesting and significant than what *is* depicted. The problematic, tense aspects of family life are usually left outside the frame. Filmmakers such as Alan Berliner, Michelle Citron, Morgan Dews, and Adrianne Finelli have tried to expose the repressive and silencing effects of home movies by reediting personal home-movie material and/or mixing the material with explanatory texts. In *Must Read After My Death* (Dews 2007) and *Too Soon Too Late* (Finelli 2009), seemingly cheerful home movies are accompanied by either spoken or written diaristic texts produced by one of the central women in the movies. Whereas the film clips portray these women as happy mothers and wives, the diary fragments expose their unhappiness and depression. In *Daughter Rites* (1979), Citron shows the disconnection between herself and her mother through a montage of happy home movie material in which mother and daughter seem to run towards each other. However, at the end of the scene, they do not fall into the expected warm embrace. Instead, they miss each other, and continue their trajectory without meeting at all.

Films such as *Too Soon Too Late* and *Daughter Rites* can be seen as visual expressions of Zimmerman's ideological thesis. They show that home movies are integrally related to the ideology of the family, and should therefore not be understood as transparent documents of family life. However, Citron goes one step further by pointing out that the repressed is nevertheless visible in home movie material. This exposure does not entail the rearrangement of home movie footage; it is carried out through a close reading of film strips. In her book *Home Movies and Other Necessary Fictions* (1989) Citron analyzes a piece of family film in which she is about seven years old and hugs her sister. Then, she gives her younger sister a kiss and laughs. The filmmaker points out that when the film fragment is frozen (the still is printed in the book), it becomes visible that this seemingly endearing gesture of one sibling to another is actually an aggressive act. The still film frames show how Citron pushes her tongue into her sister's mouth in a pretty obtrusive way. The unamused expression of the sister confirms that the kiss was indeed a ferocious intrusion. In addition, the slightly sardonic smile on Citron's face after she has offended her sister is not innocent. Citron explains that this film fragment illustrates the incest of which she was a victim as a child. In the film images, we can see how she unconsciously imitates the actions of the uncle who abused her.

Citron's close reading does not merely reveal what is repressed within the home movie, it even reveals what is repressed or has remained unnoticed within her family. By applying film as a medium by which hidden family secrets can be uncovered, Citron subscribes to the idea of the technologically produced image as an epistemological tool that makes the invisible visible. In doing so, she demonstrates the advantages of film over photography. Film offers the possibility to study small facial and physical movements both in real time and in successive still images on a film strip. These small gestures—which can hardly be perceived by the naked eye—can expose the possibly problematic nature of the relationship between family members.

Next to the fragment of the aggressive kiss, Citron analyzes a piece of family film in which her mother puts slides in the girl's hair. The young Citron shows discomfort, she recoils from her mother's hands. As soon as the distracted mother notices her daughter's resistance, she persistently continues to shove the pins in the little girl's hair with a grim and a determined expression on her face. These small interactions seem insignificant when they unfold in real time in a couple of seconds. The scene of a mother who is trying to do the hair of a struggling daughter can easily be understood as an endearing moment in the life of a happy family. However, when the scene is studied per frame, the mother's attitude towards her daughter appears to be pretty insensitive. Her physical gestures and expressions show that she is not bothered by her daughter's discomfort at all.

Even without additional information of an insider, a detailed examination of the short film fragment could lead one to suspect that Citron's mother might not have been very attentive towards her children. Citron points out that it is indeed important to understand the small frictions which one can discover in a few seconds of home movie as subtle manifestations of general and persistent—yet most often covert—dysfunctions within the family. Citron's mother could not easily be recognized as a cold mother. However, the subtle insensitivity she displays towards her daughter in the short hair-slides scene characterizes their entire relationship—and with that, Citron's life—in important ways.

Instead of using the home movie as a genre for ideological repression, Citron deploys it as a tool for discovery and recovery. This doesn't merely *expose* the ideological nature or "falseness" of home movies. By showing that the home movie can do quite the opposite of covering up and excluding, Citron's strategy also *counters* the repressive effect of the genre's ideological character. The filmmaker's approach points out that the home movie's typical focus on cloistered family interactions can turn the effect of the genre around: if the focus is sharp enough, idealizing and worshipping can become critical dissection.

From family film to home video

Another approach to the ideological character of home movies can be found in the theoretical writings of media scholar James M. Moran. Like Citron, he looks for moments in home movies in which the ideological conventions of the genre do not hold. However, instead of searching for manifestations of a family's repressed dark side within film clips, Moran advocates a focus on the personal and individual aspects of home movies. The author criticizes Zimmerman for her representation of the "home mode" as a form of amateur filmmaking corruptly domesticated by familial ideology. He argues that the home mode has relative autonomy within the social order, not because the genre is a self-identical practice immune from its historical relations, "but because its cultural functions, depending on the communities that they serve, may or may not express dominant ideology" (2002: 56).

In his *There's No Place Like Home Video* (2002) Moran opposes Zimmerman's ideology thesis by emphasizing that, besides its possible perpetuation of familial and capitalist ideologies, the genre of the home has positive functions and possibilities. Much at odds with Zimmerman's ideas on the isolating effect of the genre, Moran claims that by providing an active mode of media production, the home mode constructs "a liminal space in which practitioners may explore and negotiate the demands of their public, communal, and private, personal identities" (60). In addition to the genre's inclination to enable the deliberation of personal and public identities, it enables a material articulation of generational continuity over time, and constructs an image of home as a cognitive and affective foundation situating our place in the world. According to Moran, the genre provides a valuable narrative format for communicating family legends and personal stories (61).

In the 1980s, video supplanted celluloid as the dominant amateur motion picture medium. The home video quickly became the new home movie. Since the advent of this new medium, the positive functions of the home mode have expanded and gained in force, while the influence of the ideology of the patriarchal nuclear family has declined. Moran argues that the expansion of the home mode's expressive possibilities for a large part can be explained by specific technological differences between the medium of film and that of video. Amateur film equipment consists of a camera that lacks sound recording, and holds relatively expensive reels of film which can only record for three minutes. The celluloid substrates, moreover, need high light levels in order to record sharp images, cannot be recycled, and need lab processing for proper exposure and development. The home video apparatus, on the other hand, typically consists of a camera with synchronous sound recording. The relatively inexpensive videocassettes allow up to eight hours of shooting, may be recycled, operate in low light levels, and do not require lab processing. Videotapes can be viewed immediately after recording, and can easily be played back and copied at home (Moran 2002: 41). According to Moran, these basic differences precipitate differences of production and reception, which in turn "extend home video's range of content and space for interpretation beyond the limitations of home movies" (41).

One of the most important differences between home movie and home video production is that home videos often include the downsides and boring aspects of (family) life which are absent from most home movies. This difference in content can be explained by technological disparities between video and film. As Moran points out, home movie production methods emphasize brevity, control, and selection because of the limited length per reel. "Thus, rather than expose random moments of everyday life, which would require a much greater financial investment, home movie makers generally film only the highlighted moments of ritual events wherein participants could be posed and conventions controlled in advance" (Moran 2002: 41). A video camera, in contrast, may be left running on a tripod for hours, where it may ultimately be forgotten. Moreover, video's sensitivity to low light levels allows the camera to be present at virtually all indoor family scenes. Therefore, moments of embarrassment, distress or defeat are less stringently excluded from home videos than they are from home movies.

In addition, video's synchronous sound recording allows for on-camera narration. This allows the camera operator to interpret the scene while shooting, and invites interview-like conversations with subjects in front of the lens. Like the long running time of video, the medium's synchronous sound relaxes some of the artificial conventions imposed by home movies. The subjects on view do not have to pose or pretend that they do not see the camera; they either freely interact with the camera operator or forget that they are being videotaped. Now that the amateur video camera has become a regular onlooker of family life, its presence often goes unnoticed. In sum, many of video's technological features enable a representation of the family that is less censured and contrived than the depiction of the family by film. Because of this, "home video reveals that families have always been more complex and contradictory than home movies have generally portrayed them" (Moran 2002: 43).

When it comes to reception, one of the most important differences between home movies and home videos is that the latter are viewed by larger audiences than the former. While family films were viewed within the private sphere of the living room by family members only, home videos are shared with friends and acquaintances, or released to the public domain via television shows or the Internet. This expansion of the audience elevates some of the isolating effect which Zimmerman attributed to the genre of the home movie. The family no longer sits in solitude in front of a screen in their own living room; they share their family footage with others. This sharing involves social interaction between the family members and outsiders. The viewers who are not a part of the represented family are supposed to react to the clip, preferably with compliments or moved "oohs" and "aahs." In this respect, the video medium can again be said to satisfy the narcissist impulse of its users, whose pride and self-love is fed by the admiration of others.

Through explicit, overt reactions to home material, viewers not only sustain the narcissism of the family on view; they also connect themselves to this family. Zimmerman has argued that some home videos even need sentimental outbursts from the audience in order to *be* home videos. When viewers of a home video are not related to the family by consanguinity, their responses are necessary to show that they acknowledge the images as *home* video. Without spectator interaction, the video would be reduced to disengaged, inconsequential surveillance (Zimmerman 1995: 144). Showing or posting a reaction is a polite and reassuring gesture towards the family in question. It affirms that, as a viewer, you do not watch their private life in a disengaged, uninterested way, but that you affectively relate to the people in the video. By responding to the material, the viewer includes herself provisionally in the family, thus escaping the compromising position of silent voyeur. A familial viewing community, then, is both a prerequisite and a result of home videos.

It is remarkable that when home movies are compared to home videos, many genre conventions that defined the family film can suddenly be understood as the outcome of technological factors. The genre's initial exclusive focus on the happy highlights within family life can for instance no longer be interpreted as the representation of familial ideology alone; it was just as much dictated by technical limitations of the filmic medium. Likewise, the isolation of the viewing situation was prompted by the cumbersome equipment which had to be installed in order to project home movies. The medium of video has exposed that these forms of exclusion and isolation can be diminished by technological changes. In the words of Moran: "... video has liberated the constraints of the photographic apparatus, pressuring home mode practitioners toward [...] eliminations, patterned just as much by material and economic choices as by ideology" (2002: 43).

However, as Moran rightly notes, the revolutionary impact of video technology should not be overestimated: "... rather than assume that video itself may 'revolutionize' amateur practice because it changes conventional perceptions of domestic living [...], we more properly should conclude that the new medium is more likely to represent the fuller range of domestic ideologies already present in culture" (43). It cannot be denied, however, that "the fuller range of domestic ideologies" which Moran mentions has gained force over the last couple of decades. The ideal of the nuclear family has lost terrain, while alternative family forms have made their entry. Can we assume that video has had a hand in the transformation of domestic ideologies, without falling into the trap of technological determinism? Moran leaves his answer hanging when he concludes that video has expanded the aspects of family life which the home mode can represent. Yet, by focusing on the representation of what is already in place within the social sphere, Moran overlooks the performative effect of these representations on their social context. Although the transformation of family ideals within society should certainly not be understood as the result of video technology alone, it is reasonable to suspect that video has supported these changes.

This performative effect of medium-specific family representation *is* emphasized in the functions which Moran has attributed to the home mode: it constructs a space in which we explore identities, it articulates generational continuity, constructs an image of home, locates our place in the world, and provides a narrative format for communicating personal family stories. These functions show that film and video in the home mode not only represent, but also construct during the process of representation. In comparison to film, video has not only liberated representational constraints. It has also liberated constraints concerning the kinds of identities, families, homes, and places in the world can be produced by way of moving images. The expanded expressive possibilities that video has introduced to the home mode have therefore not only affected how the family can be represented, but also how the family can be built.

Counter-cinema counters cinema

As for the field of video, film's field of application contains considerable strands of alternative practices and activist counter-movements. Just like activist videos, films produced within the alternative realm are aimed at social emancipation and empowerment. They act for the oppressed and the marginalized within society. However, some important differences can be pointed out between activist video and activist film. First of all, the metaphor of space is less applicable to films that deal with social identity and social change.

Video is often described as a contained, secluded space. The space indicated when the medium is defined as an alternative or third space often, but not always, concerns the represented space; the space in front of the camera which is subsequently visible in the video image. Video artists and activists emphasized that the spatiotemporal separation between the represented space and the space of presentation in which the video is viewed by a wider audience offers represented subjects the safety and privacy to speak their mind and experiment with social roles. On the contrary, in alternative and counter-cinemas the separation between the represented space and the viewing space is breached as much as possible. Activist filmmakers who are part of the so-called Third Cinema—an activist group of primarily Latin-American filmmakers which lived its heyday around 1970—declare continuity between the film space onscreen and the space in which it is shown. This viewing context is not limited to the boundaries in which the film is viewed by a participatory audience; it concerns a wide social context. The inside of the film is supposed to be continuous with its outside, because it deals with the real struggles of the poor and oppressed within their society.

The idea of video as a detached, private, and secluded space can also be explained by the accessibility of the medium. As contradictory as this seems, the accessibility of the video medium grants video makers a substantial degree of control over the size of the social space of their video.[3] This doesn't go for film. Making a film is more difficult and more expensive than the production of a video. The creation of a movie requires a variety of costly professional equipment, and—partly as a result of that—it depends on corporate action and professional teamwork. In addition, films often depend on distribution networks before they can reach their audience.[4] So, the social space of film cannot be limited to one person when it comes to the domain of production. In addition, the temporal distance which film requires between the moment of production and the moment of reception precludes the inclusion of a film's social space within its viewing space. Such inclusion is possible with video; in the situation of instant feedback, the viewing space in which the apparatus of video is situated potentially encloses the social space that is simultaneously produced. The closed circuit of live feedback necessarily includes the position of the viewing subject as a well as the represented subject, and can possibly contain the enunciating subject (artist/producer) of the installation as well. Although the social aspect of this set-up has been questioned because the subject positions are often occupied by one and the same person, they certainly do form a spatial web. They are separated in space yet related by the acts of looking and being looked at. Definitions of video as space—enclosed alternative space, counter-space, third space or action space—can, therefore, also be motivated by the possible coincidence of the conventionally and mechanically produced viewing space and social space which the medium produces in a closed-circuit set-up.[5]

Because of film's dependence on relatively large social groups of production, films can be said to have a social effect even prior to their completion. For, even before a film is shown to an audience—and thus before it has entered into the communication model of sender(s) and receiver(s) often applied to map out a medium's social web of interrelations—it starts to generate social relations between its producers. This idea of producing social cohesion through movie production can be discovered in some alternative film movements. The organization Women Make Movies, for instance, was established in 1972 with the idea of addressing the misrepresentation of women in the media. It funded—and continues to do so to this day—projects by female filmmakers who make movies about women. However, in the 1970s, the emphasis was not only on the content of films. The organization set up programs in which women would collectively produce films. This collective social aspect of making a movie together was just as important as the educational aspects of the training programs and the content of the films that were made.

Similar importance is attached to the collectivity of production by the Third Cinema movement. In the manifesto *Towards a Third Cinema* (1969), filmmakers Fernando Solanas and Octavio Getino explain that the revolutionary film making they have in mind already produces a collective during the production process. Third Cinema films aimed to document the daily reality of their nation's struggling people. Their films were shot on the streets, which demanded the support of the people in the street—both those inside and outside the frame of the camera's viewfinder. This support was not lacking. As Solanas and Getino point out, Third Cinema films such as *La hora de los hornos* (Solanas and Getino 1968) were made in hostile circumstances with the support and collaboration of militants and cadres of the people. As a rule, Solanas points out, "vanguard layers and even masses participate collectively in the work of the film when they realize it is the continuity of their daily life" (1969: 8). Merely the production process of the films in some cases already inspired what the Third Cinema Activists aimed for: the rise and coherence of dominated social groups.

Alternative and activist films that pursue social empowerment instead of profit often have to find, or create a network of "allies" who support the production and distribution of their film. In light of this, it is not surprising that theories and practices that deal with film as a medium of social emancipation pay a lot of attention to the aspects and modes of film production. In *An Accented Cinema* (2001) Hamid Naficy discusses what he sees as a group of stylistic traits shared by so-called accented films—films that function as the performance of the identity of individuals and communities which are situated within social interstices, as well as the interstices of the film industry (10). Alongside his primary attention to style, Naficy devotes one whole part to a discussion of different modes of funding, production, and distribution on which accented films depend because they cannot rely on the dominant, mainstream film industry.[6]

The specific appearance of accented cinema—in which Naficy includes the large body of cinematic works which deal with social identity—can be summed up as follows: it has a low-tech, often home-made quality, is mostly nonfictional and biographical, and is moreover characterized by narrative hybridity and a tactile optics. Accented films are fragmented, multilingual, epistolary, and self-reflexive. Borders and border crossings, doubled and lost characters, journeys, airports, and suitcases, as well as intermedial relationships within a film, can all be understood as part of the accented style. The appearance of video in the films of a director whose work is discussed elsewhere in this book—Atom Egoyan—is interpreted by Naficy as a marker of "accentedness." According to Naficy, instances of intermediality in film often express a concern with those who exist in between societies: interstitial, displaced subjects, and diasporized communities.

Although the accented films Naficy discusses are not the most polemical and militant ones in the field of counter-cinema, the author stresses that accented cinema "is a political cinema which stands opposed to authoritarianism and oppression" (2001: 30). However, as Naficy also makes clear, in addition to this opposition to disempowerment and social marginalization, accented cinema is positioned vis-à-vis dominant cinema. The accented style stands opposed to the unaccented style of Hollywood productions and other commercial mainstream films. The accented aesthetic of smallness and imperfection is not in accordance with the mainstream tradition, and the narrative strategies of accented films cross generic boundaries and undermine conventional cinematic realism. One of the progenitors of accented cinema, the Third Cinema group—which is, in fact, one of the most polemical and militant in the field—posits itself against mainstream cinema (First Cinema) in a similar manner. By way of a rough, unpolished "poor" style, Third Cinema wishes to differentiate itself from commercial cinema. In addition, its imperfect documentary style is aimed at social empowerment and revolution; the unfinished, unordered and violent works are made "with a camera in one hand and a rock in the other" (Solanas and Getino 1969: 5).[7]

The stylistic characteristics of counter-cinema are interesting in comparison to the counter-video movement that I discussed earlier on. The video guerillas similarly applied rough, unpolished style as a way of opposing oppression by the conventional ruling class. Yet, the video guerillas worked against television. Engaged counter-cinema fights battles within the arena of its own medium. Film is opposing film.

The Third Cinema can be related to video in two additional ways. First, as Teshome Gabriel explains in "Third Cinema Updated" (2010), third cinema has evolved and branched out since it arose in the 1960s in relation to revolutionary struggles in the third world (most particularly in Latin America, but also in Africa and Asia). Because the communities that are constituted around Third Cinema have become less fixed and more heterogeneous, Third Cinema has become an increasingly creolized form in which the myths and stories of different cultures are integrated. Moreover, as Gabriel explains, "many of the narrative communities have become more media-savvy than they might have been at the outset of Third Cinema. They have become much more adept at adopting/adapting various media for their own uses" (under "Narrative Communities"). As a result, in contemporary Third Cinema (or rather; Third Cinema*s*), stories from both different cultural heritages *and* different media are mixed. One of the most important media which Third Cinema films have adopted is video. According to Gabriel, the video camera has become a vital tool in witnessing social injustice, police violence, and other forms of oppression. He even claims that "witnessing via the video camera has become a sort of substitute for a Third Cinema style of filmmaking" (under "Third Cinema as Collective Witness"). It is in this different form (of video) that Third Cinema continues to serve as a guardian and witness for the underrepresented and marginalized, according to Gabriel.

However, although Gabriel views the substitution of Third Cinema by video as a process of the last two decades, I would say that Third Cinema and video have always had an affinity with each other—even though this affinity was not expressed within videos or Third Cinema films. The link between the video medium and the Third Cinema relies—paradoxically—on an aspect by which Third Cinema at first sight differentiates itself from video, namely the fact that—quite unlike the specification of video as a secluded space—Third Cinema makers upheld the idea of continuity between the represented space and the space of presentation. The film show was defined as a meeting, an event, and an act. The film-as-act was only completed when the members of the audience participated in the discussion, the action plans, and finally the actions to which the films gave rise. In that sense, the film spectators became producers of the film.[8]

Moreover, the filmmakers presumed a level of identity between their viewers/co-producers and the represented subjects in their films. They made films of the people for the people. In addition, viewers of Third Cinema films were transformed by the fact that they had to take some risks to attend the film meetings. In the words of Solanas and Getino:

> Every comrade who attended [. . .] showings did so with the full awareness that he was infringing the System's law and exposing his personal security to eventual repression. This person was no longer a spectator, on the contrary, from the moment he decided to attend the showing, by the moment he lined up on this side by taking risks and contributing his living experience to the meeting, he became an actor, a more important protagonist than those who appeared in the films.
>
> 1969: 7–8

The viewer/producer/actor was not only supposed to participate during the film screening by contributing to the arguments, conclusions and plans which could be derived from the movie, but was also supposed to carry out the proposals for action. As Solanas and Getino explained to the audience of their film:

> The conclusions at which you may arrive as the real authors and protagonists of this history are important. [. . .] But most important of all is the action that may arise from these conclusions [. . .]. This is why the film stops here; it opens out to you so that you can continue it.
>
> 1969: 8

Although the set-up of the Third Cinema film meetings does not resemble the set-up of closed-circuit video with live feedback at all, these forms of cinema and video are very similar in one important respect: the positions of viewer, producer, and subject of representation can all be occupied simultaneously by one and the same person. Therefore, this particular form of film accomplishes something usually believed to be specific to the medium of video.

CHAPTER 16
ELECTRONIC DIARIES, CINEMATIC STORIES

Lynn Hershman's *Electronic Diary*

> Right now I'm sitting here with no cameraman in the room. I'm totally alone. I would never, ever talk this way if somebody were here. It's almost as if, if somebody were in the room, it would ensure lying [. . .] just like eating alone.

In *Binge*, the second of three sections of Lynn Hershman's *Electronic Diary* (1985–1989), Hershman looks into the camera, and tells us how she has frequent romances with "caloric strangers" since her husband left her. In the privacy of her home, Hershman confesses, she often binges on large amounts of food. As the quote above suggests, her video project is an attempt to tell the truth about her eating disorder. It is, moreover, also an attempt to tell the truth about one of the causes of her disorder; the fact that she has repressed her incestuous childhood—until the moment that she testifies on tape that she was abused. Next to the confessional and testimonial aspect of the *Electronic Diary*, Hershman's project also has a therapeutic goal. As the videomaker herself states repeatedly in the work: "It helps me to talk about it."

For the artist, the solitary nature of the recording situation spurs self-revelation and honesty. However, like so many other video works in which artists videotape themselves, the privacy of the recording set-up is known to be provisional. Within her *Electronic Diary*, Hershman often wonders about the feelings and impressions of her future audience, and she occasionally addresses the (imagined) spectator. "Are you watching me? Are you hearing me? Am I voicing things for you?," the artist wonders in *First Person Plural* (part three of the diary). In *Binge*, she remarks that it must be quite boring to listen to someone talking about their diet. "Who cares?," she wonders. Still, Hershman believes that someone will care enough to listen, for a moment later, she starts asking personal questions to the camera/viewer about some of the topics she has just revealed about herself: "When was the last time you had sex? Or, more interesting, when was the first time you ever had sex? How do you see yourself?"

These questions seem to imply that Hershman wishes to "even the score" with her spectators. Upon exposing her own secrets and desires, she urges the viewer to undertake a similar kind of self-exposure. Such a dialogue is, of course, impossible. Michael Renov has argued that this impossibility of actual interaction between the artist in front of the lens and a future spectator problematizes the therapeutic effect of the video discourse. There is no responding interlocutor who assists the subject in her search for self-analysis and self-healing. In addition, Krauss claimed that video merely reflects its (narcissistic) subjects, it mirrors them into symmetry. This reflection offers no opportunity for reflexiveness, which would require asymmetry; a fracturing into two different entities that elucidate each other insofar as their separateness is maintained (Krauss 1976: 56). Hershman overcomes these claims on the medium for the most part, as she manages to build in levels of reflexiveness with and within video.

Splitting, cutting, inserting

First of all, Hershman is split into two characters within the tape itself. The first character is filmed in close-up. She is the one who exposes intimate secrets and repressed trauma, as well as the one who addresses the viewer with personal questions. The close-up enforces the feeling of intimacy between the narrating subject and her audience. The second character shows the same Hershman, yet she is filmed at a slightly less close range. Besides her face, we see a part of her upper body. As opposed to the personal stories of the first persona, this character reflects on wider social issues. These issues are related to the personal details revealed by Hershman in close-up. The more distant subject discusses topics such as food, nutrition, and hunger in relation to society and history, and reflects on the impact which domestic violence can have on society. These analytic expositions place Hershman's personal struggles in a social context. This procedure points toward an understanding of the self as a social construction. Moreover, it creates reflexivity within the video: the distant Hershman elucidates the problems of the Hershman in close-up by framing her personal story within the social structures—the family, American society—which are largely responsible for her problems.

Secondly, Hershman's tapes can be regarded as reflexive because they have been edited and manipulated after the story was recorded; the videos are characterized by an abundance of artifices such as split screens, dissolves, montage effects, and distortion. This postproduction is already a form of self-analysis in which the artist becomes her own responding therapist. By editing the primary material, Hershman has already arranged her diaristic material in a fairly coherent, condensed, and meaningful way. Moreover, in the editing process, the artist has added images and video effects.

During Hershman's discussion of her difficult childhood, the image of her face is mixed, through video layering and keying, with images of a crying baby and prisoners in a concentration camp. While she mentions that the scars of her past are deep, light-hearted home video footage of a family alternates with moving war pictures. In another scene, a conventional home video shot of a little girl running on a lawn are cut through with images of street fights and suffering, hungry children in abandoned houses. In addition, the footage of the running girl is slowed down, which has the eerie effect that she seems to struggle against an invisible force. We never get to see the girl properly. Her body is turned away, and she doesn't look into the camera. In the end, she disappears behind a large dark hedge. The message of these formal devices and temporal as well as layered montages is clear: behind the surface of happy family life, a battle can take place. Hershman's childhood was like a warzone. She was deprived of safety, and struggled against violence. The montages and image manipulation can be seen as straightforward rhetorical techniques which enhance and clarify Hershman's painful narration for the spectator. But they can also be seen as artifices by which Hershman tries to clarify her story for herself and to herself.

The same can be argued for the film images shown in *First Person Plural*. Hershman's starts this section by recalling that, when she was small, there were episodes of violence in her family, during which she would hide in the attic. A few moments later, the artist remarks that "most people conceive of their life's story through some myth." For her, the story of Dracula has always had a special meaning. Hershman explains how she would hear his footsteps coming to her room when she was small, how she would be both repelled and excited by that. In light of the previous details on domestic violence in her childhood, these sentences seem to suggest that there was sexual abuse too. Dracula "comes at night, when nobody is around," the artist continues, upon which her discussion is interrupted by a whispering voice which repeatedly says "You're not supposed to talk about it, don't talk about it." Then, we see suspenseful film images of a cloaked Dracula who walks into a dark home, sneaks upstairs, and quietly enters one of the rooms. These film images help Hershman to expose something which she cannot tell. She is not supposed to talk about the incest, a soft inner voice tries to suppress the story, even if it is disguised by a myth. However, whereas talking about it is still too difficult, Hershman is able to show what happened in a suggestive way: through ready-made film images.

In addition, the many video effects which the artist abundantly applies can be understood as therapeutic acts to expose the truth. Hershman's discussion of her distorted view on her own abused body is accompanied by a distorted video image of her body. Moreover, in *Confessions of a Chameleon* (part two of *Electronic Diary*), Hershman confesses that she has been playing different personas throughout her life. She can switch between characters, but doesn't know anymore which of her performed identities is really hers, or where she has lost her sense of self. She has adopted multiple personas, but now, she doesn't seem to know who she is. Her authentic self (or at least her sense of an original singular self) got lost in the middle of layers of fat as well as layers of clothing from her different wardrobes ("for several people, in several sizes"). This unstable subjectivity is one of the main problems Hershman tries to come to terms with in her *Electronic Diary*. Unlike the childhood incest and the obviously related binge eating disorder, Hershman's split personality returns as a theme throughout the three parts of the diary. Whenever she mentions how she plays multiple personae, the moving images mirror her story through split screens. The video medium replicates Hershman's recorded image into many smaller images just as she multiplies herself into different versions in her daily life. These split screens can be interpreted as a visual representation of the verbal confession, yet can also be viewed as a therapeutic form of acknowledging or facing up to a problem, by way of video.

Moreover, another form of therapeutic reflection can be discovered in the tapes when Hershman suggests that the footage is being viewed between the recording sessions. In *First Person Plural*, she explains that she has shown some (already edited) footage on her childhood to some friends. She noted that they didn't hear or see what she was trying to make clear with the Dracula movie. They understood the fact that she was battered, but didn't pick up the reference to incest. Therefore, Hershman decides that she needs to talk more explicitly about the thing she is "not supposed to talk about." The screen turns black, upon which the artist declares: "I was physically and sexually abused." This brief and softly spoken utterance can still easily be overheard while viewing the video. However, for the artist, naming the sexual abuse outright appears to function as a talking cure. After the exposure, Hershman remarks how helpful and necessary it is to talk about it.

The final level of reflexivity can be recognized in the fact that the artist has clearly watched and edited her tapes between the recording sessions. She responds, in the video, to her own previous recordings. For instance she tells us that she has trouble looking at herself, on video or in any other way. After having avoided mirrors and other reflections for years, she doesn't recognize herself anymore when she views herself on video. She remarks how she hates the close-ups of her face, but also suggests that by only shooting her face, she avoids looking at her body. However, at the moment that the artist self-critically remarks that all she ever shoots is herself from the neck up, several images of her entire body are inserted into (or unto) the image of her talking head. Thus, in postproduction, Hershman breaks out of the habit of avoiding images of her own body. As the producer and the first viewer of the tape, she forces herself to look at her own body.

In order to show that the appearance of Hershman's whole body within the video is, however, not the end of her negative, unstable self-image, the video image of her body is replicated in several inserts. Moreover, the body turns away from the camera/viewer; it turns away in a corner. However, while her averted body appears on screen, Hershman addresses herself in voice-over with the encouraging words: "You don't have to be put in a corner." At this point, the artist has explicitly become her own interlocutor within the tape. Because of this, her *Electronic Diary* is both oriented towards a larger social viewing context, and a self-contained therapeutic interaction between the artist and her self-image(s).

Failed confession, successful secret

However, in spite of all the levels of reflexivity discussed above, it is questionable if Hershman succeeds in her quest to help herself by revealing all the repressed and hidden details of her life on video. One of the main reasons for which she uses video is—as pointed out in the epigraph—that the medium offers her the possibility to be honest. Whereas the presence of a camera operator or anyone else would ensure lying, Hershman can tell the truth about her life in solitude to the inanimate video camera.

Yet, being honest and truthful is problematic for Hershman, for several reasons. First of all, the artist always pretends; this is one of her main problems. This makes it difficult to tell the truth about herself. It is hardly possible to be honest and authentic as long as she doesn't really know how to be someone without a conscious, continuous roster of identities.

Secondly, Hershman problematizes the possibility of being truthful in her video diary by her following reflection on the society in which she believes she lives:

> I think that we've become a society of screens, of different layers that keep us from knowing the truth, as if the truth is almost unbearable and too much to deal with, just like our feelings. So we deal with things through replication, and through copying, through screens, through simulation, through facsimile, through fiction, and through faction.
>
> Hershman in *Binge*

Hershman's analysis is reminiscent of Baudrillard's idea that we live in a world of simulation and simulacra. A situation that is, for him, indebted to electronic media such as video. Hershman, in addition, argues that the simulacra around us keep us away from something vital: the truth, the real. For Hershman, it is a problem to live in what she calls a "society of screens," in a society of layers that keep one from the truth. Under social pressure, Hershman has kept her truth, her traumatic childhood, hidden for years. She has, indeed, dealt with it through replication and copying; by playing different personas, she has replicated and copied her identity continuously.

Yet, splitting into replicas has not been a satisfactory coping mechanism for the artist. It has resulted in an eating disorder and a lack of a stable identity. She tries to cure both of these problems by finally exposing the truth about her past. However, Hershman tries to tell the truth in a video, which requires that she makes a screen image or replication of herself (or selves) once more. Again, she deals with things through replication. In addition, she splits herself into different personas within the video, in the alternation between the distant and close Hershman character, as well as within the frame of singular video images through manipulation such as inserts and split-screens. Hence, the multiplication of Hershman's self-image continues by and in video onto the level of the singular frame of the video monitor.

In sum, the alleged cure for Hershman's incapacity to know and tell the truth about herself, namely the private video recording, in the end reinforces her inauthenticity, and her lack of a sense of (one singular, true) self. As one of the main producers of "screens, replications and simulations" in the postmodern era of simulations and simulacra, the video medium is perhaps even a cause of the problems which Hershman now tries to solve with it. So, the harmful effect of a society of screens and simulacra, ensuring that we are kept from the truth, is supposed to be solved with its cause, video.

In the case of Hershman, this doesn't have a healing effect: it merely replicates the problem of replication.

In Hershman's *Electronic Diary,* video is used as a tool for confession, (self-)therapy, and testimony in intricate and medium-specific ways. However, the medium is not as uncritically embraced as in many of the practices and theories which use or reflect on the medium as a wonderful tool which is nothing but helpful in the domains in question. Hershman's video contains both the utopian and the dystopian perspectives on the social effects of the medium. Hershman adopts the medium with the hope that it can offer her the opportunity to be honest, yet her discourse is also permeated by the Baudrillardian opinion that the screen shields instead of shows the truth. Therefore, in the *Electronic Diary*, the acts of confession, therapy, and testimony fail because in Hershman's work, the video image is exposed as yet another simulacrum. The medium doesn't just produce an unreality effect (as Hartman has it); it produces images without a referent in reality (as Baudrillard would claim).Therefore, video cannot provide the truthfulness Hershman needs in order to free herself from the troubled process of hiding in replication and simulation; nor can it provide the truthfulness that confession, therapy, and testimony need in order to be successful.

However, Hershman's video is successful in representing her secret. This doesn't mean that she manages to tell what she wasn't supposed to tell, for as was explained, the artist emphasized that she doesn't succeed in revealing the truth. However, she does manage to present her secret as a secret. In *Languages of the Unsayable*, Jacques Derrida wonders: "does something like the secret itself, properly speaking, ever exist?"(1989: 25). A secret is something which cannot be told; if told, it is no longer a secret. It is something that cannot be told and which has to be denied at all times. However, how can it exist if it cannot be told? As Derrida puts it:

> There is a secret of denial and a denial of the secret. The secret as such, as secret, separates and already institutes a negativity; it is a negation that denies itself. It de-negates itself [. . .] This denial [*dénégation*] does not happen by accident; it is essential and originary.
>
> 1989: 25

Leonard Lawlor explains this *dénégation* as follows: in order to possess a secret, to have it really, I must tell it to myself:

> I must have a conceptual grasp of it; I have to frame a representation of the secret. [. . .] A trace of the secret must be formed, in which case, the secret is in principle shareable. If the secret must be necessarily shareable, it is always already shared. In other words, in order to frame the representation of the secret, I must negate the first negation, in which I promised not to tell the secret: I must tell the secret to myself as if I were someone else. I thereby make a second negation, a "de-negation," which means I must break the promise not to tell the

> secret. In order to keep the secret (or the promise), I must necessarily not keep the secret (I must violate the promise).
>
> Lawlor on Derrida 2011, under "The Secret"

The closed-circuit video set-up offers Lynn Hershman the ability to possess her traumatic secret by telling it to herself as if she were someone else. At the same time, her video is released to a wider audience; she is not the only listener. Yet, her video keeps the secret as secret, for although saying her unspeakable secret out loud ("I was abused"), Hershman also keeps denying that she is capable of telling the truth, of even knowing the truth about anything, let alone herself. She is kept from the truth by screens and simulations, and can only deal with things through fiction, she asserts. In this way, the artist raises doubts as to the secret she is claiming to tell: there might not be a real secret at all. Hershman's secret is denied and told at the same time. It is negated ("I'm not supposed to talk about it") denegated (whispered to the self: "I was abused") and negated again ("but I do not know nor speak the truth about myself ever"). This leaves the existence of the secret undecided. And that is why Hershman's secret comes across as a secret, after all.

Sadie Benning's *It Wasn't Love*

Two teenage girls are standing in front of the video camera. While looking into the lens, they strike playful poses together. Between laughs and hugs, the two friends try to put on a bold face. They chew gum, arrogantly hold their chins up, and nod their heads in a macho way. With their arms folded before them, slightly leaning backwards, the girls seem to perform a rather masculine form of toughness. All the while, the song "You Go To My Head" is playing. With her warm tone of voice, Billie Holiday sings of how she is in the spell of a lover whose smile makes her temperature rise. At first, this old-fashioned romantic song on a "crazy romance" which "never can be" does not seem to fit the images of the two bold girls acting like tomboys. However, when the two young women start to dance in a sensual embrace it becomes clear that Holiday's lines on an intoxicating love affair are not entirely inappropriate in relation to the girls in view.

As the video proceeds, one of the girls turns out to be the narrator and producer of the video. Sadie Benning, the nineteen-year-old narrator of *It Wasn't Love* (1992), tells about a short-lived exciting affair she has had with a tough "bad girl." After the dancing scene, Benning points the camera at herself. When grainy black-and-white close-ups of her face fill the screen, Benning starts her story: "Yesterday night, I drove to Hollywood with this chick." The trip to Hollywood the "chick" had initiated gets Benning into a lot of trouble, for Benning's adventurous lover admits that they are driving in a stolen car. In addition, while driving, Benning's friend alters the plan. She proposes to go to Detroit instead, and to rob liquor stores on the way. Although the situation makes Benning feel tense, she also finds her friend's fearlessness very attractive: "I got nervous. She got sexy." The bold, daring way in which the friend lives her life fills Benning with longing and admiration: "Her life was my fantasy."

In addition to the fact that the girls are initially driving to Hollywood, the video relates to Hollywood movies in many other ways. As I will demonstrate, Hollywood cinema functions as an important frame of reference for Benning, the narrator. However, on a formal level, *It Wasn't Love* does not imitate or resemble Hollywood films at all. This is mainly due to Benning's plain video equipment: a Fisher-Price toy camera which tapes video images on audio cassettes. The simple technology of this video camera dictates some of the most prominent formal characteristics of the video story. First of all, the black-and-white images are very grainy—the Fisher-Price camera in question doesn't go by the name of "PixelVision Camera" for nothing. Secondly, the absence of a zoom lens necessitates Benning pushing the camera near to her face when she needs to show detail. Christine Tamblyn defined the effect of these close-ups well when she remarked that these close-ups achieve "an eerie fish-eyed sense of presence" (1996: 22). In addition, the length of the shots is limited by the camera's weak batteries. As a result, the video hurls from one clip to the next at a pace that wouldn't be out of place in popular music videos—no "boring" video art-like extendedness here. Moreover, because she could not insert titles into her images due to her limited video equipment, Benning videotapes handwritten signs when she wants to accompany the images and spoken words with written texts.

The amateuristic, home-made, rough low quality of the video is emphasized all the more by the fact that the video was quite literally home-made. The artist didn't take her video camera with her when she went on the exciting road trip. Both the spoken and written texts, as well as the video images through which the story is told, were all recorded with the Fisher-Price video camera in Benning's bedroom. Although Benning's story involves the act of running away from home, the images by which Benning tells this story always have the private house as their background, and frequently show small objects which can be found in family dwellings. When the artist tells about driving or getting into the car, her story is accompanied by a shot out of the bedroom window which shows a car pulling out of the street, or by video images of a small toy car driving across a wooden floor.

Both the limitations of the video equipment, as well as the confinement of the video camera to the bedroom, are production constraints. As I will demonstrate, they produce meaning and have important performative effects. Most importantly, they create the type of space Acconci defines in opposition to Krauss' idea of video as an antisocial, solipsistic, narcissistic medium. He describes video as an "intimate space with permeable boundaries." In *It Wasn't Love*, the space in front of the video camera is an intimate one in the sense that it is a private and closely personal space. This intimate space, then, is permeable because the video's viewers are granted visual access and physical proximity to this space. In addition, the permeability lies in the fact that Benning investigates her identity in relation to the dominant social and cultural institution of Hollywood cinema.

The private and personal character of *It Wasn't Love* depends in part on the fact that the video space coincides entirely with Benning's teenage bedroom, an important private domain for adolescents. It functions as a retreat from the world in general, and from parental supervision in particular. As a space where teenagers can be alone with themselves or with close friends, the private bedroom has a vital function in the process of establishing one's identity and becoming an independent adult. In Benning's work, the video camera works in tandem with the function of the bedroom. Like the bedroom, the medium assists her in a trajectory towards independence and the formation of identity.

In front of the video camera, Benning is able to expose personal facts about her private life. To a certain extent, video is like a diary in which (and to which) the artist reveals her thoughts and confesses (secret) experiences and desires. Benning makes the diaristic function of the medium explicit when she addresses the camera with "dear diary." However, the comparison between video and the diary fails to recognize one important aspect of the video: it is shown in public art spaces and is distributed via the Video Data Bank in Chicago. This is why the boundaries of video's intimate space can be called permeable. When Benning addresses the camera or performs in front of it, she relates to a future audience. Moreover, the video can be said to haul in the viewer by its haptic image qualities. The poor, grainy quality of the footage invites the engaged mode of looking discussed in the previous part; a tactile mode of looking that involves all the senses and which rushes up the image surface. The spectator of *It Wasn't Love* is enabled to perceive Benning's discourse on gender and sexuality with her body.

No diary, no mirror

The comparison of the medium of video to a diary is not only unsuitable in order to express the relationship between the narrator and the audience. It is also potentially problematic for the artist/narrator herself. This is most noticeable precisely within the one scene in which Benning calls her video a diary. The two spoken words "dear diary" are simultaneously shown by printed curly letters on what presumably is the front of an actual paper diary. The letters are accompanied by a picture of a ponytailed little girl and surrounded by some printed hearts. After the utterance of "dear diary," upbeat music sets in, and Benning continues with the sentence "On the way she said [...] 'I stole this car.'" The ironic tension between the curly little girl on the diary and the thrilling revelation of Benning's friend point out why Benning cannot adopt the genre of the diary in a serious way. The diary has a sweet, girly connotation, while the girls in the story Benning is telling as well as the gender identities she is interested in are precisely not the stereotypical sweet, girly types.

The gender types in which Benning is interested are more fierce. This is noticeable when she admires the powerful attitude of her daring lesbian friend, as well as in the gender types she exhibits in front of the video camera. In *It Wasn't Love*, Benning dresses up by turn as female vamps who seductively blow cigarette smoke while staring through the lens, or like masculine bad-looking bearded guys who show off their bold moves and tattooed arms in front of the camera. Although the clothes, wigs, and make-up on these female and male characters slightly differ from one scene to the next, what these gender types have in common is that they can all be recognized as well-known popular images of forms of femininity or masculinity which put their sexuality on display by being seductive or showing off. Forms in which, moreover, sexuality is related to danger: both the femme fatale and the macho man are associated with violence and threat.

The familiarity of the stereotypes Benning performs can be explained by the fact that she often imitates famous, iconic film stars. Benning for instance resembles James Dean in shots where she looks pensively into the camera with her collar turned up or a cigarette in the corner of her mouth. When she dresses in a kimono and a platinum blonde wig, the artist is clearly impersonating Jean Harlow. The combination of sexuality and danger is especially prominent in these two film stars. Both of them acquired the status of sex symbol during their short lives. In addition, the image of the rebel is inextricably bound up with Dean, while the assumed viciousness of Harlow's seductive sexuality was expressed by her nicknames; the actress was known as the "laughing vamp" and the "blonde bombshell."

Benning's performance of these stereotypical or iconic characters in front of the camera points out that the comparison of the video medium with the diary is not only problematic here, but also inadequate. In Benning's video, the medium fulfills diaristic functions, but it also offers possibilities absent from the diary. As Benning shows, it is possible to constantly change one's physical appearance in a video. The performances of dressing up and play-acting so prominent in *It Wasn't Love* are, however, by convention not a part of the genre of the diary, nor are they technically possible within the most conventional physical form of the diary, the written book.

However, like the confessions confided to a diary, the role-play Benning is carrying out in the video has a personal and private character. It can be recognized as an adolescent search for the right look or the proper image, for the appearance that best expresses the teenage identity in the making. Such experiments with different looks tend to be carried out in private before the result is shown in public. Therefore, the idea of video as an intimate space certainly applies here. In *It Wasn't Love*, the space in front of the camera is a safe and private one in which the artist is engaged in the personal and precarious process of figuring out her identity.

Benning's experimentation with different personas in front of the video camera may be compared with the mirror. Christine Tamblyn has argued that the camera functions as a metamorphic mirror in *It Wasn't Love*, because it witnesses Benning's transformation from one character to the next (1996: 22). In addition, the video equipment is able to feed the image back to its subject: Sadie Benning. Moreover, video resembles a mirror in Benning's work because the act of dressing up which she performs in front of the camera is actually carried out in front of the mirror by teenagers who experiment with their looks.

However, as the diary, the mirror has its shortcomings when it is applied as a metaphor for the function of video in *It Wasn't Love*. The notion of the mirror does not automatically express the reflexivity video offers to the subjects using it. It runs the risk of portraying video in a "Kraussian" manner; as a narcissistic medium which simply reflects the subjects it records without opening up possibilities of critical self-analysis and/or (personal) change. In contrast to this, Benning's video is an outstanding example of video's potential with regard to critical analysis and change. However, this critical potential of the video medium functions in relation to another medium. In *It Wasn't Love*, the medium of film is both a target of and a tool for poignant reflections. In her video, Benning reflects both with film and on film.

In addition to the scenes in which the artist imitates famous Hollywood film stars, the Hollywood movie enters the video in the form of videotaped fragments from some classic movies that were all produced in the first half of the twentieth century. The video images which show or refer to film are alternated by and combined with spoken and written words as well as fragments of popular music. The images, words and music clips function on different levels which gain and produce meaning in relation to one another. In the video, spoken and written words outline the story of the road trip. With her voice as well as hand-written text, Benning depicts her adventure concisely. In about a dozen short sentences, she explains how the road trip ran, what her friend said and how she behaved, and how Benning responded to all this. The words give a clear impression of the story's fabula. In addition, they provide an insight into the conflicting feelings of its internal narrator. Benning mentions how she "played it cool," but also got stressed out by the adventurous plans of her friend. Moreover, she expresses ambivalence about her attraction to the tough lesbian.

After Benning has told how her friend said "Go ahead, fall in love with me," the following hand-written phrases successively fill the screen: "Run away/Get lost/Love me/Scat/Tomboy/Forever/Faggot." In this stream of consciousness, the ideas of running away, loving a girl and being a tomboy forever are each followed by words which express aversion. On the one hand, this aversion can be attributed to the narrator and focalizor, Benning, who is still hesitant about her possible identity as a rebellious lesbian. On the other hand, the negative word "faggot" might also be said to represent a more general negative view on lesbian women within society at large—a view with which Benning has to come to terms. Benning's struggle with this broader social stance against homosexuality becomes more noticeable at a later point in the video, when the melodramatic lament song "Why Must I Be a Teenager in Love" (Dion and the Belmonts 1959) is followed by an up-beat music clip in which Prince sings: "I just can't believe/all the things people said/Controversy!"

The words and songs which depict Benning's road trip, as well as her struggle with the controversies of being a lesbian teenager in love, interact with the video images which show or refer to Hollywood film. On the one hand, the film references influence the meaning of Benning's words as well as the lyrics of the song she picks. On the other hand, as I will demonstrate later, the spoken, written, printed, and sung words have an effect on the Hollywood characters and clips which Benning shows in *It Wasn't Love*. The references to Hollywood provide the two girls' road trip with a certain grandeur. They are not only driving to Hollywood, they are on a trip which, according to the narrator and focalizor, has the air of a glamorous and exciting classic film. For example, Benning audio-visually argues that her trip was like a film when, after the disclosure of her friend's criminal plans, she inserts a cinematic fragment of policemen shooting.

Towards the end of the video, it becomes clear that the girls didn't end up as fugitives robbing liquor stores. They didn't make it to Detroit, much less Hollywood, but made out in the parking lot of a fast-food restaurant instead. "Then it happened," Benning remarks, increasing the suspense, only to continue with an ironic conclusion: "She dropped me off at home." In sum, the trip turns out to have been a short, not too glamorous one. Yet, for Benning, the small and short experience was big and important, because it made her feel worldly and powerful. As she explains: "In that parking lot, I felt like I had seen the whole world. She had this way of making me feel like I was the goddamn Nile River or something." The notion of Hollywood, with its connotations of glamour, dreams, fame, and excitement, helps Benning to express the realm of positive feelings which her short affair opened up to her.

Inside or outside Hollywood

However, although Hollywood as a frame of reference brings out some of the positive effects of the affair on the artist/narrator, it also emphasizes the difficulty of her struggle in defining her identity as a lesbian woman. The scenes in which Benning is dressed up as film star-like characters confirm the search she expresses in words. They show that she is indeed experimenting with gender roles; she is trying them on one by one. However, the question which arises is: is Hollywood the place to go for lesbians looking for role models? The stereotypical characters of the vamp and the macho-man which Benning performs seem in line with her story, since the vamp and the macho-man represent a combination of sexuality and danger, and of sexuality as danger. This relationship between sexual attraction and seduction and danger is also an important theme in Benning's story, who feels attracted by the daredevilry of her self-confident and seductive friend.

Moreover, film stars such as James Dean and Jean Harlow seem all the more suitable to express forms of queerness, because in spite of the fact that they served as heterosexual sex symbols, they inconspicuously possessed androgynous traits which transgress the conventional distinctions between masculinity and femininity. The abundantly dressed-up and made-up Harlow could, at times, have the appearance of a transvestite. Particularly in pictures which emphasize her somewhat sturdy facial bone structure and angularly shaped eyebrows, the laughing vamp looks like a drag queen. The androgyny which Harlow possessed was actually quite fashionable in the 1930s, and has been noted in other actresses of the decade too. Benning imitates some of them, such as Greta Garbo and Marlene Dietrich, as well. James Dean's slightly androgynous appearance has been understood as sign of bisexuality; the sexual orientation of the actor is still widely debated.

When it comes to the expression of a rebellious and tough form of lesbian, queer subjectivity the artist is investigating, the Hollywood icons which Benning imitates are the most suitable role models available within the Hollywood spectrum.[1] However, although they are the most suitable, they are still very poor role models. The fact that, in the 1990s, the Hollywood stars with whom a young lesbian teenager can best identify are decades-old heterosexual sex symbols who look slightly androgynous and might have been gay, shows that homosexuality has not yet been included within the discourse of dominant mainstream cinema. Naturally, this exclusion of homosexuality from Hollywood points to the marginalization of gay men and women in a larger social context. Hollywood cinema is inextricably bound up with the American society in which Benning grew up. Mainstream movies, including the stars they bring forth, express, determine, and perpetuate the prevalent values of the society in which they are produced. Therefore, in dealing with Hollywood, Benning's video deals with society at large as well.

In addition to the absence of openly gay film stars, Hollywood's exclusion of homosexuality is also visible in the fact that explicit love scenes between members of the same sex are hard to come by. Benning's video exposes this absence in a funny, tongue-in-cheek way. She shows that the part of her story which refers to criminal activities can well be expressed by available Hollywood imagery, such as policemen shooting, a crook turning in front of a prison camera, while sexual intimacy between women can only be shown by way of cinematic shots which portray other forms of physical proximity between women. In order to express sexual attraction between women, Benning resorts to clips from the classic thriller called *The Bad Seed* (LeRoy 1959). The "bad seed" in the title refers metonymically to its offspring; the film tells how housewife Christine starts to suspect that her sweet-looking adolescent daughter Rhoda is in fact a heartless killer. However, it is not surprising that film's title is explicitly shown in *It Wasn't Love*, because in the context of lesbian love, the title also seems to form a mocking rejection of the origin instead of the offspring of seed; the male sex.

After a shot of the title frame, Benning's video shows a scene from *The Bad Seed* in which Rhoda confesses her crimes to Christine. Apart from the sentences in which Rhoda asks her mother if she wants to play with her again, the dialogue between the two protagonists is omitted from *It Wasn't Love*. Thus, attention is drawn to the physical interaction between the adolescent girl and her mother. Rhoda tries to win the shocked Christine over by stroking her face and throwing herself into her mother's arms. Christine falls for these attempts at conciliation, upon which she protectively presses her daughter against her chest.

Benning's video camera not only changed the smooth film images into pixilated haptic ones which invite a sensual form of looking, it has also reframed them with a focus on these gestures of affection. For instance, whereas the film shows a large part of the room in which Christine and Rhoda hug each other, the two women fill the entire video frame when Rhoda's head rests on Christine breasts. The sensuality suggested by these videographic close-ups is confirmed as well as enhanced by the song accompanying the images. The lyrics of Prince's "I Wanna Be Your Lover" ("I wanna turn you on/ turn you out/ all night long/ make you shout") leave little doubt as to the way in which the video invites its viewers to understand the intimate gestures between the girl and woman on screen. According to Benning, the film's bad girl is indeed what the artist calls a "bad girl," yet not in the sense predicated by the film (a heartless sociopath), but in the sense proposed by the video (a tough lesbian).

Like Benning's imitation of heterosexual sex symbols in order to investigate lesbian subjectivity, the artist's reframing of the film scene points out the marginalization of homosexuality within Hollywood representations, as well as within the larger social sphere to which Hollywood movies relate. As was the case with the imitated movie stars, the sampled movie scene at first sight does not seem to express queerness or homosexuality at all. The scene clearly does not depict two lovers. Even without the sound of the dialogue that would indicate kinship, Christine and Rhoda can easily be recognized as mother and daughter. If this scene from LeRoy's 1950s film is the most suitable fragment for Benning to express her infatuation, there is obviously no place for homosexuality in Hollywood representations.

No wonder that in *It Wasn't Love*, the artist and her friend do not make it to Hollywood. The short story of the road trip mirrors the more general reflection on Hollywood presentation in Benning's video piece. In addition, the formal characteristics of the video do not quite make it to Hollywood in terms of image quality and style. The video copies and imitates Hollywood movies in many ways, yet the quality of the medium as well as the way in which the footage is edited is very poor in comparison to the smooth continuity of the classic narrative films to which it refers. In comparison to these award-winning big budget films, *It Wasn't Love*, visibly made with a toy, looks amateurish and childlike. This distinction between the old smooth medium of film and the relatively young and rough medium of video is all the more emphasized by the fact that the films and film stars which are quoted by Benning are indeed old films and film stars of the old days. In contrast to this, in *It Wasn't Love*, the medium of video is clearly in the hands of a young woman, who operates it front as well as behind the camera, and who edits it in a fashion that resembles the style of contemporary popular music clips instead of classic narrative movies.

Old and young

The discrepancy between film as an old, established medium and video as a young, flexible, rough medium is important because it is meaningful in relation to the video's themes of gender and (homo)sexuality. Throughout the video, the lesbian subjectivity Benning is trying to establish is repeatedly represented as "young." First, the murderous Rhoda who is reframed by Benning as a lesbian "bad girl" is obviously a child. Secondly, the two most prominent film stars who Benning imitates (Dean and Harlow) died young. Hence, they not only function as sex symbols but also as symbols of youth. In addition, due to his performance in *Rebel Without a Cause* (1955), Dean is widely considered a symbol for misunderstood teenagers.

Thirdly, some songs that accompany the video images mention the teenager or the child. Dion DiMucci plaintively wonders why he must be a teenager in love in the quoted song. When a fragment of Prince's song "I Wanna Be Your Lover" is playing during the film fragment from *The Bad Seed*, the theme of youthfulness is also brought to the fore. Benning has selected precisely the stanza from the song in which the pop star sings: "I get discouraged/Cause you treat me just like a child." In the context of Benning's video, the reproach uttered by Prince can be interpreted in two ways. It can be understood as a remark on Benning's friend and lover, who takes the lead and has an attitude. However, the line "you treat me just like a child" can also be interpreted as a reproach to Hollywood as an industry in general, which excludes gayness. Moreover, as *It Wasn't Love* shows, the Hollywood characters who can function as models for queers are immature, childlike characters.

Yet, in spite of the lines that express disapproval of being a teenager or being treated like a child, Benning also seems to embrace puerility. In the video, the notions of "tomboy" and "bad girl" are posited as important, positive models for Benning. This can be explained by the fact that these words transgress a conventional form of femininity. They refer to a boyish or rebellious girl, and as such, they stand in contrast to the stereotype of the sweet, girly woman. Therefore, the notions of tomboy or bad girl are suitable for women like the artist who cannot identify with the dominant stereotype of femininity. It is significant, though, that the two most common phrases by which slightly masculine, tough or daring women can be indicated are terms which simultaneously indicate immaturity.

However, it is not only in the absence of terms such as "tom-man" or "bad woman" that Benning adopts these terms. The youthfulness to which "tomboy" and "bad girl" refer is fully expressed by the artist. Not only does she use a toy camera, she also tells her story by showing childish objects such as the toy car and the girl's diary. Besides dressing up and acting like films stars, Benning occasionally dances in front of the camera or plays back a song. All these performances have a playful character, they are reminiscent of the childlike pastime of "playing pretends." Moreover, even the least naïve parts of the story are presented by way of images which refer to childhood. When the narrator, for instance, relates how she made out with her lover/friend in the parking lot, the story is accompanied by seemingly erotic images of a sucking mouth in close-up. This mouth as well as its content, however, turn out to belong to Benning herself, who is sucking on her thumb like a child.

Benning's representation of adult matters such as a love affair, a road trip in a stolen car, and a sexual encounter in a parking lot by way of childish objects and images should be understood not only as an expression of the artist's teenage angst, or as a representation of her position between childhood and adulthood. For besides this mimetic function of the toys and games, they have a performative effect. In *It Wasn't Love*, youthfulness, childishness, and play function as strategies by which the artist attempts to overcome her marginal position within the dominant cultural representation as well as society at large. As a lesbian teenager who doesn't want to conform to conventional gendered stereotypes, she is excluded, she is not taken seriously, and she is treated like a child. Yet she embraces precisely the nonseriousness and the lightheartedness of child's play in order to oppose her exclusion from dominant social and cultural forms.

For it is by way of play that Benning inscribes herself into Hollywood. Or, to put it the other way around, she appropriates Hollywood and makes it her own. First of all, Benning's marginal position not only concerns Hollywood representation; she is also an outsider to Hollywood production. Toys offer her the opportunity to make her own movie nevertheless. Her shot of a toy car with her toy camera does not hide the fact that the objects in question are childlike attributes of little value. Nevertheless, the video images of the toy car, in combination with suspenseful music, are very similar to the extreme long shots in narrative films on road trips, which show a car driving through the landscape. In addition, Benning presents her story as a film because the notion of Hollywood, with its connotations of glamour, dreams, fame, and excitement, emphasizes the feelings of excitement and grandeur the artist experienced during the trip with her friend. In this respect, Hollywood film is appropriated for its positive connotations of glitter and glamour. The fact that the story of a love affair between two girls has never been told by Hollywood doesn't mean it cannot have, or borrow, Hollywood's air of magnificence.

The word "inscription" is more suitable than "appropriation" with regard to Benning's imitations of film celebrities. By dressing up like famous Hollywood icons, the artist puts herself in their shoes. By imagining herself in their position, Benning enters the domain of Hollywood, albeit imaginatively. In the privacy of her bedroom, through play, Benning can be any star she wants to be. Near the end of the video, the artist states: "We didn't need Hollywood. We were Hollywood. She was the most glamorous woman I'd ever met. And that made us both famous." This conclusion expresses the idea that young lesbian women do not need to be represented by Hollywood imagery in order to represent Hollywood images, including its stars, themselves. They can just be Hollywood—glamorous and dramatic—without being in Hollywood, be it a place or a discourse.

Moreover, instead of being oppressed by or forced into the gender types Hollywood dictates, Benning enters into Hollywood's stereotypical characters voluntarily. This makes her the one in charge, and moreover shows how gender can be played or changed at will. *It Wasn't Love* presents gender identity as flexible. This brings me back to my earlier statement that the discrepancy between film as an old, established medium and video as a young, flexible, rough medium is meaningful in relation to the video's themes of gender and (homo)sexuality. In *It Wasn't Love*, the characteristics of the two media reflect the way in which they represent gender. The old, established medium of film is ruled by inflexible, old-fashioned conventions when it comes to the representation of gender. The young and malleable medium of video represents gender as a form of play, open to a multitude of possibilities. The accessible, flexible medium functions as an alternative space in which possibly alternative subjectivities and identities can be tried out. In addition, unlike the smooth surface of film which keeps the passive film viewer at bay, video's haptic low-quality images invite the viewer to participate and fill in the blanks. This mirrors the way in which Benning fills in different forms of masculinity and femininity. It also brings out the politics of inclusion the video calls for, a politics that contrasts with the cinematic tradition of exclusion, concerning both the audience in general as well as queer subjectivities in particular.

The word "inscription" is also applicable to Benning's performances as film stars in the sense of "re-writing." By playing several specific famous Hollywood icons, Benning changes the meaning of stars such as James Dean and Jean Harlow, who mostly stand for conventional masculinity or femininity as well as heterosexuality. The performances of the artist look amusingly contrived because they show a tomboy getting into the skin of conventional sex symbols. This not only brings out the "misfit" between Benning as a rebellious lesbian and the conventional Hollywood stereotypes she is trying out, it also brings out and enhances some of the queerness and androgyny which—as mentioned above—are already present in the Hollywood icons. After having seen how well Dean can be imitated by a girl, his soft feminine features can be recognized far more clearly. After Benning's boyish impersonation of Jean Harlow, the actress can never be seen again without somehow recognizing a young man underneath her layers of make-up. In sum, Benning not only stresses that the queerness which is excluded and covered up by Hollywood can be inscribed into it by way of play, but also that it is already there.

This also goes for the film clip Benning playfully includes in her video. The suggestion of reading a scene between a mother and daughter from *The Bad Seed* as a lesbian encounter can be understood as a bold appropriation of Hollywood material. The artist inscribes gayness into the scene by presenting it in a new context as a representation of homosexuality. The effect, then, is slightly mocking and amusing; we know that this scene from a classic movie is not representing lesbian sexuality at all, but Benning's video allows us to read it against the conventional grain. However, the representation of the scene can also be interpreted as an indication that the film does secretly refer to homosexuality. In the vein of articles and documentaries which suggest that many covert yet intentional references to homosexuality can be found in classic Hollywood movies, Benning's video can be said to claim that the queer and the gay have always had a place in Hollywood. You just have to know how and where to look.

In addition to the fact that playfulness grants Benning the ability to appropriate and inscribe herself, and with that, a queer type of subjectivity into Hollywood, the aspects of puerility, lightheartedness, and nonseriousness related to her playfulness have one other important critical effect. The funny and playful character of the video stands in contrast with one of its serious revelations, namely the fact that explicit gay role models are absent from Hollywood discourses. The result is an ironic tension between the serious and the nonserious. In "Female Transgression" (1996) Laura Kipnis argues that Benning's irony signals an exit from some of the more constrictive aspects of an earlier feminist video politics, when the charge of "not feminist enough" or "not queer enough" rained down frequently. In contrast to this, Kipnis states, Benning's video issues a dissenting "fuck you" to any dictates of correctness and pleasure, whether social or sexual. Kipnis praises *It Wasn't Love* for its exuberant, energetic play, and for its generosity towards the audience. She remarks that "Benning's invitation to join her in her room and party on the margins makes so much political video seem, by contrast, pinched and joyless" (341).

Although I agree with Kipnis that Benning's video stands out for its facetiousness, I contend that the irony within the video is not merely amusing. The effect of irony on the video's audience is far more complex. Indeed, Benning invites her audience to join her in her room. Although the viewer is drawn close by the haptic qualities, and Benning seems to address her audience when she looks into the lens while talking, her irony should not be understood as a generous invitation to the audience to laugh and party with the playfully mocking artist. As Sharon Willis (1997) has convincingly argued in an article on Tarantino's funny yet horrifying nouvelle violence films, an ironic combination of fun and grave matters can tweak our internal social censorship mechanisms. It can cause the sensation of "being caught with one's pants down" (Willis 1997: 190). For when serious problems or crimes are ironically represented in a funny way, the viewer can find herself laughing when perhaps she shouldn't. Most frequently, this results in feelings of embarrassment and discomfort.

Because the imitations and citations of Hollywood film within *It Wasn't Love* are both playful and serious, both lighthearted and grave, both funny and painful, every response seems "off." As viewers, we supposedly shouldn't cry over the video, for the predominant tone of the video is a cheerful one. Yet the inclination to laugh also seems wrong. Benning's openness makes the matter even more precarious. We are invited into the private domain of her bedroom, where her fantasies and secrets are confided to us. It would be harsh to betray this vulnerability and trust by laughing when one actually shouldn't. The discomfort which is caused by this uncertainty is an affect rather than an emotion. As physical urges and sensations such as laughter or abhorrence have to be rapidly deliberated and/or repressed while watching the video, the resulting self-conscious embarrassment and doubt can be experienced with the body. Willis would say that this affect of discomfort is the result of affective excess. The viewer gets embarrassed because she has to manage the many conflicting affects which are produced in her by the work.

The uncomfortable affective access is combined with the work's invitation to haptic looking. Because of this combination, it is reasonable to conclude that, in spite and because of the video's amusing qualities, looking at *It Wasn't Love* can be a pretty uncomfortable physical experience. This effect on the viewer is important in relation to the issues of gender and sexuality which are dealt with in the video. In addition to the fact that these issues concern the body, they are often related to physical discomfort and insecurity for subjects like Benning whose gender identity and sexual orientation hold a marginal position within a society and its dominant discourses. The viewer of *It Wasn't Love* can, to a certain extent, share the experience of the artist through the medium of film, the medium of video, and the trope of irony.

Although *It Wasn't Love* points out suppressing sides of film, and manages to create discomfort by way of video, the positive, productive sides of film and video have the upper hand. This can be said to apply to this entire part; in spite of discussions of negative evaluations of film (e.g., the isolating home movie) and video (the narcissistic close-circuit set-up), the emphasis was on the curing, helping, and emancipatory applications of both media. This tension between negative and positive features suggests that the two media are "Janus-headed": on the one hand, they create, help, and relate subjects, but on the other hand they are involved in hurting, oppressing, and harming their users—sometimes simply by enabling users to hurt or oppress each other. In the next part, I will turn to the other side of the Janus heads, and focus specifically on the darker sides of film and video. The specifications and applications that will be discussed next stand in stark contrast to some of the more utopian, positive specifications of film and video that were addressed in this part.

PART IV
VIOLENT FEATURES

Supervision and Subversion—so could one, in a Foucauldian manner, formulate the tensions between these media interests regarding vision by means of modern technology.

Siegfried Zielinski, interview by D. Senior (2007)

INTRODUCTION

In David Cronenberg's film *Videodrome* (1983), video is a very dangerous medium. It causes brain tumors, hallucinations, and murderous intent in its viewers. Malicious videotapes send out invisible signals, which slowly manipulate the people who watch the video images. When Max, the film's protagonist, falls under the spell of such a hazardous videotape, he is no longer safe in front of a television screen. Because ever since video infected his mind, he can be touched and hurt physically by the videos he watches. Max seems, for instance, to be eaten alive by a video image when his head disappears momentarily into a large mouth which appears on a television screen. In a later scene, Max is again watching a videotape when the form of a hand suddenly emerges from the flat and grainy surface of the screen. The hand is holding a gun. The male protagonist is shot by a video image.

In *Videodrome*, video's malignant powers may seem extraordinary and highly imaginary; yet the film doesn't depict the medium in an entirely unheard of way. Cronenberg's film fits in with a widespread tendency to portray video as a violent medium. Although the victims of the medium are mostly shown to be the filmed instead of the viewing subjects, harmful characteristics of video are regularly pointed out by both theoretical texts and visual objects. When the medium is theorized in relation to the surveillance practices it serves, it is frequently considered to be a tool of oppression and control, with the camcorder functioning as a "source [. . .] through which the power exercised by the surveilling gaze circulates" (Renov and Suderburg 1996: xv). That filming someone with a video camera can be an aggressive act is also exposed by many videos posted on internet sites such as YouTube. In amateurish cell-phone shot videos that show fights and beatings, the act of recording can violate the victims as much as the blows, punches and terms of abuse which are unleashed. The short clip *Bully gets beat up* (2008), for example, shows how a young man tries to fend off his attackers by defending himself against their provocative insults, shoves, and hits, as well as their video camera which is filming him up close.

Video is not the only lens-based medium the aggressive or harmful traits of which are often brought to the fore. It has two allegedly violent ancestors: photography and film. The lethal effects of video in *Videodrome* can, for instance, be traced back to Susan Sontag's comparison of photography with murder in *On Photography* (1979). Although Sontag asserts in her book that—unlike video in Cronenberg's film—photography doesn't really kill, shoot, or rape, the act of taking a picture should certainly not be understood as an innocent deed: "To photograph people is to violate them" (1979: 14). The metaphors of murder, hunting, and rape, so often used to indicate the violent character of photography, are also frequently applied in discussions of film. In particular, the filmed female subject is often said to be assaulted or shot by the film camera

(Weinstock 1984: 41). In some instances, figuratively used terms such as murder and rape are shown to apply to the act of filming in a more literal sense. Women are, for example, stabbed to death with a film camera in Michael Powell's *Peeping Tom* (1960). As in *Videodrome*, a lens-based medium has lethal consequences in Powell's film.

The capacity to act violently is ascribed to lens-based media by a large body of works, of which the abovementioned films, videos, and texts form only a small part. I contend that the negative specifications of film and video—both in theory and in practice—dominate the more positive views of the two media. Even objects which do not explicitly confirm or expose the violent sides of film and video can nevertheless respond to the more negative side of the lens-based media by trying to discard or work against it. Near the end of this part I will discuss how feminist films (e.g., Potter 1979, Akerman 1975) as well as videos (by, among others, Johanna Householder and b.h. Yael) aim to overcome misogynist film conventions in different ways.

While film and video frequently (self-)reflexively work against, expose or confirm the harmful characteristics of each other's or their own medium, the aggressive features of one specific other, third medium need to be taken into account if the violent effects of film and video are to be fully understood. In previous parts, media such as literature, painting, sculpture, and television functioned as interlocutors of film and video, as their similarities and differences with the two lens-based media shaped the specification of film and video. In this part, photography will play a pivotal role in outlining the differential specificity of film and video. The photographic medium is more than a related, specifying interlocutor; it is the ancestor of the two lens-based media. Although the harmful features of the photographic apparatus as well as photography's stilled images differ in many ways from the moving images and mobile cameras of film and video, the two last-mentioned media relate in one way or another to the violent heritage of their progenitor.

As I will show in this part, this relationship between film and video, and their joint ancestor takes many forms. Films and videos under analysis (e.g., Fiona Tan's *Facing Forward* and *Countenance*, Michael Haneke's *Caché*) show how the two younger lens-based media form a continuation of photography's harmful abilities, and aim to overcome this violent legacy by way of video-specific or cinematic features such as editing techniques, the movement of their images, or a medium-related dispositif. In these instances, films and videos specify film and video as media that are able to unravel and possibly overcome the aggressive impact of their predecessor. On the other hand, whether self-critical or not, many films and videos—from anonymous juvenile YouTube clips to self-reflexive art films such as Samuel Beckett's *Film*—lay bare the specific, typical harmful capabilities of their own medium. These specific capabilities become all the more noticeable when the two media are contrasted with photography. Mapping the similarities and differences between photography's aggressive sides and the distinct, medium-specific violent features of its lens-based "offspring" will complete the portrayal of film's and video's respective Janus heads which already started in the previous part.

CHAPTER 17
OBJECTIVE REPRESENTATION

In many respects, this part hinges on the idea of "soft determination" I discussed in Part III. Without overlooking the reciprocity between a medium's physical base and the human subjects who apply and shape this base, I will focus on the (violent) effects which the material, technological structures, and apparatuses of the three lens-based media have on their users; their viewers, the subjects represented in their images, as well as the producers of photographs, films, and videos. For the question of how film, video, as well as photography are able to hurt their users cannot be answered without addressing the effects of the media's technological abilities and material forms.

However, this attention to the material and technological abilities of the media in question goes hand in hand with a concept that will redirect attention to the conventional layers of medium specificity and medium specification, namely, the concept of *discourse*. Many of the violent features of film and are tied to specific discourses; scientific, medical, colonial, racist, orientalist, ethnographic, disciplinary, and misogynist discourses. My understanding of the concept of discourse is based on the work of Michel Foucault, who has defined discourse as a group of statements; "an entity of sequences of signs in that they are enouncements (*enoncés*)" (Foucault 1972: 141). For this philosopher, a group of statements is a discourse insofar as they belong to the same discursive formation (117). A discursive formation is a group of statements in which "one can define a regularity (an order, correlations, positions and functionings, transformations)" (117).

As Stuart Hall puts it in his discussion of the Foucauldian term, as a group of statements, a discourse "provides a language for talking about—a way of representing the knowledge about—a particular topic at a particular historical moment [...] Discourse is about the production of knowledge through language" (Hall 1997: 44). By producing specific forms of knowledge, discourses work to govern and empower certain understandings of the subject, while ruling out or delegitimizing others (Procter 2013: 60). For Foucault, discourse is therefore inseparable from power. Discourse defines as well as produces the objects of our knowledge. It reinforces certain identities already established and creates subject positions. Moreover, the rules and regularities which define a discursive formation display and perform hierarchical relations. Discourse determines what can and what cannot be said, what criteria of "truth" are and what is false, who is allowed to speak with authority and who is not, where such speech can be spoken and where it cannot be uttered.

Hall rightly emphasizes that it is important to note that the concept of discourse is not a purely linguistic concept. It doesn't only involve language in the narrow sense, but can also indicate thematic choices, types of statements, concepts, (visual) objects, and architectural, spatial forms. The notion of statements which together form of a discourse can therefore be understood in a very wide sense. In an interpretation of Foucault's concept, Hall moreover argues that since all social practices entail meaning, and meanings shape and influence our conduct, all practices have a discursive aspect. "Discourse is about language *and* practice" (1997: 44).

Media and discourses are interrelated in a number of ways. Put briefly: a medium *is* discourse, a medium *produces* discourse, and a medium *is part* of discourse. First, as I pointed out in Part III with the help of ideas by Moran and Green, a medium's specificity is in itself a largely discursive object. It is produced by the discourses which define it. The large body of representations that depict film and video as violent media—including (self-)reflexive films and videos themselves—can therefore be understood as a discursive formation which produces film and video as dangerous objects by representing them as such. However, next to being discursive objects or discursive formations, media are applied in the production of discourse. Film, video, and photography produce discursive representations (statements, if you like); films, videos, photographs. The technological possibilities and limitations of specific media, as well as their specific sets of representational conventions, have a decisive influence on the representations they bring forth. The specific structure of media thus influences what can and what cannot be said, and as such, it influences discourse.

What is more, media can become part of certain discursive formations as technological objects. Previously, I stated that the concept of discourse directs attention to the conventional layers of a medium's specificity. However, the concept also brings to light that the technological set-up of a medium's apparatus is in itself inseparable from its discourse. The spatial organizations or material characteristics of media's technologies can be understood as meaningful statements or practices that, like architectural forms, assign specific places and functions to subjects.[1] Lens-based media, for example, create subject positions in front of and behind the device of the camera. Such mechanical ordering of looking and looked-at subjects can and has become part of larger discourses involved with the production of knowledge on others, or more accurately, with the production of others. In addition, certain specific discursive specifications of lens-based media have sustained wider discursive formations: they have been posited as technological tools by which we can objectively see, represent, and get to know the world. In these instances, discourses on media sustain specific empirical discourses.

Having said this, I will start a more detailed exploration of the relationship between the three lens-based media and discourse by discussing a seminal work on the meaning and impact of some of the first optical, lens-based technologies: Jonathan Crary's *Techniques of the Observer* (1990).

Camera junctions

In *Techniques of the Observer*, Crary states that optical devices such as the stereoscope and the camera obscura should be understood as "points of intersection where philosophical, scientific, and aesthetic discourses overlap with mechanical techniques, institutional requirements and socioeconomic forces" (8). Instead of regarding optical media as technologies which impose themselves on social fields or disciplines, transforming them from the outside, Crary suggests that interplay exists between optical devices and the discursive fields in which they are embedded.

This interplay between optical medium and discourse can be noted in the position of the camera obscura in the seventeenth and eighteenth centuries. Crary writes that from the late 1500s onwards, the apparatus of the camera obscura was highly influential on discursive explanations of human vision, as well as on representations of the relationship between an observing, knowing subject and an external world. Through the model of the camera obscura, the observer was defined as an isolated and autonomous subject. Hidden in the dark confines of the camera, the spectator was withdrawn and cut off from the outside world. This world could, however, be viewed by the observer inside the camera obscura's black box, for the camera was considered to be a device that created a perfect representation of the exterior reality. The observer did not have any influence on this representation and therefore remained invisible to the camera's projection. The monocular, mechanical, and disembodied apparatus of the camera obscura was believed to offer an entirely undistorted, objective image of the world. Human vision was modeled on the camera obscura's infallible, disembodied way of representing the world. The act of seeing was sundered from the physical body of the observer, vision was decorporealized.

Although the camera obscura was an influential force in the crystallization of philosophical and scientific discourses on human perception, the camera was not necessarily the origin or instigator of these ideas. Rather, the camera obscura can be understood as concomitant or even subordinate to the discourses it seems to have enforced. The fact that the camera obscura was glorified as the perfect form of objective perception in the seventeenth and eighteenth centuries depended in part on surrounding discourses concerning perception and knowledge. Important seventeenth-century thinkers such as René Descartes considered the bodily senses as deceptive and therefore inadequate in gathering veritable knowledge about the world. Hence, a more disembodied, objective view of reality was pursued. What is more, many philosophers of the enlightenment, for instance David Hume and John Locke, insisted on distance and division between interiorized subject and exterior world as a precondition for knowledge about the latter. The camera obscura, with its disembodied lens and dark interior, was used as a model by which these particular modes of thought could be further refined, explained, authenticated, and legitimized.

Today, the media of photography, film and video are still frequently thought of in ways resembling seventeenth- and eighteenth-century thought on the camera obscura. Apart from the reality-effect producing devices discussed in Part I, images produced by the three lens-based media are—through conventions stemming from early applications—often understood as perfectly transparent, objective registrations of reality as it appeared in front of the lens (Mack 1991: 63–64). Moreover, the idea that the person looking through the lens of the camera is a detached onlooker who is invisible in the produced images is not unheard-of today. In spite of the obvious similarities between the apparatuses of the camera obscura and the three modern three lens-based media, it is remarkable that the paradigm of the camera obscura still seems to influence how the capabilities of photography, film, and video are viewed. For the most important idea in which the camera obscura was embedded—the idea that the world can be perceived and represented in an entirely objective and detached manner—was already questioned in the same century in which photography was invented, and it has been repeatedly undermined in the century that followed.

The presumed capability of photography and film to capture reality objectively has done much harm. Yet, the supposedly objective representation by these lens-based media is not violent in itself; it only functions aggressively when it is applied in particular ways within specific practices, discourses, or disciplines. Crary's idea of the interplay between the optical medium and the discursive fields in which it is embedded is of use here, because the violent effect of photography and film's presumed objectivity arises precisely from the interplay between the media and the specific fields in which they operate.

Two fields in which photography and film have played an important part ever since their arrival are medicine and science. In some historically and socially specific scientific and medical discursive practices, moreover, the two media were used as tools for objective representation. While this use sustained and confirmed specifications of photography and film as infallible reality-reproducing media, their presumed objectivity in turn confirmed and sustained the objectivity of those medical and scientific practices, as well as the truthfulness of their findings, and the superiority of their ideas. These findings and ideas, underpinned by photography and film, were not innocent or neutral; they often considered negative notions of other human beings who were turned into an object of scientific or medical investigation.

One of the medical practices in which photography was used as an objective tool that sustained the objectivity of the practice itself is the neurological study of hysterical women in the nineteenth century. As Ulrich Baer argues, the spatial relationship photography creates between photographer and photographed contributed to the apparent objectivity of this strand of medicine: "When the camera's *objective* (its lens) is positioned between doctor and patients, the photographic set-up offers the illusion of objectivity—the empirical existence of an objective distance between observer and observed that the medical establishment had long sought" (2005: 33). The highly misogynist medical treatment of hysterical females was carried out by doctors who sought to establish the positivist and objective quality of their work by linking it to the "guarantees of inherent veracity" they found in photographic images (2005: 33).[2] Another instance of harmful interplay between the presumed objectivity of photography or film and certain discourses can be discovered in nineteenth- and early twentieth-century Western ethnographic practices, which will be addressed in the next section.

Ethnographic film, in video

> What we have been missing is this: that the photographic machine should unite itself definitively with the hypsometer, with the thermometer, with the sextant, in this ideal conquest of the Dark Continent.
>
> Cordeiro, in Moraes 1885: vii

The above sentences from an introduction to a nineteenth-century book of ethnographical photographs convey dominant historical scientific ideas on photography. According to Luciano Cordeiro and many of his contemporaries, the "ideal conquest" of Africa would take place through knowledge of the continent as gathered by, among other scientific devices, the photo camera (Hartmann et al. 1998: 10). The idea that photography would help in conquering a continent clearly indicates the relationship between photography and colonialism. Photographing the other was used in the process of taking possession of the other. However, the conquest was not enabled by photography's production of veritable knowledge through transparent, objective images of the world and its inhabitants. It was supported and justified by specific, highly constructed, Eurocentric images of the other that ethnographic photographs produced. The harmful effect of these images did not lie solely in their biased and racist representation of African human subjects, but was also caused by the fact that they were nevertheless understood as true and real by the public because they were delivered by the trustworthy medium of photography.

Like photography, the slightly younger medium of film was applied by ethnographers in order to capture the "Dark Continent." The cinematic medium inherited three conventional representational forms from ethnographic photography. First of all, the group portrait in which long horizontal rows of indigenous people were lined up, the composition stressing that the portrayed people are one group, characterized by sameness—not diversity. Secondly, the "natural" image: images which allegedly show indigenous people living in nature, while performing typical rituals or carrying out their daily business without overtly posing for the camera. Thirdly, anthropometric visual documents, which presented the body as the essential defining characteristic of "primitive" peoples. Those photographs and films were to capture parts of the colonized other's body, focusing particularly on the genitalia, as well as face and skull structure. The pictures were used as allegedly scientific support for racist evolutionary theories; they were believed to demonstrate European physical superiority in a human hierarchy of development (Harris 1998: 22).[3]

Because film can record movement, it had some advantages over photography. Film could, for example, portray much larger groups of people than photography, because the film camera could pan across a group, and that way show lined up bodies one after another, but still as a whole. Moreover, unlike photography, film was able to record the movement of indigenous people while they performed their daily businesses within their natural surroundings. When it comes to anthropometric mapping, film did not have to represent all sides and pieces of the other's body in different still images. Bodies could be captured on film when they were scanned by the camera, or move around in front of the lens so that all sides came within view. Filming bodies may therefore seem less aggressive than photographing them because, unlike photography, film does not "dissect" the other's body into fragmented still parts.

Nevertheless, early ethnographic films had a degrading impact on the human subjects under examination. This is clearly visible in artist Fiona Tan's video *Facing Forward* (1999), a skillfully composed assemblage of a disparate range of colonial film material recorded all over the globe. Most of the archival footage in *Facing Forward* is ethnographic, with anthropometric recordings as ethnography's most extreme and racist form. In Tan's video, these recordings show a couple of naked natives rotating in front of the camera. First, they are filmed *en face* from the waist upwards. After holding a still pose for a while, they all make a quarter of a turn to the left. The simultaneous poses and movements show that the filmed people are clearly subordinated to the camera and the camera operator, who invisibly and inaudibly orders the subjects in front of the lens to hold still or turn around at his will.

Although the ethnographic film material Tan has sampled in her video piece is in itself visibly degrading to the filmed subjects, the manner in which the artist has selected and edited the archived films brings out the aggressive character of this type of film all the more. It is telling that the medium of *Facing Forward* is video, not film. The former medium is often used to expose, rewrite, or criticize ethnographic film practices. Tan mainly deconstructs the violent discourse of ethnographic film by bringing several moments to light in which ethnographic films themselves undermine the objectification they tend to produce. Thus, in the footage that Tan has selected and edited, small slippages occur in the anthropometric process of capturing and controlling the bodies in view by way of film. Slippages that, moreover, would be less noticeable in comparable photographic material.

For example, one thing that seems to slip out of the camera operator's control is eye movement. While the filmed subjects in the anthropometric film sequences in *Facing Forward* are forced to stand still in front of the lens, their eyes turn in many directions. Sometimes, when looks are turned downwards, the eyes express feelings of humiliation. At other times, glances of the filmed subjects at each other, or straight into the camera, function as questions: "What are we doing? And what are we supposed to do now? Why?" Mostly, the agile eyes of the subjects in view seem to indicate agitation and fear, *not* the docile, indifferent acceptation of their objectification which is expected of them by the filmmakers. Another dent in the camera operator's mastery is made by a man in a row of three people who doesn't turn in the right direction when the group is ordered to show yet another side of their bodies. Although this wrong turn may not have been a conscious act of resistance, it does undermine the authority of the filmmaker. For it shows that the filmed bodies belong to human beings who cannot be fully subjected to the objectifying rules and demands of scientific research.

Besides showing these slippages, *Facing Forward* disturbs and counteracts the objectification and typicalization in a few more ways. First, the convention of portraying the other as a body in nature is thwarted in Tan's video by fragments of tourist-like film. These images of Indonesian city life lack the focus on specific subjects and their typical activities, as is characteristic of ethnographical film. More importantly, they miss the rural setting common in that genre. Whereas the type of the "savage" can be recognized in many of the ethnographical film clips in *Facing Forward*, the tourist film fragments provide a different view of reality: the "others" wear clothes, drive cars, and live in cities, too.

Another important counteractive type of film in Tan's video is the counter-shot. Halfway through the video, ethnographical recordings of "savage" men in nature are interrupted twice by a counter-shot of a cameraman who is cheerfully operating a film camera. On his head, he has stuck some of the feathers the other men were shown to be wearing too. The cameraman's attempt to look like the other that fascinates him is a rather comical infantile gesture—he is playing Indian—as well as a form of hostile appropriation. It can be understood as an allegory for the act of filming; like taking the feathers, taking images is a way of taking possession of the other. This ethnographical visual appropriation of the other moreover sustained the colonial appropriation of other people.

In addition, the counter-shot is meaningful because—in conventional ethnographic discourse as well as in other discourses which apply the media of photography and film as tools of objective representation—the camera operator usually remains invisible.[4] When *Facing Forward* reveals that the film camera is operated by a white, Western, male human subject, the recorded images of "savage" men can hardly be understood as objective representations of reality: they are recorded from a culturally specific, gendered, and interested point of view.

A final disturbance of colonial ethnographic conventions occurs in Tan's video when a few white men are inserted in a large group portrait of native people. *Facing Forward* starts with images in which a row of indigenous people is panned by a camera from left to right. Before the end of the row is reached, the film switches to footage of a new group of people which is scanned by the camera in a similar fashion. This process is repeated, until after a couple of minutes, the right end of a row is reached. By editing all these fragments of filmed groups together; Tan has created one very large group out of different filmed ethnographic group portraits. One of the fragments of which the group portrait is composed, however, is not ethnographic; it is a colonial portrait that shows approximately ten white men, surrounded by their indigenous servants. Within the flow of images, these Western colonizers stand out because some of them wear light-colored military uniforms, whereas the other people wear more plain clothes, or no clothes at all. Yet, although they do catch the eye for a moment, in the end the Western men are caught up in the effect large panoramic group portraits have: they homogenize, make everyone the same. Therefore, in *Facing Forward*, the colonizers don't benefit from the homogenizing othering effect of ethnographic group portraits. Absorbed within the form that backed them up, colonizers are now represented as being similar to their others: the colonized.

Video looks: self-reflexive and involved

Facing Forward is not the only video in which representational conventions of ethnographic photography and film are breached, as the medium is quite often used to respond critically to the scientific practices of visual ethnography and anthropology. In the case of *Facing Forward*, the choice of the medium of video was not inevitable. Although editing video footage is easier than the montage of analogue film, Tan's piece could have been made with film as well. When it comes to rewriting objectifying conventions of ethnographic photography and film, the benefits of video mostly lie in medium-specific traits, which are largely conventional. One of these traits is the video convention of artists pointing the camera at themselves, an act which has—as we have seen in the previous part—a long tradition within the field of video art. Fiona Tan has applied this convention in her video installation *Countenance* (2002) in order to break the illusion of objective anthropological representation. The installation consists of three large black-and-white video projections (initially shot by the artist on 35mm film stock) in which film portraits of individuals or small groups of people are shown in steady succession. For a period of about a minute, the subjects in question are shown posing patiently for the camera, until their image is replaced with the next portrait. Although the subjects remain as still as possible, small movements are visible in the images.

All portraits, moreover, are preceded by titles which categorize the people on view. Main headings such as "SOCIAL CONSTELLATIONS" or "WORKING PEOPLE" point out in which broad category the portrayed people should be seen, while many subtitles (e.g., newly-weds, flatmates, geriatric home residents, butcher, baker, student, beggar, pensioner) indicate which sub-category they represent. By extensively categorizing social and cultural categories, Tan's project clearly draws on August Sander's photographic portraiture project *Citizens of the Twentieth Century* (1910–1964). Like Tan, Sander portrayed a large number of (paired or grouped) human subjects, each of which stood for a whole type, be it a profession or a social group. With his project, the German photographer aimed to provide an accurate document of twentieth-century German society.

The most important difference between *Citizens of the Twentieth Century* and *Countenance* lies not so much in the fact that Sander's medium is photography while Tan filmed her images (although this difference between stillness and movement is not without consequences—more on this later on). The most influential difference between the two projects is rather produced by a videomatic convention. Before entering the room in which the projected portraits are screened, the visitor of the installation passes through a room in which a small self-portrait of Tan is projected. While looking into the camera, Tan talks, albeit implicitly, about the project which the viewer is about to see in the next room. The artist tells how her "hungry eye" observes people's faces in the underground and at the market of the foreign city she has moved to, Berlin. In the monologue, Tan reveals her propensity for categorization:

> Almost automatically I try to guess someone's background and origin. I don't stop to wonder what determines which details I notice and which I let slip by. [...] I gather together impressions and snapshots like an amateur biologist in the nineteenth century would collect butterflies. Type, archetype, stereotype. An irrational desire for order; or at least for the illusion thereof. However I am constantly reminded that all my attempts at systematical order must be arbitrary, idiosyncratic and—quite simply—doomed to fail. [...] Could I possibly collect, collate a time in history? Whose history?

Unlike Sander's positivist attitude, Tan's self-portrait attests to a self-reflexive awareness of the shortcomings and impossibilities of systematical ordering. Tan compares herself to a nineteenth-century biologist, but not a professional one. She calls herself an amateur, an enthusiastic, "hungry," yet imprecise and unscientific collector of types. Her systematic ordering, Tan concedes, fails as an objective positive fact. For her exposition of types is arbitrary and, most importantly, idiosyncratic.

By way of her self-reflexive monologue, Tan distances herself from older scientific ethnographic, anthropological, and sociological discourses in which lens-based media were applied as tools for objective registration and collection. The self-reflexive content of Tan's words is underpinned, or perhaps even enabled, by a conventional video set-up; that set-up in which the artist sits in front of her own camera. In addition, the videomatic *dispositif* of the multi-screen installation sustains Tan's self-reflexivity. Showing the monologue in a room adjoining the larger hall in which the Berlin types are projected doesn't merely serve as a prologue to the larger three projections of portraits. For when the visitor moves from the first room to the next, Tan's looped portrait video doesn't disappear. The portrait of the artist, her confessions and doubts, remain present in the room nearby. Although she is no longer visible to the viewer, her voice remains audible. Therefore, the installation will never seduce its viewer to take the represented types as objective slices of social or historical reality; they are Fiona Tan's types.

Tan's *Countenance* is closely related to an important field in which video is used to create such alternatives to the ways in which the "other" is represented by conventional ethnographic photographs and films, namely the field of so-called domestic ethnography. However, whereas Tan categorizes a foreign city which is simultaneously her home, domestic ethnography maps an even smaller personal domain. Michael Renov, who coined the term, explains that domestic ethnography is:

> [...] a mode of autobiographical practice that couples self-interrogation with ethnography's concern for the documentation of the lives of others. But the

> Other in this instance is a family member who serves less as a source of disinterested social scientific research than as a mirror or foil for the self. Due to kinship ties, subject and object are embroiled in each other. The result is a self-portraiture refracted through a familial other.
>
> 2004: 216

What Renov fails to mention here is that social scientific research is hardly ever disinterested, and that subject and object are always embroiled in one another, with or without kinship ties. But his definition of domestic ethnography is useful because it indicates the self-reflexivity of these video practices. Like Tan's *Countenance*, domestic ethnographical videos replace the myth that the other is represented objectively and transparently, with the idea that an interested self is always visible or audible in the images she produces of others. Unlike photography and film, video is not used as a tool which offers a transparent view of reality, but as a means by which the observer produces personal images of private relations within the domestic sphere.

Mindy Faber's *Delirium* (1993) is a paradigmatic example of domestic ethnography. In this video, the artist examines her relationship with her mother, who had various mental breakdowns when Faber was a little girl. The artist investigates her mother's illness by interviewing her, and by, more broadly, looking into the history of women and madness. It is very clear that the tape doesn't serve disinterested scientific or artistic research. Faber states that she is frightened by the pattern of female madness in her family history; her grandmother was mentally ill as well. Especially now that she has recently become a mother herself, it has become important for Faber to find out if she can break the cycle of family horrors. The object of her investigation is not spared from the reasons for which her daughter films her: "You used to tear up my room. I used to come home from school and you would throw pots and pans at my head. You used to chase me around the house hitting me." While her mother denies having done any of those things, Faber persists: "You did mum, it's true. That's why I'm making tapes about you."

These accusations are not made off-screen by an invisible Faber hidden behind the camera; she is making them while her mother is filming *her*. As Renov has noted, such an exchange of the camera is a recurrent trope in domestic ethnographic videos. Like the counter-shot of the camera operator in *Facing Forward*, the exchanged camera renders the conventionally invisible ethnographic observer visible. The difference with Tan's counter-shot in *Facing Forward* or with her self-portrait in *Countenance*, however, is that with an exchange of the camera "the object of the gaze is temporarily allowed to become its subject" (Renov 216). In other words: the filmed other is allowed to temporarily become the camera operator. That the camera swop between filmed and filming subject is more common in video than in film practices can in part be explained by the fact that video cameras can be more easily held and operated.

In *Delirium*, it is vital that Faber's mother points the camera back at her daughter. Without this reversal, the video would not have differed from the representations it condemns; that is, (melodramatic) films and (medical) photographs which portray rebellious women as hysterical, thereby keeping them in their passive place, "at a distance" and "imprisoned on the edge," as Faber says. Her video does run the risk of doing precisely this when it places emphasis, sometimes accusingly, on the mother's abnormal behavior, such as dancing in the street, running away from her family with a gun, and throwing pans at her children. Mainly because she gets to hold the camera, Faber's mother is not merely a passive, distanced object of her daughter's representation, but a subject involved in the act of representing both mother and daughter.

In addition to this application of video as a medium that breaches the barrier between the invisible, detached camera operator and the object of representation, video has also been praised as a medium which gives rise to an involved, intimate and embodied mode of looking through its haptic image qualities (as discussed in Parts II and III). These haptic qualities not so much shape the relationship between camera operator and filmed object; they most of all have an effect on the way in which the viewer of the representation relates to the represented others. In *Delirium*, the grainy quality of Faber's video footage aggrandizes the hapticity of speckled old black-and-white film images of hysterical women Faber has incorporated into her piece. Through video keying and layering, old film footage of "crazy" women is overlaid with low-quality video close-ups of female bodies. The haptic qualities of the video images force the viewer to relate to the peculiar medical "objects" on view in an involved, embodied way. In addition to the fact that the layered yet opaque surface of the scenes emphasizes that the images on view are not a transparent window, it also stimulates the spectator to look at the suffering, collapsing, or jolting naked bodies of the hysterical women on screen with their own body. Hence, in *Delirium*, the hapticity of the video images precludes a disembodied, distant mode of looking.

The other video look: detached

In stark contrast with the above specifications of video as a medium that rewrites the history of detached, objective observation to which lens-based media are tied, video is just as often specified as a medium that keeps the detached observer in place. In many discourses, video is pictured as an "ice cold eye" which objectively registers reality, and gives rise to an uninvolved mode of looking at the world.

This view of video can be recognized in two films by Michael Haneke; in *Benny's Video* (1992), and *Caché* (2005). As discussed in Part I, the adolescent protagonist of *Benny's Video* watches video all day. The young boy has adopted an unempathetic, detached way of looking similar to the cool and mechanical way in which his video camera registers the world, which in the end results in Benny killing a friend without remorse. The male protagonist of *Caché* is not a cold-blooded murderer, yet he is just as much a detached observer as Benny is. This does not become immediately apparent in the film. Middle-aged Georges Laurent is a loving husband and father, who presents a book show on television with an intellectual touch. His life goes by pleasantly until he receives videotapes on his doorstep on which his house is being surveilled. After a while, he also starts to receive unsettling childlike drawings together with the videos, which bring Georges to suspect who has sent the tapes.

When Georges was six years old, an Algerian boy named Majid came to live with Georges and his parents at their farm. Georges' parents wanted to adopt the young boy, but because Georges told an incriminating lie about Majid, the child was taken to an orphanage. When Georges meets Majid decades later in order to confront him with the video recordings, a stark contrast becomes visible between Georges' bourgeois life and Majid's residence in a poor Parisian suburb. Although Georges is in part responsible for Majid's poverty, Majid denies having sent the tapes. Georges refuses to believe this, and angrily visits Majid once more. Then, an unexpected event takes place. Without warning or explanation, the Algerian man slits his own throat with a knife.

Majid's puzzling suicide in the presence of Georges, as well as the tapes he has presumably sent him, can both be interpreted as attempts to breach Georges' uninvolved disposition. The vile drama and threatening videos should be able to instill some shock or fear in this cool onlooker. That Georges is in fact a cool observer is made clear by the film through video, in a flashback (Verstraten 2008: 58). A short while after Majid's suicide, Georges decides to go to bed early after a nasty confrontation with Majid's son. The scene in which Georges goes to sleep is followed by a shot of the farmyard of his parental home. A car arrives, and someone enters the house that is seen from a distance. Seconds later, when a few people walk out the door, a little boy tries to escape from the small group, screaming that he doesn't want to go. It is plausible to assume that these images are Georges' recollection or dream of Majid's removal from the family. It is surprising, however, that the images are bright, whereas earlier on in the film, Georges' childhood memories were shown in pale colors. What is more, the images look like the video recordings of Georges' home: recorded from a distant viewpoint, they steadily frame whatever moves by. The dreamed or memorized images of the farm which are in all probability focalized by the six-year-old Georges are thus formally similar to the surveillance video images of his house.

Peter Verstraten has convincingly argued that this similarity can indicate two things. Either Georges has internalized the procedure of the threatening surveillance videos he received on his doorstep, and now looks at the past as if it is mediated by video, with a cool eye. Or, Georges has always been an aloof observer. In that case, the outlook of a registering video is a suitable imitation for Georges' way of looking. Either way, in the flashback at the end, the medium of video is used to illustrate Georges' lack of compassion. He is a man with the cool outlook of a registering video, who can perceive things from an appropriate distance and can wallow in the safe enclave of his intellectual class (Verstraten 2008: 58–59).

Together with Georges, the viewer of the film is confronted with her own (dis)engagement through the last shot of the film. The long continuous shot shows students hanging around a flight of stairs in front of a school. As the young people are shown from a distance, it is impossible to learn more about them. Their facial expressions or conversations cannot be discerned, and nothing special seems to be going on between the students. The static shot does not seem to be related to the film's story in any way. What is more, because the video-like images of the ordinary everyday scene cannot be attributed to an identifiable internal focalizor, it is the spectator who is put in the position of a frighteningly cold video eye (Verstraten 2008: 59). As the film's credit titles start rolling, the (intellectual art-house) viewer is left with the question of whether she looks at the world in an overly detached manner. Moreover, as the relationship between Georges and Majid is set within a framework of postcolonial relations, the previous question can subsequently be narrowed down by replacing "the world" with "the colonial past." Do I look at the European colonial past with compassion and a sense of responsibility? Or do I, like Georges, regard the suffering of the previously colonized other from a distance, without getting involved?

The fact that the film prompts the above questions in the viewer with the help of video shows that the medium of video does not always create or encourage a detached observer. Although Haneke's films represent video as a medium that registers reality in a detached mechanical manner, it is applied in such a way that the detached observer is encouraged to get involved. The video camera might look with a cold mechanical eye; but this is not a mode of looking that should be adopted by human beings. In *Caché*, film and video together undercut a long tradition in which photography and film were applied as tools of objective representation that allowed the spectator to look at the cultural, colonized other as an object. *Caché* shows how inhumane and violent such a mode of looking really is.

CHAPTER 18
THE PRODUCTION OF PORTABLE OBJECTS

In contrast to objective registration, the capability which will be discussed in this chapter is not attributed to photography, film, and video by convention. The three media are technically able to produce portable objects, with the word portable indicating that those objects can be held or carried and can be transported through space. The fact that photographs, films, and videos are usually material objects which can be taken in one's hands, and the fact that they are transportable, can have violent consequences, but in different ways.

Of the three media, photographs are the only objects which can be viewed and held at the same time. Videotapes can be carried, and film reels can be held, but they cannot be viewed at the same time. When their images are shown, videos and films are no longer objects easily handled, as their projection mostly depends on multiple elements such as a cathode-ray tube for video and a screen and a projector for film. Moreover, the projections are not material; they consist of light, which cannot be held as an object in the way photographs printed on paper can be.[1]

The violent impact of photography's ability to produce objects has been widely noted and demonstrated. Thus, Susan Sontag has remarked that photographing people is a violent act because it turns them into objects (1979: 14). According to Sontag, photographs function as symbolic images. When photographs stand, as symbols, for the person they depict, the objecthood and disembodiment of flat photographic prints can be read as if they were done to the person on view, as acts of objectification and disembodiment inflicted on the real person who lives or lived outside of the frame. When the referent is believed to be part of the photograph itself (following Roland Barthes (1980)), the objectification and disembodiment are more literal; the photographed subject is turned into a disembodied object because she is present in this object as its referent. In both possible senses, however, the body of the photographed subject is not really hurt; it remains intact when photographed, even if it becomes part of the picture as a trace.

Yet, the objectification of the photographed subject through the objecthood of photographs is often used as a metaphor for forms of objectification that do not leave the body of the subject unharmed, such as rape or murder. Moreover, pictures which stand for those they depict can be used as a way of appropriating someone. When Sontag remarked that photographing people turns them into objects, she continued with "objects that can be symbolically possessed" (1979: 14). Symbolically possessed, that is, because photographed human beings can be "owned" by way of the photographic objects which symbolize them or carry them within. In addition, photographed subjects can be hurt through a violation of their photograph, that is, in the eyes of the beholder/violator who reads pictures as human subject. Lovingly caressing a photograph as if it were a living human being has a violent equivalent in aggressively touching or damaging a photo which stands for the person it depicts.[2]

While photography's objecthood is often regarded as a harmful capacity of the medium because it seems to, or is believed to, objectify the represented subject, the fleetingness of film images can equally be understood as a violation of the represented subject's body. Consider for instance the following passage on the experience of the (silent) film actor in Luigi Pirandello's novel *Si Gira* (1915):

> With a vague sense of discomfort he feels inexplicable emptiness: his body loses its corporeality, it evaporates, it is deprived of reality, life, voice, and the noises caused by his moving about, in order to be changed into a mute image, flickering an instant on the screen, then vanishing into silence.
>
> Pirandello quoted in Pierre-Quint 1927: 14–15

The passage hints at the limitations of the cinematic representation, for the sounds made by the actor are not recorded by silent film. However, the emotions of the actor cannot be explained as feelings of indignation over the inadequacies of his representation. He experiences emptiness and has the feeling that his body evaporates, is killed even, deprived of life. This experience appears to stem from the fact that the film images are so fleeting; the narrator mentions how they flicker for only an instant on screen before they vanish. It seems as if, in the experience of the actor, the transitory character of the film is inflicted on his body. And in a way, of course, his body has become a film image, because it is caught on celluloid in the same way it would have made a photographic image. Because of their similar technical and chemical support, analogue film and photography have their indexical nature in common. As a result, film images are also often regarded as co-natural with their referent. This is noticeable in the passage from Pirandello's story in which the difference between the actor's real body and its representation isn't marked: the narrator doesn't say "his represented body," but "his body" when he describes how it evaporates through film.

While the above remarks on the fleetingness of film are also applicable to the ephemeral moving video image, it is important to note that, over the last couple of years, a change in the objecthood of video has taken place. Today, video recordings no longer depend on a bulky apparatus in order to be shown; clips can also be viewed on cellphones. As such, video images can easily be carried and viewed at the same time. Played on a cellphone, the video images are still composed of light and they still disappear without electricity. Yet, this impalpability and ephemerality become less noticeable because the screen on which the images appear is so small. Thus, the impression arises that videos can be held and touched as material objects, like photographs. Videos played on a cellphone can therefore function in the same ways as photographs. They can be understood as a symbol or a trace of their referent, and as objects displayed on the small screen of a GSM device, they can easily be carried, held, and touched. As such, they can function as objects for symbolic appropriation in a manner similar to photographs. Yet, an important discrepancy lies in the fact that videos cannot be damaged in the same way by hand as printed photographs can. Apart from erasing them all together, or destroying the device which displays them, videos cannot easily be "injured," making them unsuitable to function as voodoo-doll-like objects in which the physical separation between representation and represented subject is obliterated in the eyes of the user/beholder.

Relocating violence, violent relocations

When locating the violent consequences which spring from the ability of the three lens-based media to produce portable objects, more emphasis can be put on the violent effects of portability as in transportability. The fact that photos, films, and video images can be moved to another place and spread around can harm the photographed or filmed subject. The objecthood of the image is less important in this line of approach; the harm arises more from the fact that a person's image can be taken away from her and can be viewed when she is not around, than from the fact that she is turned into a material object when photographed, filmed, or videotaped. When it comes to transportability, electronic and digital images are the main concern. Precisely because they lack material objecthood, these images are transportable par excellence through the digital highway.

Walter Benjamin pointed out the possibly violent effect of the transportability of images in a discussion of film in the pre-digital era. A person's subjectivity is in danger when her representation can be shown at one or more places apart from the subject's own location. In "The Work of Art in the Age of Mechanical Reproduction," Benjamin mentions this loss of subjectivity in relation to the film actor. The actor before the camera is overcome by feelings of strangeness, oppression, anxiety, and fear of the apparatus of film. The feeling of strangeness is basically the same kind of estrangement as is felt before one's image in the mirror, according to Benjamin. The difference between the mirror and film, however, is that with film, the reflected image has become separable, transportable. The filmic apparatus will take the actor's shadow, her mirror image, away from her—and expose it in the absence of the performer.

Benjamin provides two reasons for which this "abduction" of the actor's image by the apparatus of film instills feelings of anxiety in the actor. First, the subject is robbed of her aura when she is reproduced in the form of film images, because this aura is connected to the here and now of the single and unique living person. In the case of the actor, both the aura of himself and of the character he plays are lost when he is filmed. In the words of Benjamin:

> For the first time—and that is the effect of film—man has to operate with his whole living person, yet foregoing his aura. For aura is tied to his presence;

> there can be no replica of it. The aura which, on stage, emanates from Macbeth, cannot be separated for the spectators from that of the actor. However, the singularity of the shot in the studio is that the camera is substituted for the public. Consequently, the aura that envelops the actor vanishes, and with it the aura of the person he portrays.
>
> 1999: 223

A second reason why the actor fears the film apparatus is that it transports his image to the public, who represent the market. Through his film image, the actor will become absorbed by the market, to which he offers "not only his labor, but also his whole self, his heart and soul" (1999: 225). Besides being reduced to a commodity, the actor is robbed of his self-determination. He cannot control the market, and therefore he cannot control his position within it. Instead, the market determines him. Capital decides what he does, where and when his shadow performs for the public, and who he is. It can turn the actor into a star, a constructed personality, or a nobody.

Compared to video and photography, the effect of turning subjects into well-known commodities is more common to film images because of the star system which is so typical of the movie industry. However, photography and video have their own share of handing over subjects to the market. Especially within the music industry, video clips and, to a lesser degree, photographs, have become indispensable factors in gaining fame—and losing self-determination in the process. What is more, not only movie actors or musicians become a part of the market via their images. Practically everyone can become a bankable celebrity when their portrait or home video is picked up by the media or "goes viral." Everyone's image, moreover, can serve as a commodity. A famous example in this regard is Steve McCurry's picture of a displaced Afghan girl, looking straight into the camera with piercing green eyes, the color contrasting with the red shawl loosely wrapped around the girl's head. The image first appeared on the cover of *National Geographic* in 1985 and has been for sale ever since in the form of reprints, posters, stationery, and other forms of merchandize.

Such commodification of one's image can be harmful because, as Benjamin notes, the market in which a commodity functions cannot be controlled. When lens-based images become a popular object, the circulation and exposure can hardly be stopped.[3] The measure of harm done to a person by her limited control over the circulation of her representation depends on a number of factors. To be exposed in the form of an image is especially damaging when you haven't given permission for it, or when you are exposed against your will. Moreover, the intensity of the violation depends on the extent to which what is exposed usually remains hidden, or is supposed to remain private according to those depicted. In addition, as Mieke Bal notes, showing or circulating images of people without their endorsement is all the more a theft of their subjectivity when they do not get paid, or are not paid in proportion to their exposure (2006: 95). Without compensation, showing images of others is a form of exploitation, especially in light of the fact that "their exposure is someone else's merchandise" (95). As we will see in Chapter 20, video has an especially dominant role in uncovering things that are supposed to remain hidden, and in secretly stealing subjectivity without compensation.

The harmful effects of the exposure and circulation of a person's image should, moreover, not be understood in emotional or psychological terms only; the exposure of pictures can have material consequences. For Sharbat Gula, the exposure of her face could have had grave results for her, as she lived in a segregated society in which most women are veiled. She wasn't punished or repudiated only because the famous picture of her face never circulated in her own community. In addition to the violent effect of exposing pictures that show things or parts of people they themselves would like to keep out of sight, the beauty of the images (like the one of Gula) can sometimes aggravate the violation of the photographed, filmed, or photographed subjects. The beauty of images is especially damaging when those images show death or suffering—pain, poverty, disease, injury, and deprivation. Beauty distracts, and threatens to neutralize acts of violence (Bal 2006: 103). It is important to note this violent effect of beautiful images in relation to photography, film, and video, because all three media are applied both in journalistic and aesthetic ways; applications which do not automatically rule each other out.[4,5]

Finally, a represented subject can be hurt through the transportability of her representation, because together with the subject's lack of control over the circulation of her image, control over the image's meaning is also lacking. This meaning depends largely on the context in which the representation is viewed, and without control over the circulation, the context of the image cannot be decided either.[6] To come back to the Steve McCurry's portrait of Sharbat Gula, after having been published in *National Geographic*, the photograph of the beautiful Afghan girl was repeatedly used in various humanitarian campaigns. Serving as a visual lynchpin for philanthropic efforts to raise money for causes ranging from the education of Afghan girls to repressed people all over the globe, Gula's image came to stand for, among other things, repressed and poor women to be rescued, poor and suffering people in general, Afghanistan as a whole, and Afghan girls and women in particular. First of all, it is questionable whether Sharbat Gula would approve of being appropriated as a *pars pro toto* of these causes. Secondly, as humanitarian causes are often closely intertwined with political interests, it is necessary to wonder whether Sharbat Gula would agree to the political agendas her image was made to serve.[7] Besides the fact that particular political forces may contradict her own ideals, they can ultimately disempower her and influence her environment against her will. When a person's image is appropriated within a certain context, its resulting meaning can thus violate the represented subject.

CHAPTER 19
FROM FREEZING TO TOUCHING

With straightened backs and deadpan expressions, about forty police officers pose together in what seems to be a conventional group portrait. Because of the static poses held by the portrayed figures, the large image projected on the wall of a gallery seems to be a photograph. Only after close inspection, it becomes clear that this is not the case. Very small movements can be detected within the image. An eyelid flutters rapidly, a foot is slightly repositioned, a chest is lifted, or a head slightly tilted. They are the kinds of movements a person cannot avoid making when holding a pose for a long time, which is precisely what these officers are doing. For sixty minutes, they remain as silent and as still as possible.

60 Minutes Silence (1996) by British artist Gillian Wearing exposes something important about the related specification of photography, film and video. Wearing's video shows that in general, photography is defined as a medium that produces immobile images. As soon as photographic images start to move, they are rather recognized as film or video images, no matter how many associations with photography are evoked by the representation in other respects. The stasis of its images is one of the ways by which photography is able to freeze the represented subject. When a person's photograph is taken, his movements in space and time are stopped, frozen within the immobile image. In this chapter, I will discuss the violence inherent in this and other kinds of freezing performed through photography, film, and video. In addition to the fact that moving film and video projections such as Wearing's can provide insight into the aggressive character of photography's freezing effects, photography's stasis, and the movement of film images gain meaning in relation—often in opposition—to each other. However, I will demonstrate that film's movement should not merely be understood as the antithesis of photography's stilled images; moving film and video images can violently freeze their subject, too. Some of these forms of freezing or capturing the subject by way of moving images will ultimately lead me to consider violent modes of touching and invading the human body with the video camera.

Filmic fluxus vs. photographic fastening down (like butterflies)

The movement of film images is generally associated with life.[1] In the following fragment from an interview, Hungarian artist Péter Forgács for instance states that movement *is* life when he discusses the effect of film's moving images:

> If we make here and now a black-and-white photograph of ourselves, we can observe this event already as being from the past: history. [...] But when we have moving images from the past, we always have the fluxus of life, the contrapuntal notion between Barthes's photo thesis and the movement (=life) on film, which proves that we are alive. So my viewers—and you—know that they (the amateur film actors, my heroes) are physically dead, yet, they are still moving. They are reanimated again and again by film.
>
> Forgács in Spieker, 2002, under "Each photograph is a tombstone."

Roland Barthes made a similar claim by when he said that "the cinema has a power which at first glance the photograph does not have: the screen (as Bazin has remarked) is not a frame but a hideout; the man or woman who emerges from it continues living [...]" (1980: 55–56). However, for Barthes, represented people do not live on in film because the film shows their movements, as Forgács has it. Rather, they live on because *film moves on*. Even when looking at a single stilled film frame, there is always what Barthes calls "a blind field"; something we cannot see but which is there: (the possibility of) a next frame. Film images thus always carry future continuation in them, and because of that, the represented people can live on, even if they do not move at all.

Besides the fact that Forgács as well as Barthes think of film as a medium which (re)animates the human beings it shows, both theorists contrast this effect of film's movement with the effect of the stasis of photography. According to Barthes, the motionlessness of a photographic image not only means that the figures it represents do not move. Unlike the continuation of life in moving film images, the people appearing on photographs "do not emerge, do not leave, they are anesthetized and fastened down, like butterflies" (1980: 57). In addition to this, photographs do not reanimate their referent in the present, as films do, but have the effect that a photographed person immediately belongs to the past. For as Barthes has argued, and Forgács endorses, photographs claim the "that-has-been" (56). Because of photography's technique, people shown in a photograph have irrefutably been there, in the past, in front of the lens when the photograph was taken. And because of photography's immobility, they remain frozen in that past moment forever; anesthetized, fastened down, or dead.

Theorists or filmmakers like Forgács, who are of the opinion that film reanimates people because it shows their movements, are likely to subscribe to the widespread viewpoint that photography "kills" the subjects it depicts because it cannot capture their movements, and therefore pictures them as static (=dead). According to Barthes and other thinkers who relate the animating effect of film to the progressive movement of the images rather than to the depicted mobility of the shown bodies, the death of the photographed subject is not so much caused by the immobility of the single photographic image. Rather, it is the result of another kind of movement the photographic medium lacks; movement beyond or outside the single frame in order to show what is next, both in a spatial and a temporal sense. Whereas something depicted in a single film frame possibly has a future in the next frame on the film reel, "every thing which happens within the [photographic] frame," writes Barthes, "dies absolutely once the frame is passed beyond" (1980: 57). And because we know nothing comes next, the depicted subject not only dies when the frame is passed beyond, but is in a way already dead within the frame itself.[2]

Although this killing or death of the photographed subject should not be understood in a too literal sense (in spite of metaphors such as shooting and aiming, the camera is not a lethal weapon), for Barthes dying is so inherent in being photographed that he does not phrase the relation between death and photography as a comparison: "Whether or not the subject is already dead, every photograph *is* this catastrophe" (1980: 96, emphasis added).

What is more, to see yourself (as if) dead when looking at your picture, is a confrontation with your own, actual death in the future. The paradox here is that precisely because photographs only show static things that have been, things without a future, without continuation in time like film images, they do point to the future after all. Together with and because of the "that-has-been," a "this-will-be" is announced by photographs. What they announce is death in the future, according to Barthes (1980: 96). For him, the death of the viewer is not only announced when she watches her own photograph; every photograph announces this future death, and therefore "each one [. . .] challenges each of us, one by one, outside of any generality" (97). This means that photography's stasis has two victims. Not only are the photographed subjects touched by the catastrophe of death; the viewing subjects of photographs are without exception confronted by it as well.

Captured by video

The movement in film and video footage often gains the meaning of "liveliness" and "freedom" in relation to the stillness of photography, which is understood as restricting and murderous, as (a reminder of) death. In Fiona Tan's previously discussed *Countenance*, the movement of the installation's projected images not only provides the portrayed people with more presence and liveliness than they have in Sander's comparable photographic project, but the movement within the images, as well as the movement of their succession on the projection screens, also affects the status of the types both Tan and Sander create. Whereas the bakers, butchers, beggars, and farmers in Sander's project seems to be stuck in their category forever, Tan's looped moving images indicate that the presented ordering of types is an ongoing, unending process. In comparison to Sander's photographs, the types in Tan's moving video projections look less fixed. The small movements within the video images, such as waving hair or twitches of an eye, not only suggest that these people are alive, but also that they will live on, and subsequently change. Butchers will become pensioners, newly-weds will turn into residents of geriatric homes, teachers may turn into politicians, and so forth.

In addition, the movement of images in *Countenance* also structures the relationship between the viewing subjects and the portrayed ones. While standing in front of the projected portraits, museum visitors resemble the subjects on screen. The size, the pose and the nearly stilled position of the viewing and the viewed subject are approximately alike. Whereas people in Sander's photographs have the form of small, frozen figures on a piece of paper, the people in Tan's video piece are broadly the viewer's mirror image. The resemblance between the viewer and the portrayed subjects stimulates a form of self-reflexivity in the beholder that Tan herself exposed in the self-portrait preceding the large projections in an adjacent room. For the resemblance summons questions: "We are alike, but how alike precisely? Do I belong to this type? Or to this one as well? What is my social position? With which social group do I identify most?" Such questions obliterate the possibility of looking at the portrayed others in a distant, neutrally observing way. Instead the viewer is stimulated to categorize *herself* by way of the large number of portraits passing by on the projection screens. Therefore, in *Countenance*, the movement of images not only forms a response to the aggressive freezing effects of photography's stasis. It also counteracts the detached, objectifying mode of looking which the photographic medium sustains.

However, although the movement of cinematic and videomatic images is often understood as a positive, resuscitating or liberating abrogation of photography's aggressive stillness, this movement can violently capture the represented subject just as well. How such freezing by way of movement can proceed is shown by Hester Scheurwater's video *Heal Me* (2000). This piece starts with a shot of a woman who is standing bare-foot on the tiled floor of an empty room. She is standing in the middle, while the camera is positioned somewhere in a corner, showing her from a distance, from the back. Although the shot only takes a few seconds, it lasts long enough to show the viewer that the women is average-sized and dark-haired. A black dress covers the upper part of her bare legs, and a large part of her lower back.

After this quick first overall shot, the camera approaches the woman, and starts circling her body at close range. Starting with a view of her back, the camera zooms in on her buttocks. From there it descends to the woman's lower legs, showing her ankles and calves. After having paid considerable attention to the woman's lower legs, the camera slightly tilts upwards. It tries to peer between her thighs, but moves on when only darkness can be seen under the dress. Slowly circling upward, the camera moves to her side, where one of her arms hangs down by her body. A hand with polished fingernails comes into view. After that, the camera turns to her chest. Although the woman is wearing a dress, it does not cover her breasts. The camera films the bare chest from a very close range, especially nearing the nipples. In addition, the movement of the camera seems to decelerate a little when the breasts are brought into view, although it quickly resumes its slow yet continuous pace. After swerving further upwards around the body, the camera finally moves around the woman's head and shoulders. Although her overall posture is straight, her head is hanging down a little and her shoulders stoop slightly forward. The woman's face is invisible, as it is covered by her hair. After tilting up and downwards again, the camera circles back down to the buttocks, and zooms out in order to give a final overall shot of the woman before the video ends.

During the four minutes the video takes, the represented woman does not move at all. It seems as if she is frozen by the circling camera, which captures her within its spiraling movement. The fact that she is filmed at close range suggests the near physical presence of the someone or something that is looking at her, a physical presence that retains her body without actually touching it. In addition, the woman is held in place by the look of the camera that surrounds her because it scans her body in an aggressive way. By focusing for a long time on her buttocks, peering between her legs, zooming in on the long red finger nails, and taking a close look at her bare breasts, the camera turns the female body into an object of sexual desire. Her objectification is emphasized all the more by the fact that her face is covered: she cannot look back in order to become a viewing subject. However, the objectifying and freezing power of the camera's gaze in *Heal Me* relies for the most part on its ability to move. Especially because of the particular movements it makes (circling, decelerating, tilting, and zooming) when filming the woman it has a forceful, violating strength. Its intimidating and objectifying mode of looking requires mobility.

Although the relatively small circumscribing movements in *Heal Me* are made with a lightweight video camera, Scheurwater's video could technically have been recorded with a film camera as well. That the work can be recognized as video is more due to the fact that it doesn't follow an important narrative film convention: the so-called 180-degree rule, which dictates that the camera cannot cross an invisible line running through a film set. The circling movement in Scheurwater's video clearly doesn't follow this convention. The video does refer to another strong film convention though: to represent women as the object of the male look, as well as his desire. In Chapter 21 I will further discuss this convention, of which *Heal Me* can be understood as a subversive exaggeration.

As in Scheurwater's *Heal Me*, a woman is the object of the camera's attention in another important video by the Dutch artist: *I Wanted You* (2001). The woman who is filmed in that video work is lying on the floor at full length. She is clearly trying to move forward and get up. Her arms and legs make swirling and crawling movements. The woman manages to drag her body forward a little, while the front side of her body scrapes over the floor. Yet despite her seemingly desperate attempts she isn't able to move forward or upwards very much. The struggle of the woman seems to indicate that she is somehow restricted in her movements by something. Is her body too heavy for her to lift? Or is the air surrounding so thick that it works as tar? What is holding her down? Upon closer inspection, it becomes apparent that the oppressive, suffocating effect of the video is caused by the manipulation of the video footage. The movements of the women are shown in slow-motion, which creates the impression that she is countered, captured, and smothered by an invisible force. This force does not lie in the weight of her own body, or in the atmospheric pressure, but in the medium that depicts her.

The female subject in *I Wanted You* is not frozen. She isn't killed by the stillness of the images; the images do show movement. Yet, because of the deceleration of the video material, the life seems to be drained out of her. She isn't frozen (dead) yet, but she is slowed down (dying). As mentioned previously, Forgács and others have argued that the movement of images brings filmed subjects back to life. According to Forgács, the manipulation of film time, such as stilling, slowing down, or speeding up the footage, only emphasizes the movement of the images, and hence the liveliness of the depicted people. *I Wanted You* demonstrates that this is not always the case. For, in this video, the manipulated movement of the images doesn't reanimate the represented subject. Rather, it seems to be in the process of murdering her.

Kicking with the camera

As mentioned previously, photography, film, and video are often specified as media that give rise to a detached mode of looking. A mode of looking, that is, with possibly violent consequences, because it presumes a distinction between observer and observed which objectifies the represented subject. In part, the assumption that the three lens-based media enable detached observation can be explained by the fact that a literal distance is required between the camera and its object in order for the lens-based media to record images at all. If the camera's lens were to touch the object when photographing or recording, the resulting images would turn out black. For the light necessary for the production of photographs, videos, and films can only enter the camera if there is some distance between objective and object.

When the distance between camera and represented object is reduced to a minimum, the detached mode of looking is not necessarily hindered or diminished. In fact, close-ups often give rise to the impression that the object or subject on view is appropriated, because it is scrutinized and exposed in greater detail. This appropriation can be a sexual one; think about the close-up of the woman's bare breasts in *Heal Me*. Because the camera approached them, it seemed to take hold of them. Moreover, when human bodies are represented in close-up, an objectifying effect can be caused by the association with scientific and medical examination. This association quickly arises in relation to close-ups, as they are used to document and represent objects of research.

The distance between the camera and its object of representation can be more convincingly minimized by video than by photography and film, through a procedure that requires a medium which can record movement, and whose apparatus can moreover easily be moved itself. The movements made with a handheld, so-called kinetic video camera can mimic, follow, or resemble movements which are made by the human body. Movements, that is, which are made by one body when it touches another. A stroking movement made with one's hand when caressing another, can be mimicked by a tracking movement of the camera when it films a person. This can successfully create the impression that the camera touches what it records, as is shown by Celio Braga's *Dalice* (2006). In this video installation, a camera slowly pans over the face of a sad-looking woman. Its slight movements seem to touch the woman's skin, to caress and console her with gentle strokes. Because the movements clearly indicate that the camera is hand-held, and moreover moves in precisely the way a stroking hand would, the technical device seems to function as an extension or prosthesis of the human body holding it. An extension, that is, which reaches up to the face of the sad woman.

The camera in *Dalice* seems to touch the subject in the most loving way possible with video. The possibility of gently touching with the camera does, however, have its downside in that the camera can be used to seemingly touch the filmed subject in a violent or aggressive way too. Then, the movements of the camera do not resemble soft strokes, but the slaps a person can give with the hand. This aggressive application of the video camera is widespread and dominant in video's field of application. A gentle use of the video camera such as in *Dalice* is an exception to the rule; the possibility to touch lovingly is a rarely applied possibility of the video medium. The dominant, violent mode of touching with the video camera can be identified in many amateur video clips posted on internet sites such as YouTube. Very often, the clips are recorded with cellphones. These small and lightweight devices are, of course, suitable for the hand-held effects by which violent movements of the body are copied with the camera.

Unlike many videos of violent crimes, the clip *Mobile Phone Cam Reveals Murder* was not posted on the Internet by those recording the clip with a cellphone. The crime the video exposes is too grave for that, and the perpetrators' faces are too identifiable. Before it was uploaded on YouTube, the clip appeared in a television news program, in which the newscaster explained that the video was discovered by the police in the GSM device of one of the perpetrators. Thanks to the clip, the unsolved murder of a homeless person in a Moscow park was no longer a mystery, as the video reveals how a group of young men bludgeoned the man to death at night. The video is clearly recorded by a member of the group, as the filmed boys communicate with the person who is filming. In addition, they signal the camera operator to come closer, in order to bring the crime properly into view. Moreover, the perpetrators repeatedly look into the camera, and sometimes make cheerful gestures of victory into the camera after having kicked the homeless man, who is lying helplessly on the ground. One of the boys even climbs on top of the man's body, and while looking into the camera, he raises his arms with clenched fists so as to indicate his domination of the victim. The gestures into the camera clearly show that the violators draw the camera in while murdering the man. It is involved by the young men in the crime because they want their "funny" deed to be recorded.

The involvement of the camera in the killing is furthermore exposed by the fact that the camera mimics the blows, punches and kicks the youngsters inflict on the vagrant. One shot shows how one of the boys runs up to the man, and in the same flowing movement smashes a glass bottle against the man's head. Immediately the camera, which filmed the scene from a distance, rapidly zooms in on the injured head until the image becomes a blur. This could be interpreted as an attempt to show what spectacular injuries the smashed bottle has caused. However, the zooming moves at such a speed that the camera has no time to automatically focus the image of the man's head. Before this can be done, the zooming-in has already continued up to a point where nothing can be clearly discerned within the images anymore.

Instead of an attempt to show, the zooming movement seems to be an attempt at hitting the man once more. The speed of the zoom movement, as well as its point of impact, resemble the previous movement of the filmed blow. In another instance, the camera rapidly zooms in and out a few times while filming the victim; a movement that resembles a number of kicks in the stomach the man has to endure. What is more, at the beginning of the beating, when the man still tries to get to his feet a few times, the boys one by one run into him, in order to push him over with the weight of their entire bodies. The swerving camera slightly follows the sideways and downward movements of the falling bodies that press the victim against the ground.

By mimicking the violent gestures acted out by the body, the video camera can be seen as an accomplice to the violence it shows. The blows and kicks of the camera do not, of course, injure the victim physically. Yet the resemblance between the camera movements and physical acts of violence draw attention to the violent effect of filming violence. By following the same trajectory of punches or slaps, with the same speed, the camera reveals that the act of filming can be an aggressive act that contributes to the violence it records.

The anonymously uploaded YouTube video *Bully gets beat up* (2008) shows that its violent impact on victims of violence is, although not physical, certainly not virtual. In the introduction I already mentioned how, in this amateur online video clip, a young man tries to fend off his attackers. He is abused, pushed, and shoved. However, while defending himself both verbally and physically, he is mostly occupied with attempts to evade the camera that keeps approaching him in order to film him in close-up. This act seems to provoke the assaulted man the most, as he either looks angrily into the camera while saying "don't," or evasively turns away from the lens while making averting gestures towards the camera with his hands. To the young man, the act of being filmed is clearly just as violating as the physical and verbal attacks.

Being filmed while being physically attacked or threatened is often experienced as an act of aggression because it is a double objectification of the subject under attack. The first form of objectifying acts concerns the physical hindrance and disempowerment of the victim, possibly accompanied by verbal degradation. Secondly, the violated subject becomes an object of representation because of the recording video camera. This second objectification, then, is especially aggressive because it means that the victim's desubjectification through violence is recorded, captured on tape. This visual preservation and appropriation of one's degradation is itself degrading. What is more, in the current digital age, being recorded with a video camera implies that the undignified "spectacle" can be put on show on the Internet afterwards, to be viewed by anyone, anywhere, without the victim's approval.

In *Mobile Phone Cam Reveals Murder*, the idea that the video could be viewed later on seemed to occupy the men. This idea didn't frighten them, though. The presence of the camera clearly added to the "fun" of the beating for the aggressive young men. They did not merely hit the man just for the pleasure of hurting him, or to have a good time together, they also performed for the camera. The performing quality of their behavior is shown by the fact that they look into the lens before handing out another blow ("Is this being filmed? Watch this!"), and because they adopt aggressive positions while turning to the camera, such as the expression of victory. Such gestures make the camera a part of their crime, yet they also seem to anticipate future viewings. Why show off and put oneself out for the "dead eye" of the video camera, if it isn't for the expectation that what the video lens sees will be witnessed by an audience later on too? Even if this audience consists only of oneself, the expectation of future viewing can be a stimulation to put on a violent show in front of the camera.

Invading the body

Whereas metaphors such as shooting, stabbing, and penetrating abound when the acts of photographing and filming are discussed, it is the video camera that nowadays seems to be best able to enter the body. Jerry Bruckheimer's television series *Crime Scene Investigation* (2000–2015) is one of the most popular programs in which video is used to provide a view inside a body. In the series, a group of forensic experts solves murder cases with the help of state-of-the-art techniques. After a thorough inspection of the crime scene, the corpse of the victim is taken to a lab to be meticulously examined by a pathologist. Once the pathologist has established the cause of death, he informs the members of the team of his findings while they stand near the dead body. The briefing starts with a short introduction by the pathologist on the methods he has used, and on the blemishes and injuries he has discovered on the victim's skin. These are pointed out by him to the team, and to the viewer. Then, when the naked body of the victim is in view, the pathologist reveals the cause of death. When he does so, the images illustrate his words, by showing what has killed the victim.

Neither the murderer nor the murder weapon are shown in a flashback of the event, however, but the production of the internal injuries that caused the death of the murdered person is depicted. If a victim was, for example, hit over the head, resulting in a shattered skull and damaged brain tissue, the camera swiftly zooms in on the victim's head, pierces through hair and skin, and then shows how the skull cracks into pieces and cuts through grey matter. Similarly, the camera sometimes follows the trajectory of a bullet, again by penetrating the skin, and subsequently showing how the bullet hits the victim's internal organs or bones. Chemical murders such as poisonings are visualized too. In such cases, the camera shows the effects of the poison. For instance, it enters the body to show how the lethal toxicant is digested, or how it travels to vital organs through blood vessels.

CSI forms an interesting parallel with the previously discussed YouTube video *Mobile Phone Cam Reveals Murder.* In both cases, the camera approaches the body in a manner copying the trajectory and speed of a violent act inflicted on it by somebody else. In *CSI*, however, the camera doesn't stop at the skin. It pierces through it, and enters the body. The camera does not so much mimic the aggressive act of a perpetrator, as in *Mobile Phone Cam Reveals Murder.* The camera in *CSI* seems to coincide with the murder weapon, because the video images of the inside of a victim's body seem to be focalized by the murder weapon. Video functions as the eyes of the murder weapon, so to speak.

The visual effect of the camera as murder weapon, or of a murder weapon with video eyes, is created with the help of animation. Digital video recordings have been adapted and modeled so as to create the illusion that the camera can break through skin and bones with force, while retaining its ability to record clear images of messy insides. In a TV series covering medical or forensic topics such as *CSI*, these insides are represented in a fairly realistic way. The images show a stylized, beautified, and rather clean version of the body's inside, but they show what most people expect underneath the skin; blood, tissue, and bones.

In many art videos, animation techniques have been used as a way of suggesting the penetration of the skin by the camera. However, as in *Blood in Blossom* (Merel Mirage 1995), the world exposed beneath the skin by such videos does not always consist of blood and bones. Unlike any suggestion made by the title, Mirage's video depicts a dreamlike reality once the camera has slowly breached the skin of a girl's folded hands. Bright colored, transparent figures appear, only to quickly dissolve into the background again. In contrast to the images in *CSI*, the images of *Blood in Blossom* are out of focus, blurred. Sometimes the passing forms can be discerned as people; sometimes the images are abstract. They are in no way reminiscent of the physical insides of the human body. Instead, they could be interpreted as representations of memories, thoughts, feelings, or dreams. It seems as though the camera has not so much entered the girl's body, as her mind or soul when it pierced through her skin. The penetrating act of the camera may seem less violent in Mirage's art video than in *CSI*, as it doesn't involve murder. Yet, the suggestion that the camera is able to enter the mind or the soul as a "peeping Tom" is perhaps more frightening than that it can enter one's internal organs.

Whereas, fortunately, the former option can only be visualized by way of video animation, the latter can actually be realized. Microscopically small video cameras are used nowadays by scientists and medical examiners in order to look at the body from the inside. The difference with *CSI*'s (virtual) camera is that these medical cameras do not violently break through the skin of the subject under investigation. They are inserted into orifices of the body, which may be painful but leaves the body intact. On the one hand, such visual invasion of the body happens for the benefit of the violated patient, as it is applied as a means of detecting diseases and disorders. On the other hand, these internal viewings of the body through video can nevertheless be understood as a violation of the subject, whose body is hurt and penetrated, and who is moreover turned into an object of medical or scientific investigation.

That the viewer of medical videos can, to some extent, be a victim of what she sees, is emphasized by Mona Hatoum's video installation *Corps étranger* (1994). In this installation, the viewer gets to watch medical video recordings of Hatoum's own body. In order to create the piece, the artist had a camera travel through her entire body, entering all orifices. The images are shown on a circular screen installed into the floor of a cylindrical white chamber that can only be entered through a slender aperture. There is only a small gap between the wall of the chamber and the screen. Hence, for the viewer, there is not much room to move around when watching the video. In order to see the images, one has to stand erect, but with a bent head and lowered eyes; a pose that can be associated with subordination and punishment. At the same time, the low position of the images could instill a feeling of domination instead of subordination in the spectator. That is unlikely, however, because through the translucency of the images on the circular screen, the projection looks like a well. A well at the edge of which the viewer is very close, and into which she could disappear if gravity had its way. Disappear, that is, into the frightening, repulsing, moist, pulsating tunnels of the body shown below. For, enlarged on the big round screen, the representations of the inner body will not be experienced as comforting. Although they may fascinate, they are not pleasing aesthetically.

What is more, Hatoum's installation can be disconcerting to the spectator because on its prolonged journey through the body, the camera doesn't discover anything. As the entire body is scanned, the video lacks the specific goal of a medical examination, which is in general aimed at detecting for instance a tumor or inflammation in a particular area of the body. The lack of such a medical goal raises the question of what it is the camera in *Corps étranger* is looking for or trying to show other than a defect. Is it perhaps trying to reveal, as Chloe Scott (2010) wonders, "a glimpse of something spiritually significant within the living body (traditionally the house of the soul), or metaphysical truths divined from the body as a microcosmic representation of the cosmos?" But no matter for how long one follows the camera's journey, no such things become noticeable. With her video, Hatoum represents a body that is "if anything, dispossessed: no agency, no mind, no soul, no centre" (Scott 2010). Previously, I stated that Mirage's suggestion of a camera entering the mind or the soul may be more frightening than the possibility of a video camera intruding the body. Hatoum's *Corps étranger* demonstrates, however, that it can be equally unsettling to see, by way of video, that neither soul nor mind can be found anywhere inside of the living human body.

CHAPTER 20
SURVEILLANCE

> PERROT: And there's no point for the prisoners to take over the central tower?
> FOUCAULT: Oh yes, provided that isn't the final purpose of the operation. Do you think it would be much better to have prisoners operating the panoptic apparatus and sitting in the central tower, instead of the guards?
>
> Foucault 2002: 101

As soon as video arrived, this medium largely became the most dominant mode and medium for guarding and monitoring, taking over most of the applications of film and especially photography in the field of surveillance. What is more, the practice of surveillance became—next to artistic and domestic usages—one of the dominant applications of the video medium.

Video's utility for surveillance is often regarded as violent or as harmful. The harmful impact attributed to video surveillance, however, is intertwined with the negative aspects ascribed to surveillance in general. Therefore, only when it is clear which discourses and connotations surround the issue of surveillance in general, is it possible to define which surveillance practices are specific to video, and specifically violent.

Some of the most negative aspects associated with surveillance are the controlling and repressive discourses of punishment and discipline. They can be said to produce paranoia and suspicion. The subject of surveillance is harmed by surveillance because she is watched without consent and robbed of her privacy. According to Foucault, however, everyone who is engaged in the structure of surveillance—both those carrying it out and those subjected to it—can be understood as victims of that structure. For, in his opinion, it is an apparatus of total and circulating mistrust that spares no one. Not everyone, however, experiences surveillance as victimizing; it is often carried out and defended with conviction. The positive evaluations of surveillance include terms such as order, regulation, crime prevention, and again, control. We all benefit from surveillance, is a frequently heard argument, because it keeps us safe—"we" and "us" indicating both the surveilling and the surveilled people.

Both perspectives on the matter, however, underline the idea that surveillance is a way to exercise power by way of looking. Merely through being watched by a controlling gaze, people under surveillance are subjected to the power the gaze represents and acts out.[1] According to Foucault, the power exercised by the gaze cannot easily be attributed to the people who do the watching alone. Although the highest power can be identified in the pyramidal form which systems of power often take, the summit doesn't necessarily form the "source" or "principle" from which all power derives (Foucault 2002: 100). It is dispersed over different levels, as is the origin and the object of the gaze itself.

A famous structure of surveillance which is used to illustrate the power of the gaze, is Jeremy Bentham's famous concept of the Panopticon, which became especially well-known from Foucault's discussion of the concept in *Discipline and Punish* (1975). By being ceaselessly under the control of a guard residing in a tower in the middle of the circular prison, Bentham explained, inmates would lose power and even the idea of wrong-doing would be almost cleared from their minds. Whereas in the eyes of many, the Panopticon is a cruel concept that oppresses the prisoners, the inventor himself considered his idea to be a perfect solution to the problems of discipline posed by a great number of persons in the hands of a very few—with order and safety as a result.

As the good or evil of both surveillance in general and specific surveillance practices in particular is a matter of opinion, depending moreover on views on who is allowed to surveil and who deserves to be controlled and dissuaded by the gaze, it is impossible to declare surveillance by video as a violent act per se. It is however important to examine how video shapes surveillance, and with that, the exertion of power through looking. One of the most important contributions of video to surveillance is that it has significantly expanded the field that can be observed by one person. The range of observation possible in Bentham's Panopticon pales in comparison to contemporary video surveillance circuits. In such circuits, the tower of the guards can be said to consist of different parts.

First, it consists of a large number of cameras. The views which these cameras provide on the surveilled space are linked up, so that together, they form a closed circuit that can show an entire area, without so-called blind spots. The footage is sent without delay to the second part of "the tower": a control room, where a security guard can watch it in real time on different monitors, which all show a part of the surveilled area.[2] From a control room, the guard can operate cameras which can tilt, pan, or zoom. The video cameras can be understood as an extension of human vision into space, as well as a multiplication of a single person's sight. For they enable one person to look at a space in which he is not present, from multiple points of view at the same time.

As the size of video cameras can vary from undisguisably big to imperceptibly small, the apparatus can be used for two kinds of surveillance: manifest surveillance or secret surveillance. The Panopticon's system of surveillance is an overt form; the prisoners behave well because they know they are under inspection. They can not only be watched from the tower, they can also see the tower from their cells. Like the tower of the Panopticon, video cameras are often positioned so that they can be seen by the people under surveillance, which has a preventive function; people will refrain from misbehaving if they realize that they are being watched. The visible video surveillance camera shares another important characteristic with the Panopticon's tower. The prisoners of the Panopticon can never really know for sure if they are being watched. Similarly, it is not always possible to see if a security camera is operative, and moreover, if anyone is viewing the footage. Therefore, both the Panopticon's tower and the video camera even function as the eye of power in the absence of surveilling human eyes.

Rather than being preventive, hidden video cameras mostly have a corrective function. This correction can be an intervention at the moment the crime is carried out (e.g., by security guards when hidden cameras detect a hold-up). Yet it can also be carried out after the fact, for instance when raiders are arrested later because they were videotaped. The corrective function which is more specific to hidden surveillance cameras is not entirely absent from overt video surveillance, as these cameras can show wrong-doings as well. In addition, the recorded footage of both hidden and exposed cameras can serve as a means of solving and proving crimes after they have been committed. Hence, as video not only shows but also records what is in front of the lens, it not only exercises power through its controlling gaze at the spot, but, as evidence of a past event, it can also sustain other exercises of power, such as arrest, trial, conviction, and punishment. This adds to the power of the surveillance gaze of video. It is a gaze that not only looks, but also captures what it sees.

Hidden cameras, moreover, not only have a corrective function; they can have a preventive effect as well. That is, the idea of hidden cameras, the mere possibility of their presence, can prevent crime. Foucault is of the opinion that each individual under surveillance will ultimately interiorize the gaze "to the point that he is his own overseer, each individual thus exercising his surveillance over, and against, himself" (2002: 98). Today, video surveillance has become such a widely applied method that most people are familiar with it and have been under its gaze. The result is that many people have interiorized this gaze, the video gaze of power. They are aware of the fact that video cameras can be hidden anywhere, everywhere; that the gaze is potentially omnipresent. It is not so much unclear if the guards are watching, it is unclear whether there is a tower, and if so, where. Because of that uncertainty, it is presupposed to be everywhere; people who have internalized the video gaze can feel as though they are being watched by video cameras at every step. Even if they are not watched at all, they see themselves as being watched, and therefore constantly watch themselves through the eyes of a virtual, imagined video gaze. This may prevent them from wrong-doing, but it also can be understood as a form of suffering.

In sum, video has enlarged the possibilities of surveillance, and because of its ubiquity in contemporary society, it is often experienced as an omnipresent gaze of power. It is not always clear, though, who is in power—who is in charge of the video eye. And this indicates precisely the most important way in which video as a medium shapes the exercise of power through looking. For although, on the one hand, video has facilitated the exercise of power through surveillance, on the other hand the medium has dispersed the power to surveil. Because video cameras can easily be acquired and operated, video surveillance can be exercised by almost anyone. It is not reserved for specialists or to those who are already in power. Foucault's question of whether it would be better to have the prisoners sitting in the Panopticon's central tower instead of the guards, cannot easily be answered absolutely in the affirmative or negative. With video, however, it has become pretty easy for the prisoners to take over the tower, or to place their own camera right across from the guards' tower.

Seizing video power

The possibility to seize power through the surveilling gaze of the video camera has been widely utilized by artists, not to come into power themselves but to criticize video surveillance practices as such. Video art on video surveillance hardly ever welcomes the latter application of the medium; it rather tries to counteract or question the surveillance applications. By aiming their cameras at surveillance cameras, many artists have acted out what I have described as prisoners building a tower across from the guards' tower. The various forms, places, and situations in which they designed their "towers" undermined the distinction between "prisoners" and "guards" in different ways.

The title of Peter Weibel's early video installation *The Guard as Bandit* (1978) indicates that the piece is concerned with the identity of the guard. The work was temporarily installed in the main branch of the Savings Bank in Vienna. It consisted of a monitor and a video camera, the latter being directed at the surveillance camera of the bank. The Saving Bank's surveillance camera was thus filmed and surveilled by Weibel's camera. The image of the bank's surveillance camera could, moreover, be watched on a monitor covered in a mesh stocking, similar to those used by gangsters during bank robberies to hide their identity. Therefore, the monitor showed the Savings Bank camera wearing a mesh stocking, the "guard as bandit," so to speak (Levin et al. 2002: 76). The artist himself aptly explains how the covering stocking also reveals something:

> What also becomes evident is that this video system [the bank's], which is supposed to warn against violence, itself has inherent aspects of violence. [...] By providing the monitor itself with a symbol of violence, namely, the anonymity provided by the mesh stocking, the anonymity of the violence of control is removed. The covert surveillance, the concealed threatening element of surveillance, becomes apparent.
>
> Weibel in Levin et al. 2002: 76

Like Weibel, Steve Mann has filmed video surveillance cameras in public places with a video camera, yet unlike Weibel, he never did this with the approval of the bank or store manager. This is an essential difference. Weibel's camera is the camera of an artist, an artist who uses it to expose his view on surveillance cameras—which he is allowed to do by the bank only because he is an artist.[3] Mann's camera rather functions as a camera of the public. His work circles around the reactions of authorities to civilians who point a video camera at surveillance cameras, and the possibly subversive effect this act of "shooting back" can have when it doesn't use its artistic ground as a cover-up. The artist has designed several devices with built-in video cameras, devices which can be worn on the body when entering a place under surveillance. Mann himself has made many reports of his experiences while wearing his devices. But in principle, he presents them as equipment that could, and should, be worn by anyone.

Mann's "shooting back" practices mainly undermine surveillance practices because they mirror them. One of his most famous pieces is a device called *WearCam* (1995). It consists of a small camera that can be worn as a prosthesis on the head, looking somewhat like headgear from a science-fiction movie because all kinds of wires and two antennas stick out of the helmet. The camera, which is not immediately visible, can be operated leaving both hands free. In this way, filming with a video camera during daily activities is made just as easy as being filmed by surveillance cameras while carrying out those activities. The possibility of filming at random while doing some shopping is important because, then, the act of filming does not have the appearance of intentionality or selectivity. As such, it resembles the nonselective and slightly covert way in which surveillance cameras operate. What is more, the *WearCam* doesn't reveal whether it is actually recording or not, just as it is impossible to see whether a surveillance camera is capturing images. In addition, Mann's device resembles conventional surveillance systems in that it makes an offsite back up of the recorded pictures. As the artist puts it: "Just as an individual cannot rob a bank and then destroy the video record [...] my apparatus of détournement puts the images beyond the destructive reach of members of the establishment" (Mann 2002: 535). The *WearCam* can store the images because it includes a computer with a wireless connection to the Internet. Through that, all the recorded video images are backed up and shown at various internet sites around the world.

The subversive effect of *WearCam's* resemblance to the surveillance system it records arises when representatives of this system, such as security guards or store managers, approach Mann (or anyone else wearing the apparatus) in order to find out if the weird-looking headgear poses a threat. Their interrogation of the person wearing the device will soon lead to a reversal of roles; they will be interrogated by the person wearing the device, or simply by the device. When the guards learn the characteristics of the *WearCam,* which must be revealed by its carrier, their first reaction tends to be that filming is prohibited in the establishment. That remark can easily be parried with the reaction that the establishment is filming too, with their surveillance cameras. In addition, the reply can be that although *WearCam* is a camera, it doesn't necessarily record. Such remarks mostly create confusion in the interrogators, who are moreover uncertain about the action they should take because their behavior is possibly recorded and stored out of their reach. Any slip or misstep could later backfire on them. Suddenly, the guards become aware of the repressive power and violent impact of the video surveillance they carry out. Although the power measurement set up by *WearCam* mostly affects the lowest representatives of the surveillance system, their possible discomfort might affect higher authorities too. These are dependent on the blind obedience and resolve of the guards on site, qualities that may be disrupted by the mirror-like structure of the *WearCam*.

CHAPTER 21
VOYEURISM

The practice of cinema, wrote Christian Metz, is only possible through "the desire to see," in other words, through voyeurism. The concept of voyeurism has over the years dominated definitions of cinema. According to many film theorists, characteristic aspects of cinema's conventional *dispositif*, such as the set-up of the film projection and the conventions of cinematic storytelling, put the film viewer in the position of voyeur. The definition of voyeurism by the French film theorist can be rephrased as "to see with desire." Desire, that is, for the object on view.

One of the meanings which voyeurism has is *secret* looking; watching with desire without being noticed by the object of desire in view. This mode of looking points to the possible violent impact of "the desire to see." To be looked at with desire by a voyeur is not damaging to the subject when she assents to the gaze that rests upon her. The voyeur can be in perfect harmony with the exhibitionist; the one who wants to see and the one who wants to show can fulfill each other's wishes. However, when voyeurism is a form of spying, peeping, or looking without permission of the viewed subject, it is a violating act. The secretly watched subject is turned into an object of desire without consent; her self-determination is infringed and her privacy is violated.

In his influential discussion of the relation between film and voyeurism, Metz has argued that film specifically gives rise to this violent mode of voyeurism. The voyeuristic pleasure to which cinema gives rise is what fills cinema seats with viewers. A starting point in Metz' explanation of how film meets voyeurism is the assertion that in order to obtain voyeuristic pleasure, the voyeur needs to maintain a gulf, an empty space, between the object and the eye, between the object and his own body. The object has to be at the right distance from the voyeur; both far from it but close enough to see it. Although the voyeur desires the object he looks at, his pleasure depends on the act of looking. Because of this, the object of desire has to be kept at a distance.

Film first of all offers this necessary distance because of the conventional viewing position that is part of the medium's specific, dominant *dispositif*. The gulf between viewer and filmed objects is all the more secure by the fact that the screen forms an impenetrable barrier between the two. Interaction between the world of the viewer and the represented space on screen is practically impossible.[1] Not only does the film show a physically inaccessible *elsewhere*, it also represents an *elsewhen*.

Metz compares the absence of the film actor to the presence of the performer in the theater. As with film, a distance is to be kept between the audience and the performance in a theater show, both media uphold the proscenium. Yet, for Metz, looking at theater performances, as well as at stripteases and peepshows, is less scandalous than looking at film because of the presence of the actors on stage. The presence of the actor can be read as a form of consent to being watched: "In the theater, [. . .] the actor (the one seen), simply because he is bodily present, because he does not go away, is presumed to consent, to cooperate deliberately" (1982: 62). In other words, because he is there, he must like it (62). This presumption is hypocritical or deluded, because performers can be forced to act on stage, if only by economic factors—Metz mentioned the example of the impoverished stripper. Still, voyeurism that is not too sadistic, rests on the fiction that the viewed subject agrees, that it is therefore exhibitionist. Video is able to accommodate the desires of the nonsadistic voyeur very well. Today, exhibitionist amateur videomakers can show their most intimate (often sexual) acts to the world by posting clips online or by performing in front of a webcam. Exhibitionist video clips do not necessarily please the voyeuristic onlooker alone; viewers can gain pleasure from identifying with the exhibitionist subjects on the (computer) screen who willfully offer themselves to the gazes of a potentially infinite number of online video viewers.[2]

However, although video is in many respects the opposite of film when it comes to the voyeuristic structure of the latter medium, it is important to realize that the exhibitionism enabled and stimulated by video technology is by no means a beneficial cure for, or a compensation for, cinema's violent voyeurism. The online exhibitionism that has boomed since the arrival of the webcam has its own violent side. One of the most harmful offshoots of the webcam is probably the fact that ignorant, poor and/or underage subjects are seduced or threatened into exposing themselves in front of webcams.

In addition to these sexually oriented criminal activities, the exhibitionism which webcams spur on has fundamentally altered—or rather, invaded—contemporary society. Today, online exhibitionism is an obligatory rather than a liberating option. In order to be a part of social networks, one must "share" private information. This private information hardly ever includes bedroom scenes; the most tedious, boring little facts of everyday life will do when it comes to escaping social isolation. With a comprehensiveness bordering on compulsiveness, pictures and videos of the most ordinary things—meals, pets, Christmas trees, traffic jams, new shoes—are widely shared via online social media platforms such as Facebook. Although the images in question are willingly uploaded by the users of those platforms, the voluntariness of this exhibitionism is something of a chimera. Under the influence of the webcam, the imperative in the age of social media has become: exhibit yourself to your friends, or have no friends at all.

Films, on the other hand, usually do not offer (a fiction of) exhibitionist agreement to their spectators. The film viewer's act of looking is turned into a secret, offensive deed all the more by the conventional darkness in the cinema. Not only is the viewer unauthorized to watch, she is also put in the darkness, hidden and anonymous, like a peeping Tom who spies on other people through the keyhole of a dark closet. In addition, narrative film conventions reinforce the film viewer's hidden position, who is not addressed or acknowledged as an onlooker.

All this suggests that, although film meets the demands of the voyeur, it also creates the voyeur. The viewing position which films produce for the spectator leave her no choice but to adopt the position of an unauthorized voyeur. The film viewer is not necessarily a beneficiary of the voyeuristic structure of looking which films set up; the viewer can also be its victim. The role of sadistic, aggressive voyeur can be an unwanted and uncomfortable one—and it can only be rejected by not being a film viewer at all. Most spectators, however, adopt this role willingly because it gives them pleasure. Guilty pleasure, maybe, but an accepted form of guilty pleasure. Because, as Metz has argued, the nonauthorized film voyeurism is authorized in one important respect: by the mere fact of its institutionalization. Watching a movie is a very normal thing to do. That it nevertheless has the connotation of a slightly prohibited activity too, may be its strength:

> For the vast majority of the audience, the cinema [...] represents a kind of enclosure or "reserve" which escapes the fully social aspect of life although it is accepted and prescribed by it: going to the cinema is one lawful activity among others with its place in the admissible pastimes of the day or the week, and yet that place is a "hole" in the social cloth, a *loophole* opening to something slightly more crazy, slightly less approved than what one does the rest of the time.
>
> Metz 1982: 66

According to Metz, the viewer thus likes to escape from "the fully social aspect of life" through the loophole that is cinema. But what about those he sees through this loophole? How are the represented subjects on screen negatively affected by the fact that they are looked at in a voyeuristic way? Film actors *act* as if they are not aware of the camera. The sadistic voyeuristic structure of film is thus created with the knowledge of the people who form the objects of this structure, which is why film voyeurism is less sadistic and violating to the viewed subjects than the voyeuristic viewing of people who really do not know they are secretly being watched with desire. "Because he *was* there, he must like it" is not as convincing as the previously mentioned "Because he *is* there, he must like it," but the fact that the actor did not hide from the camera can be understood as some form of consent. Yet, even if the actor is indeed an exhibitionist who agrees to being watched—and thus not an innocent unknowing victim of the voyeuristic look—she still can somehow be considered a dupe of the cinematic structure. Metz has stated that, in the cinema, the exhibitionist and the voyeur always fail to meet. In spite of this, the voyeuristic film viewer still gets to watch—albeit in a slightly sadistic, unauthorized way. The exhibitionist actor, on the other hand, can never see herself being watched while exposing herself. Except for the eye of the camera (operator), she is never entirely assured of a public. She always misses her audience. What the cinema offers her though, is multiplication and circulation of her image, so that the audience she always misses is at least, hopefully, a large one.

Other loopholes

In *Rear Window* (Hitchcock 1954), a disabled man in a wheelchair spies on his neighbors through the telephoto lens of his photo camera. As viewers, we join his perspective. In *Sliver* (Noyce 1993), an evil yuppie programmer has wired an entire high-class Manhattan high-rise with invisible video surveillance, through which he secretly spies on various women who live in the building. The protagonist of *La mort en direct* (Tavernier 1980) has a video camera installed in his brain, with the lens hidden in one of his eyes. He is hired by a television producer to secretly record the death of a terminally ill woman, in order to provide footage for a television show called "Death Watch." *Gigante* (Biniez 2009) tells the story of a security guard at a large supermarket, who falls in love with one of the cleaning ladies who appears on the monitors he has to watch at night. Instead of approaching her in person, he tracks all her moves throughout the store via remote PTZ (pan-tilt and zoom) video surveillance. Films in which voyeurism is an important theme are often interpreted as reenactments of the voyeuristic structure of film (Verstraten 2008: 145). However, when the voyeuristic viewing in the film is carried out with the help of media such as photography and video, as is the case in the examples just mentioned, the films can also be understood as reflections on the voyeuristic applications of these other media. *Rear Window, Sliver, La mort en direct*, and *Gigante*, among other films, reveal that photography and video, like film, serve the needs of the voyeur.

In fact, the harmful aspect of film voyeurism, namely its nonauthorized character, can be found in certain photography and video applications in a stronger way. Whereas the film actor only *pretends* not to notice the camera, photographs and videos can truly be shot without the knowledge of the represented subject. Most importantly, photo and video cameras, as opposed to film cameras, can easily be kept from sight when they are operated as they can be very small. As *Gigante* shows, hidden video surveillance can produce voyeuristic pleasure for those who watch the footage. The gaze of control is then combined with a gaze of desire. Because of their technical properties, as well as their conventional applications, both photography and video are more suited than film to what Metz calls the sadistic voyeur; the voyeur who spies on his object of desire without their approval.

The gulf between eye and viewed object necessary to the voyeur is maintained by photographs too, in that the represented space on a photograph is not accessible to the viewer, and no interaction is possible between the subjects who are depicted on printed photographs and their viewers. As with film, the photographed subjects are removed from the spectator in time and space in that the moment and place shown on a photograph are not the time and place the viewer resides in. Therefore, Metz' argument that the filmed subject's willingness to be looked at cannot be guaranteed by bodily presence also goes for the photographed subject.

This is different as far as video is concerned. Video can easily bridge the division between viewer and viewed subject. First of all, the viewer and her object of vision can reside in the same moment in time through live video broadcastings. What is more, due to its open structure, video can be used interactively. Webcams and the Internet, in addition, have enlarged the possibilities of interaction between viewing and viewed subjects to the point that the distinction between them can no longer be made. People interacting through webcams can both be looking at each other and watched by each other at the same time. The spatial distance between viewing subject and viewed object which is not canceled out in these instances is completely obliterated in video-based Virtual Reality (VR) environments. The viewer of VR is enveloped by this world, and the distances between herself and the virtual objects on view can be bridged. There is no longer a screen which forms a physical boundary between the two.

Thus, while video is technically more capable than film of offering images of secretly spied-on subjects to a voyeuristic viewer, the medium is at the same time more capable than film of obliterating the distance between viewing and represented subject, a distance which is a prerequisite for voyeurism. When this distance or gap is indeed bridged by video, for instance through interactive set-ups, the represented subject is no passive victim of voyeurism but a person who can influence and control her own representation and exposition. Moreover, unlike the film viewer, the viewer of interactive video images is not forcefully put into a voyeuristic position. Instead of remaining at a secret distance, the spectator can make contact with the subject shown.

This contact is also enabled by the fact that unlike film, video and photography are not dominated by a *dispositif* that dictates distance between viewer and image. Although videos and photographs can be watched from a distance, and moreover can easily be watched in private, it is not uncommon to approach a video projection in a museum.[3] Photographs, moreover, often have to be touched or held close in order to be seen. Such approximations threaten the distance between the body of the onlooker and the object in view which is a necessity for the voyeur. The secret voyeur is furthermore thwarted by photography and video because these media do not share another important convention with film, namely the cinematic convention which forbids actors from looking into the camera. Unless they are truly photographed or filmed without their knowledge or permission, the represented subjects of photography and video often do look into the lens. It is by convention appropriate and desirable to look into the photo or video lens when one agrees to being captured by the camera. As a result, the viewers of the images are looked at too; they are addressed by the look, and hence acknowledged as onlookers. For this important reason, the viewer of photographs and videos is—if a voyeur at all—not a well-hidden voyeur: often, the object of desire looks back.

When watching Samuel Beckett's *Film* (1965), it becomes clear that the convention not to look into the camera is very dominant within the field of film's specificity, while represented subjects looking into the camera are regarded as common to video. The unnamed protagonist of Beckett's short movie is afraid; afraid of all the things around him that look at him or seem to look at him: other people, animals, a mirror, an image of a mask, holes in a chair.[4] In addition to all these looking subjects and objects which frighten the man, he is terrified by one other looking instance: the film camera and the film viewer. When hurriedly running up a flight of stairs as if chased by something, the scared figure suddenly turns around, and looks fearfully into the camera. This image of the man's scared look is not sutured; the film doesn't show what the man was looking at in a next shot. Because of that, his fear seems to be directed at the camera and the viewer, who, after all, like all the other eyes in the film, are looking at him, too.

When *Film*'s protagonist looks into the camera, the viewer is no longer an unacknowledged, hidden voyeur. The violating impact of voyeuristic looking isn't entirely canceled out by *Film,* however. For although the frightened man has shown that he is aware of the camera's presence, he certainly doesn't give permission to be filmed or looked at. Instead he tries to run and escape from the gaze, and attempts to hide his face from view. In spite of this, the camera keeps looking at him. By retreating into his apartment, the man can escape from the looks of other people. The animals can be thrown out of his living room. His own reflection doesn't look back at him anymore when the mirror is covered with a sheet. Images of looking faces are torn apart. Yet the piercing spying eye of the film camera cannot be avoided. *Film* ends with a close-up shot of the man's left eye, which is blind. Framed in this way, the film's object can be looked at by the viewer from an invisible position again; for although it looks back, it cannot see.

On the one hand, it is remarkable that *Film* is titled after its medium, because it violates one of the most dominant film conventions; the ban on looking into the camera. On the other hand, the title of *Film* is appropriate because it is very much a film about film. Precisely by violating the convention that forbids actors to look into the camera, the movie is able to reveal the aggressive voyeurism of film which is for the most part produced by this convention. By looking fearfully into the camera, and by trying to escape from it, the protagonist shows what the film camera usually does; it spies on filmed subjects without their permission. It is indeed a device to be feared. *Film* can be understood as a critical exposition of the persistent voyeurism specific to film, and therefore as an attempt to adjust the medium's specificity.

When *Film* is looked at from a contemporary perspective, however, it is impossible not to recognize another medium in the movie, or rather, to recognize the movie *as* another medium. *Film* is a film about film which looks like video today. When a represented person in a sequence of moving images looks into the lens, most present-day viewers will associate the representation with video instead of with film, because such a look is common in video while it is not in film. In 1965, the year in which *Film* was produced, video already existed as a technology, but not quite yet as a medium, for the technology still had to be inscribed with medium-specific conventions, such as the one which stipulates that it is common for subjects in front of a video camera to look into the lens. It is remarkable that *Film* was produced precisely at the moment video was about to arrive as a medium. For it opposes a film convention with film, while a new time-based medium was in the making in which this cinematic convention was done away with, too. Because of the absence of the voyeurism-sustaining convention in video, the voyeuristic structure of film became all the more apparent. It is no coincidence that this structure was critically discussed in film theory at the height of video's popularity, during the late 1970s and early 1980s. Although the voyeuristic structure is still specific to film today, these critical reflections—of which *Film* is remarkable forerunner—had its effect on the medium's specificity. Film could no longer produce a secret voyeur in secret.[5] *Film*, in conclusion, is a film about film, but also a video before video, as well as a film about film-before-video.

Feminist perspectives

The critical theoretical discussions of film voyeurism were in a large part conducted by feminist film theorists who, like Metz, analyzed film from a psychoanalytic perspective. These feminist film theorists exposed the voyeuristic structure of traditional film as being a *gendered* one. The division between looking subjects and looked-at objects in voyeuristic cinematic patterns is simultaneously a division between men (who look) and women (who are looked at).

One of the first critics who pointed out this intertwinement of cinema's voyeuristic conventions with patriarchal gender conventions is Laura Mulvey.[6] In her influential essay "Narrative Pleasure and Narrative Cinema" (1975), she discerns three looks associated with narrative cinema: first, that of the camera as it records the pro-filmic event; second, that of the audience as it watches the final product; and third, that of the characters looking at each other within the screen illusion. The conventions of narrative film deny the first two looks, and as a result, the film viewer is turned into a voyeuristic spectator. The conventional application of the third look within narrative cinema, in addition, turns the film viewer into a male, heterosexual voyeur. This is caused by the fact that the look of characters within the film diegesis is generally attached to male characters in conventional Hollywood films. In those films, it is men who look at each other and at women. Female protagonists, on the other hand, hardly ever function as internal focalizors in narrative fiction films. They are on display as passive objects, not active bearers, of the look.

The internal focalization of male characters forcefully invites the film viewer to identify with these characters. Because the spectator gains access to the film world by looking, as it were, through the eyes of these male protagonists, it is hardly possible for the viewer to disassociate from the male perspective on the film's diegesis. As Mulvey explains, the enforced act of identification is not necessarily uncomfortable or harmful to the film viewer. In fact, identification with characters in fiction films is one of two aspects that produces pleasure for the spectator, because identification with the object on screen satisfies the viewer's narcissistic fascination with likeness. The second aspect which makes looking at film pleasurable derives from the previously discussed voyeurism cinema gives rise to. As Mulvey points out, the two structures of voyeurism and narcissism are highly contradictory, because "one implies a separation of the erotic identity of the subject from the object on the screen, the other demands identification with and recognition of his like" (1975: 18). Yet, cinema beautifully solves this contradiction. It offers the viewer the possibility to look desirously and voyeuristically at one category of objects on screen (women), while identifying narcissistically with another category (men).

For the female viewer, however, pleasure in looking is highly problematic when it is produced by the conventional film structure that compels voyeuristic desire for women and narcissistic identification with men. For, when the female spectator accepts the position this structure imposes on her, she has to "become" a male spectator and identify, as it were, against her own gendered self. When she does what the film incites her to do, and looks at the women on screen as objects of male sexual desire, the female spectator turns into a transvestite masochist.[7,8]

According to Mulvey, the only option for female spectators, besides experiencing films masochistically, is to reject the many traditional films that impose a male perspective on their viewers. Some later film theorists who elaborated on Mulvey's ideas, however, have investigated whether traditional films in which the power to focalize is exclusive to male characters can nevertheless leave some room for the desire and power *of*, and not merely *for* and *over*, women. Tania Modleski has, for instance, scrutinized some of Hitchcock's films in order to find out if these films are as utterly misogynistic as feminist critics such as Mulvey have argued. On the one hand, Modleski sides with these feminist film theorists, as she agrees with their conclusion that women are treated with considerable violence in the work of Hitchcock. On the other hand, Modleski wishes to "save" the brilliant director from the critics who see only the darkest misogynist vision in his films.

In her deconstructionist readings of films such as *Rear Window* (1954) and *Vertigo* (1958), Modleski points out that Hitchcock's films are resistant to patriarchal assimilation because they are characterized by thorough ambivalence about femininity (1989: 3). In Hitchcock's *Vertigo*, for instance, women and their femininity at first sight seem to be fully controlled by men. The male protagonist, Scotty, focalizes all the female characters, who appear to function as the passive objects of his look. What is more, Scotty turns one of them, Judy, into his ideal image of femininity, by picking out specific clothes for her.

However, when taking a closer look at the film, it becomes noticeable that Scotty's power over the female characters is undercut in many instances in the film. For example, in a scene in which Scotty's gaze rests on Judy—his object of desire—the camera shows us a side of her face Scotty cannot see. From this angle, her expression reveals disdain for the male protagonist. In addition to this hidden disdain, Scotty is mocked openly by his friend Midge, who scornfully calls him "big boy." Most importantly, Scotty's masculinity is undermined by his strong fascination for women. It leads to hallucinations and blind obsession which disable Scotty from functioning as a stable, all-seeing, and omnipotent man. According to Modleski, such impediment to masculinity by a fascination for femininity characterizes the work of the famous director: "[...] time and time again in Hitchcock films, the strong fascination and identification with femininity revealed in them subverts the claims to mastery and authority not only of the male characters but of the director himself" (1989: 3).

Counter-cinema and counter-video

In addition to rejecting existing misogynist films (Mulvey), or the strategy of reading them deconstructively (Modleski), a third reaction feminist film theorists have summoned in opposition to traditional films is the transformation of cinematic conventions by cinematic practices. Some of the early feminist film critics declared that a counter-cinema had to be developed in which traditional narrative and cinematic techniques should be shunned (Smelik 1999: 355). Mulvey, who was one of the critics who advocated the creation of such counter-cinema, placed her hopes in radical, experimental, avant-garde filmmakers who knew how to strike blows against "the monolithic accumulation of traditional film conventions" (1975: 26).[9]

However, as Teresa de Lauretis has pointed out, the transformation of traditional narrative film forms, for which Mulvey and others argued in the early and mid–1970s, is a harsh and slow journey. In her *Alice Doesn't* (1984), de Lauretis argues that whenever films expose female perspectives and desires, these are still colored negatively or canceled out by the plot of the films:

> [...] when a film accidentally or unwisely puts in play the terms of a divided or double desire [...], it must display that desire as impossible or duplicitous [...], finally contradictory [...], and then proceed to resolve the contradiction much in the same way as myths and the mythologist do: by either the massive destruction or the territorialization of women.
>
> 1984: 115

In this respect, de Lauretis adopts a different position than Modleski. Whereas Modleski finds instances and moments of female desire or power in narrative films meaningful and important as resistance against patriarchy, de Lauretis argues that such instances lose their importance when they are negated by the narrative closure of a film. The fact that the women whose desire is displayed usually die or "surrender" to the opposite sex in many old, new, mainstream, or alternative narrative films, demonstrates that a feminist transformation of cinema is a tough job, according to de Lauretis.

Yet, it is not a lost cause. In her book, written approximately a decade after Mulvey's seminal essay, de Lauretis states that she sees it as very possible for women's cinema to respond to the plea for a "new language of desire" expressed in Mulvey's text. In fact, many feminist narrative films which "tell the story differently" have been produced from the 1970s onwards.[10] Most feminist films that intervene in patriarchal mainstream cinema are characterized by two aspects. First, they critically thematize the oppression of women, and secondly, they create new narrative forms which express instead of suppress female perspectives and desires. The short feminist film *Thriller* (1979) by Sally Potter, for instance, splits its female character in two: Mimi I and Mimi II. The first Mimi is placed outside of the melodramatic story in which she is a character. From this outside position, she investigates how she is constructed as an object in and by the narrative. She asks many questions on her tragic fate in the story: "Was I murdered? Who killed me and why? What does it mean? Would I have preferred to be the hero? What if I had been the subject of this scenario, instead of its object?" In Potter's film, the narrative strategy of a split character in a divided diegesis enables the expression of a female perspective on the oppression of women by means of narrative film conventions.

In Chantal Akerman's *Jeanne Dielman, 23 quai du Commerce, 1080 Bruxelles* (1975), the subordinate position of women in a patriarchal society is addressed by the oppressive life of its female protagonist called Jeanne, who is shown to serve men all day during her regimented daily routine of cleaning and cooking for her son, and prostituting herself to male clients who visit her at her home. In contrast to many patriarchal films, the oppression of the female character is not aggravated or confirmed by the formal structure of Akerman's film. One of the most important reasons for this is that the look of the camera is not sutured to the looks of characters in the film. The view on Jeanne is a voyeuristic one, because she doesn't acknowledge the presence of the camera. Yet, as it is not attached to characters in the film's diegesis, it is not a masculine, desirous, objectifying view. Rather, the view has been called "objective," "neutral," and "realistic" by many of the film's critics. Because of the long and static shots of Jeanne's repetitive daily business, the film creates a reality effect. It gives rise to the impression that it shows the stifling slowness and dullness of real life; real women's domestic life.

Another reason why the structure of the film doesn't aggravate the oppression of Jeanne is that the uneventful narrative ends with sudden pleasure and revenge for the female protagonist. Jeanne unexpectedly has an orgasm with her day's client, and then stabs him to death with a pair of scissors. Whereas many films "correct" or "punish" instances of female emancipation when the story ends (de Lauretis), the narrative closure of *Jeanne Dielman* instead forms a sudden correction or punishment of patriarchal oppression.

In addition to the considerable field of feminist counter-cinema in which the medium of film was used against conventional aspects of film, the medium of *video* has been applied even more widely to counter the traditional patriarchal cinematic conventions. As explained previously, video is cheaper and easier to work with than film, and except for its lower image quality, video can imitate film rather well. Because of these qualities and abilities, the video medium offered feminists the opportunity to make counter-movies without having to become highly skilled and funded filmmakers.

Feminist videos which form a reaction to traditional cinema can roughly be divided into two categories. First, feminist videos have been produced which copy or imitate fragments of mainstream films. Those videos offer a critical perspective on the films they copy through slight or overt differences between the video works and the original films. Before discussing this type of video practice, however, I will first turn to a second category of feminist video, namely, videos which create new forms of telling stories; telling stories, that is, with moving images, from a female point of view. The aim of creating a new visual language which characterizes this second category very much resembles a dominant aspect of feminist counter-cinema: the replacement of old film forms with new ones.

A Spy in the House that Ruth Built (1989) by Vanalyne Green is of one of the most poignant videos in the area of what I will term "counter-video." Green's tape is well known as a feminist video which creates a new, feminine, visual language of desire, and is often cited as a work that reverses the regime of the male gaze. When compared to traditional patriarchal cinema, *A Spy in the House that Ruth Built* can be said to turn the tables. In the video, men are the objects of female desire, and they are spied on by a female voyeur. This female voyeur is Green, who is the protagonist as well as the narrator of the story. She tells in the first person about her relation to the male world of baseball. For a three-year period, Green's fascination with baseball dominated her life. She would read all about the game in the newspapers, and visit as many games as possible.

Her main interest, however, is not so much in the game itself, but in the players. Green has strong sexual fantasies about the men on the field, and explicitly states how she "wants them," how she feels the need to possess them. When she acquires a press pass, she is granted the privilege of entering the baseball field, and looking at the baseball players at close range. What is more, from this position, she is allowed to film them with her video camera. The video images of the male baseball players are incorporated in *A Spy in the House that Ruth Built* in such a way that they are sutured to Green's look of desire. That they do indeed represent her desirous way of looking becomes visible all the more by the way the camera has been operated while filming the playing men. The images do not so much bring the game in view, they rather put the bodies of the baseball players on display. Often, the camera zooms in on the bodies of the men, showing their bulging crotches and round posteriors, or roving up and down pairs of muscular thighs packed in tight white baseball outfits. Green shows awareness of the objectifying, voyeuristic manner with which she operates the camera when she wonders: "Could they tell where I was angling the lens of my camera, or the passion with which I took aim?" In addition, her desire for the men is made all the more explicit through video keying: on top of the close-up of a player's groin the artist has inserted a video clip in which a faceless woman takes off her panties.

Green's awareness of the fact that she objectifies and appropriates with her camera results in feelings of guilt in the artist. On the one hand, the aggressive act of filming the players is pleasurable, but on the other hand, she feels sorry for the players when she pins them with her viewfinder. They have no idea that they are being pictured as objects of lust, and willingly let themselves be filmed. As Green pitifully remarks, "their passive acceptance of my camera made them look like show animals on display." In addition to her feelings of guilt, Green is uncomfortable in her role of voyeur because she feels demeaned and captured by her own fascination with the baseball players. In the course of the video, the artist's main goal appears to change from sleeping with a baseball player to finding out why she so desperately wants to have sex with the men on the baseball field.

In the end, Green's self-reflection provides her with new insights into male desire for women, and about the relationship between her own sexual desires and her family history. This knowledge, she claims, came as a sense of reunion; it has liberated her from her anxious, aggressive desires. This plot might be understood as a final (anti-feminist) renouncement of female desire—as a form of narrative closure which Teresa de Lauretis recognized in so many films. Laura Kipnis has critically remarked on *A Spy in the House that Ruth Built* that "the journey of the tape has been one of victory over transgressive desire and the narrative return of the good girl" (1996: 339). For Kipnis, Green's video is mainly valuable because it shows how the voyeuristic gaze can be adopted by women. This is an important reversal in light of the dominant dichotomy between looking men and looked-at women in visual culture. Yet, Kipnis regrets the fact that the tables do not remain turned in *A Spy in the House that Ruth Built*. I would argue, however, that it *is* important that the voyeuristic, objectifying gaze is reflected on and finally rejected by the woman who adopts it, for a mere reversal of poles or roles would still leave the dichotomy between the sexes intact. Although Green may too positively propose insight as a miraculous solution to the aggressive aspects of sexual desire, her idea that insight into gender and sexuality can reduce the oppression of one sex by another is quite reasonable.

Unlike the production of new forms and languages of female desire, which is executed in both film and video, the strategies of copying and imitating are specific to counter-video. Artists and artistic duos such as John Knoop and Sharon Hennessey, Bruce and Norman Yonemoto, Matthias Müller and Christoph Girardet, Johanna Householder and b.h. Yael, among others, have produced videos which mimic or sample conventional film scenes. Remarkably, the strategies of copying and imitation are largely absent from feminist films, which shun resemblance to the films they aim to work against. An explanation of the fact that feminist videos use copying and imitation as critical strategies, while feminist films do not, can be that the reflective edge of copying and imitating mostly lies in the difference between original and copy. When films are copied by video, the difference between media ensures that there is always already a (potentially critical) difference between original and copy. An imitation of film by film would not have this automatic difference with its original, which enhances the risk of an obliteration of critical distance and difference.

One form of copying used by feminist video artists who reflect on traditional film structures is the appropriation of original film footage. Mainstream films are transferred to video or simply bought as a VHS tape or DVD. Subsequently, they are edited by the artists in a way which exposes the misogynist traits of the cinematic works. Two artists who have applied this method in their work are Matthias Müller and Christoph Girardet. Together, they have created a piece called *Kristall* (2006) in which they have collected and reedited a large number of film scenes showing women and men in front of a mirror. The montage of the scenes exposes a mainstream film convention which stipulates that whenever men are looking in the mirror, they are shown to feel complete and satisfied with themselves. When female characters are looking in the mirror, however, the cinematic narrative in which they are embedded implies that something is missing for them. They are waiting for a man to complete them, and are dressing up in front of the mirror for *him*.

Another video by these two German artists, *Phoenix Tapes* (1999), is a compilation of material from a large number of films by Alfred Hitchcock. The artists have chosen fragments and scenes from Hitchcock's films that are very similar to each other. These fragments have been pasted in succession in the video. One group of scenes for instance shows how women are trapped and brutalized in a similar fashion by men over and over again in the films. Another group of fragments exposes the way in which the look of the camera is attached to the look of male characters by Hitchcock's mode of editing. Müller and Girardet's work clearly underlines Mulvey's theory of narrative cinema in general, and Hitchcock's work in particular. The advantage which the work has over Mulvey's theory, though, is the impact created by the repetition of the similar scenes. When the structures and conventions so often condemned are shown quickly one after another in large numbers, it becomes impressively clear how dominant these conventions are. What is more, when the repetitiveness of the misogynistic aspects is brought fully into view by *Phoenix Tapes*, the violent voyeuristic and patriarchal features in the films lose their normalized character. The repetitions point out an obsessive, compulsive fascination with women which is not consonant with sound and stable masculinity. In this sense, *Phoenix Tapes* joins in with Modleski's opinion that the strong fascination and identification with femininity revealed in Hitchcock's films subverts the claims to mastery and authority, not only of the male characters but of the director himself.

A second mode of copying which has been adopted by feminist videomakers is the form of the remake. Films or film scenes are restaged and shot with a video camera. Some of the most precise shot-by-shot recreations of narrative cinema scenes have been produced by Johanna Householder and b.h. Yael. In their videos *The Mission* (2000) and *December 31* (2001), the two artists imitate scenes from Francis Ford Coppola's *Apocalypse Now* (1979) and Stanley Kubrick's *2001: A Space Odyssey* (1968).

In both films, women play no part whatsoever. The stories center entirely around male heroes who serve and save their country.

In *The Mission* and *December 31*, the cinematography of these films is imitated with precision; the remade scenes are shot-by-shot copies of the original ones. An important difference is, however, that the male heroes are replaced by females. In the videos, Householder plays the part of the male hero. In *December 31*, her sex is not immediately visible, as she plays the role of a male astronaut (Dave), which means her body is covered with a bulky space suit. In *The Mission*, on the other hand, Householder performs a scene in which Willard, the young protagonist, prepares for his important mission in a hotel room while wearing nothing but underpants on his well-toned body. Householder perfectly duplicates his masculine acts of drinking whisky and practicing battle movements. In addition, she wears men's underpants in order to look like the male hero. Yet, her body is that of a middle-aged woman.

In *December 31*, femininity does not so much enter the scene in the form of the performer's female body, but through the *mise-en-scène*. Householder and Yael recorded their tapes in Householder's apartment. The backdrop as well as the props they use are therefore domestic ones. This is especially visible in *December 31* because in this video, space travel and space technology are mimicked with the help of a refrigerator, a tiled bathroom floor, and a washing machine. In *2001: A Space Odyssey*, Dave dismantles the computer on board his spaceship with the help of sophisticated tools. In the video imitation, Householder carefully "dismantles" a CD-rack with a kitchen knife.

When performed by a woman in a feminine environment, the performed character of masculine behavior becomes noticeable in these videos by Householder and Yael. The fact that masculinity can be copied by a woman with conventional women's utensils has a rather comical effect that undermines the natural authority and seemingly innate masculinity of the films' heroes. In addition to exposing the artificiality of masculinity, *The Mission* and *December 31* point out that in spite of the fact that Kubrick's and Coppola's narrative films carefully construct and confirm conventional masculinity, they do contain moments which subvert this stable and conventional masculinity. The scenes Householder and Yael have chosen and copied, are scenes in which the male protagonists are in distress. They feel insecure and afraid; afraid to fail in their important masculine task. Although they attempt to remain calm and strong, it is clear that they are riddled with doubt about their own abilities. Willard even seems to face a full mental breakdown. In the films, these moments of psychological instability are, of course, overcome by the male characters. They bravely get their acts together, complete their mission, save the world, and hence fulfill their role of reliable hero after all.

These videos by Householder and Yael pull the scenes they recreate out of their original narrative, cinematic framework. The artists do not show the happy ending which follows the scenes. In *The Mission* and *December 31*, the weakness and instability of the heroes therefore remain unresolved. This recontextualization, or rather decontextualization of the film scenes, stresses that the gender roles played by the male heroes are not as stable as they seem. The male protagonists display fear and ambiguity towards their conventional male task of saving the world by way of violence or complicated technology. The fact that the heroes are replaced by a female actor further emphasizes the instability and ambiguity of the male heroes' gender roles. The video works read the films against the grain in a fashion similar to Modleski's deconstructionist readings of Hitchcock films. The videos, however, use the opportunities offered by their own medium to present their readings of two cinematic works in the form of an adaptation of the films, by copying the films with a difference.

The critical reflections on film by feminist film theorists, as well as the feminist movements of counter-cinema and counter-video, have not left the specificity of film untouched. First, counter-cinema has "invaded" the field of film; it has "conquered" pieces of the medium's field of application that determine the specificity of the medium. What is more, both the visual and textual critical reflections on the patriarchal structures of film have affected the dominant application of the medium. Mainstream narrative cinema has not disposed of its gendered voyeuristic patterns entirely, yet they have become less stringent. In many contemporary films, men are not the only ones who look. Because of the feminist views on narrative films, women in mainstream films now get to look, too.

CONCLUSION

An inverse(d) voyage, back to the waves

Hang your eyes on the sail of my sleeves
The way is open on the murky path
Ten thousand waves take us to the shore
Home will arrive under our feet

Wang Ping, "The Great Summons," in: *Ten Thousand Waves*

This study started with the claim that many contemporary visual objects combine features which are specific to the media of film and video. Such intermedial pieces, I argued, can be better understood if the differences between film and video are not overlooked. For the meanings, effects, and affects contemporary moving image objects give rise to are to a large extent shaped by combinations of videomatic with cinematic elements. However, the aim of gaining insight into these combinations called for a delineation of the separate components of the combinations: film and video. In the four parts of this book, I have explored how film and video can be defined as closely related, yet distinct media; an exploration that necessarily entailed an investigation of the concept of medium specificity itself.

As it turned out, the relation between film and video could not be analyzed without expanding and rewriting definitions of the medium. In Part I, the differences between film and video concerning their production of the reality effect turned out to lie not in unique properties, but in typicalities and commonalities; in dominant versus marginal functions and applications. Therefore, Rosalind Krauss' definition of medium specificity as a changeable layered structure was expanded with George Baker's notion of "field" in this part. Unlike Krauss' predominantly temporal definition, Baker's spatial notion of the field offers us the possibility to account for the sometimes internally conflicting heterogeneity of media, as well as the overlapping functions and shared abilities of different media, without losing sight of their specificity.

In Part II, the concept of the medium was rewritten along the lines of Jean-Louis Baudry's notion of *dispositif*, in order to investigate how the differences and similarities between film and video lie in the ways in which they (dis)embody their viewer. Not only did this concept prove helpful in explaining the (dis)embodiment of the film and video viewer; it also formed an important contribution to definitions of the medium by including the viewer as well as the spatial, institutional, and conventional aspects of the viewing situation into the structure of the medium. In addition to the fact that this inclusion formed a welcomed breach with dominant theorizations of the medium as an autonomous material entity, an inclusion of the seemingly contextual features of the viewing situation within the notion of the medium also enabled the investigation of a realm of intermediality often left undiscussed. As I have demonstrated in this part with the help of cinematic video installations by David Claerbout and Douglas Gordon, intermedial interactions, including mutual specification, between film and video often take place at the level of the *dispositif*.

My discussion of the differences and similarities between film and video in the social field were preceded by a reflection on the relationship between medium and society in Part III. In this part, I defined this relationship according to Raymond Williams' idea of soft determination. With this notion, Williams makes clear that although media technologies produce social structures, they are not all-powerful. Technology is never immune to or even untouched by the agency of human subjects. Therefore, it doesn't ever stand apart from the social, cultural, and historical conventions and expectations which shape the way in which humans envisage, create, and apply technology. Williams' understanding of technology points out that Krauss' division between the technological and conventional layer of a medium implies that technology might be a pristine origin. The idea of soft determination forecloses such an essentialist return to the idea of origin. Moreover, it informed my analyses of video and film in relation to the social realm: in Part III, I discussed how the two media produce social relationships and how they are produced by social structures, occupations, and needs.

Part IV rests on Williams' idea of soft determination in many respects. However, the violent features of film and video that are the topic of investigation in this part cannot be explained by the reciprocal relationship between technology and socialized subject alone. Some of the most prominent harmful and oppressive effects of film and video are wedded to specific scientific, medical, colonial, disciplinary, and misogynist discourses. Some of which, moreover, arose even before the invention of the two media, as they circled around the progenitors of the lens-based media such as the camera obscura and photography before they tied up with or informed the use of film and/or video. Foucault's concept of "discourse" is thus indispensable in understanding some of the most notable differences between the violent features of film and video, as those features spring from the manifold ways in which medium and discourse are entangled. Moreover, together with the notions of field, *dispositif* and soft determination, the concept of discourse forms a last breach with the modernist idea that this study aimed to undermine and rewrite; the idea of medium specificity as an autonomous, unified material essence.

However, alongside this rewriting of the concept of medium specificity, this book explored the differences and similarities between film and video. The result is, I would say, a map of some of the most prominent ways in which film and video are specified by, and vis-à-vis, each other. A map of similarities and differences, moreover, which can guide the analysis of the many contemporary intermedial films and videos that combine videomatic with cinematic elements. To conclude, I will take up my map, and return to the piece with which I started out: Isaac Julien's *Ten Thousand Waves*. How can the differences and similarities between film and video that were outlined in the previous parts guide us through the nine screens and three stories of *Ten Thousand Waves*? Which differences between film and video can provide insight into the ways in which Julien's installation produces meanings and affects in its viewer?

Traveling along

As mentioned in the introduction, *Ten Thousand Waves* interweaves several stories. First of all, there is the tragic story of the twenty-three Chinese immigrants, who drowned while working as clandestine cockle-fishers because they were unfamiliar with the tides in Morecambe Bay. The second story concerns the Chinese myth about the goddess Mazu, who saves drowning men and escorts them to a beautiful, pristine Chinese island. Thirdly, *Ten Thousand Waves* imitates parts of the classic Chinese movie *The Goddess* (Wu 1934), which tells the story of an unnamed prostitute who walks the streets at night in order to provide for her son. Let us first turn to the last-mentioned story, which applies some of the videomatic strategies I discussed with regard to feminist video practices in Part IV, namely copying and imitation. As explained, feminist video pieces tend to be more comfortable with critically imitating misogynist narrative fiction films, as the difference between their own medium and the medium of film automatically ensures some critical distance. In *Ten Thousand Waves,* this strategy of imitation with a difference plays an important part.

The close resemblance between the prostitute's story in Julien's piece and that of Wu first of all lies in the fact that both take place in the exact same décor. Both the 1934 film and its 2010 version were recorded in the Shanghai film studios. Hence, when actress Zhao Tao is shown to be walking the streets in *Ten Thousand Waves,* these streets are exactly the same as those walked by actress Ruan Lingyu in *The Goddess.* Not only can the architecture of the houses as well as the many shop windows be recognized from the original film; Julien imitates some of Wu's close-ups of these façades. Although the images of *Ten Thousand Waves* are in color instead of the original's black-and-white, the atmosphere of the dark streets at night is copied exactly in Julien's version. In addition, Zhao Tao is dressed and coiffured in the same 1930s style as Ruan Lingyu was in Wu's film.

In Wu's film, the prostitute falls prey to an evil male gambler, who first helps her to hide from the police, but then considers her to be his property. He forces her to give him her earnings, and threatens to take her son away if she doesn't. The prostitute hides some savings from him so that she will one day be able to escape with her son. However, when she decides to run, the gambler turns out to have stolen all her money. The prostitute kills him in a rage and ends up in prison. She will be forever separated from her son. For, in order to save him from the shame of having a prostitute and a murderer as a mother, she asks his guardian to tell her son that his mother is dead.

The story of *The Goddess* is copied only partially by Julien's installation. *Ten Thousand Waves* most comprehensively mimics scenes from *The Goddess* in which the prostitute is walking the streets at night, and travels through the old city during the day. Like *The Goddess*, Julien's installation shows how the woman waits painstakingly to be picked up by a stranger in the dark streets. In *Ten Thousand Waves*, however, these scenes are not embedded in a story about blackmail and murder. Although Tao is shown to be accompanied by a man who looks somewhat like the evil gambler in *The Goddess*, this man doesn't seem to be treating her in an overtly aggressive way. Whereas the gambler is constantly frightening or humiliating the female protagonist in Wu's film, the man in *Ten Thousand Waves* (played by artist Yang Fudong) just silently sits with her at a table. Although the woman doesn't seem comfortable or happy in any way, she isn't as violently approached by men in Julien's story as she is in Wu's. She isn't robbed, chased, laughed at, or scolded.

She is looked at though, in both works. As a prostitute, she is gazed upon—visually inspected, so to speak—by male passers-by who occasionally pick her up. In addition, the prostitute is looked at by the man who accompanies her the most; the evil gambler in *The Goddess*, and the silent male table-companion in Julien's installation. In both pieces, these male gazes can be witnessed within the frame, when the prostitute is shown with men in a single shot. However, she also becomes the object of the male gaze through the cinematic procedure of suture. Although *Ten Thousand Waves* does not completely do away with this procedure, it seems to protect the female protagonist from an objectifying gaze in two ways.

First, the sutures aren't tight in Julien's installation. Like many cinematic video installations, *Ten Thousand Waves* sutures images spatially instead of temporally. The videomatic *dispositif* of the multi-screen installation offers artists and filmmakers the possibility of attaching the look of characters to opposing screens. Instead of being stitched to a temporally preceding or succeeding shot on the same screen, their gaze is sutured to another screen; the screen they seem to be looking at in the exhibition space. In *Ten Thousand Waves*, this form of suturing first appears when the gaze of goddess Mazu is sutured to adjacent images of the billowing sea. When the technique is employed in relation to the prostitute, however, the male gazes that rest upon her seem to "misfire." Whereas the eyes of Mazu can hardly miss the surface of the sea, which fills entire screens, the gazes of men never seem to fall precisely on the figure of the prostitute. Because the match between their gaze and the female protagonist depends both on the position of the spectator in front of the screens, as well as the precise angle between screens, the men in *Ten Thousand Waves* seem to look slightly *past* instead of *at* the prostitute when they do not reside in the same frame. Although the viewer is likely to understand that the male gazes are aimed at the female protagonist, the sutures don't fit precisely enough in space to be effective.

These "missutures" not only protect the prostitute from the male gazes within the diegesis; they also disable the installation's viewer from looking at her as an object of desire. As sutures forcefully invite film viewers to share the looking character's point of view, the visitors of *Ten Thousand Waves* will look past the prostitute if they adopt the gaze of her male onlookers. In this respect, the installation hinders the viewer. What is more, like the missutures caused by the installational video *dispositif*, this second form of hindrance can again be understood as a videomatic intervention in a cinematic quality. Although the prostitute mostly appears in bright, sharp, and smooth cinematic looking images of a high quality, they are occasionally drastically out of focus. Although the old, original 1930s version of *The Goddess* has its own small haptic blots and scratches, the extreme opaqueness which Julien's installation displays is not common to the popular cinema which *Ten Thousand Waves* refers to. It can rather be recognized as a quality that has become well-known through video.

The result of the blurred opaqueness is that the female protagonist is hardly visible anymore. Whereas the projected images first invite the viewer to plunge visually into the depth of the illusionistic spaces on screen, they cast the viewer out as soon as the images are out of focus. The depicted prostitute can no longer be mastered or appropriated with the eyes. This is not only relevant in relation to the male gaze; it is also a significant strategy when it comes to the occidental gaze. With the exception of one show in Shanghai, *Ten Thousand Ways* has been exhibited in Western countries alone. The resulting Western point of view holds the risk of being orientalist in the contemplation of Julien's installation which, very basically, is "about" China—or, to put it slightly less narrowly: about China's social, political, and economic history, and the resulting Chinese migration to the West. The haptic, opaque image surface disables the Western viewer from visually obtaining the oriental other. Moreover, it prevents the spectator from a disembodied mode of looking in which the viewer forgets herself. Instead, it invites an embodied mode of looking in which the beholder is aware of her own position in time, space, as well as place.

However, the opacification of the screen has a paradoxical dimension. On the one hand, the screen protects the female protagonist by problematizing visual access to her. On the other hand, the impenetrable screen reinforces that category of the "other." It sets up a boundary between the presumably occidental viewer and the oriental other on screen, behind the limitation of the blurred image surface. This exclusion of the occidental viewer, and inclusion of the oriental subject, is established through a couple of other features of *Ten Thousand Waves*. First of all, the reference to the Chinese film classic in itself creates insiders and outsiders. As I discussed in Part III, films can create communities among those who know them—and exclude those who don't. For many Chinese film viewers, the reference will be obvious. *The Goddess* was a very popular movie, and has recently received new critical attention and acclaim in China. For, in spite of the fact that it can be criticized from a feminist perspective, the film has also been praised as a valuable social document. It represents its female protagonist as a victim and object of men, but in doing so, it might be said to critically expose problems of impoverished working class women in early twentieth-century China.

Western viewers might, however, only pick up on the imitation of *The Goddess* through the additional information museums often provide alongside the piece, for Wu's film is less likely to be part of their cultural frame of reference. However, the viewer who completely misses the installation's resemblance to *The Goddess* will not feel excluded by the piece—for such a viewer simply doesn't know that she doesn't know the film in question. The imitation of Wu's film is more likely to instill feelings of belonging in the viewers who do know the original movie. The occidental viewer who does not recognize that the installation copies a film classic will, however, nevertheless feel excluded from and by the story of the unnamed prostitute because her monologues are inaccessible to most Westerners. Although the basic story of a suffering, sad prostitute can be understood by most viewers, her Mandarin speech is not subtitled or dubbed. Therefore, most viewers will be in the dark when it comes to the prostitute's monologues. Only her lamenting tone of voice forms an indication to the meaning of her words.

In addition to the woman's speech, the installation shows many close-ups of Chinese characters which are unintelligible to most members of an occidental audience. Notably, some of them are written on the surface of the screen by a Chinese calligrapher. The large sweeps of ink drip down on what now seems to function as a besmeared window between the exhibition space in which the viewer resides, and the represented on-screen space in which the calligrapher is painting his human-sized signs. Like the opaqueness of the blurred images, these large written ideograms instill a cleavage between viewer and "foreigner." Only now, the boundary is produced by a presumably illegible sign, a sign of alterity itself.

However, the blurred and smeared boundaries which *Ten Thousand Waves* occasionally creates between the space of the beholder and the illusionistic space on screen are not permanent. In a manner comparable to the installations by David Claerbout and Douglas Gordon, the represented space on the screens fuses with, or expands into, the space between the screens. One of the most poignant examples of this occurs in a scene in which the unnamed prostitute travels through the old city by tram. Whereas the carriage would have to be mapped out by successive shots and reverse shots in a conventional single screen movie, *Ten Thousand Waves* forms the interior of a tram by way of several, simultaneously projected images in the exhibition space. Six of the installation's screens roughly form a rectangle which resembles a tram in both size and shape. Each screen, then, shows a part of the tram: at the front, we see how the tram driver navigates the streetcar through traffic, while the screen at the back of the rectangle shows how buildings and people in the streets disappear in the distance as the tram continues on its way through town. On the screens which form the sides of the tram, passengers sit on their benches. Although the female protagonist seems to sit alternately on each side of the tram, we see how she travels through the city while powdering her nose or staring out of the window. Her staring gaze is never sutured in the installation. Therefore, as a viewer, you cannot adopt her point of view. In this sense, the depicted woman remains an inaccessible other.

However, the viewer of *Ten Thousand Waves* is occasionally invited into her world. The spectator is not enabled to become the unnamed prostitute through (visual) identification, yet the installation does offer its viewer the impression of traveling along with her—in the tramcar, through town, but also through time.

For, as mentioned in the introduction, the unnamed prostitute appears to move forward through time. First, she seems to belong to the 1930s. However, as she rides the tram through the old-looking city, the cityscape is suddenly exposed as a film set. In the background, men are moving pieces of scenery; house fronts are lifted and some pieces of film equipment enter the frame. These exposures indicate that the prostitute is actually an actress who has been playing a part in a film studio. However, she doesn't escape from her role completely, for when the old setting is left behind, the woman still ends up at a (not so old-fashioned) table with a man who looks like the evil gambler from *The Goddess.*

In this scene at the table, however, historical time seems to have moved forwards by decades. Whereas the scenes in the old film studio were interspersed with black-and-white images of an old city, the scene in which the female actress/prostitute is sitting at a table with a male companion is combined with archival film images of the Cultural Revolution. Both the black-and-white and the color footage of China's Cultural Revolution show that, in addition to its dominant application in the field of narrative fiction film, film is well able to create what I have called a "referential reality effect" in Part I. The images have some quality defects (graininess, flickering, color distortion) which give them a documentary, indexical appearance. They signal that what they show is real. Yet, the moment they show is a historical moment from the past, a moment that subsequently defines the temporal location of the female protagonist as well. While sitting at the table, she seems to have moved from the 1930s to the 1960s.

After the scene at the table, the temporality of the images switches to the "now" in two ways: through architecture and through the temporal indexicality of video. Although the female protagonist remains dressed in a slightly old-fashioned way, the architectural surroundings of the prostitute/actress turn highly modern as her storyline in *Ten Thousand Waves* progresses. She is depicted in what seems to be the contemporary interior of a high-class restaurant or luxurious hotel lobby. In addition, we see her staring out of the window of a hotel room, which offers a magnificent view over Pudong's skyscrapers. The association with prostitution hasn't disappeared completely, for the manner in which the woman is strolling and sitting around in the hotel lobby is not unlike the way in which she was walking the streets before. However, the staring gaze of the woman attaches her to another story—precisely because the gaze itself hardly ever attaches itself to anything. The sad looking prostitute (or actress) keeps staring into the distance as if she is longingly thinking of someone who is not there. So who is she thinking of?

In *The Goddess*, the prostitute was separated from her son. Given the installation's initial resemblances with this early film classic, it seems obvious to suspect that the sad female protagonist might be missing her son. The installation confirms this presumption when shots of the staring actress/prostitute in the modern interior are alternated with shots from a video documentary on the Morecambe Bay victims. These show how an older family member, presumably a parent, of one of the drowned immigrants lays out some of the victim's personal belongings on a blanket, and folds up clothes of the deceased relative. Then, the installation shows a video image of two hands holding a photograph of one of the drowned young men. Although the photograph is clearly not held by the prostitute, the fact that her image is juxtaposed with this shot strongly implies that she is missing a son, too. However, the fact that the picture of the drowned man is shown by way of video embeds the "that-has-been" of the photograph into the "now" of video's temporal indexicality. In addition, the referential reality effect of the video documentary further questions the presumed fictionality of the prostitute's cinematic story. This photographed man is really dead, right now. And the character of the prostitute is related to the reality of this moment in the present.

This presentness is further sustained when images of the female protagonist are mixed with video footage which has an even stronger temporal indexicality: surveillance video footage of the rescue operation at Morecambe Bay. As explained in Part I, the genre of surveillance video is strongly associated with live feed. When images of the prostitute are mixed with these images (including the audio recording of a panicking woman begging for help), the story of the female character can no longer be seen apart from present tragedies involving Chinese migrants.

In the same boat

Although the installation doesn't establish an implicit link between the prostitute and a specific victim of the Morecambe Bay tragedy, it suggests that many contemporary Chinese women lost relatives because of migration to the West. *Ten Thousand Waves* makes clear that the lethal disasters which happen to Chinese migrants are manifold. While the nine screens of the installation are filled with images of traffic circling on an incredibly complex cloverleaf between high rises, a staccato female voice rapidly recites one of the poems Chinese poet Wang Ping contributed to Julien's piece:

> We know the tolls: 23—Rochaway, NY; 58—Dover, England; 18—Shenzen; 25—South Korea and many more.
>
> We know the methods: walk, swim, fly, metal container, back of a lorry, ship's hold.
>
> We know how they died: starved, raped, dehydrated, drowned, suffocated, homesick, heartsick, worked to death, working to death.
>
> We know we may end up in the same boat.

In sum, *Ten Thousand Waves* creates a relationship between Wu's film classic and migratory tragedies which are pointed out by poems like this one, as well as by video footage that affirms their presentness. In doing so, *Ten Thousand Waves* seems to suggest that the problems of China's working class are not new. In the 1930s, poverty ripped families apart as it (for instance) forced mothers to prostitute themselves and distance themselves from their children. In the twenty-first century, after the Cultural Revolution, family members try to cross the ocean in the hope of a better life. Julien's installation points back in time even further when it comes to the problems of China's working class. For, as mentioned in the introduction, it relates the Morecambe Bay tragedy to the mythical goddess Mazu. This goddess, who is known for saving fishermen at sea whose lives are in danger, rescues three of the drowning cockle-fishers in *Ten Thousand Waves*. By representing this myth, which dates back to centuries before the Ming dynasty, Julien's installation indicates that "working to death" (or at least nearly to death) is a process that is endlessly repeated through the centuries in China.

The fictionality of the Mazu myth, as well as the imitation of Wu's *The Goddess*, may seem to stand in the way of such a conclusion, though. Whereas the Morecambe Bay tragedy is what we call a real story which was recently relayed on news channels and in newspapers, the Mazu myth and *The Goddess* are less firmly tied to what we understand as referential reality. Although both stories are certainly related to real social and economic circumstances of China's working class, the stories of Mazu and the tragic prostitute are more fictional than the twenty-three drowned cockle-fishers in Morecambe Bay. This is not so much, or not merely, an ontological distinction; Julien's installation presents the Mazu myth and the prostitute's story line as more fictional than the Morecambe Bay tragedy. First, both stories are told by way of sharp and colorful cinematic-looking images. These images partially create a reality effect by their smoothness, but this reality effect is what I have termed a "constructed reality effect." The high resolution of the images hides the materiality of the medium, but at the same time points out that the images are probably part of a *fictional* film story, as this reality-effect producing device is typical of conventional fiction film.

Secondly, the constructedness of the film stories is revealed in the case of both goddesses. As mentioned previously, the prostitute suddenly appears to find herself in a film studio where the set is remodeled as she passes by. Mazu, in addition, does not only fly around skyscrapers and through green valleys; she is also depicted hanging between a large ventilator and a green screen. Her appearance in the sky, with waving hair and fluttering robes, turns out to be the result of highly professional digital video keying and CGI. Thus, in spite of the cinematic smoothness and sharpness of the Mazu scenes, these shots are high-definition digital video images manipulated and partly generated by the computer. Insofar as the images of Mazu flying through the air are still indexically tied to something, they can only be a trace of Maggie Cheung dangling on ropes in a green-screen studio.

However, paradoxically, this exposure of cinematic digital constructedness not only separates the Mazu myth and the prostitute's struggle from the Morecambe Bay tragedy. In fact, it emphasizes that these old fictional stories are tied to the present reality of Chinese workers. For they are re-presented, re-told, today, by Julien's installation. Moreover, the fact that the Mazu myth is told by way of state-of-the-art digital video imagery appropriates the centuries-old myth as a contemporary story. A story that deals with a topical theme (Chinese men risking their lives at sea in order to make money), as well as a story that can offer comfort, satisfy a longing for home, and instill a sense of belonging—all of which are needed by Chinese migrants and/or their (surviving) relatives today.

Hence, the overtly digital character of the images may point out that the cinematic image is severed from referential reality in the sense that it is no longer a trace of a pro-filmic event as analogue film images used to be. Yet, at the same time, the digital constructedness functions as a temporal index in *Ten Thousand Waves*, as the contemporaneity of the technology points to the "now" of the image production. In this sense, the reality effect of the grainy surveillance video footage which appears in between shots of Mazu does not merely function as a rhetorical strategy which lends the digital film images some of their lost indexicality, as Thomas Levin would argue. For the temporal indexicality of the grainy surveillance video footage supplies the film images not so much with something they do not have; but, rather the video images are complementary to the temporal indexicality which the cinematic-looking images, to some extent, already possess because they turn out to be generated with the help of a video-specific technique that remains invisible when it is applied in contemporary digital narrative films.

Although the smooth digital artificiality of contemporary HD chroma-keyed images in no way resembles the rough look of the video surveillance footage, but rather looks exactly like high-quality film, both of these image types are video forms that point to the present. However, the temporal indexicality of keyed video images is not a general given. As mentioned previously, digitally manipulated HD video images cannot always be recognized as such. Therefore, they are often understood by their audience as fictional film images whose indexicality is simply uncertain in the digital age: they could refer to something which caused them, they could be entirely computer-generated. The temporal indexicality of HD digital video images depends entirely on the explicit confirmation that the chemical indexicality of the cinematic images in question is indeed nonexistent. In other words, their indexicality depends on the exposure that, in spite of their filmic look and their embeddedness in a cinematically told fictional narrative, the images in question are in fact the result of state-of-the-art digital video manipulation. This state-of-the-art manipulation, moreover, especially signals "now" in Julien's installation because its contemporaneity stands in contrast to what it helps to represent: an age-old myth. In *Ten Thousand Waves*, the ancient myth of Mazu is both presented as an actuality by the fact that it is narratively tied to the drowned cockle-fishers, and through the (disclosure of the) technological way in which it is tied to those Morecambe Bay victims.

In relation to the theme of migration, the coarse video images differ from the cinematic-looking ones in one important respect, however. The medium-typical low image quality and hand-held character of the videomatic material produce an embodied mode of viewing which shapes the way in which the spectator can relate to the Chinese migrants. When the nine screens of the installation are filled with rapidly moving grey video pixels and black surging waves, the viewer loses the ground under her feet. Without a horizon or recognizable point of orientation, the spectator of Julien's installation is likely to feel lost and disoriented between the screens. Previously, I described how the piece doesn't enable its spectator to identify with the character of the prostitute through the conventional film strategy of suture, because her point of view is not made accessible or visible to the viewer. However, the viewer is occasionally offered the possibility of seemingly traveling along with her, to accompany her in the tram, for instance. The same goes for the video footage of the rescue operation. The high angle from which most of the surveillance images are recorded indicate that they do not represent the immigrants' point of view. However, their disorienting effect enables the viewer to share the experience of the immigrants to some extent. This goes for the particular Chinese men who were lost at sea in Morecambe Bay, but can also be understood in a more general sense; the experience of migration is often described in terms of disorientation and being lost.

The installation's devices of exclusion I described before can be regarded in this light as well. When the high-quality cinematic images in the installation occasionally opacify and turn haptic, this change from cinematic image qualities to video-specific features excludes the viewer from the depicted world, and puts up a boundary between the viewer and represented other. This visual exclusion of the viewer from the world on view can in itself be understood as an act that makes the viewer more like the other: similar to migrants in a strange country, the viewer is not allowed to visually enter the onscreen world. This exclusion is, of course, strongest in the case of Western viewers, who are not only excluded by the impermeability of the videomatic image surface, but who are also left in the dark when it comes to the spoken and written Chinese signs. Moreover, in addition to the fact that the Mandarin language is incomprehensible to the Western spectator, she may be unable to grasp the installation's culturally specific cinematic references. As a result, the viewer will to some extent experience a few of the most dominant negative feelings that can accompany migration. Through *Ten Thousand Waves*' specific combination of film and video features, we may end up in the same boat, indeed.

NOTES

Introduction

1. Even Elleström, who deliberately returns to (a heterogeneous definition of) the medium in order to study intermediality, does not brush the idea of a medium's essence aside very firmly when he states that "All of the four modalities [. . .] must hence be considered when attempting to find the core of one medium or another—if there is one" (2010: 27).
2. In addition to *A Voyage on the North Sea*, Krauss has reflected on the concept of medium specificity in a number of articles, such as: "'. . . And Then Turn Away?': An Essay on James Coleman" (1997), "Reinventing the Medium" (1999), and "'The Rock': William Kentridge's Drawing for Projection" (2000).
3. Schröter terms differential medium specificity "ontological intermediality" (2011: 5).
4. A well-known example of such a change is the invention of photography. Because of the creation of this new medium, the specificity of painting had to be drastically revised. Of all existing media, painting was best able to depict reality. This feature of painting lost its uniqueness with the invention of photography. With the latter medium, it was possible to depict reality in a more real, more direct, faster, and cheaper manner. Consequently the specification of painting had to be defined by other qualities.
5. I am using the English translation ("discourse") of Foucault's French term *discours* throughout this book.

Part I Introduction: From Real to Reel in *Benny's Video*

1. This dialogue between Benny and a friend in the film *Benny's Video* was translated by the author.

Chapter 1 Reality Effects: Literature, Film, and Video

1. My attempt to apply a theory to the media of film and video doesn't rule out the fact that those two objects will, as it were, answer back when a straightforward application of Barthes' theory proves to be problematic.
2. Only film is mentioned by Chatman; I have added video here because Chatman's argument also applies to this medium.
3. This magnetization, or electromagnetic charging, of the particles on video tape was mostly analogue in the first three decades of video's existence. Yet, when the DV format was introduced in 1995, it quickly became commonplace to charge the magnetic particles on video tape digitally (i.e., only positively or negatively).

Chapter 2 Devices in Video

1. In comparison to film, video has long had a low contrast ratio; video equipment could not record the high contrast between dark and light areas in one image. As a consequence, video images tend to look dark or extremely light when they are recorded in a situation where the contrast between light and dark shades is very high.
2. I use the terms viewer and reader interchangeably.
3. The viewer is not necessarily aware of this activity on her part, though. She simply has the impression that reality is represented by a text or image. For although many of the devices producing a reality effect are on the one hand understood by the viewer as signifiers signifying "this is reality," they are on the other hand often not consciously recognized as such. This is why the truth behind the referential illusion remains hidden according to Barthes; the insignificant detailed descriptions in realist texts are not recognizable as signifiers the signified of which is the category of the real while they function as such. And, I would add, they do function as such because the reader does recognize and understand them as signifiers at some level.
4. Like the documentary in general, home video (or home movie) is a genre which video has for a large part taken over from film. Because of this, the devices producing a reality effect within home movies became more typical to and therefore more effective in video than in film.

Chapter 3 Devices in Film

1. Of course "realness" is relative in this sense, even without treating it as a philosophical concept, simply because the presence of a camera is often already enough to direct events or influence the behavior of people. Similarly, the "not realness" of narrative fiction film can be put into perspective by the remark that the actors playing in these films are nevertheless real people of flesh and blood.
2. As Verstraten aptly remarks, acting which was perceived as natural and true-to-life in the 1950s looks very artificial today (2006: 61). Thus, it is historically relative what good acting is, or which modes of acting are least recognized as acting.
3. See also Heath 1981: 19–76. Interesting in this regard is Heath's remark that on the one hand, a narrative is needed in order to relate successive shots, while on the other hand, the successive shots enable a narrative to unfold in film to begin with.
4. Besides the demand that the temporal relationship between represented events be clear, it is also a narrative convention in Hollywood to establish cause and effect relations between those events. So-called neorealistic filmmakers have argued, however, that it is much more natural and realistic when the course of events is directed by haphazard coincidences instead of by logical chains of cause and effect (Verstraten 2006: 66). Of the two films I am discussing here, Egoyan's film is more strongly composed of cause-and-effect relationships, while *Benny's Video* leans towards neorealism in this respect. Yet, both films produce reality effects. Thus, although I cannot establish which narrative composition produces a stronger reality effect, I would say that neither of them—a composition of cause and effect or one of coincidences—is truly a prerequisite to the creation of a reality effect by narrative film, while for instance the surveyable arrangement of time and space are needed if the viewer's illusion of overview which produces a reality effect in narrative film is to be upheld.

Chapter 4 Sliding Scales

1. The manipulation of digital film and video images will be addressed later in the book.
2. The distinction between "the" reality we believe we live in and the imaginary realities produced by discourse has been convincingly deconstructed by linguists and philosophers who argue that reality is always a product of discourse. What matters in light of my argument on the reality effect, however, is not so much the philosophical tenability of the distinction between the reality and constructed imaginary realities, but the fact that this distinction exists as an idea which governs the thoughts of viewers and readers when assessing and experiencing representations. As an idea, the distinction influences the viewer's belief in the truthfulness of the representation and the reality effect such a representation produces.
3. The fact that the viewer's understanding of reality, which is historically, culturally, and socially relative, influences the reality effect proves again that the reality effect is not only an effect *on* the viewer, but also an effect *of* the viewer.

Chapter 5 Medium Specificity and the Reality Effect

1. This search for the unique capabilities of a medium is, of course, prominent in Greenberg's essentialist discourse on medium specificity. Moreover, as Noël Carroll has pointed out in his writings on medium specificity (1988, 1996), this search can be traced back to ancient discussions on the word–image relationship. In addition, Carroll argues that descriptions of the specificity of media often take the form of recommendations or requirements.
2. Whereas Cubitt states that "discussions of video need to be prefaced with a caveat against essentialism" (1993: xv), it is also possible to argue that video itself forms this caveat. It is not a coincidence that Krauss discusses video's hydra-headedness in her declaration of the post-medium condition; through its heterogeneity, video obstructs essentialist conceptualizations of the medium.

Chapter 6 Interaction: Between Reality Effects

1. Another medium which was similarly specified in a narrative film by the protagonist's understanding of the medium is photography in Antonioni's famous film *Blow Up* (1966). In this film, protagonist Thomas blows up a photograph because he expects that something will become visible that cannot (or can no longer) be perceived in reality by eyesight alone. Besides the fact that the visual media of video and photography have thus been specified within film as media by which more can be perceived than by human eyesight alone, it is worth noting that film itself has often been specified as a medium which offers an unprecedented view on reality, a view which reveals, penetrates, and analyzes reality in ways the human eye cannot match. This specification of film was, however, provided not so much by other media, but by famous theorists and filmmakers such as Walter Benjamin and Dziga Vertov.
2. In Part III, I will demonstrate why theorists have attached great social and political value to the functions of pausing, rewinding, and slowing down moving image material. In

Part IV, I will discuss some of the negative consequences and premises of the application of lens-based media as epistemological tools.

3. As in *Family Viewing*, video is also shown to be a medium which penetrates and exposes reality in *Benny's Video*, with the difference that the latter film stresses this ability of video by the way video functions as an actor and is understood by the characters in the film, whereas the former film mainly shows the revealing capacities of video through the way the medium functions as an internal narrator.

Chapter 7 *Dispositif*: An Expanded Layered Structure

1. I am quoting Judith Mayne's English translation of Baudry's text here, as she has expounded the latter's theory with attention to the differences between the French terms and their English translations (see Mayne 2002).
2. Baudry does discuss how these formal features of classical narrative films sustain the effect of cinema's *dispositif*, yet he does not consider them to be a part of it.
3. In the past decade, this form of exhibition has become less typical for the artist.
4. My somewhat simplified list of the *dispositif's* components resembles outlines of the concept by Kessler (2006, 2007) as well as Parente and Carvalho (2008), and Joost Raessens (2009).
5. McCall's solid light films deviate from cinema's dominant *dispositif* in a very overt way. However, film theorists such as Mary Ann Doane (2003) and Philip Rosen (1986) have pointed out that relatively inconspicuous formal and narrative features of classical fiction films can form subtle deconstructions of the disembodied viewing subject in cinema's traditional *dispositif*.
6. His negation of an absolute division between the implied and real spectator/reader can be traced back to some of the ideas by reader-response critic Walker Gibson (1950) as well as literary theorist Ernst van Alphen (1988), and is based on pragmatic approaches to the relation between text and spectator as theorized by film scholars such as Francesco Casetti (1983) and Nick Browne (1986).
7. Since the film and video works I will address are contemporary Western European productions, their general spectator is, at this point, specified as being a contemporary, Western European one.

Chapter 8 (Dis)Embodying *Dispositifs*

1. As Richard Rushton has pointed out, the sense of bodyliness he and others ascribe to the film viewer is "actually more of a loss of self-consciousness—for example, the loss of awareness that one is sitting in a movie theatre—or a loss of 'self-theorization'" (2002: 114).
2. Likewise, disembodied spectators do not necessarily physically occupy the single static viewpoint which perspectival images produce in front of their image frame (this would cause problems in crowded museum galleries and cinema halls). They rather imagine themselves in this (or *as* this) center.

3. In light of embodied spectatorship, this interactivity should be further specified as what Ryan (1999) has termed "literal interactivity." As opposed to "figural interactivity," which concerns the collaboration between reader and text/image in the production of meaning and affect, literal interactivity depends on physical interaction between the viewer and object.
4. In fact, linear perspective images also interpellate the viewer as a "you" by the viewing point they construct in front of them. Likewise, the viewer of narrative film can be regarded as its addressee; when it is assumed the film's story is told by a narrator, an addressee is implicated. However, this I–you structure is not visible in the case of linear perspective, and it is invisible or implicit in the case of film. This invisibility makes all the difference; it leaves the division between the "here and now" of the spectator and the "there and then" of the representation intact. I will discuss this issue in relation to film more extensively later on.
5. The effects of closed-circuit (surveillance) video on the viewing subject will be further discussed in Part III.

Chapter 9 Film's Disembodying *Dispositif*: An Effect of an Effect

1. This attention to the ideological and psychological effects of the *dispositif* remained central in later applications of the concept, both within and outside of the field of film studies. In studies by, for instance, Jean-Louis Comolli (1980) and Michel Foucault (1980), the concept came to refer to a much wider array of related elements (e.g., discourses, economic factors, laws, institutions, scientific statements). Yet, the notion of *dispositif* nevertheless remained linked to power and desire in these redefinitions of the term. I am leaving this association largely undiscussed in this chapter, as the power structures which are put up or sustained by the media of film and video will be investigated in Part IV.
2. Although the film screen is often theorized as a division between the illusionistic film space and the projection room, it is important to note that sound doesn't obey this border. In addition to the fact that diegetic film sounds do not remain isolated within the film's diegesis as they necessarily escape into the viewing room, sound is often the one thing which does penetrate the film screen: speakers are frequently positioned behind the film screen. The played film sounds then reach the audience through millions of invisible tiny holes in the film screen.

Chapter 10 Other Views on Film Viewing

1. Williams rightly notes that although most body genres produce a physical reaction in their spectator, they do not always produce mimicry. She gives the example of physical clown comedy as a body genre which does not lead to mimicry: the audience's physical reaction of laughter does not coincide with the deadpan reactions of the clown who performs gross activities such as eating shoes and slipping on banana skins (1991: 4).
2. Even though she does not write on cinema of exhibition specifically, it is remarkable in this regard that Ágnes Pethő claims in her book *Cinema and Intermediality* that "reading" intermedial relations in film requires an embodied spectator (2011: 04).

3. In an article titled "What Do We Really Know About Film Audiences?" (2012), Ian Christie points out that empirical studies in the UK have found that only 6 percent of the total number of film viewings takes place in the traditional cinema. Although these numbers seem to prove that cinema's traditional viewing set-up in the movie theater is no longer dominant in a quantitative respect, I hold that it is still dominant, or at least pervasive, as an idea. As such, it shapes many of the nontraditional *dispositifs* films are watched in today. In addition, the newer viewing set-ups which Christie discusses have often incorporated aspects of the traditional *dispositif*. For this reason, it would be a mistake to discard the traditional *dispositif* as an irrelevant, marginal viewing situation.

Chapter 11 Surfaces and Screens: Video's Embodying *Dispositifs*

1. For this reason, studies which focus on the production rather than the reception of medium objects tend to characterize film as a haptic medium instead of an optic one. The tactile, embodied experience of working on analogue film strip is for instance celebrated by Tactita Dean in *Film* (2011), a publication which accompanied her monumental film piece with the same title.
2. Uhlin does not use the phrase of "time that weighs on the body" in relation to video art, but in reference to Andy Warhol's films, which are indeed characterized by the slow and extended uneventfulness which has become typical of video. This shows that the expression of the temporality in question is not unique to the video medium. Only, within in the field of film, this expressive possibility is less widely applied than in the field of video.
3. Today, some video artists even soften or tune down the sharpness and brightness of high-definition video images in order to give them a more cinematic look. This cinematic look concerns a slightly old-fashioned feature; we tend to regard images as more filmic when they have the warm, soft look which characterizes many movies of the 1950s.
4. Although the video projector entered the museum because the TV monitor was already there, it is more suitable for the production of multi-screen pieces than the average film projector. As video projectors were initially developed with the idea that they would replace data projectors such as the overhead projector and episcope in classrooms and business meeting rooms, many video projectors are equipped with a so-called short-throw lens. This allows them to project large images while being relatively close to the projection surface. When it comes to video installation art, this short throw is not only a prerequisite for the production of large video projections in small museum rooms, it can also prevent the appearance of unwanted shadows of visitors on the projection screen. The distance between the projector and the video projection can be made so small that viewers need not stand in the projector's light beams when they behold the image. When the spectator's shadow does play a part in video installations (which it often does), this is not an inevitable flaw.

Chapter 12 In Between: Three Intermedial Installations

1. Frohne adds an important historical remark to her discussion of the participating viewer in installation art: "Just as the viewer has become a participant in the scene, the

parameters of the aesthetic of reception criticized by Michael Fried have become the actual principle of impact" (Frohne 2008: 269). The author is referring to Fried's influential "Art and Objecthood" (1967) here, in which he argues against the focus on the viewer's experience which is commanded by Minimal Art. A few decades later, this focus appears to have become one of the most important hallmarks of both contemporary art practices and art theoretical writings. It is telling in this regard that, in a recent article on Douglas Gordon's *k.364* ("Another Light" 2011), Fried limits his analysis to the movie version of the piece, and only briefly mentions the installation version in a footnote.

2. The viewing process I will describe is based on what a general, Western contemporary viewer who is acquainted with video and film is most likely to see and do. Moreover, the spectator I describe is not a resistant spectator, but a spectator who is susceptible and open to the influence the work acts out on her.
3. My discussion of *American Car* is based on the way it was exhibited in the Van Abbe Museum in Eindhoven, The Netherlands, 2005. As the position of a door close to the projection surface is essential to the perception of the video installation, *American Car* can be considered as a site-dependent installation. When exposed in rooms different from those in the Van Abbe Museum, it changes considerably.
4. This trajectory is mostly an imaginary one, for narrative films are not usually recorded with only one camera. However, if a shot shows an object in close-up, and a second shot shows the same object from a distance, the spatial distance between the two viewpoints and the trajectory crossing through the space connecting the two viewpoints can be imagined by the viewer. Moreover, especially if the two viewpoints are not point-of-view shots, this trajectory can be understood as the distance the camera has traveled—albeit instantaneously.
5. At first sight, 3D cinema may even seem more able to fill the viewing space with a fictional world than multi-screen video installations which reproduce an illusionistic space within an exhibition space. On the one hand, the flatness of the screen becomes invisible during a 3D viewing experience, whereas the screens of a video installation remain recognizable as flat surfaces—sometimes this flatness is even more apparent in spatial set-ups. On the other hand, 3D cinema is not as three-dimensional as a video installation, in that the images can only be viewed in 3D from a fixed viewpoint. If the film spectator of a 3D film turns her head, the illusionistic world is no longer there. In sum, video installations are able to produce the impression that the represented world enters into the viewing space in a *dispositif* which involves a (more or less) embodied, mobile viewer, whereas the illusion of 3D cinema only unfolds in a traditional cinematic *dispositif*, including an immobile disembodied spectator.
6. In the case of film, any contact between characters in the representation and the spectator is illusive, because the characters are not really present when they seem to look at the viewer, and the spectator was not present when the actors looked into the camera. However, the visual address of the viewer still provides the viewer with the strong impression that the division between the time and space within the film and outside of it is lifted. This *impression* of the viewer is of influence on her embodiment.
7. Both of these arguments illustrate my previous assumption that the spectator doesn't necessarily experience a work of art passively, but can apply conventional or intertextual modes of looking at a work. The previously discussed effects of *American Car* on the spectator depend for a large part on the spectator activating her knowledge of film's traditional *dispositif*, including narrative film conventions.

8. It is worthwhile, however, to briefly consider whether sound in itself could produce an embodied listener. For in itself, sound has the manifest capacity to envelop the listener, for it is never a limited object, but something which can—and often does—fill a space. When it does, the listener can be understood to be embodied because she shares a space with the sound. The question is, however, whether (by definition immaterial) sound alone can give rise to an embodied mode of looking by simultaneously occupying and constructing a three-dimensional space as installation art often does. On the basis of contemporary soundscape installations by artists such as Justin Bennett, I would say that this might be possible. For further thoughts on this subject, see *Site Specific Sound* (2004) by Brandon LaBelle and *Resonances: Aspects of Sound Art* (2002) by Bernd Schulz.
9. It was, for instance, shown this way in MUHKA and in Gallery Micheline Swayzer, both in Antwerp.
10. *Bordeaux Piece* was recorded with a state-of-the-art HD digital video camera.
11. In this regard, *Bordeaux Piece* confirms some arguments by Stephen Heath. As mentioned in Part I, Heath argued that, on the one hand, film shots can map a space, which enables a narrative to unfold. On the other hand, the space mapped by film shots can only be reconstructed if a narrative sustains the relationships between the shots. Similarly, the looks and voices of characters can connect film shots and as such enable a narrative to unfold, but the characters themselves need to be related by or embedded in a narrative which clarifies their nonspatial relationships in order for their looks and voices to construct meaningful relationships between shots. *Bordeaux Piece* shows that within this reciprocal process, dialogue can incite such relationships.

Part III Introduction: Framing the Medium

1. In this regard, is not surprising that, in the United States, early media studies arose from the discipline of sociology.

Chapter 13 The Medium, the Media, and the Social

1. Note the pedagogical effect which Croteau and Hoynes attribute to media.
2. In *Marxism and Literature* (1977), Williams also argues against the idea of the medium as a neutral, transparent organ and the medium as a solely artistic material.
3. A similar claim was made by André Bazin on the origin of cinema (Bazin 1967: 17).

Chapter 14 Video: Flow and Feedback

1. The term "flow" is used by Jameson in order to refer to the signs that the medium of video is able to produce without intermission. However, the concept has also been used to indicate the processual character of video images; even those which seem not to change or move at all contain an invisible flow, namely the ceaseless flow of electrons scanning the image surface from left to right and top to bottom. For this reason Yvonne Spielman

understands video as "transformation imagery." Video distinguishes itself from photography and film by the fact that instead of containing single images, transitions between images are central; video images are always in the process of being produced (2005: 4).

2. The uneventfulness of video artworks has not been understood as an objectifying characteristic by all video critics and artists. Bill Viola for instance explained that he favored seemingly uneventful actions in his videos in order to increase the spectator's sensorial, attentional, and cognitive faculties, so that "one might liberate oneself from the habit of viewing objects as we see them" (1976: 277).
3. Some closed-circuit art video installations explicitly raise this question. Consider, for instance, the following title of a closed-circuit video installation by Bruce Nauman: *Video Surveillance Piece: Public Room, Private Room* (Nauman 1969–1970).
4. In an interview in *Afterimage* with Florence Gilbard, Acconci consistently addresses the video medium as an "embodiment of [. . .] intimate space" (1984: 9).
5. Christine Ross has pointed out how important this remark by Acconci is in relation to Krauss' evaluation of his work and of video in general (2006: 86–87).
6. Renov correctly notes that "Rouch's insight brilliantly anticipates what the video apparatus (with the playback monitor mounted alongside the camera) realizes" (83).
7. This is the conclusion of Mimi White (1992), who examined American television programs.
8. Although artistic video confession certainly relates to the explosion of confessions that can be witnessed on television, on the radio or in magazines, the confessional art videos which are under discussion here operate in a different domain. Although artworks do have an exchange value, they are often considered to be counterindustrial in comparison, for instance, to confessional TV shows, as they are produced at a relatively low cost and have a limited audience.
9. Alongside the therapeutic analytical value of video keying, the political usefulness of medium-specific technique had been recognized by film and video artists. In their film essay *Ici et ailleurs* (1976), Jean-Luc Godard and Anne-Marie Miéville, for instance, apply chroma-keying as a form of spatial montage that allows them to make political and historical analyses as well as statements. After *Ici et ailleurs* Godard has frequently applied video in less activist works. It is telling in this regard that in a relatively recent work the French director has told the history of cinema by way of video. In *Histoire(s) du cinéma* (1998), video keying and layering function as the piece's core rhetorical tools in postulating and visualizing interrelations in film history. Interrelations, moreover, which film itself would not be able to expose.
10. The application of video as a therapeutic device is addressed in *Onourown* (1990), a video documentary by Joe Gibbons and Tony Oursler. The documentary shows how two psychiatric patients are deinstitutionalized. As part of their outpatient therapy they are asked to keep a video diary.
11. Ginsberg was one of the members of the alternative video collective "Video Free America." Although he deals with a small social community in the *Continuing Story*, Ginsberg was concerned with the way in which video could change American society in general.
12. The genre of video testimony is also widely applied by human rights organizations and other organizations which aim to address, expose, prosecute, and/or help to remember

acts of injustice and crime. Today, such organizations sometimes use or create online video sharing sites on the Internet in order to reach a global audience for their collected testimonies. See for instance www.engagemedia.org; an online video sharing site focused on social justice and environmental issues in the Asia-Pacific.

13. In 1972, the U.S. federal mandate required local origination programming on cable and opened the wires to public access. In 1973, the stand-alone time-base corrector was introduced; a black box that stabilized helical scan tapes and made them broadcastable. Because of that, it was finally possible for small-format video to become a stable television production medium, which paved the way for guerrilla television (Boyle 1997: 229).
14. Some media theorists have argued that guerilla television has evolved into video sharing sites on the Internet such as YouTube, albeit in a less critical and less collective way (see Merrin 2012). Today, new guerilla television collectives sometimes reappear in times of conflict. For instance, during the 2011 riots in the United Kingdom, a small guerilla group called Sangat TV reported as well as intervened in the riots.
15. See, for instance *Video for Change: A Guide for Advocacy and Activism* (Gregory et.al 2005). This publication was produced within the scope of an activist video project called WITNESS.

Chapter 15 Film: Private/Production

1. A similar tension between the private lives depicted by home movies and the historical, social, and political context in which they exist can for instance also be noted in *Private Century* (2010) by Jan Sikl, and *Y In Vyborg* (2006) by Pia Andell.
2. See van Alphen (2011).
3. The conventional understanding of the concept of space as a purely mathematical, geometrical category has been questioned by a group of influential social theorists (e.g., David Harvey, Edward Soja, Manuel Castells), of whom Henri Lefebvre is the most important forerunner. This sociologist and philosopher has argued in his seminal book *The Production of Space* (1974) that space is first and foremost produced by social actions and relations: "(social) space is a (social) product" (26). The idea of social space has been related to media theory by Manuel Castells. In comparison to Lefebvre, Castells places more emphasis on physical, material properties of social space: "space is a material product, in relation to other material products—including people—who engage in [historically] determined social relationships that provide space with a form, a function, and a social meaning" (1996: 41). In addition, he assumes that media can act as the material support of spaces. In *The Rise of the Network Society*, Castells describes how electronic media technologies constitute a network of electronic impulses which forms the support of a contemporary space which he calls "the space of flows." Alongside a material spatial network, this is also a social space, for the electronic media in question connect physically remote people as they allow them to communicate with each other. In conclusion, the communication network established by electronic media such as the Internet should be understood as a social network as well as a spatial one, and can therefore be called a social space. Here, I have combined Castell's notion of social space with the idea of a conventional viewing space (enforced by the material apparatus).
4. This especially goes for analogue films. Television, as well as digitalization and the Internet have made the dissemination of films less complicated. However, these electronic

forms of distribution do not always leave the image quality of the film images intact. In addition, films that have to be remunerated still depend on distribution companies or organizations.

5. Definitions of video that use space as a metaphor for the medium are therefore partly motivated by another trope: as *pars pro toto*, the feedback set-up with its enclosed character has come to stand for the medium as a whole.
6. I will not discuss all the production details which Naficy maps. An impression of the variety of such production modes can be provided by the following titles and subtitles from sections in this book: "Interstitial and Artisanal Mode of Production," "Postindustrial Production," "Coproduction," "Multisource Funding," "Distribution to Academic Institutions," to name but a few.
7. As the Third Cinema movement produced films as a group, and moreover centered on the expression of the people's interests instead of the artistic ideas of one individual, it also dissociates itself from "Second Cinema," the European, artistic "auteur cinema." Accented cinema, on the other hand, is engaged less with "the people" and "the masses" than with specific individuals, ethnicities, nationalities, and identities, and with the experience of deteritorialization itself. Therefore, accented films tell both private and social, public stories. In addition, Naficy claims that accented films perform the identity of the author, implying the author should be taken into regard when accented films are analyzed.
8. The co-productive role of the audience was also important to the so-called art "happenings" performed in the 1960s.

Chapter 16 Electronic Diaries, Cinematic Stories

1. I am using the concept of queer in addition to the word lesbian in order to emphasize that Benning is not merely investigating her homosexuality, but also a form of gender identity which transgresses the conventional forms of femininity and masculinity. Whereas the term lesbianism does not refer to such a transgression of gender norms, the concept of queerness has (through a reappropriation of the term in the 1990s) come to refer not only to gay and lesbian subjectivities, but also to transgendered subjects (*Norton Anthology*, first ed., 2433).

Chapter 17 Objective Representation

1. In this respect, the concept of discourse is not incompatible with Williams' opinion that there is no such thing as a pristine, meaningless medium technology outside of social structures. Foucault's concept, however, helps to theorize and analyze the power relations involved in these social structures, as well as the way in which knowledge is produced within social structures through and on media technologies.
2. Baer's *Spectral Evidence* (2005) includes an intricate analysis of the application of the flash by French psychiatrist Charcot in the nineteenth century, who would lead female patients into a pitch black room where the light of a flash would suddenly flood the darkness. The effect on the women in front of the camera was that they fell into a state of catalepsy. Their bodies froze in the position in which they had been flashed. Baer

convincingly argues that while the flash was thought to expose a symptom of hysteria in female patients; it actually produced this symptom.

3. Anthropometric "racial science" measurement was not limited to colonial projects; it also played a role in, for instance, nineteenth-century criminology and in the Nazi regime in early twentieth-century Europe.
4. A convention that can be traced back to the paradigm of the camera obscura.

Chapter 18 The Production of Portable Objects

1. Although some theorists insist on the materiality of light, I have decided to call it nonmaterial here, because when compared to the paper on which photographs are printed a stark difference is noticeable between the palpability of the two.
2. Appropriation and violation by way of photographic objects does not physically harm the photographed subjects, except when the acts of collecting or damaging photographs trigger aggression towards people outside the photographic frame—a possibility that is demonstrated in cinematic stories such as *One Hour Photo* (Romanek 2002) and *The Comfort of Strangers* (Schrader 1990) in which photography is a prelude to hostage-taking and murder.
3. However, it should be noted here that, although the circulation of photographs, films, and videos is hardly ever controlled by a single person or institution, the images do not spread themselves. Someone is responsible for their exposure and distribution. The power over the images starts with their producer; the person who handles the camera. In addition, the many possible channels through which images are made public exert power over the exposure of images, and like the producers, can decide to share this power with the represented subject by giving them the chance to endorse the circulation of their image, or not.
4. The combination of aesthetic pleasure and journalistic value is most prevalent as well as accepted within the field of photography, as it is common for documentary news photos to be exhibited in art galleries.
5. The beautification of suffering cannot be condemned as an immoral act per se. For many victims, it is better to be seen suffering beautifully, than not to be seen at all. For more detailed discussions of the complicated matters encompassing the representation of suffering, see Sontag (2003) and Reinhart et al. (2006).
6. The context and meaning of a representation can never be fully controlled, but in spite of the fact that it is always partial, the amount of control can differ.
7. For instance, when a humanitarian campaign convinces the public of the neediness of a particular group, this may serve the justification of military intervention.

Chapter 19 From Freezing to Touching

1. But not always; the movement of film images is sometimes associated with death instead of life, see the excerpt from Pirandello's *Si Gira* in this chapter.
2. Barthes' general ideas on photography which I have discussed here are by no means put as absolute truths in *Camera Lucida* (1980). Rules are shown to have exceptions and

different perspectives are adopted. For instance, Barthes believes that some photographs—the rare ones which have *punctum*—are in fact able to reanimate their represented subjects in the same way that film does.

Chapter 20 Surveillance

1. Although I restrict my discussion to surveillance as a visual practice here, it should be noted that surveillance can also imply eavesdropping.
2. Video surveillance by multiple cameras is often referred to as CCTV: closed-circuit television.
3. Indicating that artists have power, even without video cameras.

Chapter 21 Voyeurism

1. That is, when interaction is understood in a literal sense.
2. See also Ernst van Alphen's "Explosions of Information, Implosions of Meaning, and the Release of Affect" (2013).
3. By convention, photographs, "except for an embarrassing ceremonial of a few boring evenings, are looked at when one is alone" (Barthes 1980: 97).
4. In light of the seriousness of the role, it is remarkable that the protagonist of the film is played by Buster Keaton.
5. Unlike Beckett's *Film*, later critical reflections on the voyeuristic structure of the cinematic medium are characterized by a feminist perspective; they emphasize that women specifically are the victims of film's voyeurism. This shift to feminism is well illustrated by Yoko Ono's *Rape* (1969), a film that can be understood as *Film*'s feminist successor. Like *Film*, *Rape* depicts a person who is frightened and harassed by the camera's incessant gaze. In Ono's piece, however, the protagonist is a young woman instead of a man. What is more, in *Rape*, the camera approaches the victim more closely through aggressive close-ups from which the woman constantly tries to hide. Especially near the end of the film, the woman seems to be touched by the camera in a manner not unlike the kinetic camera strokes distributed by the bullies in the YouTube videos. Hence, the cinematic gaze is eventually presented as a physical form of harassment in *Rape*. It goes without saying that the film's title stresses the sexual nature of this harassment. Like Beckett's film, moreover, Ono's *Rape* responds to voyeuristic film conventions by way of features (e.g., the filmed subject looking into the lens, kinetic camera used a tool to "touch" the filmed subject) that would be recognized as videomatic characteristics today.
6. Feminist film theorists who criticized mainstream films before Mulvey published her ideas in 1975, did not address the gendered voyeuristic structure in films because they did not work within a psychoanalytical framework. Early feminist film critics such as Molly Haskell, Marjorie Rosen, and Claire Johnston rather focused on female stereotypes in mainstream films, which they analyzed from structuralist or semiotic points of view.
7. Although Mulvey states that the female spectator is uncomfortable and "restless in her transvestite clothes" (1981: 37), she claims that transsexual identification with a male

character *can* be pleasant to women when it signifies a rediscovery of a lost aspect of their sexual identity. This argument is based on the idea that in the pre-oedipal phase, the phallic fantasy of omnipotence is equally active for girls as for boys. Girls, however, have to shed this aspect of their early sexuality in order to acquire conventional femininity. In films which offer the possibility to identify with the perspective of omnipotent men, they can recover their lost sense of power and competence. Yet, the downside remains that they have to "become" a man in order to do so.

8. For a more thorough discussion of the relationship between female spectatorship and masochism, see "Film and the Masquerade: Theorising the Female Spectator" (1982) by Mary Ann Doane.
9. In addition to this, Mulvey created a "counter-movie" herself: *Riddles of the Sphinx* (1977), in cooperation with Peter Wollen.
10. For Mulvey, "telling the story differently" means telling a cinematic story without taking recourse to patriarchal, Oedipal structures and forms. This implies that cinematic visual pleasure has to be destroyed, as it derives only from these structures and forms. When de Lauretis refers to films which tell the story differently, however, the sentence can be rephrased as "tell the *Oedipal* story differently." For according to de Lauretis, neither Oedipal structures nor the pleasure they incite have to be obliterated entirely in order to produce feminist films. She holds that the most exciting work in feminist cinema is "narrative and Oedipal *with a vengeance*, for it seeks to stress the duplicity of that scenario and the specific contradiction of the female subject in it, the contradiction by which historical women must work with and against Oedipus" (1984: 157, emphasis added).

BIBLIOGRAPHY

Alphen, E. van (2005), *Art in Mind: How Contemporary Images Shape Thought,* Chicago: The University of Chicago Press.

Alphen, E. van (2005), "Peter Forgacs en de persoonlijke tijd: naar een nieuwe historiografie," *De Witte Raaf* 118: 26–7.

Alphen, E. van (2011), "Towards a New Historiography: The Aesthetics of Temporality," in B. Nichols and M. Renov (eds), *Cinema's Alchemist: The Films of Péter Forgács*, 59–74, Minneapolis: University of Minnesota Press.

Alphen, E. van (2013), "Explosions of Information, Implosions of Meaning, and the Release of Affect," in P. Spyer and M.M. Steedly (eds), *Images that Move*, 219–36, Santa Fe: SAR Press.

Applefeld, A. (1988), "After the Holocaust," in B. Lang (ed.), *Writing and the Holocaust,* 83–92, New York: Holmes and Meier.

Assmann, A. (2006), "History, Memory, and the Genre of Testimony," *Poetics Today* 27(2): 261–73.

Baer, U. (2005), *Spectral Evidence: The Photography of Trauma*, Cambridge, Mass: MIT Press.

Baker, G. (2005), "Photography's Expanded Field," *October* 114: 120–40.

Bal, M. (1991), *Reading Rembrandt: Beyond the Word-Image Opposition*, Cambridge: Cambridge University Press.

Bal, M. (2006), "The Pain of Images," in M. Reinhardt, H. Edwards, and E. Dugann (eds), *Beautiful Suffering: Photography and the Traffic in Pain*, 93–115, Chicago: The University of Chicago Press.

Barker, J.M. (2009), *The Tactile Eye: Touch and the Cinematic Experience,* Berkeley and Los Angeles: University of California Press.

Barthes, R. ([1980] 2000), *Camera Lucida*, trans. R. Howard, London: Vintage.

Barthes, R. (1982), "The Reality Effect," in T. Todorov (ed.), *French Literary Theory Today,* 11–17, New York: Cambridge University Press.

Baudrillard, J. ([1981] 1995), *Simulacra and Simulations,* trans. S.F. Glaser, Michigan: University of Michigan Press.

Baudry, J.L. (1978), *L'Effet cinéma,* Paris: Albatros.

Baudry, J.L. (1986a), "Ideological Effects of the Basic Cinematographic Apparatus," in P. Rosen (ed.), *Narrative, Apparatus, Ideology,* 286–98, New York: Columbia University Press.

Baudry, J.L. (1986b), "The Apparatus: Metapsychological Approaches to the Impression of Reality in the Cinema," in P. Rosen (ed.), *Narrative, Apparatus, Ideology,* 299–318, New York: Columbia University Press.

Bazin, A. ([1958–1965] 1967), *What is Cinema?,* trans. H. Gray, Berkeley and Los Angeles: University of California Press.

Bell-Metereau, R. (2011), "A Review of 'Haunted Images': Film, Ethics, Testimony and the Holocaust," *Quarterly Review of Film and Video* 28(5): 424–8.

Bellour, R. (2013), "The Cinema Spectator: A Special Memory," in I. Christie (ed.), *Audiences: Defining and Researching Screen Entertainment Reception,* 206–17, Amsterdam: Amsterdam University Press.

Bibliography

Belton, J. (1996), "Looking Through Video: The Psychology of Video and Film," in M. Renov and E. Suderburg (eds), *Resolutions,* 61–72, Minneapolis: University of Minnesota Press.

Benjamin, W. ([1936] 1999), "The Work of Art in the Age of Mechanical Reproduction," in *Illuminations,* 211–45, London: Pimlico.

Berner, M. (2009), "The Nazi Period Collection of Physical Anthropology in the Museum of Natural History, Vienna," in A. Rényi, *Col Tempo,* 34–48, Budapest: Masterprint Press.

Bolter, J.D. and R. Grusin (1999), *Remediation: Understanding New Media.* Cambridge, Mass.: MIT Press.

Bordwell, D., J. Staiger, and K. Thompson (1985), *The Classical Hollywood Cinema: Film Style & Mode of Production,* New York: Routledge.

Boyle, D. (1997), *Subject to Change: Guerilla Television Revisited,* Oxford: Oxford University Press.

Browne, N. (1986), "The Spectator-in-the-Text: The Rhetoric of STAGECOACH," in P. Rosen (ed.), *Narrative, Apparatus, Ideology: A Film Reader,* 102–19, New York: Columbia University Press.

Bryson, N. (1983), *Vision and Painting: The Logic of the Gaze,* New Haven: Yale University Press.

Burnett, R. (1995), "Video Space/Video Time: The Electronic Image and Portable Video," in J. Marchessault (ed.), *Mirror Machine: Video and Identity,* 142–86, Toronto YYZ Books.

Burnett, R. (1996), "Video: The Politics of Culture and Community," in M. Renov and E. Suderburg (eds), *Resolutions,* 283–303, Minneapolis: University of Minnesota Press.

Carlson, J.M. (1985), *Prime Time Law Enforcement: Crime Show Viewing and Attitudes Toward the Criminal Justice System,* New York: Praeger.

Carroll, N. (1988), *Problems of Classical Film Theory,* Princeton: Princeton University Press.

Carroll, N. (1996), "Questioning Media," *Theorizing the Moving Image,* 1–74, Cambridge: Cambridge University Press.

Casetti, F. (1995), "Face to Face," in W. Buckland (ed.), *The Film Spectator: From Sign to Mind,* 118–40, Amsterdam: Amsterdam University Press.

Castells, M. (1996), *The Rise of the Network Society, Volume 1 of The Information Age: Economy, Society and Culture,* Massachusetts: Blackwell Publishing.

Chatman, S. (1980), "What Novels Can Do That Films Can't (and Vice Versa)," *Critical Inquiry* 7: 121–40.

Christie, I. (2012), "What Do We Really Know About Film Audiences?" in *Audiences: Defining and Researching Screen Entertainment Reception,* 225–34, Amsterdam: Amsterdam University Press.

Citron, M. (1989), *Home Movies and Other Necessary Fictions,* Minneapolis: University of Minnesota Press.

Clover, C.J. (1992), *Men, Women and Chain Saws: Gender in the Modern Horror Film,* Princeton: Princeton University Press.

Coleridge, S.T. (1983), "Biographia Literaria," in J. Engell and W.J. Bates (eds), *The Collected Works of Samuel Taylor Coleridge,* 1–19, Princeton: Princeton University Press.

Comolli, J.L. (1980), "Machines of the Visible," in T. de Lauretis and S. Heath (eds), *The Cinematic Apparatus,* 121–42, New York: St. Martin's Press.

Cooke, L. et al. (1995), *James Coleman: Projected Images 1972–1994,* New York: Dia Art Foundation.

Crary, J. (1990), *Techniques of the Observer: On Vision and Modernity in the Nineteenth Century,* Cambridge, Mass: MIT Press.

Croteau, D. and W. Hoynes (2003), *Media/Society: Industries, Images, and Audiences*, Thousand Oaks: Pine Forge Press.

Cubitt, S. (1993), *Videography: Video Media as Art and Culture*, Houndmills, Basingstoke: Macmillan.

Culler, J. (1981), *The Pursuit of Signs: Semiotics, Literature, Deconstruction*, Ithaca: Cornell University Press.

Culler, J. (1988), *Framing the Sign: Criticism and its Institutions*, Oxford: Basil Blackwell.

Dean, T. (2013), *Film*, Melbourne: Acca Publications.

Derrida, J. (1989), "How to Avoid Speaking: Denials," in S. Budick and W. Iser (eds), trans. K. Frieden, *Languages of the Unsayable*, 3–70, New York: Columbia University Press.

Doane, M.A. (1982), "Film and the Masquerade: Theorising the Female Spectator," *Screen* 23: 74–88.

Doane, M.A. (2003), "The Close-Up: Scale and Detail in the Cinema," *Differences: A Journal of Feminist Cultural Studies* 14(3): 89–111.

Doane, M.A. (2007), "The Indexical and the Concept of Medium Specificity," *Differences: A Journal of Feminist Cultural Studies* 18(1): 128–52.

Eaton, M. (1979), "The Production of Cinematic Reality," in *Anthropology-Reality-Cinema: The Films of Jean Reich*, 36–53, London: BFI.

Edwards, H. (2006), "Cover to Cover: The Life Cycle of an Image in Contemporary Visual Culture," in M. Reinhardt, H. Edwards, and E. Duganne (eds), *Beautiful Suffering: Photography and the Traffic in Pain*, 75–92, Chicago: The University of Chicago Press.

Elleström, L. (ed.) (2010), *Media Borders, Multimodality and Intermediality*, Houndmills, Basingstoke: Palgrave MacMillan.

Elsaesser, T. (2000), "Inleiding: Hollywood op Straat," in T. Elsaesser and P. Hesselberth (eds), *Hollywood op Straat: Film en Televisie in de Hedendaagse Mediacultuur*, 9–26, Amsterdam: Vossiuspers AUP.

Foucault, M. ([1969] 1972), *The Archeology of Knowledge and the Discourse on Language*, trans. A.M. Sheridan Smith, New York: Pantheon.

Foucault, M. (1980), *Power/Knowledge: Selected Interviews and Other Writings 1972–1977*, C. Gordon (ed), New York: Pantheon Books.

Foucault, M. (2002), "The Eye of Power," in T.Y. Levin, U. Frohne, and P. Weibel, *CTRL Space: The Rhetorics of Surveillance from Bentham to Big Brother*, 94–101, Cambridge, Mass.: MIT Press.

Fried, M. (1967), "Art and Objecthood," *Artforum* 5: 116–47.

Fried, M. (2011), "Another Light: Douglas Gordon's *k.364: A Journey by Train*," in *Douglas Gordon*, 106–17, Frankfurt: MMK.

Frohne, U. (2008), "The Dissolution of the Frame: Immersion and Participation in Video Installations," in T. Leighton (ed.), *Art and the Moving Image: A Critical Reader*, 355, 370, London: Tate Publishing.

Furst, L.R. (1995), "Let's Pretend," in *All is True: The Claims and Strategies of Realist Fiction*, 29–47, Durham, NC and London: Duke University Press.

Gabriel, T. (2010), "Third Cinema Updated: Exploration of Nomadic Aesthetics & Narrative Communities." Available online: http://teshomegabriel.net/third-cinema updated (accessed July 15 2015).

Garnham, N. (1990), *Capitalism and Communication: Global Culture and the Economics of Information*, London: Sage.

Gilbard, F. (1984), "An Interview with Vito Acconci: Video Works 1970–1978," *Afterimage* 12(4): 9.

Godfrey, M. (2005), "Fiona Tan's *Countenance*," in *Fiona Tan: Countenance*, 60–80, Oxford: Modern Art Oxford.

Graham, D. (1979), "Essay on Video, Architecture and Television," in B.H.D. Buchloh (ed.), *Dan Graham: Video, Architecture, Television,* 62–76, New York: New York University Press.
Green, D. (2005), "Beyond Narrativity: Time, Space and the Embodiment of the Viewer," in *David Claerbout*, 19–43, Berlin: Walther König.
Greenberg, C. ([1961] 1966), "Modernist Painting," in G. Battock (ed.), *The New Art: A Critical Anthology,* 100–10, New York: E.P. Dutton.
Gregory, S. et al. (2005), *Video for Change: A Guide for Video Advocacy and Activism,* London: Pluto Press.
Gunning, T. (1990), "The Cinema of Attractions: Early Cinema, Its Spectator and the Avant-Garde," in T. Elsaesser (ed.), *Early Cinema: Space, Frame, Narrative*, 56–62, London: BFI.
Hall, S. (ed.) (1997), *Representation: Cultural Representations and Signifying Practices*, London: Sage Publications.
Harris, B. (1998), "Photography in Colonial Discourse: The Making of 'the Other' in Southern Africa, c.1850–1950," in W. Hartmann, J. Silverster, and P. Hayes (eds), *The Colonising Camera: Photographs in the Making of Namibian History,* 20–4, Cape Town: University of Cape Town Press.
Hartman, G. (1995), "Learning from Survivors: The Yale Testimony Project," *Holocaust and Genocide Studies* 9(2): 192–207.
Hartman, G. (2000), "Memory.com: Tele-Suffering and Testimony in the Dot Com Era," *Raritan* 19(3): 1–18.
Hartman, G. (2002), "Testimony and Authenticity," in *Scars of the Spirit: The Struggle Against Inauthenticity,*" 85–102, New York: Palgrave Macmillan.
Hartman, G. (2006), "The Humanities of Testimony: An Introduction," *Poetics Today* 27(2): 249–60.
Hartmann, W., J. Silverster, and P. Hayes (eds) (1998), *The Colonising Camera: Photographs in the Making of Namibian History.* Cape Town: University of Cape Town Press.
Hayward, S. (2000), *Key Concepts in Cinema Studies.* London and New York: Routledge.
Heath, S. (1981), "Narrative Space," in *Questions of Cinema.* 19–76, London: MacMillan Press.
Hesselberth, P. (2014), *Cinematic Chronotopes: Here, Now, Me,* New York: Bloomsbury.
Hirsh, M. (1997), *Family Frames: Photography, Narrative, and Postmemory,* Cambridge, Mass.: Harvard University Press.
Holert, T. (2004), "Die Erscheinung des Dokumentarischen," in K. Gludovatz (ed.), *Dokumentarische Strategien in der Kunst,* 25–41, Vienna: Mumok.
Iles, C. (2000), "Video and Film Space," in E. Suderburg (ed.), *Space, Site, Intervention: Situating Installation Art,* 252–62, Minneapolis: University of Minnesota Press.
James, D.E. (1996), "Lynn Hershman: The Subject of Autobiography," in M. Renov and E. Suderburg, *Resolutions,* 124–33, Minneapolis: University of Minnesota Press.
Jameson, F. (1991), *Postmodernism, Or, the Cultural Logic of Late Capitalism*, Durham, NC: Duke University Press.
Julien, I. (ed.) (2010), *Ten Thousand Waves,* London: Victoria Miro Gallery.
Kessler, F. (2006), "The Cinema of Attractions as Dispositif," in W. Strauven (ed.), *The Cinema of Attractions Reloaded,* 57–69, Amsterdam: Amsterdam University Press.
Kessler, F. (2007), *Notes on Dispositif,* Utrecht: University of Utrecht. Available online: www.let.uu.nl/~Frank.Kessler/personal/notes%20on%20dispositif.PDF (accessed July 16 2015).
Kim J. (2009), "The Post-medium Condition and the Explosion of Cinema," *Screen* 50(1): 114–23.
Kipnis, L. (1996), "Female Transgression," in M. Renov and E. Suderburg, *Resolutions: Contemporary Video Practices,* 333–45, Minneapolis: University of Minnesota Press.
Kracauer, S. (1960), *Theory of Film: The Redemption of Physical Reality,* New York: Oxford University Press.

Krauss, R. (1976), "Video: The Aesthetics of Narcissism," *October* 1: 50–64.

Krauss, R. (1986), "Notes on the Index: Part 1," in *The Originality of the Avant-Garde and Other Modernist Myths,* 196–209, Cambridge, Mass.: MIT Press.

Krauss, R. (1986), "Notes on the Index: Part 2," in *The Originality of the Avant-Garde and Other Modernist Myths,* 210–21, Cambridge, Mass.: MIT Press.

Krauss, R. (1997), "'. . . And Then Turn Away?': An Essay on James Coleman," *October* 81: 5–33.

Krauss, R. (1999), *A Voyage on the North Sea: Art in the Age of the Post-Medium Condition,* London: Thames & Hudson.

Krauss, R. (1999), "First Lines: Introduction to Photograph," in *James Coleman,* 9–25, Barcelona: Fundació Antoni Tàpies.

Krauss, R. (1999), "Reinventing the Medium," *Critical Inquiry* 25(2): 289–305.

Krauss, R. (2000), "'The Rock': William Kentridge's Drawing for Projector," *October* 92: 289, 305.

Kweek, P.M. and K. Yankah (2004), *African Folklore: An Encyclopedia,* New York: Routledge.

LaBelle, B. (2004), *Site Specific Sound,* Los Angeles: Errant Bodies Press.

Lant, A. (1995), "Haptical Cinema," *October* 74: 45–73.

Lauretis, T. de (1984), *Alice Doesn't: Feminism, Semiotics, Cinema,* Bloomington: Indiana University Press.

Lawlor, L. (2011), "Jacques Derrida," in E.N. Zalta, *The Stanford Encyclopedia of Philosophy,* Stanford: Stanford University. Available online: http://plato.stanford.edu/archives/fall2011/entries/derrida/ (accessed August 28 2013).

Lefebvre, H. ([1974] 1997), *The Production of Space,* trans. D. Nicholson-Smith, Oxford: Blackwell Publishing.

Levin, T.Y., U. Frohne, and P. Weibel (eds) (2002), *CTRL Space: The Rhetorics of Surveillance from Bentham to Big Brother,* Cambridge, Mass.: MIT Press.

Levin, T.Y. (2002), "Rhetoric of the Temporal Index: Surveillant Narration and the Cinema of Real Time," in T.Y. Levin, U. Frohne, and P. Weibel (eds), *CTRL Space: The Rhetorics of Surveillance from Bentham to Big Brother,* 578–93, Cambridge, Mass.: MIT Press.

Lütticken, S. (2000), "From Media to Mythology: Art in the Age of Convergence," *New Left Review* 6: 134–43.

Mack, J. (1991), "Documenting the Cultures of Southern Zaire. The Photographs of the Torday Expeditions 1900–1909," *African Arts* 24(4): 60–100.

Mann, S. (2002), "'Reflectionism' and 'Diffusionism': New Tactics for Deconstructing the Video Surveillance Superhighway," in T.Y. Levin, U. Frohne, and P. Weibel (eds), *CTRL Space: The Rhetorics of Surveillance from Bentham to Big Brother,* 530–43, Cambridge, Mass.: MIT Press.

Manovich, L. (2001), *The Language of New Media,* Cambridge, Mass.: MIT Press.

Maras, S. and D. Sutton (2000), "Medium Specificity Re-visited," *Convergence* 6(98): 99–113.

Marchessault, J. (ed.) (1998), *Mirror Machine: Video and Identity,* Toronto: YYZ Books.

Marks, L. (1998), "Video Haptics and Erotics," *Screen* 39(4): 331–48.

Marks, L. (2002), *Touch: Sensuous Theory and Multisensory Media,* Minneapolis: University of Minnesota Press.

Mayne, J. ([1993] 2002), *Cinema and Spectatorship,* New York: Routledge.

McLuhan, M. ([1964] 1997), *Understanding Media: The Extensions of Man,* Cambridge, Mass.: MIT Press.

Merrin, W. (2012), "Still Fighting 'the Beast': *Guerrilla Television* and the Limits of YouTube," *Cultural Politics* 8(1): 97–119.

Metz, C. (1974), *Film Language: A Semiotics of the Cinema,* Oxford: Oxford University Press.

Metz, C. (1976), "The Fiction Film and Its Spectator," *New Literary History* 8: 75–105.

Metz, C. (1982), *The Imaginary Signifier: Psychoanalysis and the Cinema,* Bloomington: Indiana University Press.

Modleski, T. (1989), *The Women Who Knew Too Much: Hitchcock and Feminist Theory,* New York: Routledge.
Molon, D. and B. Schwabsky (2002), *Gillian Wearing: Mass Observation*, London: Merrell.
Moraes da Cunha, J.A. (1885), *Africa Occidental, album photographico and descriptivo,* Lisbon and Rio de Janeiro: David Corazzi.
Moran, J.M. (2002), *There's No Place Like Home Video,* Minneapolis: University of Minnesota Press.
Morse, M. (1990), "Video Installation Art: The Body, the Image, and the Space-in-Between," in D. Hall and S.L. Fifer (eds), *Illuminating Video,* 153–67, New York: Aperture.
Müller, J.E. (1996), *Intermedialität: Formen moderner kultureller Kommunikation,* Münster: Nodus Publikationen.
Mulvey, L. ([1975] 1989), "Visual Pleasure and Narrative Cinema," in *Visual and Other Pleasures,* 14–26, London: Macmillan.
Naficy, H. (2001), *An Accented Cinema: Exilic and Diasporic Filmmaking,* Princeton: Princeton University Press.
Nash, M. (2010), "Electric Shadows," in I. Julien (ed.), *Ten Thousand Waves,* 38–44, London: Victoria Miro Gallery.
Odin, R. (1995), "For a Semio-Pragmatics of Film," in W. Buckland (ed.), *The Film Spectator: From Sign to Mind,* 213–26, Amsterdam: Amsterdam University Press.
Parente, A. and V. de Carvalho (2008), "Cinema as *Dispositif*: Cinema and Contemporary Art," *Cinémas: Journal of Film Studies* 19(1): 37–55.
Peirce, C.S. (1932), *Collected Papers of Charles Sanders Peirce,* Vol. 2, *Elements of Logic,* C. Hartshorne and P. Weiss (eds), Cambridge, Mass.: Harvard University Press.
Pethő, Á. (2011), *Cinema and Intermediality: The Passion for the In-between*, Cambridge: Cambridge Scholars Publishing.
Pierre-Quint, L. (1927), "Signification du Cinéma," in *L'art cinématographique II*, 14–15, Paris.
Procter, J. (2013), *Stuart Hall,* New York: Routledge.
Raessens, J. (2009), "The Gaming Dispositif," in U. Ritterfeld et al. (eds), *Serious Games: Mechanisms and Effects,* 486–515, New York: Routledge.
Reinhardt, M., H. Edwards, and E. Duganne (2006), *Beautiful Suffering: Photography and the Traffic in Pain*, Chicago: The University of Chicago Press.
Renov, M. (1996), "Video Confessions," in M. Renov and E. Suderburg (eds), *Resolutions,* 78–101, Minneapolis: University of Minnesota Press.
Renov, M. (2004), *The Subject of Documentary,* Minneapolis: University of Minnesota Press.
Renov, M. and E. Suderburg (eds) (1996), *Resolutions: Contemporary Video Practices,* Minneapolis: University of Minnesota Press.
Rosen, P. (1986), "Preface," in *Narrative, Apparatus, Ideology,* i–vii, New York: Columbia University Press.
Ross, C. (1996), "To Touch the Other: A Story of Corpo-Electronic," *Public* 13: 50–61.
Ross, C. (2006), "The Temporalities of Video: Extendedness Revisited," *Art Journal* 65(3): 82, 99.
Rushton, R. (2002), "Cinema's Double: Some Reflections on Metz," *Screen* 43(2), 107–18.
Ryan, M.L., (1999), "Immersion vs Interactivity: Virtual Reality and Literary Theory," *SubStance* 28(2): 110–37.
Sandoz, D. (2003), "Simulation/simulacrum," *The Chicago School of Media Theory.* Available online: http://lucian.uchicago.edu/blogs/mediatheory (accessed July 18 2013).
Saxton, L. (2008), *Haunted Images: Film, Ethics, Testimony and the Holocaust,* London and New York: Wallflower Press.
Schneider, I. and B. Korot (eds) (1976), *Video Art: An Anthology*, New York: Harcourt Brace Jovanovich.

Schröter, J. (2011), "Discourses and Models of Intermediality," *Comparative Literature and Culture* 13(3): 1–7.
Schulz, B. (ed.) (2002), *Resonances: Aspects of Sound Art*, Heidelberg: Kehrer.
Scott, C. (2010), "Mona Hatoum." Available online: www.portfolio.mvm.ed.ac.uk (accessed June 12 2011).
Senior, D. (2007), "Interview with Siegfried Zielinski," trans. W. Rauscher, *Rhizome ArtBase*, New York. Available online: http://rhizome.org/discuss/view/20967 (accessed August 16 2013).
Sharp, W. (1976), "Videoperformance," in I. Schneider and B. Korot (eds), *Video Art*, 252–67, New York: Harcourt Brace Jovanovich.
Silverman, K. (1983), "Suture," in *The Subject of Semiotics*, 194–237, New York: Oxford University Press.
Slack, J.D. (1984), *Communication Technologies and Society: Conceptions of Causality and the Politics of Technological Intervention*, Norwood: Ablex.
Smelik, A. (1999), "Feminist Film Theory," in P. Cook and Mieke Bernink (eds), *The Cinema Book*, 353–65, London: British Film Institute.
Sobchack, V. (2004), *Carnal Thoughts: Embodiment and Moving Image Culture*, Berkeley and Los Angeles: University of California Press.
Solanas, F., and O. Getino (1970), "Toward a Third Cinema," *Cineaste*: 1–10.
Sontag, S. (1979), *On Photography*, London: Penguin.
Sontag, S. (2003), *Regarding the Pain of Others*, New York: Picador/Farrar, Strauss and Giroux.
Spieker, S. (2002), "At the Centre of Mitteleuropa, A Conversation with Peter Forgács," *ArtMargins*, 21 May. Available online: www.artmargins.com/index.php/interviews (accessed August 3 2016).
Spielmann, Y. (2008), *Video: The Reflexive Medium*, Cambridge, Mass.: MIT Press.
Stam, R. (2000), "Beyond Fidelity: The Dialogics of Adaptation," in J. Naremore (ed.), *Film Adaptation*, 54–76, London: The Athlone Press.
Tamblyn, C. (1996), "Qualifying the Quotidian: Artist's Video and the Production of Social Space," in M. Renov and E. Suderburg (eds), *Resolutions*, 13–28, Minneapolis: University of Minnesota Press.
Turner, G. (2006), *Film as Social Practice*, London: Routledge.
Uhlin, G. (2010), "TV, Time, and the Films of Andy Warhol," *Cinema Journal* 49(3): 1–23.
Verstraten, P. (2006), *Handboek Filmnarratologie*, Nijmegen: Vantilt.
Verstraten, P. (2008), *Kernthema's in de filmwetenschap*, Amsterdam: Boom, 2008.
Viola, B. (1976), "The European Scene and Other Observations," in I. Schneider and B. Korot (eds), *Video Art: An Anthology*, 268–78, New York: Harcourt Brace Jovanovich.
Walton, K.L. (1980), "Appreciating Fictions: Suspending Disbelief or Pretending Belief?" *Disposito* 5: 1–18.
Weinstock, J. (1984), "Sexual Difference and the Moving Image," in *Difference: On Representation and Sexuality*, 41–5, New York, New York Museum of Contemporary Art.
Weyergraf, C. (1980), *Richard Serra: Interviews, Etc. 1970–1980*, New York: The Hudson River Museum.
White, M. (1992), *Tele-Advising: Therapeutic Discourse in American Television*. Chapel Hill: University of North Carolina Press.
Williams, L. (1991), "Film Bodies: Gender, Genre, and Excess," *Film Quarterly* 44(4): 2–13.
Williams, R. (1974), *Television: Technology and Cultural Form*, Hanover: University Press of New England.
Williams, R. (1977), *Marxism and Literature*, New York: Oxford University Press.
Willis, S. (1997), "Borrowed Style: Quentin Tarantino's Figures of Masculinity," *High Contrast: Race and Gender in Contemporary Hollywood Film* 189–216, Durham, NC and London: Duke University Press.

Zielinski, S. (1992), *Video: Apparat/Medium, Kunst, Kultur,* Frankfurt am Main: Lang.
Zielinski, S. (1999), *Audiovisions: Cinema and Television as Entr'actes in History,* Amsterdam: Amsterdam University Press.
Zimmerman, P. (1995), *Reel Families: A Social History of Amateur Film.* Bloomington: Indiana University Press.

LIST OF FILMS AND VIDEOS

. . . and Europe will be Stunned: The Polish Trilogy. (Comprises the three videos *Mary Koszmary, Mur I wieża* and *Zamach*). Yael Bartana, 2011. Multi-channel video installation.

2001: A Space Odyssey. Dir. Stanley Kubrick. MGM, 1968.

60 Minutes Silence. Gillian Wearing, 1996. Single-channel video projection.

A Movie. Krassimir Terziev, 2004. Two-channel video installation.

A Spy in the House that Ruth Built. Vanalyne Green. Video Data Bank, 1989. Single-channel video.

Air Time. Vito Acconci, 1973. Single-channel video.

American Car. David Claerbout, 2004. Double-channel video installation.

Anger. Maxie Cohen. Electronic Arts Intermix,1986. Single-channel video.

Apocalypse Now. Dir. Francis Ford Coppola. United Artists, 1979.

Approximations: Part 1–3. Includes *The Mission* and *December 31*. Johanna Householder and b.h. Yael, 2000–2001. Video project consisting of three single-channel videos.

Battles of Troy. Dir. Krassimir Terziev. Prod. The Belluard Bollwerk International, 2005.

Benny's Video. Dir. Michael Haneke. Pandora Filmproduktion, 1992.

Binge. Lynn Hershman. LUX Artists' Film, 1987. Single-channel video.

Blood in Blossom. Merel Mirage, 1995. Single-channel video.

Blow-up. Dir. Michelangelo Antonioni. MGM, 1966.

Bordeaux Piece. David Claerbout, 2004. Single-channel video.

Caché. Dir. Michael Haneke. Les Films du Losange, 2005.

Centers. Vito Acconci, 1972. Single-channel video.

Chronique d'un été. Dir. Jean Rouch and Edgar Morin. BFI, 1961.

Claim. Vito Acconci, 1971. Single-channel video.

Confess All On Video. Don't Worry You Will Be In Disguise. Intrigued? Call Gillian. Gillian Wearing, 1994. Single-channel video.

Confessions of a Chameleon. Lynn Hershman. LUX Artists' Film, 1987. Single-channel video.

Contacts. Vito Acconci, 1971. Single-channel video.

Corps étranger. Mona Hatoum, 1994. Video installation.

Countenance. Fiona Tan, 2002. Four-screen video installation.

Crime Scene Investigation. Dir. Jerry Bruckheimer. CBS, 2000–2015.

Crouching Tiger, Hidden Dragon. Dir. Ang Lee. Warner Bros, 2002.

Dalice. Celio Braga, 2006. Video installation with two monitors.

Daughter Rites. Dir. Michelle Citron. Iris Films, 1979.

December 31. Johanna Householder and b.h. Yael, 2000. Single-channel video. Part 2/3 of *Approximations* (Householder and Yael, 2000–2001).

Delirium. Mindy Faber, 1993. Single-channel video.

Electronic Diary (Incl. *Confessions of a Chameleon, Binge* and *First Person Plural*). Lynn Hershman. LUX Artists' Film, 1985–1989. Video series.

Facing Forward. Fiona Tan, 1999. Single-channel video.

Family Viewing. Dir. Atom Egoyan. Cinephile, 1987.

Fight Club. Dir. David Fincher. Twentieth Century Fox, 1999.

Film. Screenplay by Samuel Beckett. Dir. Alan Schneider. Milestone Film & Video, 1965.

List of Films and Videos

Film. Tacita Dean, 2011. Film projection.
First Person Plural. Lynn Hershman. LUX Artists' Film, 1987. Single-channel video.
Gigante. Dir. Adrián Biniez. Imovision, 2009.
Heal me. Hester Scheurwater, 2000. Single-channel video.
Histoire(s) du cinéma. Dir. Jean-Luc Godard. Gaumont, 1998.
I Wanted You. Hester Scheurwater, 2001. Single-channel video.
Ici et ailleurs. Dir. Jean-Luc Godard and Anne-Marie Miéville. Gaumont, 1976.
Intimate Interviews: Sex in Less Than Two Minutes. Maxie Cohen. Electronic Arts Intermix, 1984. Single-channel video.
It Wasn't Love. Sadie Benning, 1992. Single-channel video.
Jeanne Dielman, 23 quai du Commerce, 1080 Bruxelles. Dir. Chantal Akerman. Olympic Films, 1975.
k.364: A Journey by Train. Douglas Gordon. Lost but Found Film, 2010. Single-channel film or two-screen video installation.
Kristall. Matthias Müller and Christoph Girardet. Arsenal experimental, 2006. Single-channel video (35mm widescreen transferred to DVD).
La hora de los hornos. Dir. Fernando Solanas and Octavio Getino. Tricontinental, 1968.
La mort en direct. Dir. Bertrand Tavernier. Contemporary Films, 1980.
Le mépris. Dir. Jean Luc Godard. Les Films Concordia, 1963.
Lord of the Universe. Michael Shamberg et al. TVTV, 1974.
Mary Koszmary. Yael Bartana, 2007. Single-channel video.
Menace II Society. Dir. Albert Hughes and Allen Hughes. New Line Cinema, 1993.
Mur I wieża. Yael Bartana, 2009. Single-channel video.
Must Read After My Death. Dir. Morgan Dews. Gigante Releasing, 2007.
Now. Linda Benghlis, 1973. Single-channel video.
Observation of the Observation. Peter Weibel, 1973. Closed-circuit video installation.
One Hour Photo. Dir. Mark Romanek. Twentieth Century Fox, 2002.
One on One. Wendy Clarke. Deep Dish TV, 1991–1994.
Onourown. Joe Gibbons and Tony Oursler. Video Data Bank, 1990. Single-channel video.
Peeping Tom. Dir. Michael Powell. Anglo-Amalgamated Film Distributors, 1960.
Phoenix Tapes. Christoph Girardet and Matthias Müller. Sixpackfilm, 1999. Single-channel video.
Private Century. Dir. Jan Sikl. Ceská Televize, 2010.
Rape. Yoko Ono. ORF, 1969.
Rear Window. Dir. Alfred Hitchcock. Paramount Pictures, 1954.
Rebel Without a Cause. Dir. Nicholas Ray. Warner Bros, 1955.
Red Road. Dir. Andrea Arnold. Eclipse Pictures, 2006.
Riddles of the Sphinx. Dir. Laura Mulvey. BFI, 1977.
Shoah. Dir. Claude Lanzmann. New Yorker Films, 1985.
Sliver. Dir. Phillip Noyce. Paramount Pictures, 1993.
Stagecoach. Dir. John Ford. United Artists, 1939.
Ten Thousand Waves. Isaac Julien, 2010. Nine-channel video installation.
The Bad Seed. Dir. Mervyn LeRoy. Warner Bros, 1959.
The Comfort of Strangers. Dir. Paul Schrader. Paramount Pictures, 1990.
The Continuing Story of Carel and Ferd. Arthur Ginsberg. Prod. The TV Lab. Electronic Arts Intermix, 1975. Single-channel video.
The Conversation. Dir. Francis Ford Coppola. Paramount Pictures, 1974.
The Goddess. Dir. Yonggang Wu. Lianhua Film Company, 1934.
The Grapes of Wrath. Dir. John Ford. Twentieth Century Fox, 1940.
The Guard as Bandit. Peter Weibel, 1978. Video installation.

The Maelstrom: A Family Chronicle. Dir. Péter Forgács. Lumen Film, 1997.
The Mission. Johanna Householder and b.h. Yael, 2000. Single-channel video. Part 1/3 of *Approximations* (Householder and Yael, 2000–2001).
The Sixth Sense. Dir. M. Night Shyamalan. 1999.
The Stopping Mind. Bill Viola, 1990. Four-screen video installation.
The Truman Show. Dir. Peter Weir. Paramount Pictures, 1998.
Thelma and Louise. Dir. Ridley Scott. MGM, 1991.
Theme Song. Vito Acconci, 1973. Single-channel video.
Thriller. Dir. Sally Potter. Women Make Movies, 1979.
Time Code. Dir. Mike Figgis. Screen Gems, 2000.
Too Soon Too Late. Adrianne Finelli, 2009. Single-channel video.
Trick or Drink. Vanalyne Green. Video Data Bank, 1985. Single-channel video.
Troy. Dir. Wolfgang Petersen. Warner Bros, 2004.
Vakvagany. Dir. Benjamin Meade. Corticrawl Productions, 2002.
Vertigo. Dir. Alfred Hitchcock. Paramount Pictures, 1958.
Video Surveillance Piece: Public Room, Private Room. Bruce Nauman, 1969–1970. Video installation.
Videodrome. Dir. David Cronenberg. Universal Pictures, 1983.
Wag the Dog. Dir. Barry Levinson. New Line Cinema, 1997.
WearCam. Steve Mann, 1995. Video project.
Y in Vyborg. Dir. Pia Andell. Of Course My Films, 2006.
Zamach. Yael Bartana, 2011. Single-channel video.
Zidane: A 21st-century Portrait. Douglas Gordon and Philippe Parenno. A-film Distribution, 2006. Single-channel film or installation with 17 TV monitors.

APPENDIX: FILM AND VIDEO STILLS

Ten Thousand Waves. Isaac Julien, 2010. Nine-channel video installation. Installation view.

Benny's Video. Dir. Michael Haneke. WEGA-Filmproduktion, 1992. Still.

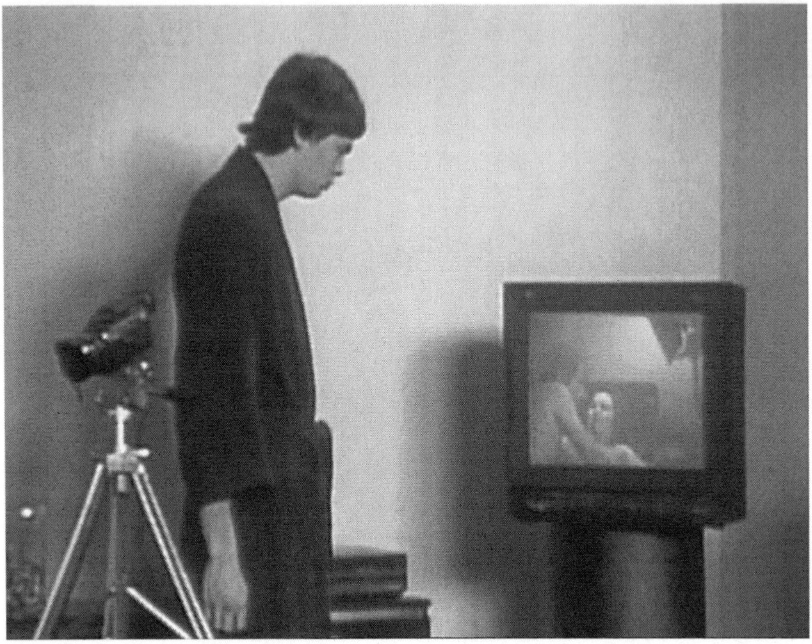

Family Viewing. Dir. Atom Egoyan. Cinephile, 1987. Still. © Ego Film Arts.

Bordeaux Piece. David Claerbout, 2004. Single-channel video with sound. Still.

American Car. David Claerbout, 2004. Two-screen video installation. Still, screen 1.

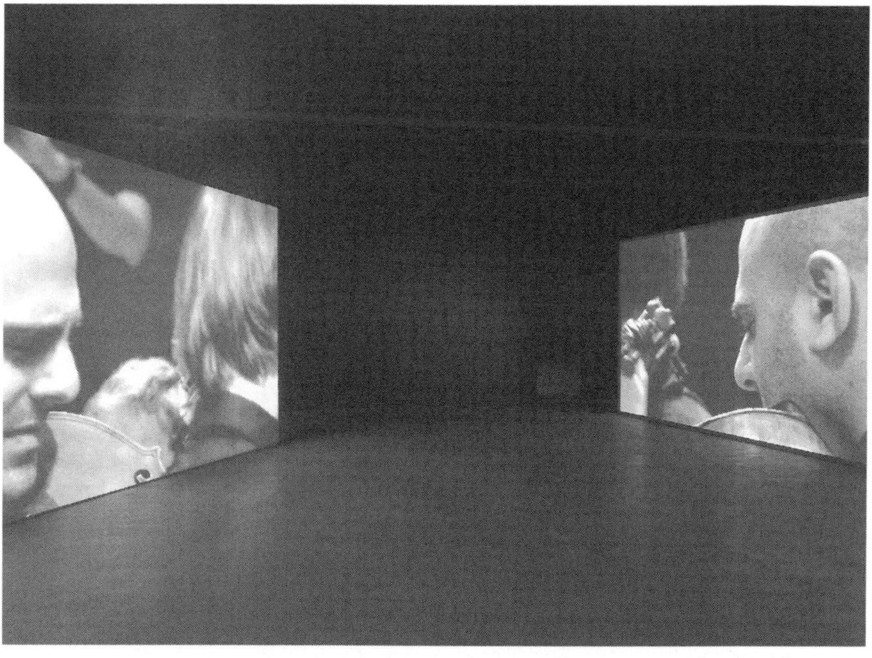

k.364: A Journey by Train. Douglas Gordon. lost but found Film, 2010. Single-channel film or two-screen video installation with sound. Installation view, Gagosian Gallery 2011. Courtesy studio lost but found and Gagosian Gallery. © D. Gordon, studio lost but found c/o Pictoright Amsterdam 2016.

Electronic Diary. Lynn Hershman. LUX Artists' Film, 1985–1989. Still.

Approximations: December 31. Johanna Householder and b.h. Yael, 2000–2001. Still.

INDEX

Index